United Nations-sponsored world confe

United Nations-sponsored world conferences: Focus on impact and follow-up

Edited by Michael G. Schechter

**United Nations
University Press**

TOKYO · NEW YORK · PARIS

© The United Nations University, 2001

The views expressed in this publication are those of the authors and do not necessarily reflect the views of the United Nations University.

United Nations University Press
The United Nations University, 53-70, Jingumae 5-chome,
Shibuya-ku, Tokyo, 150-8925, Japan
Tel: +81-3-3499-2811   Fax: +81-3-3406-7345
E-mail: sales@hq.unu.edu
http://www.unu.edu

United Nations University Office in North America
2 United Nations Plaza, Room DC2-1462-70, New York, NY 10017, USA
Tel: +1-212-963-6387   Fax: +1-212-371-9454
E-mail: unuona@igc.apc.org

United Nations University Press is the publishing division of the United Nations University.

Cover design by Joyce C. Weston

Printed in the United States of America

UNUP-1048
ISBN 92-808-1048-0

Library of Congress Cataloging-in-Publication Data

United Nations-sponsored world conferences : focus on impact and
follow-up / edited by Michael G. Schechter.
    p. cm.
Includes bibliographical references and index.
ISBN 92-808-1048-0
1. United Nations. 2. Congresses and conventions. I. Schechter,
Michael G. II. Title.
JZ4954 .U55 2000
341.7–dc21
00-011975

Contents

Tables and figures

Acknowledgements

The origins of this project can be found in a Ford Foundation funded project of the American Society of International Law (ASIL). Our intent in that project, administered by Charlotte Ku, the Society's Executive Director, was to try to influence the outcomes of world conferences through a series of issue papers and related media effects. Rebecca Cook, one of the contributors to this volume, also authored one of the *Issue Papers on World Conferences*. As a follow-up to that undertaking, I organized a panel at the 1997 Annual Meeting of the American Society of International Law, with Dr. Ku's enthusiastic support. Rebecca Cook, Thomas Yongo and Masumi Ono all delivered short papers on the panel, which focused on the implementation of decisions taken at UN-sponsored world conferences. Subsequent to that, I used world conferences as the focus for the student papers in my class on International Law and Organization in James Madison College of Michigan State University. For the class, Debbi Schaubman kindly agreed to put together a web page to assist my students in conducting their primary source research. (It has been vastly expanded and complemented by a chronology for this volume.) It quickly became obvious to me that we had the core of an important contribution to the study of international law and organization that also had implications for an important international public policy question. Should conferences like this be convened in the twenty-first century?

I approached Manfred Boemeke, Head of the United Nations University (UNU) Press, with my idea and he was immediately supportive. I agreed to seek additional authors to complement the core from the ASIL panel. I was fortunate to get quick agreement from a number of participants in the international policy-making process, who also have keen analytical and critical eyes. A draft of the volume was completed in 1999 and has profited from valuable suggestions from two anonymous reviewers selected by UNU Press.

In addition to the assistance of the UNU Press, I am pleased to acknowledge the logistical support of James Madison College of Michigan State University. I would be remiss if I didn't publicly thank my wife, Ilene, whose love, support, and patience made this and all of my scholarship possible.

Michael G. Schechter

Editor's introduction

Were the UN-sponsored world conferences of the 1990s worth their quite considerable cost in human and material resources? Are UN-sponsored conferences a useful way to meet the challenges of the twenty-first century? Can the conference follow-up be sufficiently impressive to convince conference sceptics to fund another round of such conferences in the twenty-first century? The subtitle of the volume, *Focus on impact and follow-up*, is intended to emphasize not simply the focus of this particular book, but what is novel about it and what we believe is the necessary focus in order to begin to answer the aforementioned crucial research and contentious international public policy questions.

The authors of the chapters of this volume all believe that one of the best ways to respond to these sorts of pressing questions is to assess the accomplishments of some of the key UN-funded global conferences of the 1990s and the international legal and public policy processes of which they are a part. No single volume could hope to assess all of the UN-sponsored conferences of the 1990s and none of the authors believes that enough time has lapsed since the conclusion of those conferences (and their so-called "plus 5" follow-up meetings) to provide a *definitive* assessment. But all of us believe that this preliminary analysis of a select but diverse set of conferences provides evidence that although opportunities have been missed and mistakes made, accomplishments can be documented and some noteworthy trends are evolving. Perhaps, as importantly, challenges and opportunities still exist for making *more* meaningful the UN-sponsored conferences of the 1990s.

Research on UN-sponsored global conferences is not new. Most of that research, however, has focused on the conferences themselves. Some authors have described the context in which they were proposed and a few have attempted to look at specific preparations prior to their convening. Almost no writing, especially no comparative investigation focuses on their aftermath, conference follow-up and the implementation phase, key to understanding the conferences' impact and meaningfulness. In part, of course, this is because, as the writers of the chapters in this book continually note, that is methodologically tough to assess. Moreover, it is still quite early in the aftermath of the latest outpouring of such conferences. But, as this book hopes to show, those are not good excuses, or at least not sufficient excuses. Indeed, the conveners themselves of this latest round of the conferences set a five-year time frame for a first formal assessment of their implementation and impact. Some NGOs began their post-conference assessments even earlier.

Each author's contribution also makes clear that previous studies of UN conferences underemphasize one of the keys to the success or failure of past conferences and thus whether this is a meaningful, legitimate and defensible mechanism worth continuing. Most prior work focused on the conferences and parallel NGO conferences themselves, less so the preparatory work and almost never on the implementation phase. Analytical assessments of the conferences of the 1990s – such as those in this volume – inevitably lead one to identify areas in the conference processes that have inhibited greater progress from being made. Throughout the volume examples of these procedural failures and lacunae – as well as examples of remarkable innovation, contributing to meaningful outcomes – are underscored. Two of the chapters, in particular, seek to shed some light on changes in the UN itself in terms of follow-ups to various conferences and to evaluate various innovations in the roles of NGOs in relation to such global conferences. This is done in a comparative mode and mostly in terms of NGOs' roles in assisting in the implementation phases of the conferences' activities.

The volume is divided into three parts. Part One focuses on UN conferences themselves. It begins with a brief overview of the history of UN-sponsored world conferences and some of the bases for the current debate as to whether they are worthwhile or should be relegated to the dustbin of the twentieth century. In Chapter 2, Jolly uses the World Summit on Children to debunk some of what he sees as the mythology surrounding world conferences and particularly those who see no value in them. He also argues that the World Summit on Children is not so very different from other world conferences of the 1990s and thus its success cannot be explained by a unique set of factors. Then he goes on to discuss the conditions that facilitate success for world conferences, such as those convened in the 1990s. In Chapter 3, Dias meticulously reviews the Vienna conference and the various follow-up "acts" that have succeeded it. Throughout his critical assessment, he points out lost opportunities, but he also notes that some success has been achieved, especially in the years since the conference. Much of that success is attributed to work by NGOs.

Part Two focuses on the conference process. The three chapters in this part focus less on the conferences *per se*, than on work prior to and after them, underscoring the fact that success depends as much on the entire Rio or Beijing process as it does on the conferences. All three chapters also emphasize the ways in which the international legal community has been able to use conferences to achieve some very concrete and potentially significant outcomes. Chapter 4, the first in this part, continues the discussion of human rights, but focuses on the goals of women "to live with dignity in all spheres of public and private life." Although Cook believes it will be years before one can accurately assess the impact of the Beijing Conference on women's quest for equal rights, because its recommendations require major changes in entrenched social and economic practices that cannot possibly be achieved quickly, she believes it is possible now to begin to review how well the Beijing Declaration and Platform of Action have fostered states' compliance with international law regarding women, and their potential to contribute to even further advances. Central to this process, Cook notes, is the ability of Beijing attendees – governmental and non-governmental – to measure the progress of states in living up to the commitments made at the conference and about women's rights more generally.

Chapters 5 and 6 examine two of the most important treaties that are part of what has come to be known as the Rio process. Yongo focuses on the Convention on Biological Diversity (CBD), whereas Butler and Ghai look at the Climate Change Convention. All three authors have been active participants in the Rio process and its follow-up. While many see the Convention on Biological Diversity as one of the two most significant products of the Rio Conference because it was opened for signature there, Yongo see the conference's significance elsewhere. In addition to being the year when participants were most forthcoming in terms of financial support for the ends of the CBD and related environmental accords, the Rio Conference was important because it was really a conference about equity, about the responsibilities of the North and South for meeting environmental challenges, including that of biological diversity. Those discussions and negotiations have proven key to follow-up activities, including the relatively rapid ratification of the CBD. Butler and Ghai's chapter on the UN Framework Convention on Climate Change (UNFCC) documents the painstaking and multiple steps involved in trying to make progress, largely through international legal means, in coping with the immensely important and contentious issue of climate change. Their chapter, as much as any other in this volume, documents the ways in which global conferences are merely a part of ongoing struggles for international legal and political change. In 1990, the UN General Assembly established an intergovernmental process to negotiate a global treaty to address the issue of climate change; the UNFCC was its outcome in May of 1992. But it was only at the Rio Conference itself that governments called upon the UN General Assembly to establish a negotiating process to prepare a global treaty on this pressing matter. Butler and Ghai document the triumphs and travails of that negotiating process.

The third part of the volume consists of two chapters, focusing on key non-state actors in the follow-up phase. Ono's contribution describes how the UN conferences required structural reorganization of the UN to deal effectively with the new, holistic approach to development implied by the conference processes and to begin to assist in implementing and monitoring state compliance with the decisions reached by the conferees. Schechter's chapter compares the various roles that NGOs have played in the different conference processes, noting that states have increasingly empowered them, thus placing more of the burden for conference success on their shoulders. However to hold NGOs totally responsible for the success or failure of the UN conferences of the 1990s seems unwarranted from Schechter's perspective, a view that resonates with that of many of the volume's other contributors.

The volume ends with a set of tentative conclusions about the procedural and substantive contributions to date of some of the key UN conferences of the 1990s, acknowledging that the nature of those contributions will be critical to the future of the UN conferences in the twenty-first century. Because the timing of the volume's publication means that it can only be the beginning of an assessment of past conferences and thus can only provide tentative insights for the future, Schaubman's appendixes are offered as unprecedented bases for future research. They take the form of a detailed chronology of world conference-related activities and a guide to resources, primary and secondary, "hard" and web-based.

Part One

Conferences

1

UN-sponsored world conferences in the 1990s

Michael G. Schechter

Global ad hoc conferences are not new. They have existed as long as has the UN; indeed, there were some widely publicized and well-attended ones convened by its predecessor organization, the League of Nations.[1] Jacques Fomerand has put together a useful listing of the UN's conferences (reproduced as Table 1.1 below).[2] Debbi Schaubman has provided us with a chronology of meetings associated with some of the most important recent conferences, including all of those described in depth in this volume (see Appendix A).

While global ad hoc conferences may not be new, the size, number, and publicity of such conferences have grown, both in the 1970s and again in the early to mid 1990s. 30,000 attended Habitat II in Istanbul; 47,000 convened in Rio for the Earth Summit and nearly 50,000 went to Beijing to discuss women's rights. Moreover, beginning with the 1990 World Summit for Children, presidents, prime ministers and other heads of states have been counted among those present. Conferences were fewer, smaller, and more narrowly defined in the 1980s. This was during the so-called crisis of multilateralism, that is, when the US especially chose to rely on the UN and its specialized agencies as little as possible, as the US government sought to meet its domestic budgetary challenges and as a consequence its increasingly neo-liberal public policies. Reitano provides a straightforward explanation for their resurgence in the early 1990s: "The number of conferences has increased because it is clear

Table 1.1 Selected UN conference dates

Name	Date	Venue
Trade and Employment	1947–1948	Havana
Prevention of Crime and Treatment of Offenders	every five years	
Law of the Sea	March–April 1960	
New Sources of Energy	August 1961	Rome
UNCTAD	every four years as of 1964	Geneva
Human Rights	May 1968	Tehran
Human Environment	June 1972	Stockholm
Law of the Sea	1963–1982	New York, Caracas, Geneva
Population	August 1974	Bucharest
Food	November 1974	Rome
Human Settlements	May–June 1976	Vancouver
Employment (ILO)	June 1976	Geneva
Water	March 1977	Mar del Plata, Argentina
Technical Cooperation Among Developing Countries	September 1978	Buenos Aires
Primary Health Care (WHO)	September 1978	Alma-Ata
Agrarian Reform (FAO)	July 1979	Rome
Science & Technology for Development	August 1979	Vienna
Desertification	September 1979	Nairobi
Decade for Women	July 1980	Copenhagen
New and Renewable Sources of Energy	August 1981	Nairobi
Least Developed Countries	September 1981	Paris
World Assembly on Aging	August 1982	Vienna
Population	August 1984	Mexico City
Conclusion of the Decade for Women	July 1985	Nairobi
Drug Abuse and Trafficking	July 1987	Vienna
Social Welfare for Development	September 1987	Vienna
Disarmament and Development	August–September 1987	New York
Education for All (UNESCO)	March 1990	Jomtien, Thailand
Least Developed Countries	September 1990	Paris
Water and Development	June 1992	Rio de Janeiro
Human Rights	June 1993	Vienna
Natural Disaster Prevention	May 1994	Yokohama
Population and Development	September 1994	Cairo
Social Development	March 1995	Copenhagen
Sustainable Development of Small Island Countries	April–May 1995	Barbados
Women and Development	September 1995	Beijing
Habitat II	June 1996	Istanbul
Food (FAO)	November 1996	Rome

that many problems are so universal in nature that older forms of diplomacy are inadequate and often inappropriate, especially in implementing proposed solutions."[3] Of course, the re-emergence of large numbers of such conferences only came in the aftermath of a return of economic prosperity to the OECD countries and a significant decline in the numbers of interstate conflicts, allowing for more attention to so-called postmaterialist issues. In addition, there was a change in leadership in the US toward one seemingly more committed to multilateral solutions to global problems.

In many ways, however, the conferences' purposes have remained constant over time: to raise popular and elite consciousness; to mobilize public and official attention to and support for particular issues; to develop or cultivate support for particular responses to global problems; to bring the moral force of the UN to bear on societal abusers, and to generate and eventually implement mechanisms (including international law) for coping with ongoing problems.[4] More recently, a "dialogue" with civil society has come to be viewed as a necessary ingredient in achieving these purposes.[5] Thus NGOs, sometimes simply by being present in large numbers and sometimes in very creative ways, have come to be seen as essential to the conferences' success. Smith exemplifies their more creative strategies. In order to facilitate journalists' coverage of the signing of the International Convention to Combat Desertification, NGOs developed news hooks with local angles. These were sent to several thousand editorial writers around the world. In some instances, the NGOs followed up the mailings with phone calls. Smith concludes that there were "more news stories than might otherwise have been" written.[6] (This, of course, did not have to be done for the Rio Conference, which was covered by some 19,000 journalists.)[7] Van Rooy recounts a creative strategy aimed at mobilizing official support: letter writing campaigns to members of parliament and peppering their question times. NGOs have also organized mass meetings in national capitals and waged publicity campaigns, including through local churches.[8]

Before launching into a discussion of the impacts of UN-sponsored world conferences, including the roles of NGOs in that process, it seems useful to summarize the literature as it relates to the meaningfulness of such conferences. This is done even though most of the literature is written without benefit of a systematic and comparative consideration of conferences' impacts. Perhaps this explains why there is a wide division of opinion as to their meaningfulness, a phenomenon that obviously contributes to why some call for their cessation and others look to NGOs, in the implementation phase, to lend credibility and support for them.

Conferences have been criticized for: (1) being a waste of money, which would be better spent confronting the problems or fulfilling promises already made or needs already identified rather than just talking about the problems;[9] (2) being duplicative[10] (i.e. although "... the main reason for holding major UN specialised conferences is to shift a particular issue higher up on public and formal agendas,"[11] most focus on some aspect of issues related to development and issues falling within the purview of the missions of multiple formally established UN bodies); (3) diverting attention from other serious issues, especially problematic, given that small countries can ill afford to devote their limited diplomatic and technical expertise to many issues at the same time; (4) being pervaded by a primacy of politics that "eventually leads to debates driven less by the need to make substantive progress than to reach agreements on ambiguous texts lending themselves to conflicting interpretations"; (5) either avoiding or redefining key problems "in a such a manner as to weaken proposed paths of action";[12] (6) seeking to pre-empt more radical solutions to key problems by having states rather than NGOs deal with them and by controlling the selection of NGOs that participate in such meetings; (7) resulting in compromises rather than commitments to real change; (8) foreshadowing too much regulation, and (9) focusing on human rights, democratization, the advancement of women and environmental protection deemed by some as really a thinly disguised effort to impose a new world order favouring the values of a few powerful countries. As these last two points emphasize, opposition to and criticism of such conferences cuts across the ideological spectrum.

Defenders of such conferences, of which there are many inside as well as outside the UN system,[13] portray them as: (1) mobilizing national and local governments and NGOs to take action on major global problems; (2) establishing international standards and guidelines for national policy; (3) serving as fora where new proposals can be debated and consensus sought; (4) setting in motion a process whereby governments can make commitments and report back regularly to the UN; (5) attempting to counter the hierarchy of most of the UN system and the bureaucratic inertia that is seen to plague many IGOs; (6) contributing to the creation, sharing and dissemination of information on vital global issues; (7) assisting in the establishment of mechanisms for monitoring of states' progress in meeting particular global challenges; (8) providing vital early-warning functions (as in the case of famines or overpopulation) in a state-centric world where that is not very easy to do, even for NGOs or IGOs, much less other states; (9) offering opportunities to think globally and operate along functionalist lines, forging appropriate linkages among issues that might otherwise be separated owing to the UN structure, and (10) serving a set of explicitly normative functions.[14] Two recent

UN Secretaries-General's summary judgments warrant repetition. Kofi Annan concluded that:

The 1990s have witnessed a remarkable cycle of world conferences convened by the United Nations ... [The UN], playing the harmonizing role envisaged by its founding Charter, served as an indispensable forum where diverse points of view were aired, where proposals were debated and where, most importantly, political consensus was achieved. As a result, the international community – Governments, non-governmental organizations, and representatives of civil society – has been able to set a new course for a new era in global affairs.[15]

His immediate predecessor, Boutros Boutros-Ghali quotes a "bitter critic" of such meetings. He does this because Boutros-Ghali believes the unnamed critic described such conferences accurately:

UN meetings are not just talkathons. They are opportunities to seed international law with new norms and rights, many of them hidden in apparently routine language. Though not immediately binding on any nation, after some time they may be cited as "customary" interpretations of international law and acquire some legal force ... UN conferences now have a precise use in hardball international politics.[16]

To begin to address the relative merits of these conflicting – if not actually diametrically opposed – contentions and to uncover the ways in which NGO participation shapes the conferences and their implementation in particular directions, it is necessary to systematically and objectively assess the implementation, follow-up, actions taken and consequences of a variety of recent UN-sponsored world conferences. The reasons for focusing more attention on this phase of the policy-making process are both academic and policy-motivated.

Scholars of international relations – particularly students of foreign policy and international public administration – have long called for more attention to the implementation phase of the policy-making process.[17] Traut's recent study applies the insights of some of this literature to the Beijing Conference. Her particular goal is to the factors that make for successful implementation of a conference's goals. These include: clarity, simplicity and compatibility of and consensus on policy goals; adequate resources; supportive media; effective and authoritative leadership; capable and flexible implementers who have honed their skills in negotiation, compromise, and cooption; and an ability to control the external environment.[18]

The public policy motives behind the need to investigate the implementation and follow-up to such conferences relates to the concerns of

some of their major funders. While this is most obvious in the US case –
the Foreign Relations Authorization Act for fiscal years 2000–2001 explicitly prohibits the US funding of the sorts of conferences discussed in
this volume unless they were approved by the UN prior to 1 October
1998[19] – many other governments are of a similar mind.[20] In the US case,
most of the notoriety on opposition to UN funding is tied to the Chair of
the US Senate Foreign Relations Committee, Jesse Helms,[21] but support
for a moratorium on UN global conferences is longstanding and widespread within the US government. The need for proving their worth
through evidence of the successful follow-up has been a theme for the
Clinton administration at least since 1995, when Secretary of State Warren Christopher called for a moratorium in his address to the 50th Session
of the UN General Assembly.[22]

Notes

1. The most famous of which were the World Disarmament Conference (February 1932) and the World Economic Conferences (1927 and 1933).
2. Jacques Fomerand, "UN Conferences: Media Events or Genuine Diplomacy?" 2 *Global Governance* (September–December 1996), Appendix.
3. Richard Reitano, "Summits, Multilateral Diplomacy, and the United Nations," in *Multilateral Diplomacy and the United Nations Today*, edited by James P. Muldoon, Jr. et al. (Boulder, CO: Westview Press, 1999), p. 119, n6.
4. J. Smith, "Building Political Will after UNCED: Earth Action," in *Transnational Social Movements and Global Politics*, edited by J. C. C. Smith and Ron Pagnucco (Syracuse: Syracuse University Press, 1997), pp. 190–191. Reitano, "Summits," *ibid.*, p. 115.
5. Reitano, "Summits," p. 115.
6. "Building Political Will," p. 189, n. 4 above.
7. John M. Goshko, "U.N. Conferences Come Under Fire: Critics Say World Body Can't Afford Meetings Amid Financial Crisis," *Washington Post*, 25 November 1995, p. A16.
8. Polison van Rooy, "The Frontiers of Influence: NGO Lobbying at the 1974 World Food Conference, The 1992 Earth Summit and Beyond," 25 *World Development* (1997), p. 97.
9. Former US Secretary of State Warren Christopher at the September 1995 meeting of the UN General Assembly articulated a variant of this position: "We should adopt a moratorium on big UN conferences since the present series is completed, concentrating instead on meeting the commitments of those we have held." As quoted in Goshko, "U.N. Conferences," p. A16, n. 7 above.
10. This criticism was particularly levelled at the Social Summit. Goshko, "U.N. Conferences," p. A16, *ibid.*
11. Peter Willetts, "Consultative Status for NGOs at the United Nations," in *"The Conscience of the World": The Influence of Non-Governmental Organisations in the U.N. System*, edited by Peter Willetts (Washington: Brookings Institution, 1996), p. 49.
12. Fomerand, "UN Conferences", p. 262, n. 2 above.
13. Former UN Secretary General Boutros Boutros-Ghali was among the most passionate defenders. In late 1995, he characterized the conferences as "the UN's version of cable news – the way in which we are able to shine a light into dark corners and many parts of the world and bring awareness of these problems to people who otherwise wouldn't

have the opportunity to learn about them." Goshko, "U.N. Conferences," p. A16, n. 7 above.

14. See, for example, *United Nations Conferences* and *UN Conferences: What Have They Accomplished*, ⟨http://www.un.org/News/facts/confercs.htm⟩. On this topic, generally, see Paul Taylor, "The Origins and Institutional Setting of the UN Special Conferences," in *Global Issues in the United Nations' Framework*, edited by Paul Taylor and A. J. R. Groom (New York: St. Martins Press, 1989) and United Nations, Department of Public Information, *World Conferences*, p. 2.

15. Quoted in Reitano, "Summits,", p. 115, n. 3 above.

16. Boutros Boutros-Ghali, *Unvanquished: A U.S.-U.N. Saga* (New York: Random House, 1999), p. 174.

17. See, for example, Karen Mingst and Michael G. Schechter, "Assessing Intergovernmental Organization Problems and Prospects," 22 *Review of International Studies* (July 1985), pp. 199–206.

18. Carol Ann Traut, "Policy Implementation in an International Setting: A Case Study of China and the 1995 United Nations Conference on Women," 22 *International Journal of Public Administration* (No. 2, 1999), pp. 285–308.

19. Significantly, this allows for US financial support of the World Conference Against Racism, Racial Discrimination, Xenophobia and Related Intolerance, as it was authorized by UN General Assembly Resolution 52/111 of 12 December 1997. Accordingly, the US government has committed $250,000 toward that conference.

20. Conference Report on HR 3194, Consolidated Appropriations Act, 2000 (US House of Representatives, 17 November 1999), ⟨http://thomas.loc.gov/home/omni99/ BigReport.html⟩

21. Helms's reform and restructuring proposal for the UN included "forbidding" UN global conferences, "for example the Beijing women's summit that caused such a stir in this country and elsewhere, and the Rio Earth summit …" Of course, all the US could do was to limit US contributions and the bill signed by President Clinton included the aforementioned moratorium, something a bit less than Helms called for, i.e. "… that the American taxpayers will never, never again be forced to pay the exorbitant costs of such boondoggles as the two [Beijing and Rio] that I mentioned." Foreign Affairs Reform and Restructuring Act of 1997 (Senate, 16 June 1997), s. 903, p. S5655.

22. Address by Secretary of State Warren Christopher to the 50th Session of the United Nations General Assembly, New York, New York, 25 September 1995, ⟨http://dosfan.lib/uic/edu/ERC/briefing/dossec/1995/9509/950925dosses.html⟩

2

Implementing global goals for children: Lessons from UNICEF experience

Richard Jolly

History will judge the UN global conferences of the 1990s as landmarks of international efforts in the twentieth century to advance human rights and human development. Four of these conferences were at summit level and all involved senior representation from virtually every country in the world. The themes were lofty in their vision but down-to-earth in their human specifics – education for all, better health and nutrition for children, protecting the environment, human rights, reproductive health and family planning, poverty eradication, the advancement and empowerment of women, human settlements in an urbanizing world, food security for all. All of these priority themes were set in a frame of sustainable development, seeking and receiving government commitments but recognizing the role of community and non-government initiatives and especially important for the poorest countries, the need for international support.

Table 2.1 shows the list of the conferences, with their dates and participation. It is a remarkable list – remarkable for the range of topics covered, the vision of the goals endorsed, the practical commitments made and the process established for monitoring follow up. Beginning in 1996, the conferences were also brought into the mainstream of UN reform. Although major international conferences on development had been held in previous decades, especially in the 1970s, none were comparable – for size, level of political participation, specifics of commitments or breadth of follow-up.

Table 2.1 Participation at and follow-up targets of the major world conferences of the 1990s[1]

| Year | Title | Participation | | | Follow-up[2] targets |
		Gov'ts	HoS[3]	NGOs	
1990	World Summit for Children	159	71	45	Goals for 2000
1992	Earth Summit	172	108	2,400	Agenda 21
1993	Conference on Human Rights	171		800	Vienna Declaration
1994	International Conference on Population and Development	179		1,500	Goals for 2015
1995	World Summit for Social Development	186	117	811	Copenhagen
1995	Fourth World Conference on Women	189		2,100	Beijing Declaration
1996	Habitat II	171		2,400	Istanbul Declaration
1996	World Food Summit	186	97	many	Goal for 2015

1. Source: UN Briefing papers, *The World Conferences: Developing Priorities for the 21st Century* (New York: Department of Public Information, United Nations, 1997).
2. This is a highly selective summary of the many follow-up actions agreed, usually at national, local, and international levels.
3. Number of heads of state attending comprising presidents, vice-presidents, or prime ministers.

Notwithstanding this record, expectations of practical impact of these global conferences are often met with scepticism. Too often, a worldly, all-knowing cynicism emerges, apparently based on the belief that such global commitments have never had much practical impact, never can and never will. Even more depressing is the associated belief that none of this really matters. What happens in developing countries is the result of their people or their governments and for this – it is argued – international goals and support are of little consequence.

The purpose of this chapter is to assemble some of the evidence for suggesting that such opinions are excessively negative – both factually and as a guide to future action. The chapter focuses on experience in UNICEF, on the successes of the child survival and development revolution in the 1980s and of implementing the goals of the World Summit for Children (WSC) in the 1990s. But positive UN experience is by no means limited to UNICEF. Other UN organizations and specialized agencies like WHO, UNESCO, ILO, UNDP, and UNFPA have also had their own positive achievements. The purpose of the chapter is not to sing the praises of the UN system let alone encourage any easy complacency over future outcomes. Rather it is to identify the lessons making for success. To this end, the chapter emphasizes key points of follow-up, which appear to make for successful implementation – and which will determine the extent to which the global conferences of the 1990s achieve long-run impact.

The UN and development goals

From its beginning, the UN and its constituent agencies have focused on priorities for economic and social development and provided for countries to discuss these priorities and make commitments for their achievement. The most comprehensive early initiative was the Development Decade of the 1960s, called for by President Kennedy in a speech to the General Assembly in 1961. The central goal of this first decade was that developing countries should accelerate their economic growth – to achieve by the end of the 1960s a combined rate of GNP growth approaching 5 per cent per annum. This goal was widely dismissed as unrealistic when the decade was launched. In fact, this goal was exceeded. The growth rate of developing countries averaged 5 per cent per annum over the 1960s. Accordingly, a new goal of 6 per cent was set for the 1970s – an average that was nearly achieved – though in large part because of higher oil prices and growth rates in the oil exporting states.

Such goals were by no means limited to global macroeconomic performance. UNESCO set goals for education expansion in each of the main geographic regions from 1960 to 1980. By 1980, enrolments at secondary and higher levels had often considerably exceeded the regional targets. Even at primary levels, failure to achieve the target growth enrolment ratios (in sub-Saharan Africa for instance) was the result not of enrolments growing more slowly than targeted, but of population growth exceeding that originally anticipated.

WHO also had successes. In the 1950s and 1960s, yaws and some other infectious diseases were virtually eradicated. A major onslaught against malaria was launched globally, unfortunately failing in the objective of eradication – but nonetheless reducing cases and deaths from malaria substantially. The resurgence of malaria in the 1980s and early 1990s has recently stimulated a major new WHO effort to roll back malaria.

The great success of WHO in the 1960s and 1970s was first to set the goal for the eradication of smallpox and then to devise and lead a global strategy. After several years of debate, the goal for eradicating smallpox within ten years was agreed in 1966. Remarkably there was at that time no clear idea of exactly how it could or would be achieved. So acceptance of the goal stands as a major example of bold vision and an important reminder that a bold vision always involves some leap of faith. If the goal is important and in principle achievable, adopt the goal and then work out the strategy and specifics to achieve it!

In the case of eradicating smallpox, much progress was achieved in the 1960s – mostly by vaccinating, one by one, an increasing proportion of children in each country. By 1970, however, it was clear that such an approach would never be sufficient to eradicate smallpox in the poorer developing countries, given their limited health care facilities. Thus was born a totally different approach – the "identify, isolate, track and vaccinate" technique. Fire-fighting teams were assembled in all the countries concerned, which were rushed to the area whenever any new case was discovered. These teams then tracked and vaccinated all persons who had recent contact with the person with smallpox.

Using this approach, country-by-country progress was made over the 1970s, eliminating smallpox from Latin America, then South Asia, finally from the Horn of Africa. By October 1977 the last endemic case was discovered in Somalia. Three years later smallpox was declared eradicated. This remarkable success was achieved in little more than a decade after the global goal had been formally adopted. National and international expenditures to achieve the goal had been barely $300 million, less than the cost of three fighter-bomber aircraft, and very much less than the annual expenditures of developed and developing counties at that time on preventive programmes of vaccination and other measures of smallpox control. The savings over the subsequent two decades have been a large multiple of the modest costs of eradication. Yet the significance of the achievement is even greater. It is a clear example of a global goal that required action in every country – a global goal unachievable without worldwide effort and that was achieved.

This remarkable success set the stage for accelerated international action for health in the 1980s. WHO and UNICEF joined together in 1978 (in Alma Ata) to hold a major international conference on health for all. This formulated and then endorsed the primary health care strategy directed to the goal of Health for All (HFA) by the year 2000. Initially, this seemed to be making progress, with many countries developing primary health care programmes. But after several years, UNICEF felt that more focused and accelerated action was needed. Four years after Alma Ata, therefore, UNICEF launched "a Child Survival and Development Revolution" backed up by a "GOBI-FFF strategy" to focus on specific goals as key actions to achieve accelerated action. GOBI-FFF embodied four priorities (GOBI) with three supportive measures (FFF). The GOBI-four were:

– growth monitoring, to ensure steady weight gain for all children up to five years of age;
– oral rehydration therapy, to tackle diarrhoea, then the largest the cause of children under five deaths of some 5 million annually;
– breastfeeding and supplementary feeding for the young child, critical for nutrition and health;
– immunization against 6 vaccine – preventable diseases – measles, tuberculosis, diphtheria, tetanus, pertussus (whooping cough) and polio, between them accounting for a further 4 million deaths of children under five each year.

The GOBI actions were reckoned to address about two-thirds of the main causes of the 15 million child deaths occurring each year in the early 1980s. The Gobi-four were to be supplemented by three other actions, more expensive and recognized to be larger and be more difficult to achieve:

– food supplementation, to tackle protein-energy malnutrition;
– family planning and birth spacing;
– female education, at least to completion of primary education.

The GOBI-FFF programme was a huge success. By 1990, the coverage of immunization in developing countries had reached 81 per cent compared with under 20 per cent in 1980. Deaths from diseases preventable by immunization had fallen by over 2 million. The use of oral rehydration therapy had become widespread, and annual deaths from diarrhoea had fallen by at least a million. The proportion of mothers breastfeeding had increased and growth monitoring had become much more common. Malnutrition of the under-fives had also been reduced in most regions of the world, as recent surveys confirm.

By 1990, deaths of children under five had been lowered to 12 million, a decline of 3 million per year in spite of an increase by over a quarter in the number of children born each year over the decade. Thus by 1990, some 5–6 million children were surviving each year who would otherwise have died, if 1980 mortality rates had still prevailed. This was a larger reduction in child mortality than in any previous decade.

Notwithstanding this success, the focus on these highly specific interventions had not been without controversy, especially among health professionals (less so among politicians and development planners, whose support was often decisive). It was argued that to concentrate on a core of specific high priority goals was contrary to the spirit of Alma-Ata. Primary health care (PHC), it was said, required broad-based community-led health care, not top-down priorities. UNICEF countered that the GOBI-FFF priorities responded to the basic health needs of all children, already identified in the specifics of primary health care. By focusing initially on this core of actions, political momentum, community involvement and health care structures would be established for use later in tackling a broader range of health problems. By 1990, WHO's own review of the achievements of the first decade of PHC and Alma Ata identified immunization and oral rehydration therapy as the two priorities of PHC which had seen most progress.

Moreover, extraordinary momentum and support for child health actions had built up in many developing countries. Earlier debate over the finer points of strategy became lost in the euphoria of celebrating the remarkable successes of child survival and development – political and social as well as in public health and development. The question was raised – what next?

The next landmark became the World Summit for Children (WSC) – in fact, the first of the world summits of the 1990s, although the subsequent summits were not foreseen at the time.

The World Summit for Children was held on 29–30 September 1990, at the United Nations, New York. It was attended by 71 heads of state, including all the presidents or prime ministers of the G7 industrial countries. Ministerial representatives attended from some 90 other countries and there was participation by 45 major NGOs as well as by all the relevant UN agencies.

With this positive experience and the even larger high level attendance at the three world summits which followed, it is now difficult to recall the many doubts and heavy doses of scepticism that initially were poured on the idea of even calling for a summit level meeting on a topic like children. Many said that no more than a handful of governments would attend. Indeed, if the proposal to hold this first summit had been put as a simple recommendation to the UNICEF executive board, it probably would not have been agreed. But the ground had been carefully prepared. The proposal to hold the summit was first floated in UNICEF's annual publication as "a possibility," then supported by two friendly prime ministers, issued as an invitation from six presidents and prime ministers – those from Canada, Egypt, Pakistan, Sweden, Colombia, and Senegal. All had been persuaded and mobilized by the dynamic and visionary Jim Grant, Executive Director of UNICEF. Once committed, these six presidents and prime ministers and their representatives never wavered.

So the first summit came about and was widely hailed as a success. It served directly to stimulate the holding of the Rio Earth Summit at the summit level in 1992. And further goals and commitments for improving the situation of children in the 1990s were adopted.

These goals, set out in Table 2.2, had a triple impact for the 1990s. First, they became the basis for national plans of action, prepared in some 150 countries, mostly during 1991 and 1993. Secondly, they served as the

Table 2.2 The World Summit for Children mid-decade evaluation

Area of action	End-target year 2000	Mid-target year 1995	Status 1990		Status 1995		Specific challenges
			per cent (countries/ people)	number (countries/ people)	per cent (countries/ people)	number (countries/ people)	
	Major goals						
Under-five and infant mortality	Reduction by one third, or max 70 per 1,000 living births	In line with end-target	–	–	39% of countries in line, 17% major progress, 44% unlikely to reach end-of-decade goal	One fifth of the world's under-fives in line, whereas two thirds are unlikely to be in line	Sub-Saharan Africa (85% of countries) and South Asia (72% lags)
Maternal mortality	Reduction by half	In line with end-target	0.43% maternal deaths	585,000 maternal deaths	No evidence of progress	No evidence of progress	
Malnutrition	Reduction by half for children under 5	Reduction by 20%	30% under-fives underweight	177 million malnourished children under 5	31%, unchanged rate of malnutrition	174 million malnourished	
Safe drinking water and sanitary means of excreta disposal	Universal access	Narrow gap between 1990 and goal: 71% water and 42% sanitation coverage	61% safe water coverage, 36% sanitation coverage	1.6 billion people lacked water, 2.6 billion lacked sanitation	75% water supply coverage, 34% sanitation	Additional 780 million people access to water: 1.1 billion people lack water, 2.9 billion lack sanitation	Asia and the Pacific was the only region attaining its mid-decade goal for water, all regions fell back on sanitation but West Asia fell back on sanitation

Basic education and completion of primary education	Universal access, at least 80% completion rate and reducing gender disparities	In line with end-target	Average net enrolment rate 80% for developing countries	100 million 6–11 years old did not attend school, total 496 million enrolled: 87 out of 129 countries above 80%	Average 82% net enrolment rate for developing countries	All regions but sub-Saharan Africa and South Asia meet the goal: total 545 million enrolled	High drop-out rates and still flagrant gender disparity
Adult illiteracy rate	Reduction by half and eradication of gender disparity	In line with end-target	34% illiteracy rate in developing countries	900 million people	30% illiteracy rate (decrease of 12%)	300 million more literate people, but still 900 million illiterate	Illiteracy tends to concentrate among ethnic and cultural minorities and is highest in South Asia

Supporting/sectoral goals

Immunization, measles, DPT and polio	At least 90% immunization coverage and global eradication of polio	At least 80% immunization coverage (DPT3), eradication of polio, 95% reduction in measles death and 90% in measles cases	43% of countries already reached mid-decade target	55 countries already reached mid-decade immunization level, 74 countries below target	67% of countries have reached mid-decade goal, 9% within range. For measles, a reduction of 86%	129 countries reached goal, 17 close, 46 lag behind; 3 million children saved every year, but 2 million more could be saved	Only 24% of sub-Saharan African states

17

Table 2.2 (cont.)

Area of action	End-target year 2000	Mid-target year 1995	Status 1990 per cent (countries/people)	Status 1990 number (countries/people)	Status 1995 per cent (countries/people)	Status 1995 number (countries/people)	Specific challenges
		Supporting/sectoral goals					
Diarrhoeal disease	Reduction by half in deaths for age less than 5 years, quarter reduction in incidence rate	At least 80% use of oral rehydration therapy (ORT) and continued feeding	Average 33% usage of ORT	No developing country on the targeted level	Average 85% use in developing countries; total of 49% of under-fives represented		Only Latin America/Caribbean and Middle East/North Africa had average usage lower than the mid-decade goal
Guinea worm disease	Elimination	Interruption of transmission in affected villages			Decline of incidence by 97%		Underlines the importance of peace for successful implementation of health-related policies
Acute respiratory infections	Reduction by one third	In line with end-target			67% of target countries have implemented ARI activities	59 out of 88 countries have initiated ARI programmes	Non-measurable

18

Iodine deficiency disorders	Virtual elimination	At least 90% iodization in IDD-affected countries (in total 88 countries)	0.9 billion people obtained adequate iodine intake	55% of the population obtain adequate iodine; 24% reached goal, 16% within range	2.4 billion people (1.5 billion more or 166%), 21 countries reached mid-decade target, 14 within range, 52 countries lagging
Vitamin A deficiency	Virtual elimination	At least 80% with adequate intake for age less than 2 years		22% close to goal, 32% starting programmes, 46% lagging	17 countries close to mid-decade target, 24 starting up programmes, and 35 lagging
Breastfeeding	Exclusive breast-feeding for 4–6 months and continuation into second year	Ending supplies of infant formula and breast milk substitute			Over 100 countries have taken action to prevent distribution of breast milk substitutes: 7,762 maternity facilities designated baby-friendly since 1991

priority focus for UNICEF support of country action, especially over the period 1990–1995. Finally, most of the goals were reaffirmed in the subsequent global conferences of the 1990s. This last represented important and significant support, an indication that the adoption of the goals at the World Summit for Children in 1990 had in no sense been a casual endorsement, devoid of serious debate and consideration. Both of the main WSC documents – the Declaration and Plan of Action – were scrutinized in capitals as well as by delegates in New York, analysed, debated, adjusted, and readjusted. It was appropriate that they subsequently served as baseline human goals for the Earth Summit in 1992 and for most of the other global conferences of the 1990s.

Lessons of successful experience

At the time of writing, it is too early to give a detailed assessment of the extent to which the WSC goals will have been achieved. At best, it will be a year or two after 2000 before the position in the year 2000 is even broadly known, let alone known country-by-country for each of the 10 major goals or the 17 supporting ones.

A mid-decade assessment for 1995 was however completed by the end of 1996 and revealed some important achievements with respect to the stepping stone goals of mid-1995 and in relation to longer-run trends:
– child mortality had continued to fall;
– primary school enrolments had increased;
– malnutrition of children under five had declined, measured by stunting or underweight;
– access to safe drinking water had improved;
– dramatic progress had been made in reducing micro-nutrient deficiencies
  – through such measures as the iodation of salt and vitamin A supplementation, leading to major reductions in iodine and vitamin A deficiency.

Equally important was the quantum advance in terms of defining and implementing a wide range of country policies and actions in favour of children. In part this was the by-product of the successful implementation of the child survival and development revolution, which raised awareness of the needs of children and of the possibility of making accelerated advances towards them. But it was also the direct result of the process of ratifying the Convention on the Rights of the Child – a convention first signed in 1989 but within eight years ratified by all but two countries in the world.

As on earlier occasions, the possibilities for achieving such progress in response to global goals was initially doubted, gradually accepted, later explained away. Even today, explanations for the successes are often absurdly oversimplified. One argument is that children "naturally command popular support," another that "interventions like immunization and supplementation to deal with micro-nutrient deficiencies are no more than magic bullets, easy to organize in a top-down fashion, but of little lasting significance for development." A third is that UNICEF has the finance and field organization itself to ensure delivery – so that performance shows little more than one agency's commitment. In contrast to these is the argument that positive advances are mostly the result of positive underlying economic trends, from which progress in child indicators will follow automatically.

Several of these explanations are in conflict with one another and, in my view, all are gross misrepresentations of reality. Country-by-country experience shows that mobilization of effort and sustained action were always vital to progress. So also was a wider range of supportive actions by UNICEF and WHO in assisting national action.

Success is all the more remarkable given that the 1980s were "a lost decade" for economic development in much of the third world. The 1980s and early 1990s were years of economic setback and decline for 80 to 100 developing countries, especially in Latin America and sub-Saharan Africa. In spite of these economic difficulties, child mortality and nutrition, water and sanitation, immunization and access to iodized salt and vitamin A improved. Of course, child-focused actions in the areas of the major goals received special support – but by no means only support from the international community, let alone from UNICEF. UNICEF did indeed spend heavily in support of accelerating immunization coverage over 1988 to 1990, with UNICEF expenditure on immunization peaking at $150 million in 1990 – the year 80 per cent coverage was first achieved. But within two or three years, UNICEF expenditure on immunization had fallen by almost half – while immunization coverage was maintained or increased further in 80 per cent of the countries, which achieved the 1990 goals.

In contrast to these oversimplified explanations, 11 factors explain, in my view and experience, the dramatic success in advancing towards the goals of the World Summit for Children. These factors were conscious parts of follow-up strategy to the goals of the World Summit for Children, building from the experience of implementing the GOBI goals in the 1980s. Their broader significance is that, in principle, they all can be applied to the follow-up of goals endorsed at the other global conferences.

1. *Major commitment to implementing the goals*

Such commitment has clearly been demonstrated by a good number of countries and was made a guiding principle of organization and action in

UNICEF – and in varying degrees, others of its UN and donor and NGO partners.

But such international commitment is far from typical. Goals may be readily adopted, but are often repeated mostly as rhetorical commitments in speeches, but not as the driving principles for organization and action in the institution concerned.

2. *Strong and determined leadership*

For UNICEF the commitment grew out of the single-minded and charismatic leadership of James P. Grant, UNICEF's Executive Director from 1980–1995. Not immediately, but gradually over the 1980s, Jim Grant built UNICEF into a committed organization, decentralized in action and organization to country level (and in larger countries to sub-country level) but united by a strong and public focus on a corporate policy and commitment to goal achievement for children. Initially in the 1980s, the goals were those of GOBI, in the 1990s, the goals of the World Summit for Children.

The experience of successfully implementing the goals, country-by-country over the 1980s, built up a powerful sense of morale and commitment, as well as highly specific knowledge of techniques like social mobilization, political advocacy and low-cost approaches. It also increasingly won support and commitment from many allies outside the organization. And from the totality of success emerged the 11 elements of strategy described here.

3. *Political and social mobilization*

A remarkable leader and a committed organization can do much – but ultimately what is achieved depends on a broader process of mobilization, country-by-country. UNICEF often referred to the need for a global alliance for children to underpin such a process of political and social mobilization. This recognized that UNICEF could be catalytic but that the main actors and actions would have to be country-based and far broader.

Two examples demonstrated the power of such efforts for immunization, when mobilization went far beyond the conventional health system. In the mid-1980s in Turkey, school teachers played a critical role in mobilizing villagers for a nationwide immunization campaign. In Colombia the Catholic church and village priests played a major role in mobilizing people for a wide variety of actions for child health. In a myriad of ways, the process was repeated in countries all around the world. By 1990, the year when immunization coverage first exceeded an average of 80 per cent in developing countries, social mobilization had reached the point when the globalization immunization effort could be described by Jim Grant "as the largest peacetime process of mobilization that the world has ever seen."

This laid the foundation for the World Summit for Children and the next phase of mobilization. Following the summit, a wider frame of goals and a broader process of mobilization for children were adopted. In 1995, the mid-decade year, Jim Grant met individually with nearly 50 heads of state to emphasize the need for country-by-country commitment to achieve the summit goals, the possibility of each country accelerating progress towards them, and the political and social returns of doing so. Meetings of ministers of health and ministers of finance or foreign ministers were also held at regional level.

UNICEF always emphasized that mobilization was a social process, not just a political one. Thus UNICEF worked closely with the churches, Catholic and Protestant and with Islamic, Hindu, and other religious groups.

The Rotarians were major allies in the cause. This worldwide group of business leaders pledged in the mid-1980s to raise $100 million towards the goal of polio eradication by 2005. In fact, pursuit of the goal became so popular and so successful that by the mid-1990s the Rotarians had raised $240 million and, in parallel, had provided practical support for community immunization efforts through their 35,000 Rotarian clubs worldwide. The Jaycees, a parallel movement of younger business leaders provided support for oral rehydration therapy to reduce diarrhoea deaths.

There were hundreds of other examples. The key point is that the process of political and social mobilization for children's goals turned these priority actions into a major movement, far beyond the activities of any one group alone – be it government, NGO, community action, international agency. UNICEF saw it as proof that a grand alliance for children was emerging. In early 1991, soon after the WSC was held, UNICEF staff consciously discussed and planned how such a grand alliance could be strengthened and extended.

The other eight lessons of strategy can be presented more briefly. None stands alone and none is narrowly organizational. Each gained power by being part of a total mobilizing process of committed and determined follow-up action.

4. *Focus on the determined action and organization needed to support country-by-country activities to achieve goals*

The strength of GOBI was its clear focus on a small core of priority reinforcing goals. In contrast, the WSC was comprised of 27 goals; 10 major goals and 17 supporting ones.

If GOBI was too narrow, some have argued that the WSC goals were too many and too broad. It is still too early to judge. My own judgement is that this has not been a serious obstacle. UNICEF as an organization had gained in experience and maturity – and by 1990 was certainly able to take on a broader range of goals. If there is slippage in implementation, it is more likely the result of a change in management style than of the inherent problems in tackling the wider range of goals.

5. *Country-by-country implementation*

Goals need to be focused and adapted to local circumstances. In the case of the World Summit for Children, the goals for each particular country were set out by the country concerned in its own National Plan of Action (NPA), of which some 150 were prepared in the first five years of the 1990s.

6. *Going to scale*

Though ultimately each country had responsibility to fix its own goals, UNICEF staff were encouraged to apply heavy pressure "to go to scale" – that is, to make national plans which envisaged expansion on a scale which would reach universal coverage within a foreseeable time-frame. Again, this approach often stirred controversy and opposition, including at times from the World Bank and other UN agencies. It was argued that it was unrealistic in poor countries to be overambitious and that to plan to go to scale would lead to a distortion of broader priorities.

UNICEF argued that there was a triple benefit and discipline in planning to go to scale: it required a focus on the basics for all; it would necessitate a concentration on low-cost approaches, and it would ensure equity. One should also add that it was required by a human rights-based approach to development. But going to scale was a guideline, not a slavish formula. Thus, in the 1980s, there was careful debate as to how to define universal coverage of immunization. If interpreted literally as 100 per cent coverage, such a goal would have doomed the programme to failure – and lost early credibility with a goal that was almost always unattainable. Thus "universal coverage" was formally defined (in collaboration with WHO) as 80 per cent coverage for each of the six targeted antigens. By 1990, 72 countries had achieved universal coverage by this definition – and virtually every country was encouraged to achieve significant expansion.

7. *Doable low-cost strategies*

Goals, commitment, leadership and mobilization count for nothing unless it is clear what needs to be done and what it is practicable to do within the resources available. This is easier said than done – and often even the attempt is neglected. Many times countries embark on small-scale efforts or pilot projects, worthy in themselves but lacking the potential to go to scale because the cost per person reached far exceeded the resources available if coverage was to be universal. Such efforts and projects receive donor support precisely because their resource needs are limited. But if the net result is to encourage an approach that is not replicable on scale, the whole effort can be counter-productive.

The essential point is to develop approaches that can go to scale at reasonable cost in terms of the public or private resources available. Immunization against the basic antigens was one such approach, oral rehydration another, both implemented within a local low-cost community-based health delivery system. And there are many other elements: primary education, low-cost water and sanitation systems, PHC nutritional support, family planning and reproductive health care. The five UN main agencies involved estimated the cost of reaching universal coverage for all these interventions in all developing countries within 10 years as an additional $70–80 billion dollars per year. Although not a small sum, the total could be achieved by implementing the 20/20 formula under which developing countries would allocate some 20 per cent of public expenditure to these basic social services each year and donor countries 20 per cent of their aid budgets. Although full data are not available, it is estimated that developing countries allocate an average of about 13 per cent to basic social services and donor countries about 10 per cent of their aid budgets.

8. *Building on success*

The most powerful form of advocacy is demonstration – an example that is working or has worked. "If it has happened, it must be possible." UNICEF mobilized early support for child survival and development actions by taking a few leaders from one country to see actions underway in another – praised the progress underway and then shamelessly challenged the visiting leaders to go back home and show that they could do better. Many times the visiting leaders came not from another country but from a different district or region within the same country. Sometimes, the challenge was to learn from one approach and to apply it to a different problem – using techniques of social marketing developed for selling soap powder and applying them to family planning, to prevention of HIV/AIDS or to the promotion of oral rehydration therapy to tackle diarrhoea. Many of the new approaches were developed by people themselves.

In Peru in the early 1990s, when cholera attacked at the very period when many health workers were on strike, it was the women's groups who took action. These groups had already developed techniques for encouraging widespread use of oral rehydration salts for control of diarrhoea. These techniques were applied directly to the control of cholera – using the same organization structure for outreach but with the added twist that ORS packets were only given out in small numbers, thereby requiring persons treating cholera victims to come back for more. This provided a simple monitoring system for tracking the epidemic. In spite of there being over 600,000 cholera cases, the death rate was kept below 1 per cent, far less than the mortality rates of 15 to 20 per cent often suffered in previous epidemics.

9. *Lead agency support*

In major efforts of mobilization, nothing ever works out exactly as planned. There is a need therefore to identify an agency or organization of last resort, ready to provide whatever is needed in order to ensure that the progress towards the goals is kept on track, even when the unexpected setback or obstacle arises. UNICEF accepted this role, and set aside sufficient unallocated resources in 1990 to be in a position to fulfil it.

The point is important. Social mobilization is in part a political process, dependent on building up commitment, morale, and a sense of momentum. Once disrupted, whatever the cause, it may be difficult to re-establish momentum. So a support of last resort is needed. This is all the more so in poorer countries where basic infrastructure and the margins of re-allocable resources are very limited – and where economic setbacks and constraints can be serious. But a sense of proportion is needed. UNICEF's unallocated reserve for the worldwide support of immunization and oral rehydration in 1990 was of the order of $25 million, about one sixth of UNICEF's total expenditure on these two major interventions in that year. In relation to global expenditures on most aspects of health, it is not a large sum. But it was vital.

10. *Teamwork with others*

The above presentation is largely in terms of what UNICEF did and learnt from the process of mobilization towards the goals for children. It would be a great mistake, however, to suggest that UNICEF was acting alone – or even, in many cases, that UNICEF was the main actor. Undoubtedly UNICEF played a catalytic role and was expected and asked to do so by its governing body. But it was always true that UNICEF was working with and alongside the government of the country concerned and almost always with many local groups and organizations, non-government and private sector. None of the progress achieved would have been possible without the commitment and support of these groups. The fact that immunization rates have mostly been sustained over the 1990s and actions broadened into many other areas, would never have been possible without this country-by-country support. One proof of this is the way immunization coverage rates were maintained in the 1990s, even while UNICEF's own expenditures on immunization were reduced to barely half of the peak levels of 1990.

Internationally also, teamwork with other UN and donor agencies was from the beginning a major part of the effort. WHO was the outstanding partner in all the child health and survival actions and initiatives. There was a natural comparative advantage between the two organizations going back many years. WHO had the medical expertise and many contacts with the Ministry of Health and formal links with the health care professionals and institutions of the country. UNICEF tended to have its main links with the Ministry of Planning and Finance, supportive links with Health, Education, Rural Development and Women along with a wide range of less formal contacts with NGOs and organizations concerned with children. Together, this range of links made for a powerful synergy.

Other parts of the UN were in on the act, depending on the specifics of the country and the strength and capacity of the UN organization. This included WFP, UNFPA, UNDP, and the World Bank. Increasingly over the 1990s, these linkages grew in closeness and systematic organization. The goals of the global conferences of the 1990s have increasingly been used as the basis for collaboration. There is still far to go. But experience suggests that collaboration built around shared goals and efforts to reach them is both more lasting and more effective than bureaucratic procedures of formal coordination.

11. *Monitoring*

Monitoring is often seen as a somewhat boring managerial necessity for goal achievement. This is too narrow. If social mobilization is to succeed, information on progress needs to be widely disseminated. Thus in one of the Colombian immunization campaigns of the 1980s, rates of immunization coverage for each district were tracked on television, district by district, using the same scoreboard process as was developed for national elections, with the President himself following the process and urging on the districts that lagged behind the others.

Of course, monitoring is needed for use by many other parties, from local to national and by the international community. Many initiatives to improve data collection, dissemination, and monitoring have been implemented over the years and the international community has played an important role both in stimulating more attention to economic and social indicators and in improving the quality and comparability of the data collected. UNICEF's particular contribution was to develop MICS – a low cost multi-indicator cluster survey approach which provided information on progress towards a variety of the WSC goals.

Conclusions

Experience in implementing global goals for child health in the 1980s and the broader set of goals endorsed by the World Summit for Children in the 1990s have major lessons for implementing the broader set of goals arising from the global conferences of the 1990s, especially global action towards poverty reduction and human development. National efforts will always be central. But the global community also has a major role – as a catalyst for action, in sharing experience, and in providing and mobilizing direct support.

Too often such international support is treated as a matter of providing aid and development assistance. UNICEF experience shows that this is too narrow a perspective – and the 11 lessons demonstrate some of the practicalities of how a broader approach can be made to work. Many countries and the international community could gain much in impact and effectiveness if these lessons were more broadly applied.

There are also important lessons for global conference diplomacy. First, strong leadership within the international community is essential. Without this, little will happen. There are too many differing views and conflicting interests for major initiatives to emerge without strong leadership, let alone be carried through into implementation. Jim Grant provided this – and still serves as a model within the United Nations.

Secondly, follow-up is enormously helped by having the total commitment of a UN agency with programme resources, filed offices, and strong national groups of supporters. UNICEF brought all of these to bear in preparing for the World Summit for Children and subsequently in supporting country-by-country action to implement the goals. Only time will tell how well this was sustained over the whole of the 1990s. But UNICEF's immediate support encouraged countries to prepare national plans to embark on many areas of practical follow-up action, more than appears with some of the other global conferences.

Thirdly, committed non-government groups also have an important role. In UNICEF's case, there are well-organized UNICEF national committees, nearly 40 operating in virtually all industrial countries and in some transition countries. In developing countries, UNICEF has long had strong and close relationships with many NGOs, both international NGOs like Save the Children and Oxfam and with a diversity of national NGOs in developing countries. Many of these felt deeply committed to the goals of the World Summit for Children and did much to stimulate national awareness and to maintain national commitment and support for the goals.

3

The United Nations World Conference on Human Rights: Evaluation, monitoring, and review

Clarence J. Dias

The road to Vienna

The UN World Conference on Human Rights (UNWCHR) at Vienna (June 1993) ought to have been a truly historic event. After all, it was the first such UN conference in 25 years and only the second in the entire history of the UN. But almost from its very inception, this conference seemed to be the child nobody wanted. The German government, which had initially offered to host the conference in Berlin, quickly withdrew its offer, pleading, of all things, that it could not afford the expenses involved. The UN Human Rights Centre (in Geneva) was entrusted with organizing the conference. But the Centre's reluctance and indecision was evident even a year before the conference. The Department of Public Information of the UN, fresh from its success in launching a publicity campaign to promote the UN Conference on Environment and Development in Rio, had enthusiastically prepared posters, brochures and plans for a UN radio/television campaign for UNWCHR. They were kept waiting for approval from Geneva for months while the Centre dithered, in the process of undergoing a change of leadership. UNESCAP, the agency entrusted with the responsibility of organizing an Asia-Pacific regional preparatory meeting, repeatedly postponed the date for the meeting and finally held it only at the end of March – less than three months before the date for the conference itself.

A series of preparatory committee (PrepCom) meetings, at the UN, entrusted with drawing up the agenda for the conference, failed to reach any agreement and it finally took the Third Committee of the General Assembly to draw up a provisional conference agenda as late as December 1992. This delay greatly impeded preparations for the conference, especially in respect of the UN officially commissioned background and working papers.

Fortunately, the preparatory process for UNWCHR also included a number of PrepComs at the regional level all over the world and, at these meetings, thousands of human rights NGOs virtually adopted the conference and made it their own. Several regional NGO declarations from Africa, Asia and Latin America clearly set out regional perspectives on the UNWCHR and the issues before it, well in advance of the conference.[1] A group of eminent human rights leaders met in Atlanta, Georgia and issued the Atlanta Statement of 15 January 1993 making several recommendations to the forthcoming UNWCHR. Similarly, the Ninth Nordic Seminar on Human Rights, held at Lund, Sweden, was devoted entirely to the forthcoming UNWCHR and its report of 20 January 1993 also addressed key issues to be discussed at the conference.

Two other NGO meetings were of particular importance as well. A workshop held in the Netherlands from 4–6 June 1993 (by INTRAC) addressed the theme, "Governance, Democracy and Conditionality: What Role for NGOs?" Earlier, in April 1993 a Round Table on "Strengthening Commitment to the Universality of Human Rights" was convened in Amman, Jordan (by Rights and Humanity). These meetings enabled NGOs to discuss and develop a common position on two key issues that were likely to loom large at the UNWCHR, namely the issues of universality and of human rights conditionalities.

Writing just before the conference began, this author expressed the view that NGOs might anticipate four different scenarios at Vienna and would need strategies to deal with them:
1. *Pyrrhic victories*. NGOs might find that the gains they made in Vienna were very quickly eroded or proved to be illusory. For example, the conference could well piously declare that "Women's rights are human rights" and then do no more;
2. *Containment*. If the experience of the PrepComs were indicative of what lay ahead, NGOs might well have anticipated that their efforts and initiatives would be countered, deflected and contained by the intergovernmental body through a variety of devices and techniques – especially in view of the limits to NGO participation that were put into place;
3. *Cooption* of key human rights concepts and rhetoric seemed more than likely, especially at the level of specific individual countries;

4. *Division*. Polarization along government/NGO lines, or on a North/ South basis could threaten to engulf the conference proceedings and frustrate serious treatment of issues. Challenges to universality on the one hand, and imposition of rigid human rights conditionalities on the other, could lead to fruitless and futile confrontations.

The stage was set for Vienna and, thanks to the generosity of the European Union and other donors, NGOs were well set to make the first world conference on human rights in 25 years a meaningful and productive one.

Remembering Vienna

Vienna can be regarded as the most significant of all human rights conferences to date, at least so far as participation was concerned: approximately 10,000 people assembled in Vienna, including eight heads of state, nine heads of government, ministers of justice or foreign affairs from 171 countries, 3,000 delegates from NGOs and some 2,000 journalists from all over the globe.[2]

The Vienna Conference provided drama unfolding in two acts: the NGO Conference and the UNWCHR.

Act 1: The NGO Forum

The NGO Forum "All Human Rights for All" was held from 10–12 June 1993 with some 3,000 NGO delegates taking part. The NGO Forum set itself three aims: to question critically the progress and shortcomings of the UN human rights programme; to reach joint conclusions; and to submit common NGO recommendations to the World Conference. The NGO Forum organized itself around five core working groups on: the rights of indigenous peoples; human rights of women; the relationship between development, democracy, and human rights; racism, xenophobia, ethnic violence, religious intolerance, and the rights of minorities; and a general evaluation of the UN human rights programme. As with any NGO meeting, participants, anxious to address the issues of most direct concern to them, spontaneously created a number of other working groups ranging from global subjects such as the rights of the child, the disabled, the homeless, torture and disappearances, to something as specific as the caste system. The NGO Forum programme, as printed, also indicated that there would be a number of "parallel" activities and events, notably those dealing with the human rights situation in a specific country or region. These parallel activities, including an address by the

Dalai Lama, became a hotly contested issue between some of the governments and the NGOs. These governments pressured the UN into trying to prevent the holding of the NGO-parallel activities in the Austria Centre (the conference venue) and into confiscating the NGO programme booklet. It was indeed a sorry sight to watch the Director of the UN Human Rights Centre, acting at the behest of such governments, announcing to the NGO Forum organizers that certain planned activities could not be held within the Forum. A spurious form of tenancy "conditionality" was invoked. The UN had leased the Austria Centre for the duration of the conference and had made available the basement of the Centre for the NGO Forum. They argued, therefore, that the Forum would take place on territory under UN control and, therefore, activities exposing violations against a particular member state could not be permitted to take place and, most emphatically, the Dalai Lama would not be allowed to speak within the Conference Centre. This historically unprecedented attempt by the UN and its member governments to censor and control what would take place in an NGO Forum was deplorable and especially unfortunate since it was taking place on the occasion of a World Conference on Human Rights! Participants were excluded, activities were proscribed and curbs were attempted to be introduced upon what could be discussed by NGOs within their own Forum.

Not surprisingly, the NGOs resisted successfully in some cases (discussions were free and frank within the Forum and posters, displays, and materials remained incapable of being suppressed) and unsuccessfully in other cases (some events and activities were proscribed and the Dalai Lama was made to deliver his address, in a tent in pouring rain, outside the Centre). NGO frustrations boiled over and, most unfairly, manifested themselves in the final plenary session when the speech of former US President Jimmy Carter was shouted down and brought to an abrupt and premature termination by many NGOs, especially from Latin America. Nevertheless, in the end, the reports of all the working groups were adopted by consensus at the final plenary and the final document of the NGO Forum, containing several forward-looking recommendations, was presented to the UN Conference, influencing the conference discussions as a whole, and leaving an unmistakable imprint upon the Vienna Declaration and Program of Action (VDPA). However, it is worth noting that the following NGO demands were not included in the VDPA: the recognition of the right of self-determination of indigenous peoples; the abolition of the veto in the Security Council; detailed measures to protect the rights of groups such as minorities, the disabled, victims of AIDS, people of alternative sexual orientations, and other groups facing discrimination; and adoption of a holistic approach to the right to development which would include cutbacks in military expenditures, a reform of structural adjustment programmes, and the accountability of multinational corporations for human rights violations.

Act One concluded, leaving two clear messages for the future: NGO participation was vital to the success of any intergovernmental conference on human rights including future reviews of progress and implementation. Some governments would go to great lengths to restrict, and even attempt to eliminate such NGO participation.

Act 2: The UN World Conference on Human Rights

There were no illusions before it began that the conference would involve contentious and difficult negotiations. This indeed proved to be the case. What UNWCHR set out to do was clear, unambiguous and not overly ambitious. It was to address a fourfold agenda: (1) review progress made in the field of human rights, identify obstacles to further progress and ways in which to overcome such obstacles; (2) consider the relationship between development, democracy, and the universal enjoyment of all human rights; (3) address contemporary trends and challenges to the full realization of all human rights of women and men, including those belonging to vulnerable groups, and (4) strengthen international cooperation in the field of human rights, enhance the effectiveness of UN activities and mechanisms for that purpose, and secure the necessary financial and other resources.

Procedurally, there was considerable uncertainty. NGO participation in the conference and the drafting committee was drastically curtailed and there has been much backsliding since the Rio Conference. Specific country situations were not to have been discussed at the conference but once discussion was allowed on Bosnia, the floodgates were opened and participating governments became excessively defensive about their domestic human rights situations. The one notable exception was the United States which continued to act as if the US had no domestic human rights problems whatsoever!

The conference also suffered from excessive politicization of the issues. An Asian block of countries kept challenging the universality of human rights on grounds of cultural specificity and Western imposition. The Western donor country bloc insisted on development assistance being conditioned on the human rights situation in the recipient country. Behind a smoke screen of rhetoric, genuine and pressing issues were obscured and evaded. After some nine intensive days (and nights) of negotiations, the conference adopted the Vienna Declaration and Program of Action (VDPA) – a long document, which is not very systematically arranged. It is set out in three parts: a noble preamble, a set of principles and what, with some poetic licence can be called "a plan of action."

Immediate response to the VDPA was harsh as is evident from the number of post-mortem assessments made of the conference in the very first month after its conclusion, by a wide range of conference protagonists. Most critical of the conference were the human rights NGOs. Halfway through the conference itself, the Secretary-General of Amnesty International (one of the largest and most influential international human rights NGOs) denounced the proceedings as "sham." The executive director of Human Rights Watch, expressing his concern over efforts to prevent the Dalai Lama from addressing human rights groups in Vienna, stated that the UN was preoccupied with the sensibilities of its most abusive governments. By succumbing to this blackmail, the UN sinks to the level of its most repressive member states. Most NGOs from South and North alike were dismayed that a number of abusive governments used the conference to attack the universality of human rights. NGOs were especially concerned that the conference secretariat was displaying a disturbing willingness to succumb to the wishes of certain governments with abusive human rights records.

The ASEAN governments were concerned enough about the outcome of the Vienna Conference that when their foreign ministers met in Singapore, they added the issue of human rights to the final draft of the joint communiqué they issued at the end of the 26th ASEAN ministerial meeting on 24 July 1993. The communiqué reiterates their position that "the promotion and protection of human rights should not be politicized," that due regard be paid to "specific cultural, social, economic and political circumstances," that "development is an inalienable right" and "that the use of human rights as a conditionality for economic assistance is detrimental to international cooperation and could undermine an international consensus on human rights."

The outcome of the World Conference on Human Rights was also the subject of discussion in the Social Committee of the Economic and Social Council (ECOSOC) in Geneva on 21 July 1993. The discussion involved a virtual replay of discussions during the World Conference. The representatives from China criticized "the negative impact of policies representing hegemonism and power politics on international human rights activities." The representative from Cuba termed "hypocritical" the condemnation of Cuba by "a group of countries" "without having the courage to look at the situation their own people were facing." The representative from Colombia called for "streamlining the UN human rights program to avoid duplication" – a task which the Vienna Conference was supposed to have undertaken. The representative from Venezuela called for "greater coöperation and coordination between the inter-American human rights system and the UN" – again a task that the Vienna Conference was supposed to have undertaken. The universality of human rights was a *fait accompli* before Vienna. Yet the representatives of the Czech Republic, Kuwait, the Philippines, India, Peru, and the Republic of Korea, felt it necessary to emphasize "the importance of the recognition of the universality of human rights in the Vienna Declaration." This is because the declaration contains ambiguous language in respect of universality.

Paragraph 1(5) of the VDPA does state, "All human rights are universal, indivisible and interdependent and interrelated." But it then goes on to add, "The international community must treat human rights globally in a fair and equal manner, on the same footing and with the same emphasis. While the significance of national and regional particularities and various historical, cultural and religious backgrounds must be borne in mind, it is the duty of States, regardless of their political, economic and cultural systems to protect and promote all human rights and fundamental freedoms." The above represents as strong a statement on universality as was obtainable by consensus at Vienna. It has not succeeded, however, in laying to rest once and for all, the ghost of cultural relativism and of the so-called "Asian values."

Among the main losers at the Vienna Conference were the human rights NGOs. While on the one hand the Vienna Declaration recognizes the important role of non-governmental organizations in the human rights field, paragraph 25 of the declaration states that only "non-governmental organizations and their members *genuinely* involved in the field of human rights should enjoy the rights and freedoms recognized in the universal declaration of human rights, and the protection of the national law." The notion that national governments will decide upon the genuineness of their own human rights organizations and make that the basis for affording or denying them the protection of the national law is especially worrying in the field of human rights.

The biggest winners at the Vienna Conference were probably women who, at last, obtained unequivocal recognition that women's rights are human rights. But such a victory may well prove pyrrhic unless they can ensure that the UN moves from mere affirmation to the creation of effective mechanisms for monitoring and realizing women's human rights. The other contribution that the Vienna Declaration makes is its rejection of any notion of choosing between development *or* human rights and its insistence upon development *and* human rights. As paragraph 10 of the VDPA makes clear, "the lack of development may not be invoked to justify the abridgement of internationally recognized human rights."

The executive director of Human Rights Watch made his assessment of the Vienna Conference with a remark, not entirely in jest, to the effect that he was glad that UN World Conferences on Human Rights only occur once every 25 years. Vienna must serve as a rebuke on that score.

Human rights are too important to be dealt with globally only at 25-year intervals. "Five, not twenty-five" should rather be our post-Vienna slogan. But only if future World Conferences on Human Rights can learn from and be a significant improvement upon what happened in Vienna.

It was inevitable that the Vienna Conference failed to satisfy everybody. Many of the principal initiatives to invigorate the UN human rights system failed to receive strong endorsement from the conference including the major recommendations put forward by the UN's fact-finding rapporteurs, working groups, and treaty-body experts. But, with the passage of time, criticism of the Vienna Conference has become muted. Part of what could not be achieved at Vienna has been achieved in subsequent years. The VDPA called for a review of progress towards its implementation five years down the line. In this context, it is first necessary to recall, in some detail, the salient features of the VDPA.

Recalling the VDPA

At Vienna, through an arduous process of negotiations, consensus was forged that:
- All human rights are universal, indivisible and interdependent and interrelated.
- The human rights of women and of the girl-child are an inalienable, integral and indivisible part of universal human rights.
- The promotion and protection of all human rights and fundamental freedoms must be considered as a priority objective of the United Nations in accordance with its purposes and principles, in particular, the purpose of international cooperation.
- Enhancement of international cooperation in the field of human rights is essential for the full achievement of the purposes of the United Nations.
- Democracy, development, and respect for human rights and fundamental freedoms are interdependent and mutually reinforcing.

It was vital that the Vienna Review reiterate the above consensus and treat it as not open for renegotiation. The role of NGOs, worldwide, was crucial to ensure this. It was important to be clear what *was not* up for review was the consensus reached at Vienna. What *was* up for review included:
- States' performance in meeting their obligations under the Vienna Declaration.
- Progress towards the full implementation of the recommendations contained in the Vienna Declaration.

– The performance of the United Nations system in assuming a more active role in the promotion and protection of human rights as recommended by the Vienna Declaration.

Reviewing state performance since Vienna

States have made several commitments and undertaken various duties and obligations under the Vienna Declaration. These include:

1. *Duties to eliminate certain practices violative of human rights,* such as: racism, racial discrimination, xenophobia and related intolerance (section I, para. 15); apartheid (section 1, para. 16); terrorism and drug trafficking (section I, para. 17); genocide, ethnic cleansing (section I, para. 28); systematic rape of women in war situations (section I, para. 28); violations of human rights affecting the civilian population during armed conflicts (section I, para. 29); gross and systemic violations such as torture and cruel, inhuman and degrading treatment or punishment, summary and arbitrary executions, disappearances, arbitrary detentions, foreign occupation and alien domination, poverty, hunger, and other denials of economic, social, and cultural rights, religious intolerance, discrimination against women, and lack of the rule of law (section I, para. 30).

2. *Duties regarding the universal ratification of human rights treaties*

The World Conference urged the universal ratification of human rights treaties and encouraged all states to accede to these treaties and to avoid, as far as possible, the resort to reservations. It strongly recommended that a concerted effort be made to encourage and facilitate ratification of such treaties and protocols with the aim of universal acceptance.

3. *Commitments regarding national human rights institutions*

The Vienna Declaration stresses that states should eliminate all violations of human rights and their causes, as well as obstacles to the enjoyment of those rights. There is a need for states and international organizations, in cooperation with non-governmental organizations, to create favourable conditions at the national, regional, and international levels to ensure the full and effective enjoyment of human rights. Creating favourable conditions at national level involves at least three key aspects: (1) every state should provide an effective framework of remedies to redress human rights grievances or violations. This requires an independent judiciary and legal profession and a system of administration of justice (including law enforcement and prosecutorial agencies) that are in full conformity with applicable standards contained in international human rights instruments; (2) recognizing the important role of non-governmental organizations in the promotion and protection of human rights, non-governmental organizations should be free to carry out their human rights activities without interference within the framework of national law and the Universal Declaration of Human Rights; and (3) establishment and strengthening of national legislation and national institutions. The World Conference reaffirmed the important and constructive role played by national human rights institutions, in particular, in their advisory capacity to the competent authorities, their roles in remedying human rights violations, in dissemination of human rights information, and education in human rights.

4. *Protection and promotion of the rights of special groups*

The Vienna Declaration calls attention to several groups whose human rights protection and promotion warrant special attention for a variety of reasons. These groups include:

- *people under foreign occupation* for whom "effective international measures to guarantee and monitor the implementation of human rights standards should be taken" and "effective legal protection against the violation of their human rights should be provided";
- *women and the girl-child* against whom "gender-based violence and all forms of sexual harassment and exploitation" and "all forms of discrimination on grounds of sex" must be eradicated. "The full and equal participation of women in political, civil, economic, social and cultural life" must be secured;
- *minorities*, "the promotion and protection of whose rights" contribute "to the political and social stability of the States in which such persons live";
- *indigenous people* whose "unique contribution" to the development and plurality of society is recognized." "States should ensure the full and free participation of indigenous people in all aspects of society";
- *children* whose rights "should be a priority in the United Nations system-wide action on human rights";
- *disabled persons* whose "active participation in all aspects of society" and "equal enjoyment of all human rights and fundamental freedoms" should be secured;
- *refugees* who are entitled "to the right to seek asylum from persecution as well as the right to return to one's own country";
- *internally displaced persons* whose "voluntary and safe return and rehabilitation" should be ensured;
- *victims of all natural and man-made disasters* whose right to humanitarian assistance should be respected;
- persons belonging to groups which have been rendered *vulnerable* including *migrant workers* who are entitled to "the elimination of all

forms of discrimination against them" and to "the promotion and protection" of their rights;
- *trade unions*. The World Conference supports all measures by the UN and its specialized agencies to ensure the effective promotion and protection of the rights of trade unions and calls upon all states to abide fully by their obligations in this regard.
- *the media* for whom freedom and protection should be guaranteed within the framework of national law because of the importance of objective, responsible, and impartial information about human rights and humanitarian issues.

Reviewing UN system performance

The World Conference recommended that the UN assume a more active role in the promotion and protection of human rights and made various suggestions regarding increased coordination within the UN system, technical cooperation, and strengthening implementation and monitoring mechanisms in the UN system.

1. *Increased coordination on human rights within the UN system*

The World Conference stressed that UN human rights organs should improve their coordination, efficiency and effectiveness and made several specific recommendations in that respect:
- all regional organizations and prominent international and regional finance and development institutions were called upon to assess the impact of their policies and programmes on the enjoyment of human rights;
- human rights officers were to be assigned, if and when necessary, to regional offices of the UN to disseminate information and offer training and other technical assistance in the field of human rights upon the request of concerned states;
- human rights training was organized for international civil servants who are assigned to work relating to human rights;
- the importance of the role of human rights components in specific arrangements concerning some peacekeeping operations had to be recognized;
- the need to ensure that human and financial resources are available to carry out human rights activities was recognized and the Secretary-General was urged "to take immediate steps to increase, substantially, the resources for the human rights program from within the existing and future regular budget of the UN." He was also urged "to take urgent steps to seek increased extra-budgetary resources" as well;

– the importance of strengthening the UN Center for Human Rights was also stressed by the World Conference.

It was essential that the relevant bodies of the UN, present detailed and specific reports as to the progress regarding the above recommendations.

2. *Cooperation, development, and strengthening of human rights*

The World Conference recommended that priority be given to national and international action to promote democracy, development, and human rights. It therefore recommended that a comprehensive programme be established within the UN (coordinated by the Center for Human Rights) to help states strengthen and build national institutions relating to human rights. Such an advisory services programme would include electoral assistance, assistance to strengthen the rule of law, the administration of justice, real and effective participation of the people in the decision-making processes, and promotion of freedom of expression. It would include assistance on specific human rights issues such as the preparation of reports under specific human rights treaties as well as the drawing up and implementation of comprehensive national action plans for the promotion and protection of human rights and building or strengthening national human rights institutions such as human rights commissions.

In order to achieve this, the World Conference recommended "an enhanced programme of advisory services and technical assistance" with extra-budgetary, voluntary funding expanded substantially. Strict and transparent management rules would be applied and there would be regular and periodic programme and project evaluations. The Center for Human Rights was also asked "in particular, to organize, at least once a year, information meetings open to all Member States and organizations directly involved in these projects and programmes." The World Conference also made two further specific recommendations in this regard: each state should "consider the desirability of drawing up a national action plan identifying steps whereby that state would improve the promotion and protection of human rights." The UN Secretary-General was requested "to submit proposals to the UN General Assembly, containing alternatives for the establishment, structure, operational modalities and funding of the proposed programme." It was hoped that these would be carefully examined during the Vienna +5 review, otherwise it was feared that they were in danger of going by default.

3. *Strengthening the UN's implementation and monitoring methods*

The World Conference recognized the need to strengthen the implementation and monitoring of human rights at all levels: national, regional, and international. Accordingly, at the *national level*, it urged states to ratify human rights instruments without reservations, accept all "optional communications procedures," incorporate international standards into national law and strengthen national structures for implementation, monitoring and enforcement, including the provision of timely and effective redress and remedies to the victims of human rights violations. At the *regional level*, the World Conference recommended the building and strengthening of regional human rights mechanisms and strengthening cooperation between national institutions, including the convening of periodic meetings. At the *international level*, system-wide within the UN, the World Conference made many recommendations: it recommended that the International Law Commission should continue its work on an international criminal court. It welcomed the convening of emergency sessions of the Commission on Human Rights and urged "that other ways of responding to acute violations of human rights be considered by the relevant organs of the UN system." It recommended that the Commission on Human Rights "examine the possibility for better implementation of existing human rights instruments." It recommended "continued work on the improvement of the functioning, including the monitoring tasks, of the treaty bodies" and urged the meetings of the chairpersons of the treaty bodies to "continue to take steps aimed at coordinating the multiple reporting requirements and guidelines for preparing State reports under the respective human rights conventions." It urged better coordination between the existing human rights treaty bodies, the various thematic and country mechanisms and procedures, experts and working groups "with a view to promoting greater efficiency and effectiveness."

4. *Continuing adaptation of the UN human rights machinery*

The World Conference recognized "the necessity for a continuing adaptation of the UN's human rights machinery to the current and future needs in the promotion and protection of human rights." Accordingly, it made a number of very specific recommendations. These include:

(a) The adoption of *optional protocols* to the Convention on Torture; the Covenant on Economic, Social and Cultural Rights; the Convention on the Elimination of All Forms of Discrimination against Women, and by the Commission on the Status of Women.

(b) The *withdrawal of reservations* to the Convention on the Rights of the Child and the Convention on the Elimination of All Forms of Discrimination against Women (CEDAW). In the case of the latter, it specifically asks the CEDAW Committee "to continue its review of reservations to the Convention" and urges states to withdraw their reservations.

(c) To strengthen the enjoyment of economic, social, and cultural rights, additional approaches should be examined such as *a system of in-*

dicators to measure progress in the realization of the rights set out in the Covenant on Economic, Social and Cultural Rights.

(d) So far as *special rapporteurs* are concerned, it welcomed the creation of the Special Rapporteur on Racism and has successfully urged the creation of a Special Rapporteur on Violence against Women.

(e) As far as *working groups* are concerned:

  (i) it has urged the renewal and updating of the mandate of the *Working Group on Indigenous Populations*, and

  (ii) it has urged the *Working Group on the Right to Development* to "promptly formulate, for early consideration by the United Nations General Assembly, comprehensive and effective measures to eliminate obstacles to the implementation and realization of the Declaration on the Right to Development and recommending ways and means towards the realization of the right to development by all States."

(f) So far as *Declarations* are concerned, the World Conference successfully urged the General Assembly to adopt the Draft Declaration on the Elimination of Violence against Women, and has urged the similar adoption of the Declaration on the Rights of Indigenous Peoples. It recommends the speedy completion and adoption of the draft declaration on the right and responsibility of individuals, groups, and organs of society to promote and protect universally recognized human rights and fundamental freedoms.

(g) The World Conference called upon the General Assembly and the Economic and Social Council "to adopt the draft standard rules on the equalization of opportunities for persons with disabilities."

(h) The World Conference recommended "that matters relating to human rights and the situation of children be regularly reviewed and monitored by all relevant organs and mechanisms of the United Nations system and by the supervisory bodies of the specialized agencies in accordance with their mandates."

(i) So far as *decades* are concerned, the World Conference successfully urged the General Assembly to declare a Decade on Human Rights Education and a Decade of the World's Indigenous People within the framework of which it asks that "the establishment of a permanent forum for indigenous people in the UN system should be considered."

(j) So far as *funding* for human rights activities is concerned, the World Conference has supported the concept of a *voluntary fund* for the programmes of action of both of the above decades and also of the Decade for Action to Combat Racism and Racial Discrimination. It also strongly supports voluntary funding of an enhanced programme of technical cooperation to be undertaken by the UN Center for Human Rights.

The above detailed restatement of select portions of the VDPA make it obvious that there do exist, within the VDPA, very specific provisions for measuring progress in implementation of the Vienna Conference Programme of Action. The criteria to be met and the objectives to be achieved are clear and unambiguous. In this respect, the Vienna Conference, even more so than the Rio Conference, *does* provide the basis for a thorough, systematic, and comprehensive review of progress in implementation. Unfortunately, it seems highly unlikely that such a review will, in fact, take place largely because, like most of the UN global conferences, the procedures for monitoring implementation and for review are far from adequate.

Reviewing Vienna

The Vienna Declaration recommended that the UN Commission on Human Rights annually review the progress towards full implementation of the recommendations contained therein. It also asked the Secretary-General of the UN to invite all states, all organs and agencies of the UN system related to human rights, regional and, as appropriate, national human rights institutions, as well as non-governmental organizations, to report to him on progress made in the implementation of the Vienna Declaration on the occasion of the 50th Anniversary of the Universal Declaration on Human Rights (in 1998). The Vienna Declaration also requested the Secretary-General of the UN to submit his report on the implementation of the Declaration "to the General Assembly at its fifty-third session, through the Commission on Human Rights and the Economic and Social Commission" (para. 100).

The VDPA set out specific measures for its own implementation:
– Governments were urged to ratify international human rights instruments and accept all the available optional communication procedures.
– Governments were urged to accede to the Geneva Conventions of 12 August 1949 and the Protocols thereto and to take all appropriate national measures, including legislative ones, for their full implementation.
– Governments were urged to incorporate standards as contained in the international human rights instruments in domestic legislation and to strengthen national structures and institutions to promote and safeguard human rights.
– The UN was urged to strengthen programmes to meet requests for

assistance by states that want to establish or strengthen their own national institutions.

– National institutions were urged to cooperate with one another, exchange information and experiences, and convene periodic meetings to examine ways and means of improving their mechanisms.
– The Commission and Sub-Commission were to examine all aspects of the issue of impunity of perpetrators of human rights violations with a view to eradicating impunity.
– An International Criminal Court was to be established for better enforcement of human rights.
– The Commission was to examine the possibility for better implementation of existing human rights instruments at international and regional levels (paras 83–92).

The VDPA also called for strengthening monitoring methods and activities by treaty bodies through the reporting system; the system of special procedures, rapporteurs, representatives, experts, and working groups of the Commission and Sub-Commission (paras 87–89 and 95); a system of indicators to be developed to measure progressive realization of economic, social, and cultural rights. The VDPA recognized the necessity for a continuing adaptation of the UN human rights machinery to the current and future needs in the promotion and protection of human rights and called upon the UN's human rights organs to improve their coordination, efficiency, and effectiveness. This task has been entrusted to the High Commissioner for Human Rights (HCHR) and to the Chairman of the Working Group of the Third Committee, both of whom prepare annual reports on the implementation of the VDPA.

Plans for the Vienna +5 review were finalized by the General Assembly at its 52nd session (1997) and set out in a resolution (52/148) adopted by consensus on 12 December 1997. The procedure for the review was as follows: the coordination segment of the Economic and Social Commission, at its substantive session of 1998 would be devoted to the question of the coordinated follow up to and implementation of the VDPA. The UN High Commissioner for Human Rights would prepare a report to the General Assembly at its 1998 session based upon responses she received to her invitation to governments and UN agencies to provide reports on the progress made in the implementation of the VDPA and to regional and national human rights institutions, as well as to NGOs, to present their views in this regard. The General Assembly, at its 53rd session (1998), would review progress made in the implementation of the VDPA taking into account the above-mentioned report of the High Commissioner.

The above review process, unlike that used for the Rio +5 review, did not provide any opportunity for PrepComs through which NGOs could participate in the review process. Accordingly, NGOs took the initiative (with the support of the Canadian government) and organized an International NGO Forum to review implementation of the VDPA that was held at Ottawa from 22–24 June 1998. Thus, the Vienna +5 review process ended up having three Acts.

Act 1: The Ottawa International NGO Forum

The Ottawa International Forum brought together some 250 representatives of 100 NGOs and indigenous peoples to assess the overall situation of human rights, five years after the Vienna World Conference and 50 years after the adoption of the Universal Declaration of Human Rights. There was unanimous agreement among the participants that there must be no retreat from the consensus forged in Vienna and that the VDPA was not open to renegotiation. The participants noted at least three positive developments in the five years since Vienna: (1) the post of High Commissioner for Human Rights has been created, her office in Geneva has been restructured, her office in New York has been strengthened to promote integration of human rights in the activities of the UN system, and the number of field operations of her office has grown from 1 to 20 over the five-year period; (2) the Secretary-General reorganized the entire UN system, making human rights a crosscutting theme in all of the activities of the UN system: peace, humanitarian affairs, development and economic and social affairs; and (3) the Special Procedures and Mechanisms of the Commission on Human Rights were reviewed with a view to strengthening their effectiveness and improving coordination and dissemination of information among such mechanisms and between those mechanisms and the UN system.

Despite the progress made, however, the Forum also noted with concern that much more needed to be done. Reviewing state party performance, the Forum noted the continued existence of torture, the lack of progress towards ratification of the UN Convention on Torture, the failure by states to create legislation criminalizing torture, and where such legislation does exist, the failure to implement the legislation by prosecuting torturers and rehabilitating victims of torture; and the persistence of the practice of impunity and the inadequacy of mechanisms to hold public officials accountable for their acts of gross violation of civil, cultural, economic, political, and social rights.

The Forum further noted that human rights are *far from universal for all peoples* and *all human rights*. In particular, despite reaffirmation at the level of rhetoric in the VDPA, very little progress has been made since then in realizing the rights of women and in realizing economic, social, and cultural rights.

Despite acceptance at the level of rhetoric of women's human rights at Vienna, the promotion and protection of these rights had been limited during the five years thereafter. Extremist interpretations of culture, religion, and tradition continued to encourage, excuse, or condone the subordination of women. The violence and gender-based discrimination that result from these extremist positions constitutes one of the greatest threats to human rights today. Yet the responses have been, for the most part, inadequate or ineffectual. Governments have failed to fulfil their international obligations to act with due diligence to prevent, investigate, and punish violations of the human rights of women. The Global Forum emphasized that the purpose of human rights standards is to protect the inherent worth and dignity of the human person. As an elaboration of this standard, the right to bodily integrity needs to be seen as a fundamental principle derived from the UDHR. Paragraph 41 of the VDPA recognizes the importance of women's enjoyment of the highest attainable standard of physical and mental health. The enjoyment of this right is vital to their life and well-being and their ability to participate in all areas of public and private life.

The Forum also noted the lack of significant progress towards universal ratification of the Covenant of Economic, Social and Cultural Rights during the five years since Vienna. The Global Forum further noted that despite the unequivocal reaffirmation in the VDPA of the universality, indivisibility, interdependence, and interrelatedness of all human rights – civil, cultural, economic, political, and social – marginal progress had been made at national, regional, or international levels in the realization, implementation, or enforcement of economic, social, and cultural rights. The gap between rich and poor has doubled in the last three decades with the poorest fifth of the world's population receiving 1.4 per cent of the global income and the richest fifth 85 per cent. The Forum strongly reiterated that economic, social, and cultural rights have the same status, importance, and significance for human dignity, development, and well-being as civil and political rights. Economic, social, and cultural rights are rights and not just aspirational goals. The UDHR and the VDPA reaffirmed the legal obligation of states to implement such rights. Failure by states to perform any one of their obligations to respect, protect, promote, and fulfil such rights constitutes a violation thereof.

The Forum also noted the lack of progress regarding promotion and protection of the rights of a number of excluded, disadvantaged, and vulnerable groups as well as groups continuing to face discrimination such as first nations and indigenous peoples, children, the disabled, the aged, workers, refugees and displaced persons, minorities and people of different sexual orientation. Implementation of the VDPA by both states and the UN system was needed to rectify the current situation. Accordingly, the Forum called for strengthening promotion and protection of human rights by strengthening:

(i) *international and regional systems* by moving towards universal ratification of human rights instruments, removal of reservations thereto and creation of complaints procedures thereunder;

(ii) *national systems* and national human rights institutions such as commissions, ombu, the judiciary, law enforcement and correctional facilities; and

(iii) *NGOs* by respecting their rights, providing them with access, and recognizing their invaluable contribution to the promotion and protection of human rights.

The Forum also called attention to challenges and obstacles that had arisen in the five years since Vienna:

– *Human patenting and human rights*: the patenting, commodification, and trade in human genetic materials is occurring in a complete policy and regulatory vacuum.

– *Communications technologies* have developed so rapidly that they offer unique opportunities for people and civil society organizations, but are also being used to globalize trafficking in drugs, women, and children by organized crime.

– *Globalization of the economy* in a manner that is further eroding economic, social, and cultural rights with grave impacts on the rights of women, workers, and persons with disabilities. The power of non-state actors, notably transnational corporations and multilateral institutions of trade, finance, and investment has increased enormously with no commensurate increase in mechanisms to hold such actors accountable.

The recommendations of the Ottawa Forum were presented to ECOSOC during their coordination segment which reviewed implementation of the VDPA.

Act 2: The ECOSOC coordination segment

The ECOSOC coordination segment devoted to coordinated follow-up to and implementation of the VDPA took place in New York on 17 and 20–21 July 1998. The purpose of the ECOSOC segment was to identify methods of achieving a concerted system-wide approach to human rights; examples of best practices by the UN system in the implementation of the VDPA; areas of responsibility within the UN system in which efforts should be made to implement fully the VDPA; measures for ensuring the contributions by each UN body and agency to the full implementation of the VDPA; and plans for improving inter-agency cooperation and coordination to achieve better results in the implementation of the VDPA. Thus, the ECOSOC segment concerned itself with UN implementation of the VDPA rather than with state party implementation. The latter was to be dealt with during the General Assembly review. A Report of the Secretary-General served as the working document for the ECOSOC Review. The report was prepared on the basis of inter-agency consultations that were organized by the High Commissioner in 1997 and 1998. The report focuses on efforts to assist governments and civil society and efforts to enhance cooperation and coordination within the UN system to implement the VDPA. It provides an overview of the UN system's contribution to implementation of the VDPA and recommendations for future action. The report addresses eight topics:

1. *Mainstreaming human rights, cooperation, and coordination in the UN system*, which has taken the following forms:
   (a) adoption of a "human-rights-based approach" to activities carried out by the different components of the UN system (peace and security, humanitarian affairs, development, economic and social affairs);
   (b) development of programmes and projects addressing specific human rights issues;
   (c) reorientation of existing programmes as a means of focusing adequate attention on human rights concerns;
   (d) inclusion of a human rights component into field operations of the UN;
   (e) the presence of the human rights programme in all structural units of the Secretariat responsible for policy development and coordination. The main recommendation of the report regarding mainstreaming is that ECOSOC call on its functional commissions, as well as the regional economic commissions, to mainstream human rights into their activities.

2. *Democracy, development, human rights, and the right to development.* At its 1998 session, the Commission on Human Rights reiterated that, "The essence of the right to development is the principle that the human person is the central subject of development and that the right to life includes within it, existence in human dignity and with the minimum necessities of life."[3] The report's recommendations on this topic are very weak. They call for inviting the Bretton Woods institutions to increase their participation in a UN system-wide process to promote the right to development by drawing upon the expertise of those active in both sustainable development and human rights areas. The report also recommends that ECOSOC "call for continuing focus of the UN system on implementing its Agreed Conclusions on system-wide efforts for the eradication of extreme poverty."

3. *Racism, racial discrimination, and other forms of intolerance.* The report calls attention to the lack of support for the Third Decade to

Combat Racism and Racial Discrimination and recommends that ECOSOC call on all components of the UN system to participate actively in preparations for the World Conference against Racism (to be held in 2001).

4. *The equal status and human rights of women.* The report is of the view that the gender perspective in general as well as the equal status and rights of women, in particular, are being mainstreamed by the UN system-wide. The report recommends that ECOSOC call for training in the human rights of women to be provided to all UN personnel and officials; the development of guidelines for special rapporteurs, representatives, independent experts, and working groups concerning preventive and remedial action against violations of the human rights of women; and encourages the treaty bodies to develop a common strategy for monitoring the rights of women.

5. *Groups requiring special protection.* The report examines UN activities regarding children, indigenous peoples, minorities, migrant workers, internally displaced persons, the disabled, and those with HIV/AIDS. Here, again, the recommendations of the report are very weak. It urges ECOSOC to request all components of the UN system to undertake a coordinated yearly assessment of the impact of their strategies and policies on the enjoyment of human rights of such groups requiring special protection.

6. *Technical cooperation, human rights education and information.* The report notes that the technical cooperation activities of the Office of High Commissioner for Human Rights (OHCHR) had more than tripled since 1993 but there remains a need for more systematic cooperation at the country level. The report also notes the setting up of the Internet web-site of the High Commissioner since 10 December 1996. Here, again, the report's recommendations are weak. ECOSOC is asked to encourage relevant departments of the Secretariat and other components of the UN system to appoint a human rights education liaison officer/department to work with the OHCHR in the development of human rights education activities.

7. *Implementation.* The report, lacking specific implementation data, focuses on progress regarding ratification of human rights instruments and notes that the number of ratifications of the six basic human rights treaties was up by nearly 28 per cent. The level of ratification of the optional communication procedures continues to be of concern. Here again, the report is weak on recommendations merely reiterating some of the recommendations made in the VDPA. The fact that there is need for reiteration indicates the lack of progress in implementation of the VDPA.

8. *Interaction between the implementation of the VDPA and other UN*

conferences and summits. This section of the report is very skimpy since there was little to report on and the recommendation merely calls for a reiteration that the implementation of the VDPA should be perceived as an integral part of the coordinated follow up to major conferences and summits convened by the UN.

As the above analysis of the Report of the Secretary-General indicates, implementation of the VDPA had been far from satisfactory. Even more disturbing is the fact that the report is unable to come up with significant recommendations for redressing the situation. Clearly, the contribution of the UN system to the implementation of the VDPA ranged between modest and minimalist. Moreover, the report fails to provide the detailed and meticulous review needed and is often silent on a number of the VDPA recommendations that were addressed to the UN system.

The Report of the Secretary-General is the product of several inter-agency consultations organized by the High Commissioner for Human Rights. It therefore reflects very much UN agency perspectives and concerns. Since NGOs or external experts were not part of the process that produced the report, it remains focused, almost obsessively, on inter-agency cooperation and coordination and fails to problematize issues such as *what activities* are being coordinated. It lacks both the broader perspectives and the critical objectivity that NGOs or external experts could have brought to the subject. During the first three years after Vienna, UN system contribution to implementation of the VDPA was modest to the point of bordering on indifference. During the next two years this changed dramatically because of the happy conjuncture of a new Secretary-General and a new High Commissioner for Human Rights giving high priority to human rights in the work of the UN. Hence, the Vienna +5 review took place at a time most propitious for critical introspection, candid appraisal, and creative initiatives for rendering more effective the contribution of the entire UN system (and not only that of the OHCHR) to the implementation of the VDPA. But process determines outcome and this was clearly so with the ECOSOC segment. The way the issues and recommendations were framed in the Secretary-General's Report to ECOSOC clearly influenced the outcome of the ECOSOC segment.

The three-day ECOSOC segment (and the "informals" that followed the three days and produced a twelve-and-a-half page list of Agreed Conclusions that were adopted by consensus) bear close scrutiny as a potential model for future review of other UN global conferences. During the ECOSOC segment, two panels were organized dealing with policy issues. The first panel brought together the heads of UN offices and agencies (including the HCHR, the United Nations Development Programme [UNDP], UNICEF and the Office of Humanitarian Affairs) to exchange experiences regarding follow-up to the Vienna Conference, mainstreaming of human rights and a rights-based approach. The second panel focused on the right to development and brought together representatives from the OHCHR, the World Bank, the United Nations Development Fund for Women (UNIFEM) and an external expert. The panels were followed by statements and debate by member states and the rest of the time was spent discussing the content of Agreed Conclusions to emerge from the session. NGOs (largely comprising those based in New York) were present as observers during the three-day segment and a few of them, having made a prior request, were able to address the meeting. Efforts by NGOs to attend the "informals" were unsuccessful since, invariably, a government would request the Chair to close the meetings. At one stage of the informals it seemed unlikely that agreement would be reached on Agreed Conclusions. Some of the "hard liner" governments were resisting the concept of "mainstreaming" or "integration" of human rights UN system-wide. Indeed, there was even resistance to using the words "system-wide." There was similar resistance to a "rights-based approach." Such resistance reflects continuing concern about the use of human rights as a conditionality in areas of UN activity such as peace building, humanitarian assistance, and development. But at least as far as development is concerned, such concern is ill-founded since the link between human rights and development has been repeatedly reaffirmed by consensus, by *all* member states in the now well-established global consensus (reiterated in the Agreed Conclusions of the meeting) around "the right to development as a universal and inalienable right" and "an integral part of fundamental human rights." Some governments were resistant to the concept of "field operations" of the OHCHR, preferring the term "field presence." At the end of the day, however, in the Agreed Conclusions, the Council "notes with interest" the increase in the number of human rights field operations and calls for "their further improvement!"[4] Some governments attempted to use the ECOSOC Review to attempt to install new procedural obstacles between the special procedures and mechanisms of the UN's human rights system and direct access to country information or, indeed, access to the country itself. But, fortunately, such a regressive move was resisted.

The Agreed Conclusions of the ECOSOC Review, like the Secretary-General's Report to ECOSOC, are set out under eight headings:

1. *Increased system-wide coordinated follow up to and implementation of the VDPA*. This rather cumbersome phraseology replaces the earlier language of "mainstreaming human rights." Eleven agreed conclusions appear in this section, some of which are blatantly self-serving (e.g. that the inter-agency consultations organized by the HCHR to prepare for the Vienna +5 review and for the 50th Anniversary of the

Universal Declaration, should continue in the future as a forum for cooperation); others are self-evident (e.g. that the Council reaffirms the need for increased coordination in support of human rights avoiding unnecessary duplication); none of which is especially significant (as is evident from the fact that the conclusion with most practical significance, perhaps, calls for an increase in "the system-wide human rights training of UN staff" and calls upon the functional commissions of ECOSOC and their regional economic commissions and other organs, bodies, and specialized agencies "within their respective mandates to take all human rights fully into account in their respective activities"); yet others of which are purely repetitive – with no value added to the VDPA (e.g. "the Council reaffirms the importance of ensuring the universality, objectivity and non-selectivity of the consideration of human rights issues").[5] Agreed Conclusion number 8, requesting the Secretary-General to continue and strengthen his efforts to recruit staff for the Secretariat belongs more appropriately to a UN staff collective bargaining agreement and is quite out of place in a human rights document.

2. *Democracy, development, human rights and the right to development and the role of international cooperation.* Of the eight Agreed Conclusions contained in this section, five are noteworthy: (a) the call for continuing focus of the UN system on implementing its Agreed Conclusions on system-wide efforts for the eradication of poverty; (b) the call upon states to refrain from any unilateral measure not in accordance with international law and the Charter of the UN; (c) the call upon all states to adopt and vigorously implement existing conventions relating to the dumping of toxic and dangerous products and waste and to cooperate in the prevention of illicit dumping; (d) the call upon the international community to make all efforts to alleviate the external debt burden of developing countries; and (e) the call to support national and international efforts in the promotion and protection of economic, social, and cultural rights within the framework of the indivisibility, interdependence, and interrelated character of all human rights.

All of the above Agreed Conclusions represent recognition of the perspectives and concerns of developing countries regarding human rights. Such recognition may help the depoliticization of North-South debates on human rights and may help bridge the gap on these issues between North and South. The other Agreed Conclusions in this section are merely repetitive (and verbosely so) of what is contained in the VDPA.

3. *Racism, racial discrimination, xenophobia and related intolerance.* In a world rife with ethnic conflicts, this section seems pathetic and inadequate. The four Agreed Conclusions have slim practical significance

– attempting to revive a near-defunct Third Decade to Combat Racism; recommending that the General Assembly declare the year 2001 a year of mobilization against racism (presumably a year is thought of as being significant even though the decade has proven not to be so); calling upon all in the UN system "to assist the preparatory committee and participate actively in the World Conference against Racism" and "encouraging the UN system to elaborate a comprehensive approach to the elimination of racism." The section of the Agreed Conclusions veritably represents a missed opportunity. But in one sense it is even worse. The VDPA used the category of "other forms of intolerance." This document uses, instead, the phrase "related intolerance" thus limiting the concept to forms of intolerance related to "racism, racial discrimination and xenophobia" and thereby depriving the concept of intolerance of any significance whatsoever. It would be desirable that the final document resulting from the General Assembly review session revert to the language used by the VDPA.

4. *Equal status and human rights of women.* It would appear that this section was included merely because it would have been politically incorrect to have no section at all on the human rights of women. Seven of the eight Agreed Conclusions add nothing new to the VDPA. The only new element is contained in the recommendation to the General Assembly and the Commission on Human Rights "to make explicit the integration of a gender perspective when establishing or renewing human rights mandates." Implicit in such a recommendation, whether intended or not, is a slur upon those who have held human rights mandates heretofore.

5. *Those requiring special protection.* This section, with its 13 Agreed Conclusions, represents a virtual admission that the counterpart section of the VDPA (section II B) has been inadequately implemented. The 13 Agreed Conclusions represent too little too late for the groups addressed therein, namely: the child (subject of five of the Conclusions), indigenous people (subject of two of the Conclusions), minorities, migrant workers, persons with disabilities, refugees, internally displaced persons and those with HIV/AIDS (subject of one Conclusion each). If the ECOSOC Review segment had benefited from the participation of the specific human rights NGOs working for "those requiring special protection," this section would have been considerably strengthened. Moreover, as with Vienna, the human rights of those discriminated against, on the basis of their sexual orientation, continue to be denied recognition.

6. *Technical cooperation, human rights education and information.* Technical cooperation is too important a subject to be dealt with by just four Agreed Conclusions, two of which merely reiterate what was

stated in the VDPA (calling for greater cooperation within the UN system and for the assignment of human rights officers to regional offices of the UN). Two important issues addressed in this section deserve further attention: the recommendation that treaty bodies, special rapporteurs, special representatives, and working groups continue to identify possibilities for technical assistance that could be requested by the states concerned; and reiteration that special emphasis should be given to measures to assist in the strengthening and building of institutions relating to human rights, strengthening of a pluralistic society and the protection of groups which have been rendered vulnerable. Two of the Agreed Conclusions in this section dealing with human rights education and information merely repeat calls made earlier to support the World Public Information Campaign on Human Rights and the Plan of Action for the Decade for Human Rights Education. The third conclusion is almost patronizing in its recognition of the work being done by UNESCO, DPI (Department of Public Information) and OHCHR regarding the UN Decade for Human Rights Education.

7. *Implementation*. This section adopts a "business-as-usual" approach and each of its five Agreed Conclusions expresses recognition of work already in progress. Crucial elements missing from this section are an identification of problems and obstacles encountered that impede full implementation of the VDPA and measures to overcome such obstacles.

8. *Interaction between implementation of the VDPA and other UN conferences and summits*. This section merely reiterates (as does the Secretary-General's Report) that the implementation of the VDPA "is an integral part of the coordinated follow up to major conferences and summits." Missing, however, is any attempt at identifying *core* aspects of the VDPA that should be taken up in the review and follow-up processes of other UN conferences, *specific* aspects of the VDPA relevant to each of the specific conferences, and concrete proposals to ensure that the VDPA will be an integral part of the coordinated follow-up process.

In sum, the ECOSOC segment has made a useful contribution building on the VDPA in two respects: (1) recognition of some of the pressing human rights issues and concerns of several developing country governments, and (2) adopting the concept of "mainstreaming of human rights" and of a "rights-based approach."

What remained ahead, however, was the need for an assessment of state-party performance in implementation of the VDPA; an assessment of UN system performance in implementation of the VDPA; identification of developments since Vienna that call for adaptation of the

VDPA and an updating thereof; a Vienna +5 plan of action for the promotion and protection of human rights.

Act 3: The General Assembly Review

The General Assembly Review of Vienna +5 commenced on 2 November 1998. An Interim Report was presented by the HCHR to the Commission on Human Rights at its 54th session earlier in the year.[6] It was expected that the Final Report would follow the conceptual format adopted by the Interim Report. As with the ECOSOC segment, the main working document usually influences the outcome of the session. Hence, a review of the Interim Report of the HCHR can help preview the issues addressed by the General Assembly Review. The Interim Report has five thematic sections that will be analysed below. But some general comments on the Interim Report are also merited.

In her Introduction to the Interim Report the HCHR quotes from the Secretary-General's address to the 49th session of the General Assembly, "The Vienna Declaration and Programme of Action undoubtedly constitutes one of the major events in the United Nations' history of human rights. If adequately implemented, it will be a milestone in this history."[7] As the HCHR reminded us, the VDPA was the result of concerted efforts by 171 member states and of deliberations at four sessions of the PrepCom, three regional and hundreds of other pre-conference meetings. It is a comprehensive document produced by a comprehensive process. The Vienna +5 review was not expected to involve such a comprehensive process but, nevertheless, the HCHR stressed that the review should focus on the fundamental task of the international community today – implementing human rights worldwide; promote positive developments and give due credit to achievements in implementing the VDPA; identify major obstacles to full implementation and offer practical ideas for addressing these issues in the years ahead; like the World Conference on Human Rights, be comprehensive and thematically oriented; assist in identifying the goals and tasks ahead; and envisage methods of achieving a concerted UN system-wide approach to human rights. These seemed the right goals for the General Assembly Review.

Based upon responses received from 33 member states, the Interim Report by the HCHR found that while the VDPA had guided changes in national legislation and practice, it was, nevertheless evident that full implementation of the VDPA has not been achieved. However, the following "good practices" could be identified: human rights-oriented changes in national legislation; enlargement of national human rights capacities, including the establishment or strengthening of national human rights institutions (such as commissions and ombudsmen); special protection extended to women, children, and vulnerable groups; development of human rights education programmes; and adoption of national plans of action.

The responses from governments, while calling for closer international cooperation, did identify core areas for attention: the insufficient weight given to certain aspects of human rights, especially with regard to economic, social and cultural rights and the right to development; the need for greater effectiveness and efficiency of the international system in promoting and protecting human rights; the need for the human rights machinery to adapt to changing circumstances and evolving needs; and the paucity of resources earmarked for the UN's human rights programme.

Based on reports from 12 UN bodies and organizations, the Interim Report had the following comments to make on UN system performance in implementing the VDPA: coordination of human rights activities within the UN system had improved since 1993; substantive steps had been taken to better integrate issues relating to the equal status and rights of women into the work of the UN. Progress had been made in advisory services and technical cooperation in the field of human rights and related areas such as good governance and sustainable development thereby affirming the VDPA's emphasis on the interrelationship between democracy, development, and human rights. Human rights had come to play an expanded role in the work of the UN creating increasing needs for coordination and cooperation.

The section of the Interim Report entitled "The Impact of the World Conference" was unable really to report on impacts for the most part because of the limited number of reports received by the HCHR at the time of preparing the Interim Report. However, it identified seven themes as the main themes to be reviewed by the General Assembly:

1. An integrated and holistic approach to human rights emphasizing universality, nondiscrimination, and the right to development – an approach to be adopted not only by the OHCHR but by the entire UN system.
2. International cooperation with an increased role of human rights in both bilateral and multilateral relations.
3. Mainstreaming human rights in all UN activities.
4. Target-oriented human rights protection for women and children.
5. Strengthening and adapting the UN's human rights machinery, including the OHCHR, the treaty-based bodies, the special procedures and mechanisms, the Commission and the Sub-Commission.
6. Strengthening the UN's technical cooperation programme.
7. Human rights education.

A particular focus of the review was expected to be the human rights legal framework and efforts on completing work on standard setting; by working towards universal ratification of human rights treaties; and by support for incorporation and enforcement of international standards under national law.

The Interim Report stressed that the Vienna +5 Review should refer to unfulfilled recommendations of the VDPA and identify existing shortcomings in the promotion and protection of human rights. Throughout 1998, the Interim Report hoped that the world community would weigh the impact of the VDPA at national and international levels. Lessons from this process were to be a vehicle for progress. The Interim Report concluded on a sobering note, "Without prejudging the conclusions of the Review process, one can note that the progress achieved in the implementation of the VDPA does not merit self-satisfaction on the part of the international community."[8] Indeed a meaningful review of the performance of state party implementation of the VDPA was expected to result in even less ground for satisfaction. But every indication of the process and plans outlined for the General Assembly review indicated that no such meaningful review of the performance of state parties was likely to be undertaken. The state reports received by the HCHR should have been freely available (possibly on the HCHR website). But that was not agreed to. Moreover, there was to be no scope in the process for state reports to be supplemented by additional information or critique by NGOs, either international or from the country concerned. The Vienna +5 Review looked like less of a review and more of an updating of the VDPA.

In her first annual report to the Commission on Human Rights,[9] the HCHR notes three positive developments that have taken place within the UN system since Vienna: (1) UN reform to enhance its human rights programme and its integration into the broad range of the organization's activities; (2) restructuring the human rights secretariat in the OHCHR; and (3) the adoption by the General Assembly in December 1996 of a mid-term plan for the UN for the period 1998–2001 which set out clear objectives for the UN's human rights programme during that period. In order to achieve the purpose of promoting universal enjoyment of all human rights, the programme proclaimed that it would:
– provide the leading role on human rights issues;
– emphasize the importance of human rights on the international and national agendas;
– promote international cooperation for human rights;
– stimulate and coordinate action across the whole UN system;
– promote universal ratification and implementation of international standards;

– assist in the development of new norms;
– support human rights organs and treaty-monitoring bodies;
– anticipate and react to violations;
– emphasize preventive human rights action;
– promote the establishment of national human rights infrastructures;
– undertake human rights field activities and operations; and
– provide education, information, advisory services, and technical assistance in the field of human rights.

Thus the UN approached the final act of the Vienna +5 Review poised to
play an historically unprecedented role in the implementation of the
VDPA. But as always, the UN could do no more than give practical effect
to the will and resolve of the world community as expressed by the
member states of the UN.

Vienna +5 review

The final act in the Vienna +5 review took place on 2 and 3 November
1998. This two-day session of the Third Committee of the General Assembly was tasked to undertake a review, primarily of the implementation by member states of the VDPA. Implementation of the VDPA by
the UN system had already been undertaken (for what it was worth)
during the coordination segment of ECOSOC earlier that year, as described above. The basis for this review was the final report of the HCHR
on the implementation of the VDPA.[10] Only four NGOs had contributed
written inputs to her report. In her opening statement to the Third Committee, introducing her report, Mary Robinson stressed:

Just as the World Conference itself was not designed as a single event, but rather
as a process which should lead to better promotion and protection of human
rights, so, too, the "Vienna +5" review is both retrospective and future oriented.
Analyzing the achievements and failures of the last five years, we should consider,
first and foremost, what must be done to implement more effectively human
rights, how better to protect people whose rights are threatened, how to assist
victims of human rights violations in practical ways.

She presented specific follow-up tasks: strengthening the implementation
of human rights at the national level; making the system of international
human rights instruments more effective; creating a favourable environment for human rights and human development; developing comprehensive programmes for the eradication of racism; trafficking in women
and children; and mass and gross human rights violations: including
summary and arbitrary executions, torture, and involuntary disappear-

ances; placing increased emphasis on preventing human rights violations; and strengthening the role of NGOs and civil society at large.

With characteristic candour, the HCHR in concluding her brief statement cautioned:

United Nations documents, reports by NGOs and the media provide testimony of our shortcomings and failures. Therefore, I would like to reiterate on the occasion of the "Vienna +5" Review – this is a time for practical action. We have the words of the Universal Declaration and commitments of the VDPA – deeds are necessary to give them practical meaning. In short: it is time to put up or shut up![11]

Three sessions of three hours' duration each were allotted to the review over the two-day period. The perfunctory nature of the review is evident from the fact that none of those three sessions lasted, even remotely, the three-hour time limit available. Member state after member state made self-serving statements about what they were doing (or had done) to implement the VDPA.

One Ambassador used the occasion to belittle and criticize the UDHR and VDPA:

Times change. We change. The UDHR was written in 1948 when the writers were preoccupied with the problems of fascism and totalitarianism, which had led to World War II. In that historical context, it was natural for UN members [UN membership then numbered at 58, 127 less than today] to focus their efforts on rights over responsibilities, putting in as many conditions as possible to block the emergence of fascism and totalitarianism. Indeed, the word "responsibility" is not mentioned at all in the UDHR although there is a passing reference to the concept of "duties" in the second last article, Article 29 ... we should adopt a position of humility on the issue of human rights. No time and no society has found all the right answers for mankind for all time. It would be arrogant and unwise for us to pretend that both in the UDHR and VDPA we have found the perfect answers. History tells us we have not. Let us together temper our celebrations today.[12]

Several days later, the Third Committee adopted a resolution on the Vienna +5 review which "recognizes that the Vienna Declaration and Programme of Action continues to constitute a solid foundation for further action and initiatives" and calls upon states "to take further action" "in the light of the recommendations of the World Conference" including the recommendation regarding "the universal ratification of human rights treaties and withdrawal of reservations" "within the next five years".

NGOs were mere observers and whatever their category of accreditation with the UN, have no rights of participation in the committees of the General Assembly. Moreover, the Chair of the Third Committee made it abundantly clear that he was not willing to set a precedent by allowing NGO participation in the Vienna +5 review undertaken by the

Third Committee. As a result, there would have been no NGO participation at all. Some 15 NGOs, comprising those not working exclusively
on human rights, joined with a few international human rights NGOs and
appealed to the HCHR to intervene. She responded by inviting NGOs,
governments, and others interested (e.g. UN agency representatives) to a
three-hour dialogue on the Vienna +5 review. The dialogue took place
during the 2–3 November period, in the very room in which the Third
Committee was conducting its Vienna +5 review, and during a time slot
in which the Third Committee was not otherwise scheduled to meet. The
dialogue proceeded and some 20 NGOs made statements regarding the
VDPA and review of its implementation. Some 12 governments also
made statements following the NGO presentations. Missing, however,
were the governments in the non-aligned bloc who chose to schedule a
meeting of their own in the precise time slot in which the HCHR had
already announced that the dialogue with NGOs would take place.

At the end of the two-day review period there were painful lessons to
be learned from the entire Vienna +5 review process, which bids fair to
hold "worst practice" status regarding conference reviews undertaken so
far. NGOs had no opportunity to participate in the decisions that set
up the process for the Vienna +5 review. Location of that process
in ECOSOC and the Third Committee meant the virtual exclusion of
NGOs. Moreover, the approach of inviting contributions from NGOs
through electronically posting invitations on a website (rather than by
mail as before) did not work adequately, since only four NGO responses
were the outcome of such an approach. Clearly, a more rigorous methodology needs to be adopted to review specific conference commitments,
otherwise the review ends up in platitudinous generalities. The dilemma
remains in finding ways to address new concerns that have arisen in the
five years since the conference while guarding against renegotiation of, or
unravelling and regression from the consensus reached at the conference.

The final resolution adopted at the end of the Vienna +5 review can
be viewed either as a metaphorical glass half full or half empty! The
Vienna consensus remains intact and undamaged. But to assert that the
Vienna +5 review has produced any "value-added" would be indeed to
strain the boundaries of credibility. Perhaps it would be most appropriate
to quote from the final resolution adopted by the Third Committee of
the General Assembly, at the end of the Vienna +5 review. That resolution, entitled "Comprehensive Implementation of and Follow up to
the Vienna Declaration and Programme of Action": "*Calls upon* States
and the international community to adopt a comprehensive approach
for the prevention of human rights violations, addressing the economic,
social, ethnic and other root causes of conflicts from a human rights
perspective, which includes the maintenance of the rule of law and the

strengthening of democratic institutions"; and "*Decides* to continue the consideration of this question at its fifty-fourth session under the sub-item entitled "Comprehensive implementation of and follow up to the Vienna Declaration and Programme of Action.""

Concluding observations

The Vienna +5 review was conducted under a combination of circumstances that dictated both process and outcomes. States supportive of the VDPA chose not to seek the usual process of PrepComs and a Special Session of the General Assembly. They were understandably cautious and fearful that the review would be used to renegotiate and renege on the consensus reached at Vienna. This fear was prompted by the increasing politicization of the annual sessions of the Commission on Human Rights. They approached the Vienna +5 review as a damage limitation exercise and were hoping for little more than preventing regression. This view was largely shared by the OHCHR. UN specialized agencies, funds and programmes were also far from keen on a serious review of their own performance regarding implementation of the VDPA, preferring instead to emphasize prospects for future contributions resulting from UN reform and mainstreaming. These factors led to the choice of process for the review: reports requested by the HCHR; inter-agency consultations, preparation by the Secretariat of Reports which would serve as the basis for the two review events: the ECOSOC segment (at which the emphasis would be on review of UN system performance) and the General Assembly Review (at which the emphasis would be on performance of state parties). The advantages and limitations of such a process are now becoming clear. Such a process contains politicization, achieves damage limitation, and holds the line against regression. But this is achieved at the cost of a meaningful review of commitments and obligations, of serious obstacles to implementation and of renovating the Plan of Action to address changing circumstances and needs. Such a process also severely constrains NGO participation. It will require the wisdom of hindsight to determine whether the decisions regarding the process for conducting the Vienna +5 review were wise. The process does not represent best practice, but those who supported the process will claim that this was the best possible under the circumstances. There will be a need to revisit the issue of process in respect of the five-year reviews of the remaining conferences of the 1990s. Moreover, for there to be truly an integrated conference follow-up process, the Vienna +5 Review would have needed to have identified both *core aspects* of the VDPA which should feature in the review of every other conference as well as *specific aspects* of the VDPA, particularly relevant to the subject matter of each specific conference being reviewed. The UN is uniquely placed and poised to undertake such an integrated approach, thanks to UN reform based on mainstreaming human rights system-wide. It is ironic, therefore, that the word "mainstreaming" was kept out of the Agreed Conclusions of the ECOSOC segment. But mainstreaming of human rights within the UN system is a process well underway, from which there can be no turning back. Hopefully, other conference reviews can heed the lessons of the Vienna +5 review, proceeding from less defensive a starting point and, indeed, in a "best practice" participatory process.

Notes

1. Tunis Declaration of African NGOs of 6 November 1992, Bangkok NGO Declaration on Human Rights of 27 March 1993, and Quito Declaration of Latin American and Caribbean NGOs of 30 May 1993.
2. M. Nowak (ed.), *World Conference on Human Rights* (Vienna: Manz, 1994), p. 1.
3. Resolution 1998/72 on the Right to Development adopted by consensus.
4. E/1998/L-23, p. 13.
5. E/1998/L.23, pp. 2–4.
6. E/CN.4/1998/104.
7. A/49/668.
8. E/CN.4/1998/104, p. 19.
9. E/CN.4/1998/122.
10. A/53/372, 11 September 1998.
11. Statement by the High Commissioner for Human Rights, Mrs. Mary Robinson, New York, 2 November 1998, pp. 2, 5–6.
12. Statement by the Permanent Representative of Singapore to the United Nations, 3 November 1998, pp. 4–5.

Part Two

The Beijing and Rio conference processes

4

Effectiveness of the Beijing Conference in fostering compliance with international law regarding women

Rebecca J. Cook

Introduction

The effectiveness of the Fourth World Conference on Women, held in Beijing in 1995 (the Beijing Conference), in fostering compliance with international law regarding women can be predicted by considering the resulting Beijing Declaration and Platform of Action,[1] the processes that gave rise to the platform and those that will give force to its implementation. The Beijing Conference was preceded by extensive preparation through UN regional conferences, non-governmental organization (NGO) meetings and expert consultations. An NGO Forum ran parallel to the conference at Huairou, about 50 km from Beijing, which was the site of many formal and informal workshops.

Much of the preparatory work for the Beijing Conference was aspirational, but conservative and even reactionary interests were alerted to the possibility of the conference advancing international law regarding women in directions they were disposed to resist. They contested much of the language of the text proposed for acceptance in Beijing, and the draft text presented at the opening of the conference included key phrases in brackets, indicating absence of agreement on their adoption. The conference itself tended to focus on crafting consensus around the contested language, which was reached through compromises that restrained the more forward-looking advances that women's rights advocates had hoped that the conference would achieve.

The Beijing Conference addressed 12 areas of critical concern to women, namely poverty, education, health, violence, armed and other kinds of conflicts, economic structures and policies, power and decision-making at all levels, institutional mechanisms, human rights, media and other communication systems, natural resources and the environment, and the girl child. In each of these areas, the platform specifies strategic objectives and actions that governments committed themselves to pursue.

The Platform for Action indicates the extent to which the conference achieved, and failed to achieve, evolution in international law regarding women. Expressed in a somewhat unwieldy text of 361 paragraphs, the platform provides material in each of the 12 critical areas that will encourage development of international law favouring women's interests. An emerging literature critiques the Beijing Platform, Conference and the Huairou NGO Forum from many perspectives,[2] and shows how the platform can be used to advance specific areas of international law regarding women.[3] International law regarding women is evolving through four overlapping stages of development.[4] During the first stage of development, states are beginning to focus on the promotion of specific legal rights of women such as through the negotiation of specialized conventions, for instance concerning employment, trafficking in persons, and violence against women. During the second stage of development, states have succeeded in including sex as a prohibited ground of discrimination in the Universal Declaration of Human Rights and the international and regional human rights treaties designed to give effect to the prohibition. States are now working toward enforcement of these provisions. The third stage of development seeks to remedy the pervasive and structural nature of violations of women's rights, through the effective application of the Convention on the Elimination of All Forms of Discrimination against Women (the Women's Convention). The elimination of *all forms* of discrimination includes work on eliminating gender discrimination, meaning socially constructed discrimination in contrast to exclusion on biological grounds, such as the exclusion of women from positions of authority on a presumed basis of intellectual or temperamental unfitness. The fourth stage of development seeks to integrate women's concerns into more generalized treaties such as those on international trade, and, for example, the treaty establishing the International Criminal Court.[5]

Characterizing all four stages of development in principle is a lack of state compliance in practice. The Preamble to the Women's Convention expressed the concern of states parties that "despite these various instruments extensive discrimination against women continues to exist." Many of the 165 states parties to the Women's Convention have entered fundamental reservations to their acceptance of particular provisions;

some states' reservations are indeed so central to the purpose of the convention that there is legal doubt about whether they can legally be considered parties at all.[6] Many parties without such explicit reservations cannot be said to be implementing their commitment convincingly.[7] The United Nations has long recognized that its hopes for women's equality require more than declarations and even conventions. The drafting and implementation of the Women's Convention were supported by three previous UN conferences on women, held in Mexico City in 1975, in Copenhagen in 1980, and in Nairobi in 1985. However, gaining the momentum necessary to advance international law regarding women remains a challenge. The Beijing Platform observed the failure of the previous Women's Conference, finding that "[m]ost of the goals set out in the Nairobi Forward-Looking Strategies for the Advancement of Women have not been achieved."[8]

Most feminist international legal scholars have tended to focus on why nations should obey international law or international agreements such as the Beijing Declaration and Platform for Action to improve women's status. This chapter tries to stand back from the normative question, and to ask why in practice states do not obey international law and agreements regarding women. In addressing the question, the chapter looks behind the law and the agreements to the forces and processes that mould them. It identifies some of the recent literature on compliance with international law that might be useful in responding to the question. Finally, by reference to models for determining the effectiveness of international law, the chapter suggests some approaches for reviewing how well the Beijing Declaration and Platform of Action have fostered compliance with international law regarding women, and their potential to contribute to future advances.

In considering the effectiveness of the Beijing Conference in achieving compliance with international law, recourse might be made to the phrase "implementation, compliance, and effectiveness" employed in evaluating international regimes. In a work on international environmental agreements, for instance, the terms are explained in the following way:

Implementation refers to measures taken to carry out the agreement. *Compliance* addresses whether the targeted actors have changed their behavior. We need to distinguish between compliance (1) with procedural obligations, such as reporting; (2) with substantive obligations, such as phasing out the use of certain chemicals; and (3) with the spirit of the agreement. A country could comply with both the procedural and substantive obligations but still violate the spirit of the agreement. *Effectiveness* is different; it addresses both whether the agreement has achieved its stated objectives and whether the agreement successfully addresses the problem it was intended to solve.[9]

This chapter attempts to address the effectiveness of the Beijing Conference in fostering compliance with the substantive obligations of eliminating all forms of discrimination against women so as to comply with the spirit of Beijing to enable women to live and function with dignity in all spheres of public and private life. The chapter is not exhaustive but rather exploratory, recognizing that much more work is needed adequately to address this issue.

Practices, processes, and perspectives

In considering the effectiveness of the Beijing process, it is important to look behind the principles and rules of international law to the complex practices, processes, and perspectives that generate the momentum for its development. For example, the fact that advocates of women's rights overcame powerful forces of reaction to preserve the *status quo* in the context of the Beijing process can be seen as a significant achievement.

The dynamics of international law can be understood from the perspectives of:
1. social frictions resulting in legal development;
2. the problems that legal change is intended to resolve;
3. the underlying dynamics of broad social transformations marking historical movements in world affairs; and
4. components of the power (whether military, economic, political, or psychological) that directs state action.[10]

Determining the actual effectiveness of the Beijing Conference in fostering protection and promotion of women's rights awaits further study, as has been undertaken in other areas of international law.[11] Such studies will need to look behind the actual text of the Beijing Platform to understand the underlying processes at work before, during and after Beijing to understand the conditions necessary for more effective recognition, protection and promotion of the human rights of women. Although the wording of the Beijing Platform presents compromises that may disappoint many advocates of women's empowerment through international law, the process itself of agreeing the platform has created important transnational dynamics through which advances to empowerment may be more readily achieved.

Social frictions resulting in legal development

The Beijing Conference facilitated a better understanding of and sensitivity to women's circumstances that are necessary conditions for the development of law. The facts relevant to women's advancement emerged through empirical studies prepared for the Beijing Conference, women's narratives presented at the Huairou NGO Forum, which continue to emerge through reports to treaty bodies and, for example, court cases.

A source of friction between prevailing international law and feminist criticism of its failure to realize its promise is that women's interests are not made relevant to the planning, achievement, or enforcement of human rights conventions, because such steps are conditioned within male-gendered environments that exclude women's voices. International conferences increasingly attract parallel NGO fora at which women's tribunals present testimony from women whose experiences demonstrate failures of existing human rights protections.[12] The space between the promise of international law and its achievement is not a vacuum or a silence, but is increasingly filled by voices of discontent, and by friction causing heat that may melt the iron will of resistance and rise to incendiary proportions. The limited opportunities for international judicial and other authoritative interpretation of women's rights inhibit the development of normative understanding and application of international law regarding women.

In a sense, international law with regard to women is primitive. It has established primary rules of obligation, that is, commitments to eliminate discrimination against women, but has yet to develop or use sufficiently the secondary rules of process and enforcement, by which to interpret and apply legal commitments.[13] Where procedural mechanisms do exist, they are generally dominated by people who require a fuller understanding of the realities of women's lives, particularly in the most deprived circumstances, to be able to apply the primary rules in ways that are fair to women.

Problems that legal change might resolve

At first, the problem the Beijing Platform is intended to resolve appears self-evident in the face of women's continued denial of their human rights. Inevitably, certain conflicts arise from attempts to address the needs of women, but there would be little development in the law without such conflicts.[14] The Beijing process gave voice to the continuing need for women's equality with men, but more than formal sexual equality may be necessary to relieve women's enduring subservience to male-gendered power. It has been observed that

[a]lthough, at one level, the contestation in Beijing between feminist and antifeminist perspectives resulted in a hard-won reaffirmation of previously agreed "equality" commitments by states, at another level the outcomes represent few, if any, advances for women ... the traditional equality paradigm remains the domi-

nant framework for seeking women's "emancipation" ... Extending to women the rights that men currently enjoy is not enough. It is not enough because it does not challenge the underlying social, political and economic institutions that reproduce gender hierarchies.[15]

The Beijing Conference facilitated recognition of the full dimensions of women's experience of discrimination that legal change has to resolve. The platform explains that "women face barriers to full equality and advancement because of such factors as their race, age, language, ethnicity, culture, religion or disability, because they are indigenous women or because of other status. Many women encounter specific obstacles related to their family status, particularly as single parents, and to their socio-economic status, including their living conditions in rural, isolated or impoverished areas."[16]

The Beijing Platform also recognized that in many societies girl children suffer discrimination to which boy children are not exposed, and pointed to the need "to eliminate all forms of discrimination against the girl child and the root causes of son preference, which results in harmful and unethical practices such as prenatal sex selection and female infanticide."[17] The Beijing Platform identified women's poverty and vulnerabilities of the girl child as critical areas of concern, giving further emphasis to the need for governments to address the multidimensional nature of discrimination against women.

The empowerment of women requires the development of new standards that capture the multidimensional nature of discrimination against women and against girl children. Applying a single axis framework of gender alone to expose discrimination has been criticized as inadequate by minority feminist legal scholars. Some have questioned the very choice of equality as a starting point.[18] Others have shown that unidimensional enforcement of the prohibition of gender discrimination is inadequate to expose the full depth of discrimination suffered by women within social groups that experience additional discrimination on grounds unrelated to sex and gender.[19] Further, stereotyped discrimination against women may exist within racial or other social subgroups themselves that is not a feature of the wider society. The Women's Convention may become a more effective instrument to relieve discrimination when it is applied multidimensionally. The convention clearly addresses sex-based and gender-based discrimination, but its focus on "all forms" of discrimination permits it to reinforce prohibitions of discrimination under, for instance, the Race Convention and the Children's Convention. One approach is for the Committee on the Elimination of Discrimination Against Women (CEDAW) to develop a General Recommendation interpreting the phrase "all forms of discrimination against women" in the

Women's Convention to prohibit these multidimensional, composite forms of discrimination against women and girl children.

Underlying dynamics of broad social transformations

The Beijing Conference focused attention on emerging transformations in the world order that affect women's situations. It has been observed that "[t]he contribution of [this] perspective is to bring out the historical dimension" that conditions reforms in international law, emphasizing the need to relate events and circumstances to "the broad social transformations that mark historical movements affecting world affairs."[20] Developments already amenable to historical reflection on their impact on international law that emerged contemporaneously with the Beijing Conference are evolving limitations on state sovereignty, structural globalization, and cultural fragmentation.

Proposals in the Beijing Platform to relieve the feminization of poverty were founded on the observation that "[m]ore than 1 billion people in the world today, the great majority of whom are women, live in unacceptable conditions of poverty, mostly in the developing countries."[21] The Platform for Action addresses the complex, multidimensional problem of poverty, and explains that the globalization of the world's economy and the deepening interdependence among nations challenge hopes for sustained economic growth and development, but that that presents opportunities. Observing that "gender disparities in economic power sharing are an important contributing factor to the poverty of women,"[22] and that, for instance, migration and consequent changes in family structures have placed additional burdens on women, the platform finds that "[t]he application of gender analysis to a wide range of policies and programmes is therefore critical to poverty reduction strategies."[23]

Strategies to reduce poverty and its disproportionate impact on women require national and international initiatives. However, an observable modern dynamic is reduction of national governmental economic initiatives, in favour of the operation of free market forces. Further, international policies, such as pursued by the World Bank, similarly favour free market enterprise and reduced state intervention in market regulation. The collapse of socialist economies dominated by centralized governmental controls, and the parallel decline of strong right-wing, authoritarian governments, have both opened the way to democratization. Political democracy has been accompanied by economic free market philosophies hostile to governmental regulation. Twin thrusts to move government out of the market-place and to make government more democratic have precluded the introduction of democracy into the market-place. Thus, "government by the people" in political terms accompanied by "deregulation by the people" in economic terms has worked to women's disadvantage. Continuing political disempowerment of women has denied women regulatory protection by government against poverty that results in many being powerless to protect themselves against the operation of unregulated markets. Narrowing the gap between rich and poor that is widened by market forces requires governmental action, which is compromised by the spread of "minimal government" politics.

The role of government in free markets is to prevent the degradation of free market forces through monopoly and corruption, and to protect powers of entry into the market. However, the concentration of power through male-gendered institutions and activities, and the exploitation of female-gendered activities such as caring for dependent others and supplying cheap "sweat shop" labour, exacerbate female poverty. Laws or practices that deny commercial credit to women, for instance by recognizing security for loans only in freehold property that women can neither hold nor inherit, prevent women's participation in markets. Moreover, governmental tax-cutting economies that reduce children's public day-care services, de-institutionalize the elderly and disabled from public nursing home care and eliminate public services for the disabled, require women to give unpaid care to children, the elderly, and the disabled. Rendering such care excludes women from the paid labour force, which in industrialized economies may deny them not only income but also access to employer-provided health insurance, disability insurance, and pension plans. The burden of care is shifted from the public purse, to women.

Gender discrimination of this nature results from laissez-faire economic practices unregulated by governmental gender-equity policies. Such laissez-faire sexism is often reinforced by laissez-faire racism where governments are equally non-interventionist in the face of racial and other dimensions of discrimination (as noted above). The compounded injustice is masked, however, due to the inadequacy of a single axis analysis of discrimination against women.

Globalization of economic structures has not been paralleled by comparable integration of values and cultures. On the contrary, during the decade of the 1990s, the world has retreated to defensive cultural and ethnic enclaves, each stressing its own value system.[24] Many of these systems condemn international human rights law as unhistoric and Eurocentric, and thus question the universality of human rights. As a result, some scholars have stressed the need to resist cultural isolationism and to build human rights on cross-cultural foundations.[25] These and other scholars are beginning to analyse culture as an ongoing dialogue, not as static, immutable traditions that are contrary to women's interests. They are exploring "the capacity of human rights discourse to represent and foster debate over cultural norms within communities rather than to silence or marginalize it."[26] They contend that "the right to culture must guarantee access to a supportive cultural framework for all citizens."[27]

The Beijing Platform recognizes the importance of ensuring that women enjoy cultural, including religious, traditions. It acknowledges that "any form of extremism may have a negative impact on women and can lead to violence and discrimination."[28] The platform further recognizes the growing strength of the NGO community in advancing women's rights, and stresses the importance of enabling NGOs to operate freely without government obstruction.[29] The implicit suggestion is that affording support to a strong NGO community and civil society more generally is one of the best ways of counteracting extremism, and encouraging the cross-cultural promotion of women's common interests in the understanding of human rights law.

Power directing state action

The fourth perspective from which to understand the relation of fact to legal development concerns power. It is a critical variable in the development, application, and observance of law: "power (that is, the ability of states to impose their will on other states) has a central role in the relations of states. The striving for power (whatever its components: military, economic, political, or psychological) is often a dominating goal of states. It is perceived both as an end in itself and more commonly as a means for a state to attain other goals, to give it greater freedom of action and reduce the constraints on its action."[30] The Beijing Conference reinforced recognition that

femaleness, as a category, continues to be heavily policed by masculinist interests and contained within narrow, disciplinary boundaries. Women's "citizenship" within the global community is both limited to, and conditional upon, their position within the prescribed normative framework. This is contingent "citizenship" at the price of women's diversity and of fundamental global change.[31]

Women's contingent citizenship can be explained by the fact that, due to the many forces that deny women's empowerment, women possess no effective power that governments have felt it necessary to harness. On the contrary, dominant male-gendered institutions that give power to government, such as military and religious institutions, have been able to suppress and control the power that women may generate. Such gendered institutions, for instance, exclude women from their membership or leadership, confine women to the domestic sphere of national life and exploit women's roles for the support of male dominance.

However, modern tendencies to democratization of states offer a vision, though distant, of women equally enfranchised with men, concentrating their political power through the ballot box to show discontent with the *status quo* and to attract would-be leaders to seek their democratic support. Women may come to mobilize the same self-interest that has shaped democratic politics to serve the interests of men. Where women generate self-consciousness of the way their needs and priorities can be served through their votes, those ambitious for leadership within states will recognize the advantage of women's support, and that women's alienation is a deficit in their power base. Governments conscious of their need to maintain women's support will find that international investments in women's interests, as women define them, will reap domestic returns.

Until protection of women's interests becomes a feature of a government's entitlement to recognition and international stature, and until the power and prestige of governments among the community of nations is dependent on their incorporation of women as fully participant citizens in all of their domestic institutions, governments' observance of the human rights of women will not be equal to observance of the human rights, for instance, of ethnic minorities. Very few governments have become international pariahs for abusing or neglecting women, as some have for oppression of minorities or dissidents. However, democratic governments at Beijing were concerned to find a balance between maintaining their traditional power bases and doing enough for women to ensure women's support in future elections.

Fostering compliance

Significant modern work has been undertaken to address why certain rules of international law "exert more pull towards compliance than others."[32] Some suggest that nations obey rules of international law because of considerations of legitimacy and distributive justice.[33] Others have argued that "the fundamental instrument for maintaining compliance with treaties at an acceptable level is an iterative process of discourse among the parties, the treaty organization, and the wider public."[34]

One analyst has reviewed these works and shown how two intellectual traditions in international legal scholarship "have historically defended [international law] against two divergent claims: on one hand, the realist charge that international law is not really law, because it cannot be enforced; on the other, the rationalistic claim that nations 'obey' international law only to the extent that it serves national self-interest."[35] A deeper examination is suggested to show how "the [transnational legal] process of interaction, interpretation and internalization of international norms into domestic legal systems is pivotal to understanding why nations 'obey' international law, rather than merely conform their behavior to it when convenient."[36] While much work is needed to understand "the process by which nations and other transnational actors promote compliance and ultimately obedience,"[37] three steps are proposed that might be useful starting points to determine the effectiveness of the Beijing Conference in promoting compliance with international women's rights.

1. "If transnational actors obey international law as a result of repeated *interaction* with other actors in the transnational legal process, a first step is to empower more actors to participate."[38]

The Beijing Conference empowered more actors, particularly from East and South Asia, to participate in the transnational legal process. Moreover, the conference facilitated a new generation of women to engage in the process of interaction that induces state compliance with international law. The conference was especially successful in galvanizing women to engage in international humanitarian law, and especially the drafting of the Statute of the International Criminal Court.[39] Where the conference was less successful was in engaging those involved in the development and application of private international law; for instance integrating women's concerns into more generalized treaties such as on international trade and on commercial credit.[40]

2. "If the goal of interaction is to produce *interpretation* of human rights norms, what fora are available for norm-enunciation and elaboration both within and without existing human rights regimes?"[41]

Recognizing the importance of the interpretation and application of the law,[42] the Beijing Platform recommended the development and adoption of an Optional Protocol for the Women's Convention.[43] Despite many challenges,[44] the UN Commission on the Status of Women has now agreed on an Optional Protocol,[45] and it has recently been approved by the UN General Assembly.[46] The protocol enables individuals from ratifying countries to bring complaints of alleged violations and establishes a procedure of inquiry, which may include a visit to a territory, if reliable information is received indicating grave or systematic violations of women's rights by a state party of rights under the convention. Both the complaints and inquiry procedure would be submitted to and considered by CEDAW.

The Beijing Conference had the indirect effect of facilitating the work of CEDAW and other human rights committees, since it increased understanding of women's issues and the knowledge of members of human rights treaty bodies. As a result, when these committees address women's issues raised in governmental reports, they can achieve better norm enunciation and elaboration because they can now refer to data and perspectives generated during the Beijing process. Improved normative clarity is evident in Concluding Comments and Observations, developed subsequent to the Beijing Conference.[47]

Outside the treaty regimes is the UN Special Rapporteur on Violence against Women, who has facilitated norm enunciation both internationally and domestically. The UN Commission on Human Rights appointed Ms. Radhika Coomaraswamy as Special Rapporteur, with a broad mandate to eliminate such violence and its causes, and to remedy its consequences by recommending ways and means at national, regional, and international levels to eliminate gender violence. She works closely with committees established by human rights treaties and with commissions established under the UN Charter.[48] The Special Rapporteur receives communications about alleged incidents of gender-specific violence against women that have not been effectively addressed through national legal systems, and uses this information to initiate and conduct dialogue with governments about finding resolutions.[49] Reports of the Special Rapporteur[50] show that such violence may be an offence by a state itself against a broad range of accepted rights expressed in international human rights treaties already binding on the state in question.[51]

While these fora provide foundations for progress, much more work is needed to formulate the secondary rules of process necessary for the application of primary rules of the obligation to eliminate all forms of discrimination against women. One analyst has explained that "[a] rule ... is more likely to obligate if it is made within the procedural and institutional framework of an organized community than if it is strictly an ad hoc agreement between parties in the state of nature. The same rule is still more likely to obligate if it is made within the hierarchically structured procedural and constitutional framework of a sophisticated community rather than in a primitive community lacking such secondary rules about rules."[52]

3. "What are the best strategies for internalization of international human rights or international human rights norms? One might distinguish among social, political, and legal internalization. Social internalization occurs when a norm acquires so much public legitimacy that there is widespread general obedience to it. Political internalization occurs when political elites accept an international norm, and adopt it as a matter of government policy. Legal internalization occurs when an international norm is incorporated into the domestic legal system through executive action, judicial interpretation, legislative action, or some combination of the three."[53]

National representatives and NGO delegates who attended proceedings in Beijing were able to take home the visions of women's equality that were generated there, criteria by which to measure the stage of domestic achievements towards those visions, and a sharpened sense of advances still to be made. Both public and private sector participants at Beijing received a better sense of each other, and of the potential for collaboration, conflict, and divergent interests between them. Part of the opportunity of all Beijing participants was to react, negatively or positively, to conservative forces concerned that the direction Beijing might indicate towards women's equality threatened their values, and seeking ways by which such directions might be pursued compatibly with their values. This afforded the Beijing process a dynamic for domestic application.

The goals of the Women's Convention, which the Beijing Platform was intended to advance, were illuminated in ways that could be translated domestically into enlightened choices for executive action, and to inspire legal advocacy to which judges could respond sympathetically in judicial interpretation of domestic law. Executive officers advising legislators could similarly introduce the spirit of Beijing into their advice on preferences and options for legislative developments, and NGO activists could similarly press legislators to advance legislative observance of the Beijing goals already accepted by national adherence to international human rights conventions.

Review of Beijing's effectiveness

A high level plenary review to be conducted at a special session of the UN General Assembly is envisioned for June 2000 "to appraise and assess the progress achieved in the implementation of the Nairobi Forward-Looking Strategies for the Advancement of Women and the Beijing Platform for Action five years after its adoption and to consider further actions and initiatives."[54] In undertaking any review, account must be taken of the broader context of fundamental transformation of the situation of states in the international system, and of how transformation has affected the Beijing process. This era of change has been called "the new sovereignty."[55] The fundamental transformations include "the marked decline of national sovereignty; the concomitant proliferation of international regimes, institutions, and nonstate actors; the collapse of the public-private distinction; the rapid development of customary and treaty-based rules; and the increasing interpenetration of domestic and international systems."[56] Given these developments, it has been explained that:

[n]o longer is it possible for states to achieve their most important objectives (or those of their citizens) through autonomous unilateral activity. Instead, they are embedded in a dense network of organizations and relationships upon which they depend not only to gain particular objectives but for their identity as members of the international system. To continue as a viable entity in the contemporary

world, a state must remain a member in good standing of that system and of the principal organizations of that network. That, in turn, requires an acceptable level of compliance with the going norms and rules.[57]

Different models have been proposed in the literature on international law and relations by which to evaluate compliance with and effectiveness of international regimes. The regulatory model is described as an arrangement that emphasizes "behavioral prescriptions – principles, norms and rules – as essential elements of regimes, and directs attention to issues of implementation and compliance in assessing performance of regimes ... The focus of the regulatory model is on the identification of factors that affect the extent to which the actual behavior of regime members conforms to the requirements of regulatory arrangements."[58]

This conventional approach to evaluating compliance with international treaty regimes can be contrasted with the social practice model, which might be more useful in evaluating the effectiveness of the Beijing process. This model considers regimes as

institutional frameworks that give rise to social practices which feature a wide range of integrative activities that stimulate the emergence of informal communities (including both regime members and nonstate actors) and trigger processes of social learning. This model directs attention to processes through which regime members become enmeshed in complex practices that serve to influence their behavior more through de facto engagement and through their impact on discourse in terms of which issues are addressed than through conscious decisions about compliance.[59]

A review of Beijing's effectiveness might usefully begin with a diagnosis of responses to the challenges of compliance with the Beijing Platform, and de-emphasize disobedience of norms. This requires the diagnosis considered above, of the context of the social frictions resulting in international legal developments, the problems that international law is intended to resolve, and the underlying dynamics and the components of power that direct state action. A review of Beijing's effectiveness would also require assessment over time of normative developments, and of the capacity and intent of states to comply with evolving norms.

Normative developments

A particular contribution of the Beijing Platform to normative development was the cultivation of communities of interest groups around the 12 critical areas of concern identified in the Beijing Platform, which will be more able to move towards agreements on rules to serve their common goals. Normative developments were not limited, however, to the 12 critical areas, but extended to the growing understanding that norms need to address the complex and multidimensional nature of women's subordination. A review must show how the Beijing Platform has helped to foster recognition that women's disadvantages are socially structured injustices, and not simply inherent in the physiological status of woman-hood.

The effectiveness of the Beijing Platform can be assessed by its ability to develop "soft" normative standards from which more explicitly bind-ing rules of international law will emerge. While one must guard against the assumption that binding law must be the ultimate outcome of a UN conference, it remains true that softer, less determinate normative developments are a necessary precursor for the emergence of more con-crete norms of binding law.[60] The Beijing Conference promoted a greater understanding of norms necessary to women's full exercise of their rights, which in turn can lead to an increased sense of obligation among states to comply with international law regarding women.[61]

Any review of the Beijing process has to assess the degree to which the norms articulated in the platform have become binding determinate standards of international law, and how these standards have been inter-nalized by states. It has been explained that "the legitimacy of a rule is affected by its degree of determinacy. Its determinacy depends upon the clarity with which it is able to communicate its intent and to shape that intent into a specific situational command."[62] This in turn can depend on the text of the rule, its ability to avoid hair-splitting debates about its meaning, and the availability of a process for resolving ambiguities in its application.[63] In any review of normative developments, it is important to examine not only how those developments affect relations among states, but also how they are internalized by domestic legal systems.[64]

It is important that there is an assessment over time, because the Bei-jing Platform requires major changes in entrenched social and economic practices that cannot be achieved quickly. A photograph of the status of a country's compliance at any particular moment in time is likely to be misleading. The motion picture approach might be more useful to dem-onstrate the dynamics of compliance.

Capacity

In many areas of international law, reform necessary for women's em-powerment requires administrative, technical, or financial resources for effective implementation. No area of legal development, such as eco-nomic reform, promotion of trade, or security of peace, is exempt from women's demands of participation, contribution, relevance, and advancement of their interests. A review might usefully explore progress made and potentials for future progress to remedy deficiencies in capacities to address women's concerns in these more generalized areas of international legal development.

The effective improvement of women's status might be achieved through the accumulation over time of specific entitlements or of a series of interdependent rights. A particular set of rights might be more important to improving women's status in one context than in another. For example, human rights relating to women's health might be usefully applied to improve women's lives in a country where there are high rates of maternal mortality that can be prevented by cost-effective means. In another country, human rights relating to equality in employment matters might be beneficial to women's interests applied where data show that there is a wide gender gap in wages. The challenge ahead will be to determine which mixtures of laws and policies can be most effectively applied in particular contexts to the best advantage of women who function in those contexts. This might suggest a move away from the measurement of law's effectiveness premised on universal enforcement in all contexts.

Intent

The intent of governments to improve the status of women is, at best, mixed. Analysts who adhere to the rationalistic strand of international law would argue that where there is political power to be gained by the empowerment of women, the intent of governments to comply with the Beijing Platform and relevant international law would be stronger. Those who adhere to the liberal school of international law would argue that governments obey international law out of a sense of moral obligation and justice. If one evaluates the substantive rules of international law by reference to their effectiveness as agents of distributive justice for women, as some have done for other issues in international law,[65] one is not entirely convinced that governments obey international law out of a sense of moral obligation to women.

Intent might be objectively assessed by the actual measures governments take to improve women's status, and the proportion of their available financial resources they allocate for this purpose. The requisite intent might exist in some ministries, such as foreign affairs, and not in other ministries. The intent of governments to devote their resources and time to advance agendas for women limit what they can devote to governmental priorities in other sectors, so that women's agendas will always face competition within government from advocates of other causes governments want to support.

Methods to foster compliance with women's rights can be grouped into three categories:

- negative methods in the form of penalties, sanctions, and withdrawal of membership privileges;
- sunshine methods, such as monitoring, reporting, transparency, and NGO participation; and
- positive methods, such as special funds for financial or technical assistance, access to technology or training programmes.[66]

The question then becomes which methods work best under what set of circumstances?

Negative methods are rarely, if ever, invoked to foster compliance with international law with regard to women. The choice between sunshine methods on the one hand and positive methods on the other, or adoption of a mix of the two, will depend on the capacity and the intent of governments to comply.[67] For example, where there is genuine intent to comply, but limited capacity, positive methods might be more appropriate. Where there is capacity to comply, but the requisite political intent is lacking because governments apply their capacities for other causes, sunshine methods might be more effective, particularly to engage non-state actors to promote the priority of women's equality. Where both capacity and intent are limited, a mixture of both methods might be useful.

A review will have to grapple with the enduring challenge of determining how best to foster compliance with women's international human rights by different strategies or mixes of strategies. Recourse might creatively be made to the scholarship that has been generated to foster compliance with other areas of international law, and with domestic law. Comparative assessments of the applicability of such scholarship should be made, however, with an understanding of the distinctiveness of international law with regard to women, and of the dynamics that have molded it.

Notes

1. United Nations, *Report of the Fourth World Conference on Women*, Document A/Conf. 177/20, New York, 1995.
2. See Hilary Charlesworth, "Women as Sherpas: Are Global Summits Useful for Women?" 22 *Feminist Studies* (1996), p. 537; Malika Dutt, "Some Reflections on U.S. Women of Color and the United Nations Fourth World Conference on Women and the NGO forum in Beijing, China," 22 *Feminist Studies* (1996), p. 519; Eva Friedlander (ed.) *Look at the World Through Women's Eyes: Proceedings of the Plenary Sessions at the NGO Forum on Women, Huairou, China* (New York: NGO Forum on Women, Beijing '95, 1995); Dianne Otto, "Holding Up Half of the Sky, But for Whose Benefit?: A Critical Analysis of the Fourth World Conference on Women," 6 *Australian Feminist*

Law Journal (1996), p. 9; symposium issues of journals on Beijing; 2 *Issues Quarterly* (No. 1, 1996 and *Women's Studies Quarterly* Nos. 1 & 2, 1996); for further references to the international legal literature, see the Women's Human Rights Resources of the Bora Laskin Law Library, University of Toronto, ⟨http://www/law-lib.utoronto.ca/diana⟩

3. Rebecca J. Cook and Mahmoud F. Fathalla, "Advancing Reproductive Rights Beyond Cairo and Beijing," 22 *International Family Planning Perspectives* (1996), p. 115; Elizabeth L. Larson, "United Nations Fourth World Conference on Women: Action for Equality, Development and Peace," 10 *Emory International Law Review* (1996), p. 696.

4. Rebecca J. Cook, "The Elimination of Sexual Apartheid: Prospects for the Fourth World Conference on Women," 5 *American Society of International Law Issue Papers on World Conferences* (1995), pp. 4–6, 23.

5. Rome Statute on the International Criminal Court, 17 July 1998, UN Doc. A/CONF. 189.9 (1998); 37 *International Legal Materials* (1998), p. 999; see, generally, Kelly D. Askin, *War Crimes Against Women: Prosecution in International Tribunals* (The Hague: Kluwer Law International, 1997).

6. Further information on the status of states parties to the Women's Convention is available at website ⟨http://www.un.org/womenwatch/daw.htm⟩.

7. Rebecca J. Cook, "Reservations to the Convention on the Elimination of All Forms of Discrimination Against Women," 30 *Virginia Journal of International Law* (1990), p. 643.

8. n. 1 at para. 42.

9. Edith Brown Weiss, "National Compliance with International Environmental Agreements," 91 *Proceedings of the American Society of International Law* 56 (1997), p. 59.

10. Oscar Schachter, "The Natures and Process of Legal Development in International Society," in *Structure and Process of International Law,* edited by R. St. J. Macdonald and D. M. Johnston (Dordrecht: Nijhoff, 1996), pp. 745, 755.

11. See, for instance, Harold Jacobson and Edith Brown Weiss, "Strengthening Compliance with International Environmental Accords: Preliminary Observations from a Collaborative Project," 1 *Global Governance* (1995), p. 119.

12. Niamh Reilly (ed.), *Without Reservation: The Beijing Tribunal on Accountability for Women's Human Rights* (New Brunswick: Center for Women's Global Leadership, 1996).

13. Thomas M. Franck, "Legitimacy in the International System," 82 *American Journal of International Law* (1988), pp. 705, 751–2; see, generally, Thomas M. Franck, *The Power of Legitimacy Among Nations* (New York: Oxford University Press, 1990).

14. n. 10 at p. 750.

15. n. 2, Otto, at p. 29.

16. n. 1, at para. 46.

17. *Ibid.*, at para. 277(c).

18. Mary Ellen Turpel, "Patriarchy and Paternalism: The Legacy of the Canadian State for First Nations Women," 6 *Canadian Journal of Women and the Law* (1993), p. 174.

19. Kimberley Crenshaw, "Demarginalizing the Intersection of Race and Sex: A Black Feminist Critique of Antidiscrimination Doctrine, Feminist Theory and Antirascist Politics," *The University of Chicago Legal Forum* (1989), p. 139.

20. n. 10 at p. 750.

21. n. 1 at para. 47.

22. *Ibid.* at para. 47.

23. *Ibid.*

24. Michael Ignatieff, *The Warrior's Honor: Ethnic War and the Modern Conscience* (Toronto: Viking, 1997).

25. Abdullahi Ahmed An-Na'im, "State Responsibility Under International Human Rights Law to Change Religious and Customary Laws," in *Human Rights of Women: National and International Perspectives*, edited by Rebecca J. Cook (1994), p. 167.

26. Lisa Fishbayn, "Gender Equality and the Rights to Culture in the New South Africa," Work in Progress presented at the University of Toronto Faculty of Law, 13 February 1997, at p. 4.

27. *Ibid.* at p. 3.

28. n. 1 at para. 24.

29. *Ibid.* at para. 26.

30. n. 10 at p. 751.

31. n. 2, Otto, at p. 30.

32. n. 13 at p. 708 (1988).

33. Thomas M. Franck, *Fairness in International Law and Institutions* (New York: Oxford University Press, 1995).

34. Abram Chayes and Antonia Handler Chayes, *The New Sovereignty: Compliance with International Regulatory Agreements* (Cambridge: Harvard University Press, 1995), p. 25.

35. Harold H. Koh, "Why Do Nations Obey International Law?" 106 *Yale Law Journal* (references omitted) (1997), p. 2602.

36. *Ibid.* at pp. 2602–2603.

37. *Ibid.* at p. 2634.

38. *Ibid.* at p. 2656.

39. See n. 5.

40. See text above at n. 4 on the fourth stage of evolution of international law.

41. n. 35 at p. 2656.

42. Andrew Byrnes and Jane Connors, "Enforcing the Human Rights of Women: A Complaints Procedure for the Women's Convention," XXI *Brooklyn Journal of International Law* (1996), p. 679.

43. n. 1 at para. 230(k).

44. Andrew Byrnes, "Slow and Steady Wins the Race? The Development of the Optional Protocol to the Women's Convention," 91 *Proceedings of the American Society of International Law* (1997), p. 384; Aloisia Worgetter, "The Draft Optional Protocol to the Convention on the Elimination of All Forms of Discrimination Against Women," 2 *Austrian Review of International and European Law* (1997), p. 261.

45. E/CN.6/1999/WG/L.2, 10 March 1999.

46. GA/Res/54/4, 6 October 1999.

47. See, for example, *Concluding Observations of the Human Rights Committee: Peru: Peru.* 11/18/96. United Nations High Commission for Human Rights. CCPR/C/79/Add 72, para. 15.

48. UN Doc. E/CN.4/1995/42, 22 November 1994.

49. UN Doc. E/CN.4/1997/47/Add.4, 30 January 1997.

50. See particularly country mission reports of the Special Rapporteur: "Report on the mission to Democratic People's Republic of Korea, the Republic of Korea and Japan on the issue of military sexual slavery in wartime," E/CN.4/1996/53/Add.1, 4 January 1996; "Report on the mission to Poland on the issue of trafficking and forced prostitution of women," E/CN.4/1997/Add.1, 10 December 1996; "Report on the mission to Brazil on the issue of domestic violence," E/CN.4/1997/47/Add.2, 21 January 1997; "Report on the mission to South Africa on the issue of rape in the community," E/CN.4/1997/47/Add.3, 24 February 1997.

51. See e.g. *Velasquez Rodriquez v. Honduras*, Inter-Am.CHR, OAS/ser.L/V/III.19, doc.13 (1988); *X & Y v. The Netherlands*, 91 ECHR. (ser. A) (1985).

52. n. 13 at p. 752.

53. n. 35 at p. 2656.
54. E/CN.6/1998/L.11, 10 March 1998, available at web site ⟨http://www.un.org/ womenwatch/daw/csw/rev 3d.htm⟩.
55. n. 34 above.
56. n. 35 at p. 2604 (references omitted).
57. Abram Chayes, "Compliance without Enforcement," 91 *Proceedings of the American Society of International Law* (1997), 53 at p. 56.
58. Oran Young, "Two Models of Effectiveness," 91 *Proceedings of the American Society of International Law* (1997), p. 52.
59. *Ibid.*
60. Jutta Brunnee, "What's Next on Implementation, Compliance and Effectiveness? Remarks," 91 *Proceedings of the American Society of International Law* (1997), p. 504.
61. Christine Ainetter Brautigam, "Mainstreaming a Gender Perspective in the Work of the United Nations Treaty Bodies," *Proceedings of the American Society of International Law* (1997), p. 389.
62. n. 13 at p. 725.
63. *Ibid.*
64. n. 35 at pp. 2599, 2602–2603, 2645–2658.
65. n. 33 at pp. 351–371.
66. n. 9 at p. 57.
67. *Ibid.* at pp. 58–59.

5

Development, implementation, and effectiveness of the CBD process

Thomas Yongo

Introduction

The United Nations Conference on Environment and Development (UNCED) in Rio de Janeiro, June 1992, was a unique event in the annals of international affairs and international environmental law. The "Earth Summit" brought more heads of states and governments together than any previous meeting.[1] Thirty years after the publication of Rachel Carson's *Silent Spring* (1962), the "morning star of environmentalism,"[2] 20 years after the 1972 UN Conference on the Human Environment (Stockholm Conference)[3] and five years after the Brundtland Report,[4] the Earth Summit was billed as a landmark in the process which forced politicians, policy makers, and civil society to reflect on the linkages between the twin crises of development and the environment.

The 20 years separating the Stockholm and Rio Conferences witnessed the emergence of a new generation of environmental problems, including climate change, ozone depletion, and the destruction of biological diversity. The purpose of the Rio Conference was to elaborate strategies and measures to halt and reverse environmental degradation in the context of strengthened national and international efforts to promote sustainable and environmentally sound development in all countries. The UNCED process, therefore, acted as a catalyst and focus for injecting and formulating concepts of sustainable development around the world. The Convention on Biological Diversity (CBD)[5] was one of the two most significant products of the UNCED process.[6] Like other UN conferences before it, hopes and rhetoric to match accompanied Rio. The Rio Conference, like the Stockholm Conference, was successful in generating global concern about environmental deterioration, but some would argue that neither has hitherto resulted in action to match the level of international awareness and concern. Experience has shown us that rhetoric about environment is far easier to produce than action, and international fora tend on occasion to degenerate into "rhetoric-fests" where world leaders spout all the proper phrases but then return to their capitals and often fail to implement their internationally formulated promises and obligations. This chapter recalls some of the rhetoric that accompanied the negotiations of the CBD provisions, and evaluates whether and to what extent these hopes have been achieved. The chapter begins with a brief history of the convention after having identified the significant value of biodiversity. It then elaborates on specific provisions of the convention by revisiting the negotiations of these provisions, after which it identifies the successes and constraints in implementing them. We must always bear in mind that the CBD has been in force for only six years and as far as international agreements and treaties go, it may still be too early to evaluate its impact on the conservation of biodiversity and assess the measures that have thus far been taken to implement it both internationally and nationally.

Value and historical development

The loss of biodiversity is one of the major factors threatening sustainable development because biodiversity is necessary for the functioning of the biosphere as a whole. The CBD defines "biological diversity" to mean "the variability among living organisms from all sources including, inter alia, terrestrial, marine and other aquatic ecosystems and the ecological complexes of which they are part; this includes diversity within species, between species and ecosystems."[7] The Global Biodiversity Strategy defines "biological diversity" as "the totality of genes, species, and ecosystems in a region."[8] The conservation of biological diversity is necessary as a matter of ethics, survival, and economic benefit.[9] The international community came to recognize that conservation of biodiversity is also essential for the survival of humans because erosion of biodiversity lessens the earth's carrying capacity. Biodiversity also contributes substantially to the economy both directly through the consumptive use of biological resources; diverse ecosystems are more resilient against genetic defects such as vulnerability to disease and pests, and indirectly in a contribution to the development of agriculture and modern medicine (pharmaceuticals), as well as the development of biotechnology. The genetic material in wild species contributes billions of dollars a year to the world economy through improved crop species, new drugs, and medicines.[10] Human activities in the last quarter of the twentieth century have seen reducing biological diversity at an unprecedented rate. *Our Common Future*, the 1987 Report of the World Commission on Environment and Development[11] as well as the UNEP *Report on the Global Environment Perspective to the Year 2000*[12] stressed the new challenge facing the conservation and sustainable use of biological diversity.

In 1987, amidst overwhelming scientific evidence of growing biological erosion and concern about these trends, various environmental organizations and governments called upon UNEP to examine the possibility of negotiating and establishing an international legal instrument on the conservation and sustainable use of biodiversity. In view of its catalytic role in environmental affairs, UNEP decided on 17 June 1987 to convene an Ad Hoc Working Group of Experts on Biological Diversity for the harmonization of the existing conventions related to biological diversity. At its very first meeting, the Group of Experts agreed on the need to elaborate an international binding instrument on biological diversity.[13]

In May 1989, UNEP established an Ad Hoc Working Group of Legal and Technical Experts on Biological Diversity to prepare an international legal instrument for the conservation and sustainable use of biological diversity, taking into account "the need to share costs and benefits between developed and developing countries and the ways and means to support innovation by local people." The ad hoc working group, which became in February 1991 the Intergovernmental Negotiating Committee (INC) held seven working sessions, which culminated in an agreed text of the Convention on Biological Diversity.[14]

Right from the beginning of the UNEP-sponsored negotiations on the framework convention on biodiversity in November 1990, it was clear that in order to ensure success in the negotiations, the contentious issue of global economic disparities that has always characterized previous negotiations between the North and the South would have to be well taken care of lest it derail all prospects for agreement. A task of enormous magnitude lay in convincing developing countries that the international community's resolve to save the globe's fast disappearing biological resources bore genuine marks of good faith and that it was not merely part of a wider conspiracy by developed countries to maintain the *status quo*. Equally monumental was the task of getting developed countries to bind themselves legally to provide the much needed funds and technological transfer without which it would be virtually impossible for any of the steps towards the practical implementation of the convention to be undertaken. The convention's foremost significance lies in the fact that, to a great extent, it succeeded in achieving both by coalescing the multiple divergent positions held by the various countries thus making the final text eventually more acceptable to the vast majority of the states involved in the negotiation.

The convention was opened for signature on 5 June 1992 during the United Nations Conference on Environment and Development (UNCED) held in Rio de Janeiro. The convention entered into force upon the thirtieth ratification on 29 December 1993. As of February 2000, 177 countries and the European Union have ratified the convention and a further 20 countries have signed it.[15] The United States under President Bush refused to sign the convention in 1992, but it did accede after Bill Clinton became President. On 29 December 1994, the United Nations General Assembly declared 29 December, the date of entry into force of the convention, International Day for Biological Diversity.[16]

The early entry into force of the CBD suggests that the political will that had existed at UNCED has been carried forward into the next phase, namely that of implementation and compliance with the convention's provisions. The CBD, like other international treaties, will be judged to have been successful only if each state fulfils its obligations by translating international law into national legislation, regulations, policies, and institutions. The present chapter works on the premise that in order for states to implement and comply effectively with their international obligations, there needs to be both intent and capacity, in terms of the necessary human and financial resources allocated to the process, policy, and legal frameworks, access to information about applicable rules and therefore participation by the wider public, incentives and inducement such as special funds, and technical assistance and training directed at national capacity building. The chapter will briefly highlight and evaluate how effective are the specific provisions established in the Convention on Biological Diversity to enable and ensure that state parties do implement and comply with those provisions.

Obligations under the CBD

UNCED provided a symbolic recognition of the interdependence and the vulnerability of both the developed North and the developing South. It also provided an important forum for the South to vent its frustrations at what it believes to be serious economic injustice. In many respects, UNCED was a conference about equity: how to allocate future responsibilities for environmental protection among states that are at different levels of economic development, have contributed in different degrees to particular problems, and have different environmental and developmental needs and priorities.[17] The objectives of the CBD reflect the application of the principle of equity. These objectives are:

the conservation of biological diversity, the sustainable use of its components and the fair and equitable sharing of the benefits arising out of the utilization of genetic resources, including by appropriate access to genetic resources and by appropriate transfer of relevant technologies, taking into account all rights over those resources and to technologies, and by appropriate funding.[18]

Like other recent environmental treaties, the CBD put developing countries in a stronger bargaining position than previously; the threat of non-participation gives them the necessary leverage to insist on adequate benefit from regimes of common but differentiated responsibility. The principle of common but differentiated responsibility has developed out of the application of the broader principle of equity in general international law, together with the recognition that the special needs of developing countries must be taken into account in the development, application, and interpretation of rules of international environmental law.[19] The principle is endorsed in the preamble to the CBD and is explicitly reflected in various other provisions to safeguard the special interests and circumstances of developing countries.[20]

There are a number of provisions of the CBD that are ostensibly meant to apply more specifically to developing countries than to the developed country parties and vice versa. This was apparently in response to demands put forward by certain countries that there be equal clarity about emphasis on the rights and obligations of both groups of countries.[21] Prime among such provisions with respect to developing counties is the duty "to co-operate ... as far as possible and as appropriate, with other Contracting Parties ... in the conservation and sustainable use of bio-diversity" (Article 5). The other duties of developing countries include those embodied in Articles 6 to 15 which generally define the contracting parties' obligations in relation to *in situ* and *ex situ* conservation and sustainable use of biodiversity and its components, the duty to undertake environmental impact assessment and minimize adverse impacts (Article 14), and the duty to provide access to genetic resources (Article 15).

As a *sine qua non,* developed country parties have, *inter alia,* undertaken a duty to provide and/or facilitate access to and transfer of technologies relevant to the conservation and sustainable use of bio-diversity,[22] and to take all practicable measures to promote and advance priority access on a fair and equitable basis by contracting parties, especially developing countries, to the results and benefits arising from bio-technology based upon genetic resources provided by those contracting parties,[23] to promote international technical and scientific cooperation in the field of conservation and sustainable use of biodiversity, and to provide new and additional financial resources to enable developing country parties to meet the agreed full incremental costs of implementing measures to fulfil their obligations under the convention.[24] There is also the obligation of "fair and equitable sharing" of benefits derived from the utilization of genetic resources.[25]

These two sets of obligations reflect an acceptance of the economic and technological differences between them and a mutual realization that the two groups of countries cannot be expected to make exactly the same level of contribution towards conservation of biodiversity. It also reveals the understanding that this necessarily means that more exacting demands must be made on those countries that are materially better off.

Institutional arrangements and processes

It would be pointless to grant such rights and impose the attendant obligations if the contracting parties cannot be called upon to make good their promises through a specified channel. A comprehensive implementation, compliance, and enforcement regime thus takes on a crucial significance in an international legal instrument of this nature, as it ensures that contracting parties make good their obligations. Accordingly, there are a number of provisions in the convention, specifically designed to ensure the practical realization of the commitments undertaken by the parties. A Conference of the Parties (COP) is established as the supreme governing body of the convention.[26] The COP is charged with, *inter alia*, the task of keeping under regular review the implementation of the convention and to steer its development. To that end, it is mandated to establish the form and the intervals for transmitting reports and information to be submitted by the parties and to consider such information and reports submitted by any subsidiary body.[27] To date, there have been four meetings of the COP.[28] Meetings of the COP are open to all parties to the convention, and may also be attended by observers from non-parties, intergovernmental organizations, and non-governmental organizations. The fifth meeting of the COP was scheduled for May 2000 in Nairobi, Kenya.

Article 25 of the convention establishes a Subsidiary Body on Scientific, Technical and Technological Advice (SBSTTA) to provide the COP with advice and recommendations on scientific, technical, and technological aspects of the implementation of the Convention. SBSTTA is open to all parties to the convention. Specific functions of SBSTTA include, *inter alia*: providing scientific and technical assessments of the status of biological diversity; preparing assessments of the measures taken to implement the convention; and generally responding to scientific, technical and technological and methodological questions asked by the COP. To date, SBSTTA has met five times.[29] Article 24 establishes a secretariat whose principal functions are to provide administrative support to the COP, SBSTTA, and other subsidiary bodies. It represents the day-to-day focal point of the convention, organizes all meetings under the convention and provides background documentation for those meetings. The secretariat plays a significant role in coordinating the work carried out under the convention with that of other relevant institutions and conventions, and represents the convention at meetings of other relevant bodies.

The financial mechanism is a key component of the convention's institutional structure. Article 39 appointed the Global Environment Facility (GEF) on an interim basis to operate the financial mechanism of the convention. GEF is a mechanism for international cooperation for the purpose of providing new and additional grant and concessional funding to meet the agreed incremental costs of measures to achieve agreed global environmental benefits in the areas of biodiversity, climate change, international waters, and ozone layer depletion. The three implementing agencies of the GEF are the United Nations Development Program (UNDP), the United Nations Environment Program (UNEP), and the World Bank.

As the financial mechanism, the GEF functions under the authority and guidance of, and is accountable to, the COP. The GEF Operational Strategy for biodiversity, which fully incorporates the guidance of the COP, was developed to guide the GEF in the preparation of country-driven initiatives in its four focal areas. The GEF's objectives in biological diversity derive from the objectives of the CBD. In accordance with the guidance from the COP of the CBD, the GEF Operational Strategy provides for three categories of activities: (1) operational programmes encompassing long-term measures; (2) enabling activities; and (3) short-term response measures. By providing an economic incentive for developing countries to comply with international environmental treaties, GEF constitutes part of a global approach based on the principles of cooperation in a spirit of global partnership and common but differentiated responsibilities.

Recognition of common but differentiated responsibilities in the convention

During the negotiations of the CBD most developing countries emphasized the pivotal role expected of the developed country parties in ensuring the realization of the goals of the convention. Particularly important in this regard was the statement made by China at the seventh plenary meeting of the INC as it set out the common position adopted by all developing countries.[30] The language used in Article 20(4) is substantially the same as that in the statement; thus, in what appears to be a direct response to the developing countries' sentiments as presented by China, the convention acknowledges in its preamble both the case for *special provisions to meet the needs of developing countries* as well as the need for *provision of new and additional financial resources and appropriate access to relevant technologies.*[31] Within the convention, detailed provisions addressing these particular issues are made such as those relating to access to and transfer of technology, financial resources, and on the various mechanisms for their implementation.[32] Developing countries also insisted on the inclusion of other provisions recognizing the role of local communities in promoting biotechnology development, and those stressing the need for the development of mechanisms for incorporating such knowledge in promoting rational and sustainable use of genetic resources.[33] Closely related to this is the acceptance of equitable sharing of benefits between owners and developers of biodiversity as one of the convention's three most important objectives.[34]

For their part, most developed countries were keen to emphasize that *in situ* conservation should be given priority as the most effective and reliable mode of conservation. Thus the Canadian, French, and Swiss delegations were all united on this particular point of view.[35] This stand is to be contrasted with the one adopted by developing countries, many of which felt that emphasis on measures for *in situ* conservation should be "in proper balance with their socio-economic interest." Thus Brazil insisted that equal importance be given to *ex situ* conservation as well,[36] while Tanzania went even further to construe the above propositions by developed countries as tantamount to a fetter to the development aspirations of the South thereby prompting it to make a counter-demand for the inclusion of a clause placing on developed countries "an obligation to compensate developing countries for areas set aside for purposes of conserving biodiversity."[37]

In order to achieve consensus between the two camps in entering, it was crucial that specific provisions were made which would serve to neutralize the existing or potential stumbling blocks in relation to this matter. A plausible solution came from the former Soviet Union, which made a proposal in the following terms:

... Because biodiversity is unevenly distributed, those countries that are responsible for outstanding biodiversity should receive international help in conservation and utilization of their biodiversity.[38]

A number of the CBD provisions were designed to create a more favourable climate for effective participation of developing country parties. It is these particular provisions that reflect the salient features of the convention denoting recognition of global inequalities. Article 20(4) best captures the issue of global inequalities in its proper context as it clearly stipulates that:

The extent to which developing country Parties will effectively implement their commitments under this Convention will depend on the effective implementation by developed country Parties of their commitments ... related to financial resources and transfer of technology and will take fully into account the fact that economic and social development and eradication of poverty are the first and overriding priorities of developing country Parties.

There are two tiers to the above recognition. The first involves the acceptance of the reality that environmental conservation is not at the top of the agenda for developing countries but poverty alleviation and the pursuit of socio-economic development are, and secondly that it is therefore accepted that the only reasonable and realistic way of enlisting their effective participation is through an undertaking by developed country parties to provide the necessary financial resources and relevant technology needed for the convention's implementation. These are sound conclusions, and if these provisions are effectively implemented, there is every reason for optimism that the capacity of developing country parties as partners in the international law of environmental conservation will be greatly improved.

Recent international environmental legal instruments, and the CBD is no exception, have included specific provisions regarding supporting tools to improve their implementation and effectiveness. Capacity-building has proved to be one of the most important of these tools. Rather than focusing on enforcement and dispute settlement, international legal instruments in the past few years have used clauses that provide for consensus-building and enabling mechanisms, particularly in support of developing countries, as a means of ensuring compliance with international obligations and commitments.[39] The provision of financial resources, relevant technology, and the enhancement of technical expertise and capacity building are the cornerstones of efforts to enable developing countries to meet their obligations. The next section will explore the aims and objectives of these principal mechanisms and evaluate how effectively they are and have been implemented by the parties.

The obligation of developed country parties to provide financial resources

As noted above, the convention acknowledges that availability of adequate financial resources is going to be crucial for the practical implementation of its objectives. In its preamble, the CBD acknowledges that substantial investments are required to conserve biodiversity and that there is need for provision of new and additional resources.[40] The UN has estimated that the overall cost of achieving the convention's objectives will be between $5 billion and $50 billion per year.[41]

It is important to point out that whereas there was a general consensus during the negotiations that it would be meaningless to have an international legal instrument of this kind without firm commitments to funding,[42] opinion was divided as to what form of mechanism should be used. Many developed countries were outrightly hostile to the idea of establishing new institutions to serve as the vehicle for disbursing funds to developing countries. They opposed their proliferation as unnecessary at a time when there were already far too many international institutions, which could be used to achieve the same objective. Their preference lay in strengthening existing financial institutions and mechanisms, which could then be used alongside appropriate bodies in the field of environmental assistance programmes and other bilateral and multilateral aid agencies actively involved in supporting environmental programmes.

Implicit in this preference was the fact that the World Bank would be drawn in to play a leading role in the intended scheme through its surrogate, the GEF. Such likelihood haunted developing countries. In this regard, the position adopted by Malaysia on the issue, which never changed even at the time of adopting the convention, is instructive, as the following excerpt indicates:

The Malaysian delegation always maintained that we do not see any role for the GEF. It has always been our clear position that the Convention should have its own specific funds, called the Biological Diversity Fund. In view of that, we wish to express our reservations in the strongest terms that the GEF has been accepted into the draft Convention, even on an interim basis. As we all know, in spite of our best efforts and intentions, these interim measures have the habit of becoming permanent features.[43]

Developing countries argued most emphatically for the inclusion of specific clauses strictly binding developed country parties to provide the necessary financial resources, with Venezuela[44] and Malaysia[45] being at the forefront in making such calls. In some way, this was reminiscent of previous demands by developing countries calling for the redistribution of global wealth, so that it was not altogether new: in fact, developed countries are supposed to transfer at least 0.7 per cent of their GNP in the form of official development assistance to developing countries, but not many of them ever honour it. What was new however was the context in which the developing countries were making their call this time round, and the elements that constituted that call.

The positions taken by India and Brazil vividly illustrate the changed circumstances. In its proposal India submitted the following aspects for inclusion, namely that: "the special situation of developing countries should be recognized in all the relevant provisions of the Convention, – the additional burden on developing countries arising out of their protection of their biodiversity should be met by new and additional funding, to be provided by the developed country parties – such funding should be adequate, new, and additional." Reiterating India's position, Brazil proposed the inclusion of a clause recognizing the need for additional, new, and appropriate funding, and an innovative financial mechanism in order to meet the special needs of developing countries in addressing their priorities in developing and absorbing relevant technologies and measures for conservation.[46]

The above proposals by India and Brazil also reveal a significant shift from the demands previously made by developing countries in the sense that this time they were not only asking for additional funds but also that the funds be *new, adequate*, and *appropriate.* The new dimension, which emerges from this formulation, is bound to be fraught with interpretation difficulties. It is imperative that its precise meaning be worked out in order to ascertain what sums ought to be contemplated in order to meet this particular demand. This formulation can be traced back to the Belgrade Declaration of 1989, made at the conclusion of the 9th Conference of Heads of States and/or Governments of the Non-Aligned countries. At that meeting, reference was made merely on the provision of *additional* resources to developing countries and yet two years later in Beijing, this had given way to the demand that all relevant international legal instruments should include appropriate clauses obliging developed countries to provide *adequate, new*, and *additional* funds.[47]

A logical interpretation of this shift would, of course, have it that developing countries wanted to make it absolutely clear that any funds made available to them pursuant to provisions in the convention would have to be independent of any existing development assistance that they might already be receiving from the North. In the end, a mutually agreeable position was reached as a result of which the demands by developing countries on funding were largely accepted and provided for in the convention. Article 20 on Financial Resources is the principal provision in this respect. It imposes, *inter alia,* a general duty on each contracting party to provide, in accordance with its capabilities, financial support and incentives in respect of those national activities intended to achieve the objectives of the convention, "in accordance with the national plans, priorities and programs of that country" (para. 1). But it is perhaps paragraph 2 that is most important, for it is specifically addressed to developed country parties and obligates them to provide new and additional financial resources to developing country parties. It should be noted, however, that implicit in the latter undertaking is not only a summary rejection by developed countries of the notion of "adequacy of such funds" in the terms demanded by Brazil and India but also elements of substantial conditionality imposed on the recipient developing countries, albeit couched in the most polite and diplomatic language.

In any event, the additional reference to "eligibility criteria" lays it beyond doubt that the funds to be so provided are not to be simply there for the taking by any developing country that feels like having additional funds. This has proved yet another terrible disappointment for those developing countries that had hoped for such a windfall, especially in this period of severe global economic hardship. Nevertheless the acceptance by developed countries of the legal duty to provide *new* and *additional* financial resources, even under such substantially qualified terms, is in itself a significant step forward which is a good gesture on their part indicating their willingness to "put their money where their mouths are," in a bid to foster global environmental cooperation.

Provision of relevant technology to developing countries

During the negotiations the common position of most of the developing countries was that they wanted provisions in the convention that developed countries guarantee them access to and transfer of technology. Led principally by Brazil and India, they insisted that such access and transfer should take place on a *preferential* and *non-commercial* basis.[48] Unfortunately, very few developed countries would hear of such a demand. The only exception were the Nordic countries, all of which stressed the "special obligations of developed countries to contribute financially and technologically to enable developing countries fulfill their obligations under the Convention." They put this case most emphatically, pointing out the need to take into account the "highly different socio-economic conditions and enormous differences in the amount of biodiversity found in various countries."[49]

As reflected in paragraph 20 of the CBD preamble, there is no doubt that all states involved in the negotiation were cognizant of the fact that biotechnology holds the key to the profitable use of the South's vast untapped biological resources, especially in the field of agriculture, forestry, industry, health, and food security. The sticking point, however, was the fact that most technologies generated in developed countries are actually developed and owned by the private sector and not by governments.

Article 16 (Access to and Transfer of Technology) defines the basic obligations of each contracting party regarding technology transfer, the basis of transfer to developing countries and what measures are to be taken to institute the transfer contemplated. Together with Article 19

(Handling of Biotechnology and Distribution of its Benefits) and Articles 20 and 21 (Financial Resources and Mechanisms), Article 16 is probably the most controversial article in the convention. It reflects the years of North-South debate in other forums over the issue of technology transfer, and in some of the technology at stake, the related sub-issue of intellectual property rights.

During the early stage of the negotiation process, a number of governments – primarily developed countries – did not want the convention to include any provisions on technology transfer, based on the parallel discussion of this and related issues in other fora. At the same time, other governments – primarily developing countries – considered technology transfer as a counterpart to the provisions related to genetic resources access. The latter position prevailed, but the technology transfer issue remained extremely contentious throughout the negotiations as the scope and terms of the article were defined. Developed countries were particularly fearful of language that might be interpreted as requiring them in any way to force their private sectors to transfer technology (including biotechnology). Protecting intellectual property rights was a parallel concern not least because, being based on DNA, any biotechnology protected by intellectual property rights is easy to reproduce without the permission of the intellectual property rights holder.

The US certainly minced no words in letting its objection on the matter be known by expressly declaring that it found Article 16 "potentially deficient in the protection of intellectual property rights as it failed to recognize the positive role of intellectual property systems in facilitating transfer of technology and cooperative research and development of private entities."[50] But it is perhaps Switzerland's consistent obstinacy on the issue, even as the convention was being adopted, that underscored the underlying strong tide of opposition by developed countries on this particular subject. The terse language employed in its declaration at the time of adopting the convention puts this contention beyond doubt.[51]

It is with the above controversies in mind that the convention's treatment of access to and transfer of technology in Article 16 should be considered. First, having due regard to the special needs of developing countries, this article explicitly recognizes that both access to and transfer of technology, including biotechnology, to developing countries are essential elements for the attainment of the convention's objectives. In other words, if the three objectives of the convention are to be met, the contracting parties must have access to the relevant technology. Secondly, categories of technologies are defined as: technologies relevant to the conservation of biological diversity; technologies relevant to the sustainable use of the components of biological diversity; and those technologies that make use of genetic resources. An important characteristic of such technologies is established: they should not cause significant damage to the environment. The convention does not contain explicit reference to specific technologies, with the exception of biotechnology, that are relevant to meeting its objectives. Any reference under Article 16(1) to "technologies that are relevant to the conservation and sustainable use of biological diversity or make use of genetic resources" is quite general and open to different interpretations. It may, for example, mean technologies developed specifically to conserve biological diversity, or technologies developed for other purposes, but which may be deployed in conservation activities.

The above recognition is coupled with a binding obligation on developed country parties to provide and/or facilitate the process of transferring relevant technology[52] to developing country parties under fair and *most favourable terms.*[53] These provisions are significant in that under normal free market conditions, developing countries on their own could ill afford the high licence fees charged by the patent right holders. By its inclusion, the actual and potential grounds for disagreement between developed and developing countries on the issue are effectively neutralized. However, there is an important rider to the effect that any concessional and preferential terms have to be mutually agreed and that such terms do recognize and are consistent with adequate and effective protection of intellectual property rights in the case of patented technology. This is precisely where the crunch came because whereas the right of access to and transfer of relevant technology had all along been interpreted by developing countries to mean such transfer taking place purely on concessional, low profit or non-profit basis,[54] the apparently successful view put forward by certain developed countries, and Germany in particular, was that the notion of *preferential basis* was unacceptable, and that the terms *fair and most favourable basis* would be a suitable alternative.[55] That this is the actual formulation used in Article 16 is a clear victory for developed countries, many of which seemed to be fairly comfortable with the "non-discriminatory treatment" connotations that this formulation imports.

The conditions outlined in the above provisions have a number of policy implications. First, the reference to "fair and most favorable terms, including on concessional and preferential terms where mutually agreed" seems to suggest the access to and transfer of technology on terms other than the established mechanisms and conditions of the international technology market. Secondly, the convention does not define the terms for access to and transfer of technology, or indicate such terms. It leaves it to the parties to define the terms, as they deem appropriate. Its use of the language "where mutually agreed" in Article 16(2) seems to imply that a process of negotiation is established whereby the relevant parties come to agree on the terms before access to and/or transfer of technology is effected. The effect this has had on the rest of the article is to water down the very essential aspects of the provisions relating to providing technology to developing countries. Thus, for instance, it makes voidable the legal obligation of developed countries to grant concessional and preferential terms in the event that no mutual agreement or no agreement at all is reached between individual developing country parties and the developed countries. The convention's silence on what constitutes a "mutual agreement" is no doubt a potential minefield for controversy between developed and developing countries, especially in view of the latter's misgivings about the use of the Global Environment Facility (GEF) which is the mechanism envisaged under Article 21 as the appropriate mechanism.

The logical conclusion to be drawn from the entire arrangement on the question of providing technology to developing countries is that it left none of the parties fully satisfied. For material evidence in support of this conclusion, all one needs to look at are the declarations made by the various countries when adopting the convention, and in particular, those made by Ethiopia, Malaysia, the Philippines, Switzerland, and the United States as reported in the Nairobi Final Act and subsequent official UNEP documents.[56] However, it marked a significant starting point from which real progress could be made in future on this tenuous but absolutely essential ingredient for the successful implementation of the convention.

Enhancing technical expertise and capacity building in developing countries

Research is a vital component in the realization of the convention's objectives in light of the fact that very little is known as concerns the appropriate measures that need to be taken to protect biodiversity. However cheap or accessible developed countries may make it possible for developing countries to obtain relevant technology, the ultimate solution for the latter lies not so much in such acts of magnanimity as in self-reliance. Promises of financial resources and access to technology, while in themselves a giant step towards helping developing countries meet their obligations under the convention amount to no more than a mere "tool box," totally meaningless in the absence of local skilled personnel to make use of it.

There is therefore an urgent need to fill this lacuna through detailed research to establish, *inter alia,* the critical size of habitats required to preserve biodiversity at reasonably sustainable levels, the interactive nature of ecosystems and the actual number of species that have to date not been identified and classified. Such research will necessarily be on a large scale if it is to address the existing problem of general lack of knowledge. This bears far-reaching implications on the question of competent personnel to carry it out and how it is going to be funded.

Paragraph 7 of the CBD preamble recognizes that there is general lack of information and knowledge regarding biodiversity and stresses the urgent need to develop scientific, technical, and institutional capacities to provide basic understanding upon which to plan and implement appropriate measures. The demand in developing countries for trained experts, specialists, and other qualified personnel in technical fields such as taxonomy and ethnobotany is therefore something of a great imperative. Equipped with modern technical skills carefully blended with indigenous knowledge of biodiversity, it is arguable that local experts can do much more. Many developing countries argued strongly in support of binding obligations in the convention to meet this requirement. Brazil, for example, recommended inclusion of a clause obliging contracting parties to "support human resource improvement by education and training of technicians and scientific experts, research workers for the special needs of developing countries in such areas as taxonomy, molecular biology, ecology and genetic engineering as well as specific techniques for the conservation and rational use of biodiversity."[57] Chile went even further to propose that measures be adopted so that any research developed in a country as a result of foreign initiatives include "national professionals throughout its course."[58] These proposals were accepted in principle by developed countries, as long as they would be carried out in the framework of existing appropriate organizations.[59]

Article 12 provides for training and research for achieving the convention's goals. However, this involves astronomical costs that developing countries on their own cannot afford. The convention responds to this problem by providing for technical and collaborative research and training that are tailored to the specific needs of developing countries more or less in the terms proposed by Brazil.[60]

Again, in what appears to meet the above request made by Chile, Article 15(6) obligates contracting parties to "fully participate or allow such participation" in scientific research. Equally significant is Article 15(2) that urges special attention to be paid to the development and strengthening of national capabilities by means of human resource development and institutional building, alongside promotion of international technical and scientific cooperation. Similarly, the promotion of joint research programmes and joint ventures for development of technologies is also provided.[61]

The principal mechanisms for implementing the three strategies identified above

The crucial test of any international legal instrument lies in its efficiency in delivering to the parties the benefits expected to flow from it. The favoured status conferred upon developing countries in the CBD by virtue of their special needs entitles them to a number of benefits. These, as has been highlighted above, include receiving financial resources, relevant technology on *favourable terms* and technical and scientific collaboration as envisaged under the convention. However, the question of whether or not this assistance will result in meeting the desired objectives ultimately depends on the establishment of the appropriate institutional framework and mechanism through which the resources so provided can be absorbed and adapted by developing countries to meet their specific requirements.

It is in recognition of this fact that the convention sets out a number of provisions specifically designed to meet this requirement, thus there are appropriate provisions governing financial mechanisms, and the modalities for access to and transfer of technology as well as on scientific and technical collaboration, all of which are geared towards enabling developing countries to discharge their obligations under the convention. Each of these specific provisions is considered below, with an evaluation of the actions thus far taken by the COP, parties, and supporting institutions in their move towards implementing and meeting the obligations set out in the convention.

Financial mechanisms

Out of the three strategies identified above, it would be no exaggeration to consider financial resources as the most important, given that it holds the key to the rest, to the extent that an immense amount of spending is involved in the case of transfer of technology, and scientific and technical collaboration. As has been highlighted above, this issue generated the greatest controversy between developing and developed countries throughout the negotiation and it remained contentious right up to the eleventh hour, when on realizing the impending stalemate, the two sides eventually backed down to pave way for the reaching of an amicable settlement.

Article 39 of the convention's text provides for the GEF to operate its financial mechanism "on an interim basis" but its permanent adoption has been a subject of hard debate, with donor countries making further replenishment dependent on its adoption on a permanent basis, and recipient countries (i.e. developing country parties) resisting, as they are not yet convinced that it fully meets their concerns. The Conference of the Parties at its second meeting decided that this issue would be decided at COP3,[62] but at the latter meeting the interim status was retained.

However, clear signs of improvement in the relationship between the COP and the GEF emerged at COP3. First, a Memorandum of Understanding (MOU) was adopted between COP and the GEF that formalizes the relationship and continues the GEF as the interim financial mechanism for the next several years.[63] The MOU called for the GEF to specify the amount of new and additional funding to be provided for the next replenishment and to indicate the reasons for which this funding is to be considered "new and additional." The MOU also reiterates the point that the financial mechanism shall function under the authority and guidance of COP and be accountable to it, and that the COP will determine the policy, priorities, and criteria for access to financial resources. Secondly, COP3 provided further and clearer guidance to the GEF, calling for support to capacity building related to the preservation of indigenous knowledge and practices, biosafety, the clearing-house mechanism, and access to genetic resources; conservation and sustainable use related to agriculture, targeted research that contributes to conservation and sustainable use and the understanding of these elusive concepts; and the fair and equitable sharing of benefits arising out of the use of genetic resources.[64]

Regarding new and additional financial resources, COP3 engaged in a heated debate about whether developed country parties were meeting their obligations as called for in Article 20. The creation of new and additional financial resources was neither verified nor rejected; the debate did lead to progress in the decision of COP3 that "urges developed country Parties to co-operate in the development of standardized information on their financial support."[65] In addition, the decision broadened the focus on "new and additional" to include bilateral and multilateral donors, regional funding institutions, non-governmental organizations, and the private sector.

Chapter 33 of Agenda 21 provides an agreed framework for the financing of sustainable development, and is related to the implementation of all other chapters of Agenda 21. Agenda 21 acknowledges that, in general, the financing for its implementation will come from a country's own public and private sectors. However, it clearly places the financing of sustainable development within the global economic context by stating that developing countries will need substantial new and additional funds for the implementation of sustainable development programmes, and that official development assistance (ODA) should be a main source of external funding for those countries, especially the least developed countries. Under Agenda 21, developed countries have committed themselves to provide "new and additional" resources to help developing countries to achieve sustainable development. The CBD makes this a legal obligation for biodiversity and the GEF is intended to be one of the main channels for these new resources. If resources are to be genuinely "new and additional," they must be compared to the historical levels of both aid for biodiversity and total aid and these should be higher than before the CBD entered into force in 1993. OECD, UN, and GEF figures provide no evidence that donors are fulfilling their legal obligation under the CBD, or their political commitment under Agenda 21. These figures provide no evidence that current levels of aid for biodiversity are "new and additional." The available figures indicate that after a peak in the Earth Summit year of 1992, annual aid levels for biodiversity have been lower than in the pre-GEF period of 1987–1990. Non-GEF biodiversity aid appears to have fallen substantially since 1992.[66]

Accurate and transparent reporting is essential for monitoring the implementation and ultimate effectiveness of the convention and Agenda 21. Figures currently available at an international level on biodiversity aid are incomplete, and the OECD system for recording how such support is used does not clearly identify all aspects of conservation expenditure. This makes it difficult to monitor how well the OECD countries are fulfilling their obligations. In June 1997, the General Assembly held a special session to assess the progress made since UNCED in 1992 and on this issue they concluded that most developed countries have still not reached the UN target, reaffirmed by most countries at UNCED of committing 0.7 per cent of their GNP to official development assistance, or the UN target, as agreed, of committing 0.15 per cent of GNP as ODA to the least developed countries. Regrettably, on average, ODA as a percentage of the GNP of developed countries has drastically declined in the post-UNCED period, from 0.34 per cent in 1992 to 0.27 per cent in 1995, but ODA has taken more account of the need for an integrated approach to sustainable development.[67] There have been three main developments concerning the flow of public resources to developing countries since UNCED: first, a decrease of ODA in both absolute terms and with respect to donors' gross national product (GNP), which at 0.27 per cent in 1995 was far from the Agenda 21 target of 0.7 per cent; secondly, successful implementation of many debt relief programmes, which have improved the debt indicators of many developing countries or slowed their rate of deterioration (although further efforts are still needed in sub-Saharan Africa and other highly indebted poor countries); and thirdly, some shifts in official development finances toward social and environmental areas. The average ODA in the period 1993–1995 was lower than in the period 1990–1992, both in absolute terms and as a percentage of

GNP (which at an average of 0.29 in the period 1993–1995 was the lowest level in decades). Only four countries achieved the Agenda 21 ODA goal of 0.7 of donor's GNP: Denmark, Sweden, Norway, and the Netherlands. Measured at 1994 prices and exchange rates, ODA decreased by 9 per cent between 1990 and 1995.[68]

In accordance with Article 21(3) of the CBD, which requires the COP to review the effectiveness of the financial mechanism, not less than two years after the entry into force of the convention, COP3 adopted decision III/7 setting out the guidelines for the review of the GEF. A synthesis report[69] on the first review was submitted and considered by COP4. COP4 completed the first review and adopted decision IV/11 in which it took account of "the views and concerns expressed by Parties about the difficulties encountered in carrying out the first review, in particular the inadequacy of the procedures; and the insufficient information provided as compared with that requested in decision III/7." COP4 specifically called for improvement of the effectiveness of the financial mechanism; requested the GEF to take action as specified in the work programme and report back to COP5; and designated COP5 to determine the terms of reference for the second review of the effectiveness of the financial mechanism.

Mechanisms for the transfer of technology

It was recognized early in the negotiation that one of the overriding issues which ought to be provided for in the proposed convention should be the idea of giving "countries rich in genetic resources" a stronger voice in the development and application of relevant technology.[70] The task of finding and/or agreeing on a suitable mechanism through which such a transfer could be channelled raised similar problems to that of the financial mechanism already discussed. As with the financial mechanism, developed countries underlined the significance of using existing organizations, structures, and expertise in order to avoid duplication as well as lessen the level of administrative work. In contrast, developing countries came up with a wide range of new and alternative mechanisms. So divergent were opinions on this issue that Malaysia suggested that a report be prepared concerning the role of multinational corporations in the transfer of technology to developing countries, besides recommending increased public sector participation in the biotechnology industry as a possible way of remedying the existing imbalance.[71] Venezuela, on the other hand, suggested that biotechnology being a primordial instrument under the convention, it would be meaningless if no proper mechanisms to govern it were provided for,[72] while Vietnam was even more outright on the issue as it called for the creation of a clearing-house and the establishment of regional centres as the best mechanism for meeting this requirement. Others, like Brazil,[73] called for a commitment of contracting parties to encourage private companies within their jurisdiction to facilitate and make possible joint development and transfer of technologies related to the purposes of the convention, on a preferential basis, to government institutions and private companies in developing countries. In the final analysis, the GEF once again ended up being the principal mechanism provided for under the convention as far as financing of such transfers is concerned. This was a necessary compromise that developing countries simply had to accept if they were to benefit from whatever limited offer developed countries were willing to extend to them in this respect. As observed above, the issue of technological transfer is intricately linked to finance and so it is just as well that they be dealt with through a unitary central body such as the Conference of the Parties.

In recognition of the fact that issues related to access to technology and access to genetic resources form the foundation on which the convention is based, the parties wasted no time initiating work on this very important subject matter. Consequently, the first meeting of COP, in its decision I/7, requested the first meeting of the SBSTTA, in accordance with Article 25, paragraph 2(c), to provide advice to the second meeting of the COP on "ways and means to promote and facilitate access to, and transfer and development of technologies as envisaged in Articles 16 and 18 of the Convention." In its decision II/18, the second meeting of the COP also decided that in its medium-term programme of work it wished to consider "ways to promote and facilitate access to and transfer of technology, as envisaged in Articles 16 and 18 of the Convention" at its third meeting. In decision I/2, the COP further decided that "in accordance with Article 16 of the Convention, and to meet the objectives of conservation of biological diversity and sustainable use of its components, projects which promote access to, transfer of and co-operation for joint development of technology" would be one of the programme priorities for access to and utilization of the financial resources available through the financial mechanism under the convention.

For a number of reasons, however, most developing countries have been unable either to engage in R&D or to acquire technologies for the conservation and sustainable use of biological diversity. First, many of them have not built up sufficient strength in science and technology, especially in terms of human capital. Secondly, a lack of financial resources has created major limitations to any further investment in training or in collaborative projects with foreign universities or training institutions. If these countries are to implement effectively the three objectives of the convention, and particularly those provisions on the access to and transfer of technology, they need to start organizing themselves to plan for and invest in training and R&D in new technologies, as well as to upgrade some of the traditional technologies. An emphasis on training and R&D should be given to science-based areas such as taxonomy, botany, genetic engineering, and zoology. It is also crucial that the training and R&D priorities be based on specific national needs, which should be outlined in the national strategies, action plans and programmes on biological diversity required under Article 6 of the convention. Developing countries will also have to appreciate that it will not be possible to engage effectively in the international negotiations on technology transfer, or in the implementation of the convention in general, unless they have access to some basic information on the various technologies for the conservation and sustainable use of biodiversity. Most of this information can be obtained from scientific publications, workshops, conferences, and electronic media from various institutions in industrialized countries. Often, however, developing countries do not treat these as important sources of information on technology. For technologies such as biotechnology, a large portion of technological knowledge can be obtained from scientific journals and workshops. Developing countries need to give adequate attention to these mechanisms of information acquisition and use them effectively to acquire various elements of new conservation and sustainable-use technologies. They should also create systems for linking themselves to the various forms of global information networks.[74]

There is a need for developing country governments to create policy and legal measures that favour the formation of technology partnerships between their institutions and private firms on the one hand, and private sector firms and R&D institutions from some of the industrialized countries on the other. They also need to be less reliant on the CBD and COP process alone to provide these important policy and legal measures. The clearing-house mechanism (CHM), established as required under Article 18(3) of the convention, will of course play a key role in promoting technical and scientific cooperation. The CHM could be developed as: (a) a source of new information on global scientific and technical R&D activities, including information on new conservation and sustainable-use technologies; (b) a link between developing country researchers and/or institutions, including private sector firms, and the R&D centres and firms of developed countries; (c) a means of providing developing countries with information on ways of establishing technology partnerships, including assisting them to formulate legal measures (specific technology partnership contracts, for example) and appropriate technology procurement strategies; and (d) a means of access to new sources of private-sector funding by developing country institutions.[75]

The issues addressed in Articles 16 and 18 regarding technological development as well as technical and scientific cooperation are part of the larger agenda of building technological capacity in developing countries in order to facilitate the implementation of the three objectives of the convention. In this context, priority should be given to the identification of ways to promote technological capacity in developing countries. It is evident that issues related to the access to and transfer of technology cannot be addressed in isolation from other priorities in the convention. Of particular relevance are issues related to specific programme areas already identified by the COP, such as marine and coastal biological diversity, and agricultural biological diversity, as well as other potential items such as forest biological diversity and freshwater biological diversity. Such an approach would be consistent with the provisions of Article 6 on general measures for the conservation and sustainable use of biological diversity, particularly paragraph 2, which calls upon the contracting parties to "integrate, as far as possible and as appropriate, the conservation and sustainable use of biological diversity into relevant sectoral or cross-sectoral plans, programs and policies." In this regard, the COP has already taken the step of integrating issues related to the access to and transfer of technology into the relevant sectoral and cross-sectoral issues, with particular emphasis on marine and coastal biological diversity and agricultural biological diversity, among others.[76] Despite these advances, the transfer of technologies relevant for the conservation and sustainable use of biological diversity continues to be a major area of unfulfilled expectations of most developing country parties who require these technologies in order to make use of their genetic resources in a sustainable manner without causing damage to the environment, meeting their obligations under the CBD and Agenda 21.

Mechanisms for technical and scientific collaboration

The creation of national capabilities of developing countries' capacity to conserve biodiversity and manage its use on a sustainable basis is given high prominence under the convention. The principal areas identified as deserving urgent attention are the development of indigenous human resources and installation of the appropriate institutions necessary for the creation of such capabilities. The range of activities which must be carried through to realize these goals entails a high level of technical and scientific activity thus putting it well beyond the means of developing countries if left on their own. There is therefore a strong case for having binding obligations on developed countries to undertake a substantial share of this responsibility. It is in this light that the convention contains various provisions to remedy this handicap. The contracting parties are enjoined, *inter alia,* to promote and support scientific research and technical train-ing, individually or in conjunction with others as far as possible, or with international organizations where appropriate.[77] In any event, the broad obligation to cooperate imposed on contracting parties under Article 5 could also legitimately be construed to embody a general duty on them to work towards achieving that end.

The idea of creating a Scientific Committee won very little support due to lack of enthusiasm on the part of developed countries.[78] It could be said that a substitute or compromise for creating a Scientific Committee was the establishment of SBSTTA. The SBSTTA has met five times and during those occasions it has been given very extensive agendas, it has produced sound and deep recommendations to COP on some of the issues under consideration, especially on marine and coastal ecosystems and on agricultural biodiversity. Its efficiency is often measured by the fact the COP has adopted most of its recommendations, with relatively few modifications. Further, its progress in addressing issues such as the assessment of biodiversity and the available methodologies and indicators may make it an increasingly useful source of advice to support and help parties in implementing their obligations under the convention and as-sessing their progress toward that end. There is, however, a need to em-phasize this more scientific role and issues on the agenda of SBSTTA. SBSTTA is, however, on the whole attended by diplomats and relatively few of these governmental representatives are scientists. In keeping with the nature of the intergovernmental process that policy advice and poli-tics cannot be totally absent from science, it has been quite evident during the discussions that take place at these meetings that quite a number of the delegates bring with them their national priorities. It is also worth pointing out that many of the delegates who attend SBSTTA also par-ticipate in the COP, which could be one reason why the COP rarely modifies recommendations coming out of SBSTTA, because they would in effect be modifying their own recommendations. A major concern throughout the first three years of SBSTTA has been the need to have it concentrate on technical issues and maintain a knowledge-based ap-proach rather than become, in the terms used by its 1996 chair, a "mini-COP."[79]

The experience of other international environmental issues and pro-cesses is that international action has not been forthcoming until a certain level of consensus has been achieved regarding the underlying scientific knowledge. The experience of the Montreal Protocol in regulating the production and consumption of CFCs is one of the better-known exam-ples of this relationship.[80] Suggestions that have been proposed for in-jecting science into the CBD process range from limiting the composition of delegations who attend SBSTTA to qualified scientists, introducing a mechanism for scientific input that is closer to the Intergovernmental Panel on Climate Change (IPCC) which feeds into the UN Framework Convention on Climate Change process. A third option would be for SBSTTA to develop closer cooperation and draw more extensively from other international scientific institutions, major NGOs, and other independent sources of expertise such as the GEF Scientific and Technical Advisory Panel (STAP), DIVERSITAS, and the International Council of Scientific Unions (ICSU).

The issues addressed under the CBD require not only financial and political support, but also the best science available. There is a widespread view that SBSTTA, despite its mandate to be scientific and technological, is becoming somewhat dysfunctional because it has become highly political. In response to this concern, the COP at its fourth meeting in decision IV/16 on "Institutional Matters and the Program of Work" adopted a *modus operandi* for the SBSTTA that includes three changes: (1) the SBSTTA will no longer consider the budgetary implications of the issues it discusses; (2) the Executive Secretary, in consultation with the chair and bureau of the SBSTTA, will be able to create liaison groups to prepare background reports and documentation for the SBSTTA; and (3) a limited number of newly established *ad hoc* technical expert panels, composed of no more than 15 experts, will meet to discuss specific priority issues within the SBSTTA work plan. In a further attempt to tip the balance in favour of scientific input over political wrangling, COP4 decided that SBSTTA should hold two meetings prior to the next COP.[81]

Access to information and involvement of civil society

The right of access to information on the environment, whether to the public at large or to specific categories of persons (such as workers), is a recent development in international law. An increasing number of international environmental agreements includes positive obligations requiring states to improve public education and awareness on environmental matters and give due publicity to matters of environmental importance.[82] There seems to be a realization that public participation is an integral part of compliance with agreements for sustainable development. Civil society in the form of NGOs is an important vehicle for achieving public participation. The CBD is very liberal about those who can participate in and at its meetings including the COP.[83] The CBD recognizes that in many ways environmental NGOs concerned with the conservation and sustainable use of biological diversity, such as IUCN, Greenpeace, and WWF, have made important contributions to increasing transparency in international processes. The convention remains a forum in which NGOs remain deeply involved and committed. As such it represents an important forum for the principles and objectives of Chapter 27 of Agenda 21 on strengthening the role of non-governmental organizations: partners for sustainable development. The magnitude and cross-sectoral nature of biodiversity conservation, sustainable use, and equitable sharing of benefits exceed the ability of any party to successfully implement the convention by itself. At local and national levels, some NGOs are particularly well versed and represent significant public constituencies that can assist parties in addressing the complexities of conservation, sustainability, and equity. NGOs do form an important component of the decision-making process by helping to bridge the gaps between policy-making, science, and the public. NGOs also help build public awareness of the importance of biological diversity and can thereby assist in creating the suitable political climate for decision-making. Finally, NGOs can and do assist in monitoring the implementation of the CBD locally, nationally, and internationally.

The COP's transition towards implementation

The first meeting of the Conference of the Parties (COP1) took place in Nassau, the Bahamas, from 28 November to 9 December 1994. COP1 set in motion the basic implementation machinery provided for by the convention. The decisions adopted by COP1 included: the adoption of the medium-term work programme;[84] designation of UNEP as the Permanent Secretariat;[85] establishment of the SBSTTA[86] and the clearing-house mechanism;[87] and designation of the GEF as the interim institutional structure for the financial mechanism.[88] The second meeting of the COP (COP2) was held in Jakarta, Indonesia, 6–17 November 1995. In addition to designating the permanent location of the Secretariat in Montreal, Canada, COP2 marked a turning point in the evolution of the CBD. It ushered in a new phase of the CBD through the adoption of decisions aimed at facilitating the implementation of the CBD. This transition is illustrated by the practical nature of the decisions made by COP2 and their emphasis on policy guidance.[89] The COP quickly came to the realization that the nature of the issues and areas which the convention mandates it to address means that it is heavily dependent for its implementation and effectiveness on the actions of the parties and existing international institutions with previous experience in the respective areas. The need to develop institutional links with other national bodies and hence mechanisms for co-coordinating these relationships has been recognized as being fundamental to the implementation of the CBD. Acting on this realization COP2 stressed the importance of cooperation between the convention and other biodiversity-related conventions and international institutions. Since then, the Secretariat has signed memoranda of cooperation with the Ramsar Convention on Wetlands, the Convention on International Trade in Endangered Species (CITES), the Convention on Migratory Species (CMS), and the World Heritage Convention.

In a process that initiated the development of the first substantive element of the CBD, by decision II/10, COP2 adopted a programme of work known as the Jakarta Mandate, which proposes a framework for global action to maintain marine and coast biodiversity. The Jakarta Mandate identified the following five thematic programmes that have been the focus of further action by the CBD process: (a) integrated marine and coastal area management; (b) marine and coastal protected areas; (c) sustainable use of coastal and marine living resources; (d) mariculture; and (e) alien species.

COP2 activated the operation of Article 26 of the CBD that established a national reporting system under which "each Contracting Party is obligated to present reports on measures it has taken to implement the Convention and their effectiveness in meeting the set objectives."[90] It provides a mechanism to monitor the implementation of the convention. As the report must also consider the measures' effectiveness, that means a party may have to draw on information derived from Article 7 (Identification and Monitoring) to fulfil its reporting obligations. COP2 established loose guidelines for the preparation of national reports[91] and decided that the first national reports by parties would focus as far as possible on the measures taken for the implementation of Article 6 of the convention, "General Measures for Conservation and Sustainable Use," as well as the information available in national country studies on biological diversity. Ordinarily, a domestic law is required to implement an international treaty or convention. But as the CBD is a framework convention, many of its provisions, technically speaking, do not require legislation for their implementation. For example, contracting parties that have developed and adopted national conservation strategies, programmes and plans, and that have incorporated the objectives of the CBD, would be considered as having met the obligations of Article 6. Similarly, parties may want to alleviate environmental hazards, such as deforestation, by providing fiscal incentives to this end. National implementation of the CBD objectives during the first stage after the adoption of the convention has essentially focused on the establishment of biodiversity management capacities such as national biodiversity strategies and plans, biodiversity committees or task forces, and biodiversity focal points. Implementation of the requirements of *in situ* conservation includes the establishment of protected areas, the protection of threatened species, restoration and rehabilitation of degraded habitats and eco-systems.

COP2 decided that the first national reports would be due at the fourth meeting of the Conference of the Parties in 1997. At COP3 it was decided that COP4 would be held in May 1998 and so the national reports were to be submitted by the end of 1997. It is worth noting that even though parties were requested to prepare national reports by the end of 1997, only 16 reports (9 per cent) were received by the initial deadline, 104 by the COP (60 per cent), and by the revised deadline for submission of the end of 1998 there were few more. A full synthesis of national reports is unlikely until two years after the first national reports were delivered. The syntheses of the national reports are variable in content and format, making comparison difficult. The lack of indicators and targets in most of the reports also means that review of progress over time will be difficult to achieve. COP4 in decision IV/14 determined the intervals and form of subsequent national reports based on the experience of parties in preparing their first national reports. There are, however, problems with relying on national reporting as the key monitoring tool. Officials required to file reports under the burgeoning number of international agreements may find that their time is mostly occupied by preparing reports rather than by taking the actions called for under the convention, or using the time for other high priority environmental actions. Indeed, in countries with a scarcity of skilled labour, it may require a government to devote most of its time to meeting reporting requirements.

The second meeting of SBSTTA,[92] which was held just two months before COP3, considered a number of issues including agricultural biological diversity; identification, monitoring, and assessment of biodiversity; technology development and transfer; indigenous knowledge; capacity building in relation to biosafety; terrestrial biodiversity; marine and coastal biodiversity; economic valuation of genetic resources, and capacity building in taxonomy.[93] The third meeting of the COP was held in Buenos Aires, Argentina, 4–15 November 1996 (COP3). The importance of maintaining agricultural biological diversity and the dramatic impact that unsustainable agriculture practices has had on biodiversity generally and the issue of threatened food security as a result of the rapid loss of agricultural biodiversity was high on the agenda of COP3. In decision III/3, COP3 elaborated a realistic work programme on agricultural biodiversity by establishing a multi-year programme of activities aimed at arresting its decline. The COP also recognized the central role that the Food and Agricultural Organization (FAO) has to play in this area and requested the secretariat to continuing working closely with their programmes.[94] The COP3 policy statement on forests requested the Executive Secretary to develop a focused work programme for forest biological diversity, with scientific and technical advice from SBSTTA and in cooperation with the IPF, to include integration of conservation and sustainable use in forest and ecosystem management measures; to complement existing national, regional, or international criteria and indicators for sustainable forest management, and to incorporate traditional systems of forest biological conservation.[95]

COP3 initiated important steps towards including the CBD's views in other processes that have an impact on biodiversity, such as the Trade-Related Aspects of Intellectual Property Rights (TRIPs) sub-agreement to the GATT/WTO, which has some limitations in the field of biodiversity. These include the absence of an IPR regime that recognizes traditional knowledge, and certain patent regimes regarding biotechnology-derived products. COP3 requested the Executive Secretary to cooperate closely with the World Trade Organization Committee on Trade and Environment to explore linkages between the CBD and relevant articles of the TRIPs agreement and to apply for observer status at the WTO Committee on Trade and Environment, noting mutual interests between the CBD and WTO. The COP also encouraged cooperation with the conventions on climate change and desertification.[96] The COP has clearly come to the realization that it is also crucial that the ideals of the CBD be considered in other fora, especially those dealing with economic co-operation, international trade, forests, desertification, the oceans, climate, population, and the many other developments in modern society that influence biodiversity. Indeed, the CBD alone cannot be expected to deal with all the forces that affect biodiversity. Policy development clearly needs to involve all relevant sectors, lower political levels, NGOs, and the private sector.

COP4 was a meeting that promised much, yet struggled against a tide of largely self-generated obstacles to deliver. The pace and quality of deliberations exhibited the growing pains of a convention venturing tentatively, but resolutely, beyond the threshold of adolescence. COP4 marked the conclusion of the first medium-term programme of work for the convention and the Conference of the Parties adopted a programme of work that will guide the development of the convention for the foreseeable future. The decisions reaffirmed the ecosystem approach and adopted programmes of work for marine and coastal biodiversity (decision IV/5), forest biodiversity (decision IV/7), the biodiversity of inland water ecosystems (decision IV/4), and agricultural biodiversity (decisions III/11 and IV/6).[97]

Calestous Juma noted in his opening address to COP4 that the CBD is starting to influence social, economic, and political behaviour at the national level and to provide the policy framework for the international community's effort to protect and sustainably use life on earth. He went on to stress that perhaps the CBD's transition from its medium to long-term work programme presents the perfect opportunity to find its place within the constellation of multilateral environmental agreements. COP4 made strides towards streamlining its operations through the development of a new work programme and a tune-up on institutional matters. The new work programme sets out agendas for COPs 4–6 based on a revamped structure with key thematic issues, supportive cross-cutting issues and development of relationships with thematically relevant institutions and conventions. The work programme takes a constant improvement approach, and is to be evaluated and improved upon in light of developments in implementation of the convention. The focus of the programme of work for the next few years is on implementing the general commitments of the convention. With a scope as ambitious as that of the convention's, a major challenge for the implementation process as it moves into the next phase is to find a balance between pursuing the truly holistic and integrative approach demanded by the convention and, at the same time, being focused enough to allow concrete development of its provisions building, where possible, on ongoing processes and programmes. The COP also established an intersessional open-ended meeting to improve preparation for and conduct of the COP.

Biosafety

The issues of sovereignty and responsibility are clearly reflected in the CBD, as states assume the obligation not to cause or allow transboundary damage resulting from activities within its territory. The CBD also directs the parties to "establish or maintain means to regulate, manage, or control the risk associated with the use and release of living modified organisms resulting from biotechnology."[98] Although modern biotechnology has demonstrated its utility and provided tremendous benefits, there are still concerns about potential risks to biodiversity and human health posed by living modified organisms. It was with this concern in mind that COP2 established the Open-ended Ad Hoc Working Group on Biosafety: "to develop, in the field of the safe transfer, handling and use of living modified organisms, a protocol on biosafety, specifically focusing on transboundary movement, of any living modified organism resulting from modern biotechnology that may have adverse effect on the conservation and sustainable use of biological diversity, setting out for consideration, in particular, appropriate procedure for advance informed agreement."[99]

The CBD moves to the new millennium

Developments so far within the CBD process have been focused on establishing the institutional structure and clarifying the scope of the convention. COPs 1, 2, and 3 have been characterized as moving from an establishment phase into an implementation phase in the post COP4 period. The focus of the process thereafter is expected to shift to implementing the COP decisions and provisions of the convention. It has, however, been noted that the vast scope of the convention and its emphasis on an integrated approach has meant that the agenda of the process has rapidly expanded. This has led some commentators to observe that if this trend were to continue unabated then there will be a point where the process is so overburdened as to be ineffectual. The challenge for the process as it moves into its implementation phase is to develop an approach that will find a balance between pursuing a truly holistic and integrative path demanded by the convention, while at the same time being focused enough to allow development of its provisions.[100] As the COP continues to mature, a number of ideas have been put forward in an effort to improve its future operation. An example of the COP's honing of its work programme is apparent in its decision on agricultural biodiversity, which clearly delineates actions required of parties and tasks to be carried out by the secretariat. The decision places the responsibility for implementation squarely with governments.

The agenda of the CBD has expanded to a point where it is arguable that the international institutional structure for the convention is no longer adequate to cope with the demands of the process. Inadequate institutional capacity hampers many parts of the international community. The parties have came to the realization that if the way in which the convention organizes its work programme is not made as effective and efficient as possible, the overall implementation will be appreciably weakened. As a result, COP4 re-examined the institutional structure of the convention by revisiting the operation of the Conference of the Parties and its subsidiary bodies; reviewing the medium-term programme of work for 1995–1997, and a longer-term programme of work. Experience has demonstrated that the effectiveness of the COP is hampered by factors that can be summarized as follows: (a) the effectiveness of the meetings of the COP; (b) coordination of the internal institutional bodies of the process; and (c) coordination of the external parts of the systems.[101]

For most developing countries, a key reason for joining the CBD was the promise of new and additional funding as promised in Article 20. While the GEF has been established as the interim funding mechanism (and no other funding mechanism is on the horizon), the funds made available to date are widely considered to be inadequate, and the procedures to access the available funding are long and frustrating. That said, relatively few countries are yet in a position to specify clearly what their funding requirements are and how they would use the funds that may become available. Thus the GEF has given considerable attention to supporting national efforts to prepare national biodiversity strategies and action plans, as a basis for specifying the requirements.

Participation of developing countries at COPs and other CBD meetings is limited and this means that there is a reluctance to entertain an expansion in the number of working groups at the meeting of the COP. More support is needed to ensure that developing countries are adequately represented in the negotiation of international instruments and that their representatives are trained and fully informed. Capacity building is widely accepted as a priority by the development assistance community. However, little progress has yet been made by most countries in identifying specifically what capacity is required to address the CBD, at both institutional and personnel levels. The international legal instruments adopted in Rio have confirmed and strengthened the bargains between countries at different levels of development. These bargains have turned the issue of capacity building into more of an obligation. Before, the bargains were implicit and were made on the basis of good faith; now, the treaties contain an obligation for those countries with the ability to do so, to provide supporting measures for less developed countries. These are sound conclusions and if these provisions are effectively implemented there is every reason for optimism that the capacity of developing country parties as partners in international environmental conservation will have been greatly improved. As with all religions, however, the precepts are more honoured than observed – the level of action rarely matches the level of rhetoric. The ultimate challenge will be to take the leap from making verbal commitments to environmental goals to implementing these ideas.

This chapter has highlighted the divergence of opinions between the North and South on which side bears more responsibility in the conservation of biological diversity and the environment in general and how we need to reverse this trend. It is submitted that if the UNCED process is to bear fruit, the North-South dialogue will have to concentrate more on activity and less on acrimony. Just as in the past international agreements aimed at arms reduction and elimination could only be implemented by cooperation and agreement between East and West, it must be acknowledged that any serious efforts at environmental protection cannot be formulated without the cooperation of North and South. The development of international environmental law has now become largely dependent on the resolution of the North-South conflict, and solutions will only be possible if the New World Order embodies the principle of common but differentiated responsibility.

The articles dealing with technology transfer and financial resources are meant to enhance the capacity of developing states, and failure to bring about the anticipated benefits may result in far-reaching limitations on the obligations of developing states to implement the convention. Developing states have additional leverage under this convention in that they provide most of the genetic resources and will be in a position to bargain for benefits as a condition of allowing access to their resources. Developed state parties are also specifically required by Article 16(4) to ensure that the private sector facilitates access to and joint development and transfer of technology.

In the new millennium, we anticipate increased emphasis on the implementation of and compliance with international environmental instruments. Several new directions merit highlighting: the information revolution and transparency of information; public participation in developing and implementing international environmental instruments, the emergence of economic incentives and market mechanisms as a tool of implementation, and the treatment of third parties within the agreement. That availability of adequate financial resources crucial for the practical implementation of the convention's objectives is obvious.

NGOs and industry need to be provided with direct and legitimate channels for providing reports to secretariats and having those reports considered in evaluating implementation and compliance. As noted by Edith Brown Weiss, "NGOs are likely to continue to expand their influence in the negotiation, implementation, and compliance process of international environmental legal agreements. The information revolution should greatly facilitate this increased role of NGOs in international environmental decision-making."[102]

Active treaty management requires resources and people. Secretariats in the environmental area are skeletal. Parties cannot keep up with the demands of the management. Involvement of the parties is crucial for establishing the domestic priorities of each, but a robust secretariat is also needed to carry out a strategy of active management, especially in providing the assistance needed to build capacity. The bureaucratic relationships among members and the treaty organization reinforce the propensity to comply. If there is a robust organization, it can focus and apply the pressures of exposure and shaming on a member to comply where lack of capacity is not the reason for non-compliance. That may not be a treaty with teeth, but it may be a treaty with muscle.

Convention secretariats do, however, lack the capacity to enforce the convention's obligations. In most cases their power to verify implementation is limited and is often hampered in the absence of the parties' cooperation, especially in view of the fragmentation within each country of the institutions dealing with environmental issues and the large number of enterprises where activities affect the environment. This has led to suggestions of replacing the separate conferences and secretariats with a unified body following the WTO model. This view is not commonly shared however and there is room for improvement under the present fragmented structures.[103]

The Convention on Biological Diversity has established most of the elements required to be operational. Attention within the process is now moving towards implementation. The challenge of the process as it moves into its implementation phase is to develop an approach that will find a balance between pursuing a truly holistic and integrative approach demanded by the convention while at the same time being focused enough to allow development of its provisions. This will require close attention to the international institutional structure of the convention; the responsibilities of the parties; and a clear philosophical basis or intellectual *modus operandi* for the process.[104] One of the major stumbling blocks in monitoring compliance within the CBD process is that there exists no accepted mechanism for review of implementation of the convention using information that does not derive from national reports made by the CBD national focal points. As a result, there is a wealth of information from *bone fide* sources that cannot be used in assessing progress in implementing the convention. There is also no mechanism in place for systematically tracking implementation of the decisions taken by the contracting parties, particularly those that call on actions to be taken by them. The lack of consistent and systematically arranged information on implementation of the convention makes accurate assessment of progress difficult, and this in turn also affects the ability of the COP and the Secretariat to prioritize future action.

Notes

1. 175 representatives attended the conference, led by more than 150 world leaders.
2. Neville Brown, "Planetary Geopolitics," 19 *Millennium; Journal of International Studies* (Winter, 1990).
3. See generally *Report of Conference*, Stockholm, 16 May 1972; UN doc. A/CONF.48/14/ Rev. 1; Sohn, "The Stockholm Declaration on the Human Environment," 3 *Harvard International Journal* (1979).
4. UN Commission on Environment and Development, *Our Common Future,* Brundtland et al. (Oxford: WCED/Oxford University Press, 1987).
5. 31 *International Legal Materials* (1992), p. 822, ⟨http://www.biodiv.org/chm/conv/ default.htm⟩ to search the CBD full text versions or by articles.
6. The other being the United Nations Framework Convention on Climate Change (UNFCCC), also signed at Rio.
7. Article 2 of CBD.
8. WRI, *Global Biodiversity Strategy* (1992). The strategy is a document produced by the World Resources Institute (WRI), the World Conservation Union (IUCN), and UNEP as a "complementary initiative" and as "an outline for the diverse actions that will need to be taken by governments and non-governmental organizations alongside and in support of" the CBD.

9. See generally *Caring for the Earth: A Strategy for Sustainable Living, IUCN, UNEP & WWF* (Gland, Switzerland: World Conservation Centre, 1991).

10. "From One Earth to One World," in World Commission on Environment and Development, *Our Common Future* (Oxford: WCED Oxford University Press, 1987).

11. Established pursuant to UN General Assembly resolution 38/161 of 19 December 1983, WCED was chaired by Gro Harlem Brundtland (then Prime Minister of Norway). The Brundtland Commission, as it is widely known, submitted its report to the General Assembly in 1987, doc. A/42/427, through the Governing Council of UNEP. The report was later published under the title *Our Common Future* (Oxford: WCED Oxford University Press, 1987).

12. *Our Common Future.*

13. *Ibid.*

14. *Ibid.*

15. For a full account of the negotiation of this convention, see D. E. Bell, "The 1992 Convention on Biological Diversity: the Continuing Significance of the U.S. Objections at the Earth Summit," 26 *George Washington Journal of International Law and Economics* (1993), pp. 500–507, J. McNeely, M. Rojas, and C. Moronet, "The Convention on Biological Diversity: Promise and Frustration," 4 *Journal of Environment and Development* (No. 2, 1995), p. 33; W. Burhenne, foreword to *Biodiplomacy*, edited by V. Sanchez and C. Juma (Nairobi, Kenya: ACTS Press, 1994), p. ix; V. Sanchez, "The Convention on Biological Diversity: Negotiation and Contents," in Sanchez and Juma, p. 7.

16. A/RES/52/201 of 18 December 1997.

17. Philippe Sands, *Principles of International Law I: Framework Standards and Implementation* (Manchester, UK: Manchester University Press, 1995), p. 204.

18. Articles 1 and 15(7) of CBD.

19. Sands, n. 17 above, p. 217.

20. CBD. See, for example, Articles 16(2,3), 17(1), 18(2), 19(1,2), and 20(1,2,3).

21. UNEP/Bio.Div./WG.2/1/4/Add.1, p. 7 for India's argument that the special situation of developing countries necessitated such a distinction.

22. CBD Article 16.

23. Article 19(2).

24. Article 20(2).

25. Articles 1 and 15(7).

26. Article 23.

27. Article 23.

28. COP1, Nassau, Bahamas, 28 November–9 December 1994; COP2, Jakarta, Indonesia, 6–17 November 1995; COP3, Buenos Aires, Argentina, 4–15 November 1996; and COP4, Bratislava, Slovakia, 4–15 May 1998.

29. SBSTTA 1, Paris, France, 4–8 September 1995, SBSTTA 2, Montreal, Canada, 2–6 September 1996, SBSTTA 3, Montreal, Canada, 1–5 September 1997, SBSTTA 4, Montreal, Canada, 21–25 June 1999, SBSTTA 5 was held in Montreal, Canada, 31 January–4 February 2000.

30. UNEP/Bio.Div./N7 – INC. 5/4, p. 25.

31. Paragraphs 15 and 16, preamble; cf: UNEP/Bio.Div./SWGB./1/5/Rev.1.

32. Articles 16, 20, and 21 respectively.

33. Article 8(j) and para. 12, preamble. cf: UNEP/Bio.Div./SWGB.1/5/Rev.1.

34. Above, n. 25.

35. UNEP/Bio.Div/WG.2/1/4/ Add.1, pp. 6, 16 and 18.

36. *Ibid.*, p. 4.

37. *Ibid.*, p. 16.

38. UNEP/Bio.Div./N7-INC.5/4, p. 9.
39. Diana Ponoce-Nova, "Capacity-Building in Environmental law and Sustainable Development", in *Sustainable Development and International Law*, edited by Winfried Lang, (London: Graham and Trotman, 1995), p. 131.
40. Paragraphs 15 and 16 of CBD preamble.
41. The United Nations, DP1/1205 – 92285 – March 1992 – 15 m.
42. UNEP/Bio.Div/WG.2/1/4, p. 5.
44. UNEP/Bio.Div/WG.2/1/4,/Add.1 p. 2.
45. *Ibid.*, p. 14.
46. *Ibid.*
47. Kohana, P. T. B, "UNCED – The Transfer of Financial Resources," 1 *Review of European Community and International Environmental Law*, (No. 3), p. 303.
48. UNEP/Bio. Div/WG.2/1 /4, pp. 7–17.
49. UNEP conference for the adoption of the agreed text of the CBD, p. 16.
50. UNEP/Bio.Div/N7 - INC.5/4, p. 35.
51. UNEP conference for the adoption of the agreed text of the CBD, p. 23.
52. Article 16(1).
53. Article 16(2).
54. UNEP/Bio.Div/SWGB.1/5/Rev. 1, p. 11.
55. UNEP/Bio.Div./WG.2/1/4/Add.1, p. 42.
56. The Nairobi Final Act; cf: UNEP/Bio.Div./N7 - INC.5/4.
57. Above, n. 20, p. 33.
58. *Ibid.*
59. *Ibid.*
60. Article 12(a).
61. Article 12(5).
62. Decision II/6.
63. Decision III/8.
64. Decision III/5.
65. Decision III/6.
66. *Study Report*, Birdlife International (1996).
67. Program For The Further Implementation of Agenda 21 – GA Resolution, S/19-2. A/RES/S-19/2, June 1997.
68. Commission on Sustainable Development Fifth Session, 7–25 April 1997, *Report of the Secretary-General on Financial Resources and Mechanisms: Overall Progress Achieved since the United Nations Conference on Environment and Development* (E/CN.17/1997/2/Add.23).
69. UNEP/CBD/COP/4/16.
70. UNEP/Bio.Div/SWGB.1, p. 2.
71. UNEP/Bio.Div/WG.2/1/4/add.1, p. 42.
72. *Ibid.*, p. 46.
73. *Ibid.*, p. 39.
74. "Promoting and facilitating access to and transfer and development of technology," UNEP/CBD/COP/3/21, p. 13.
75. *Ibid.*, p. 17.
76. *Ibid.*, p. 17–18.
77. *Ibid.*, p. 39.
78. UNEP/Bio.Div./INC.3/11 Annex I, p. 21.
79. "Five years after Rio: Measuring Progress in the Implementation of the Convention on Biological Diversity," 9 *Earth Negotiation Bulletin* (No. 54, 1996).
80. Sam Johnston, "The Convention on Biological Diversity: the Next Phase," 6 *Review of European Community and International Environmental Law* (No. 3, 1998), p. 225.

81. 14 *Diversity* (Nos. 1 and 2, 1998), p. 27.
82. Articles 12 and 13 CBD.
83. Article 23(5).
84. Decision I/9.
85. Decision I/10.
86. Decision I/7.
87. Decision I/3.
88. Decision I/2.
89. COP2 Report.
90. Decision II/17.
91. Decision II/7 of the COP and Recommendation I/5 of the SBSTTA.
92. Held in Montreal, 2–6 September 1996.
93. SBSTTA 2 Report.
94. Decision III/11.
95. Decision III/12.
96. Decision III/21.
97. The full text of these decisions is contained in document UNEP/CBD/COP4/27, which is available from the Secretariat or can be obtained from its home page ⟨www.biodiv.org⟩.
98. Article 19 of CBD.
99. COP2 Decision II/5.
100. S. Johnston, "The Convention on Biological Diversity: the Next Phase," 6 *Review of European Community and International Environmental Law* (No. 3, 1998).
101. *Ibid*.
102. E. Brown Weiss, "International Environmental Law: Contemporary Issues and the Emergence of a New World Order," 81 *Georgetown Law Journal* (1993), p. 709.
103. Paper presented by Ibrahim F. Shihata before the Expert Meeting on Implementation and Compliance with International Environmental Agreements, Washington, DC, 20–21 May 1996.
104. Johnston, "The Convention on Biological Diversity," n. 100 above.

6

The United Nations Framework Convention on Climate Change: Implementation and compliance

Jo Elizabeth Butler and Aniket Ghai

Introduction

This chapter examines implementation of the United Nations Framework Convention on Climate Change (UNFCCC),[1] one of three environment and sustainable development conventions that were negotiated together with "Agenda 21" during the early 1990s, as part of what is sometimes referred to as "the Rio process." The chapter reviews the essential commitments of different groups of countries under the UNFCCC, and national efforts to meet these obligations, but without entering into a technical discussion of the many related methodological issues. Throughout, the focus is primarily on implementation of the convention, although reference is occasionally also made to the Kyoto Protocol. A special discussion is provided of the role of non-governmental organizations in the climate change process. A separate section focuses on the related topic of compliance, an issue that is receiving growing importance in the light of the recently agreed Kyoto Protocol, a legal instrument which contains much stronger commitments for developed countries, including "legally binding targets" that are not contained in the UNFCCC itself.[2]

The Rio process: Climate change negotiations and other environmental agreements

The United Nations Conference on Environment and Development (UNCED)[3] was held in June 1992, in Rio de Janeiro, and resulted in

122

the adoption of Agenda 21, the Rio Declaration on Environment and Development and the Forest Principles. Agenda 21 itself is a blueprint for a comprehensive plan of action at the global, national, and local levels, for all major groups, on all areas in which humans impact on the environment. A distinct but parallel negotiation process was underway on climate change issues. As a result of increasing scientific evidence and concern at the international level that anthropogenic emissions of greenhouse gases are responsible for global climate change, in 1990 the United Nations General Assembly (UNGA) established an intergovernmental process to negotiate a global treaty to tackle climate change.[4] The UNFCCC, adopted in May 1992, was the outcome of this process. While the problem of desertification was recognized at the international level at a much earlier date (1977) only at UNCED was a call made to the UNGA to establish a negotiating committee to prepare a global convention on this issue.[5] The United Nations Convention to Combat Desertification in Those Countries Experiencing Serious Drought and/or Desertification, particularly in Africa (UNCCD) was adopted in June 1994, and entered into force 90 days after ratification by 50 countries, on 26 December 1996. While the Convention on Biological Diversity (CBD) was also opened for signature at Rio, it was the result of a negotiation process initiated under the United Nations Environment Program (UNEP), in November 1989.[6] It entered into force on 29 December 1993, three months after the 30th ratification. The UNCED process arose from consensus at the international level on the need to address further environment and sustainable development issues as a whole. The issues of climate change, desertification, and biological diversity was addressed in varying detail in different chapters of Agenda 21. Owing to the critical and global nature of these environmental problems, and pressing need for related action, the international community opted to single out these questions for specific treatment under separate intergovernmental processes, adding to the text negotiated under the UNCED process.

There are complex linkages between these different global agreements of a scientific, economic, and legal nature, which have been the subjects of much discussion both within and outside the intergovernmental processes.[7] This chapter will focus specifically on implementation of commitments under the UNFCCC, although there is significant interplay between these commitments and other international agreements.

The climate change negotiation process is distinctive among global environmental agreements in a number of respects. Signatories to the UNFCCC ratified or acceded to the convention very rapidly, resulting in its entry into force on 21 March 1994, three months after ratification by the 50th signatory, which occurred less than two years after the convention was open for signature. The speed at which ratification has occurred reflects the high degree of importance attributed by parties to the issue, the political commitment of some parties to mitigating climate change and the importance felt by countries of participating in the shaping of later climate change agreements.[8]

Secondly, the negotiating positions adopted by countries display a high degree of complexity, which diverge from the traditional North-South paradigm. Political negotiating blocs reflect a complicated set of economic, political, and strategic interests, based on possible (direct and indirect) effects on national economies both of inaction and of undertaking mitigation policies, particularly in terms of the possible costs of compliance by governments and different sectors of the national economy. Under the convention itself, commitments are applicable to three groups of countries. The most stringent apply to those contained in its Annex II, which comprise most of the countries that are members of the OECD, or the developed countries. A weaker set of commitments are defined for those countries listed in Annex I, which include the developed countries as well as a number of the more industrialized Eastern European countries. A yet weaker set of commitments applies to parties not included in Annex I (or "non-Annex I Parties"), which are mainly the developing countries.[9]

While the Group of 77 and China still present a common position during climate change negotiations, this is a balance of the views of countries that are likely to experience significant negative impacts from climate change and those of countries which may experience negative impacts of policies undertaken to mitigate climate change. Interests of the Oil and Petroleum Exporting Countries (OPEC) in some cases intersect with those of larger developing countries, such as China, Brazil, and India etc., countries that have historically resisted the introduction of additional commitments for developing countries. On the other hand, the Alliance of Small Island States (AOSIS) advocates early action. Two distinct negotiating blocs can be identified among Annex II parties – those who are members of the EU[10] and a separate group known as "JUSCANNZ," which is comprised of most other Annex II parties.[11] In negotiations on some issues, countries with economies in transition, particularly those included in Annex I, form a common bloc. The usual UN regional groupings are also represented, but are vocal principally on issues related to election of officers of the Bureau of the Conference of the Parties and its subsidiary bodies.[12]

A third distinctive feature is the important role of scientific and other knowledge related to the climate change field and urgent need for improving this knowledge. Although there is increasing evidence that mankind is contributing to global warming, large uncertainties still exist with regard to the extent of this phenomenon. There are even greater uncertainties in assessing other climate change-related events, such as sea level rise, increased weather variability, precipitation patterns, frequency of extreme weather events etc.[13] There is also uncertainty in the assessment of the impacts of any of these climate change occurrences, on the environment, socio-economic sectors, and human health.[14] The effectiveness of individual mitigation polices and their impacts on other, for example fossil fuel-dependent, economies are also not well known. The need for assessing scientific and technical knowledge is addressed by the Intergovernmental Panel on Climate Change (IPCC),[15] but important gaps in scientific knowledge need to be filled by the international research community, particularly in light of the threat of serious or irreversible damage, and exceptionally high associated costs.

Commitments under the UNFCCC

The UNFCCC acknowledges the "common but differentiated responsibilities" of countries in responding to climate change, and that the "developed country Parties should take the lead in combating climate change and the adverse effects thereof," assigning different commitments to different groups of parties.

All parties must comply with a set of basic commitments, which include: the publication of inventories of national greenhouse gas emissions; the development and implementation of programmes to mitigate climate change and facilitate adaptation; promoting the transfer of technologies to reduce or prevent greenhouse gas emissions; preparing for adaptation to the impact of climate change; promoting scientific, technological, and other research, systematic observation and the development of data archives related to the climate system; the exchange of information related to climate change and the consequences of response strategies; promoting education, training, and public awareness related to climate change, and the periodic communication of information related to the implementation of commitments.

An additional set of obligations is ascribed to "Annex I Parties." These countries should "take the lead in modifying longer term trends" in anthropogenic emissions and removals by sinks by adopting national policies and measures[16] to mitigate climate change, "recognizing that the return by the end of the present decade to earlier levels" of such emissions would "contribute to such modification." Annex I parties must also communicate information on these policies and measures as well as on resulting projected emissions, with the "aim of returning individually or jointly to their 1990 levels" of emissions. Methodologies for carrying out related calculations are decided upon by the Conference of the Parties (COP). Annex I parties must also coordinate relevant economic and administrative instruments, and identify and periodically review policies and practices that encourage activities leading to increased greenhouse gas emissions.[17]

Annex II parties, the developed countries, have the added obligation to provide new and additional financial resources to meet the full costs incurred by developing countries when preparing their inventory of greenhouse gas emissions and a general description of steps taken or envisaged to implement the convention. Annex II parties must also provide financial resources to cover the incremental costs incurred by developing countries in implementing their other commitments under the convention.[18] They must also assist developing countries that are particularly vulnerable to the adverse effects of climate change in meeting related adaptation costs. Annex II parties are also required to promote, facilitate, and finance, as appropriate, the transfer of and access to environmentally sound technologies and know-how to other parties, particularly developing country parties, to enable them to implement the provisions of the convention. Article 11 of the convention defines a mechanism for the provision of financial resources, including for technology transfer.

The convention also contains provisions regarding special circumstances. Annex I parties undergoing the process of transition to a market economy (EITs) may request a certain degree of flexibility in implementing commitments, such as in the choice of reference year.[19] With regard to funding and the transfer of technology, parties must take full account of the specific needs and special circumstances of the least developed countries. In implementing commitments, parties must also give full consideration to the actions (for example, related to funding, insurance and the transfer of technology) necessary to meet the needs and concerns of developing country parties arising from the adverse effects of climate change and/or the impact of the implementation of response measures.[20]

Decisions of the subsidiary bodies and the Conference of the Parties[21]

The pace of climate change negotiations has accelerated since signature of the 1992 framework convention. Countries have further elaborated and developed the basic commitments, through decisions of the convention's two subsidiary bodies, for implementation and for scientific and technological advice, meeting two to three times a year, as well as at the annual session of COP.

The convention stipulates that the COP shall review the adequacy of Annex I party commitments under the convention. At its first session, the

COP undertook a first review of the adequacy of Annex I party commitments, and concluded that existing commitments were not sufficient to achieve the UNFCCC's ultimate objective of preventing "dangerous anthropogenic interference with the climate system." By adopting the "Berlin Mandate," it initiated a process for negotiating additional commitments for Annex I parties. This process, which ran in parallel to "regular" climate change negotiations, resulted in a text that served as the basis for the Kyoto Protocol, later adopted by the COP at its third session in December 1997 in Japan. The protocol establishes different legally binding quantified emission limitation or reduction commitments for 38 countries and one regional economic integration organization, listed in its Annex B, for the period 2008–2012. Further emissions reductions by these countries will be decided on for subsequent five-year periods. The reduction targets apply to six gases, namely, CO_2, CH_4, N_2O, HFCs, PFCs, and SF6. As agreed in the Berlin Mandate, developing countries assume no new commitments. The entry into force provision of the protocol (Article 24) requires the ratification of 55 parties to the Convention, including Annex I parties whose emissions of carbon dioxide in 1990 amounted to at least 55 per cent of the total emissions of those parties.[22] The protocol also establishes three "flexibility mechanisms" of the international trade of emission permits, joint implementation between developed countries, and a "clean development mechanism" under which developed countries may obtain credits by reduction emissions in developing countries.

The COP is also mandated to review the lists of countries contained in Annexes I and II. At its third session, it amended the list of countries included in Annex I to the convention by deleting the name of Czechoslovakia, and adding the names of Croatia, the Czech Republic, Liechtenstein, Monaco, Slovakia, and Slovenia. The countries listed in Annex B to the protocol are those in the convention's amended Annex I, with the exception of the exclusion of Turkey.

The COP decided that the restructured Global Environment Facility (GEF) should serve as the entity entrusted with the operation of the financial mechanism of the convention, and that the financial mechanism is to be reviewed every four years, based on agreed guidelines.[23] The institutional arrangements between the COP and the Council of the GEF have also been defined.[24] The GEF Council has elaborated operational policies for the disbursement of funds. Guidance has been provided by the COP at its first and fourth sessions, on policies, programme priorities and eligibility criteria on the provision of funding under the convention, with priority to be accorded to "enabling activities," such as the preparation of initial national communications, planning and endogenous capacity building, including institutional strengthening, training, research, and education. An initial set of priority areas for funding was defined, including national public awareness and education, the formulation of national programmes to address climate change, support for agreed activities of these national programmes, and "Stage I" adaptation activities, which include studies of possible impacts to climate change and related adaptation policy options. This range of activities was broadened at the recent Buenos Aires meeting of the COP to include the implementation of adaptation response measures (or "Stage II" adaptation activities), the identification of technology needs, capacity building for participation in systematic observational networks, the preparation of subsequent national communications, studies leading to the preparation of national programmes to address climate change, strengthening public awareness campaigns, and the improvement of access to international and regional technology information centres.

At its fifth session, the COP broadened the scope of activities to be funded by the GEF by adding "capacity-building activities for implementing the Convention in developing countries" (here defined as non-Annex I parties). Gaps and weaknesses in existing capacity-building efforts will be identified through an assessment, which should result in a proposal for a framework for capacity-building activities, to be agreed on at the sixth session of the COP. A separate such exercise is to be undertaken for countries with economies in transition, although the GEF has not been designated to provide funding for these activities.

Commitments related to the transfer of technology are closely linked to those on the provision of financial resources, since the convention stipulates that the provision of financial resources for the incremental costs of implementing their commitments under the convention other than those related to communication of information should include the transfer of technology. It is perhaps as an indication of the priority attached by developing countries to the issue of technology transfer that, at all its four sessions so far, the COP has taken specific decisions regarding the development and transfer of technologies. At the first three of these, the focus has largely been on requests to the secretariat for various reports,[25] while requests to Annex II parties have been limited to communicating information in conformity with established guidelines on the implementation of technology transfer commitments and to improve the enabling environment for the private sector transfer of climate-relevant technology. Requests have been made to non-Annex I parties to provide information on technology needs and the subsidiary bodies have been requested to explore options related to technology information centres and to evaluate the transfer of technology being undertaken. At the fourth session of the COP, however, there was a significant shift in focus in the decision on the transfer of technology: a lengthy text spells out the assistance to be provided by Annex II parties and Annex I parties, using for the first time language such as "building capacity and institutional frameworks" and "strengthening capabilities," while also identifying specific sectors and activities. Calls have also been extended to intergovernmental and non-governmental organizations. Most importantly perhaps, the decision launches a new consultative process to address a broad range of technical and policy issues related to the transfer of technology, which is hoped to result in a "framework for meaningful and effective action to enhance the implementation of Article 4.5" on technology transfer.

Through several separate decisions, the COP has also agreed on methodologies to be used, for example, for calculation of greenhouse gas inventories, on aggregation of emissions using global warming potentials, for assessing climate change impacts and adaptations and on other issues arising from implementation. Broadly speaking, these decisions establish the "accounting rules" for calculating greenhouse gas emissions, clarify and define the rules applicable to future commitments under the protocol, and aim to agree on one of several alternative approaches to treating technical issues. In these decisions, the subsidiary bodies and the COP draw extensively on the work of the IPCC.

The convention allows for the "joint implementation" of commitments by Annex I parties, although it does not define this notion, but requires the COP to take decisions regarding related criteria.[26] During negotiations, many Annex I parties argued in favour of a system whereby they would obtain "credits" for funding and/or carrying out projects in other countries that would result in lower greenhouse gas emissions than would otherwise occur. These credits would be used to offset actual national emissions in order to fulfil convention limitation requirements. In the face of stiff resistance to this proposal, largely from developing countries, the negotiations on this issue did not, however, result in a system of crediting. At its first session, the COP established a "pilot phase of activities implemented jointly," under which any such projects would *not* be considered as the fulfilment of current convention commitments of Annex I parties, but supplemental. The financing of these projects is also to be additional to existing financial obligations of Annex II parties under the convention. A uniform reporting format for these activities was developed, together with reporting requirements distinct from those related to national communications. A review of the pilot phase was undertaken and concluded at the fifth session of the COP, and a decision taken to continue this pilot phase beyond the end of the present decade. As the Kyoto Protocol contains provisions allowing for joint implementation with crediting (under Article 3.10, 3.11, and 6), the activities implemented jointly are not likely to play a significant role once the first commitment period under the protocol is reached, although the experience obtained from this pilot phase will no doubt prove valuable when developing the modalities, guidelines, and criteria, both for the protocol's joint implementation and clean development mechanism.

Parties have also developed in considerable detail the procedures for the communicating of information on implementation and the review of this information. Owing to the importance of these issues in the climate change process, they are discussed in a separate section below.

Communication and review

Annex I and Annex II parties

Communication of information

During the negotiation of the Convention itself, many delegations, wary of the meaning behind words such as "verification," "monitoring," and "reporting," preferred to include language such as the "communication of information." As parties gain experience in the review process, confidence has increased and parties have become more comfortable with the concept of "reporting," a feature that is possibly also linked to the fact that their obligations and commitments are less stringent than had originally been anticipated by many during the early negotiations.

Article 12 of the convention requires all parties to communicate information related to implementation. Under this article, all parties must provide an inventory of greenhouse gas emissions,[27] a general description of steps taken or envisaged to implement the convention, as well as any other information deemed to be relevant to the achievement of the objective of the convention and suitable for inclusion. Annex I parties must additionally provide a detailed description of policies and measures adopted, an estimate of the effects of these policies and measures on future greenhouse gas emissions, and on its resulting projected emissions by sources and removals by sinks.[28] Annex II parties must also provide information on measures undertaken to implement their commitments on the transfer of technology and the provision of financial resources. In addition, the COP adopted guidelines for the preparation of communications by Annex I parties,[29] which are periodically revised to reflect changing requirements and advances in methodologies and scientific knowledge.[30] These guidelines provide detailed recommendations on the type and format of information that parties must provide, including, for example, prescribed methodologies for reporting greenhouse gas inventories, *which* greenhouse gases must be reported on, minimum information requirements to ensure transparency in inventory methods and projections calculations, as well as the reporting format. These guidelines aim to ensure that information provided is consistent, transparent, and comparable, and to assist parties in implementing commitments and the COP in assessing this implementation.[31]

The first communication by Annex I parties was due within six months of entry into force of the convention for that party. The COP determines the periodicity of subsequent national communications. It decided that the second communication was due in April 1997, except for those Annex I parties with economies in transition who were accorded an additional year. Third communications are due by the end of November 2001. The COP also decided that Annex I parties must in addition submit annually national greenhouse gas data, due in April for the last but one year prior to the year of submission.

The review process

The review process, as defined by the COP in its decisions 2/CP.1, 9/CP.2, 6/CP.3 and11/CP.4, is a "thorough and comprehensive technical assessment of the implementation of the Convention commitments by individual Annex I Parties and Annex I Parties as a whole."[32] Its purpose is to "review, in a facilitative, non-confrontational, open and transparent manner, the information contained in the communications from Annex I parties to ensure that the COP has accurate, consistent and relevant information at its disposal to assist it in carrying out its responsibilities." The basic format of this process has remained unchanged for all three communications requested so far, and can be divided into three phases. The first assesses global action undertaken by Annex I parties to implement commitments by compiling and synthesizing information in their communications. To date, two such synthesis reports have been prepared, based on their first and second communications. These reports, prepared by the secretariat, draw principally on information provided by parties themselves, and do not make any policy recommendations.[33]

The second phase involves conducting "in-depth reviews"(IDRs), or country-specific assessments, of the information provided in individual communications of Annex I parties. Independent teams comprised of experts nominated by countries and a Climate Change secretariat "coordinator" conduct these assessments, over a 6–12 month period. The teams contain a balance of experts from developed countries, economies in transition, and developing countries, and are sometimes supplemented by experts from the secretariats of selected intergovernmental organizations. The IDRs begin with a "paper" review of the communication and supporting background documentation, and, at the invitation of the country in question, are followed by a one-week on-site visit, during which the team members meet with experts from a range of national ministries and technical agencies. The teams also generally meet with representatives of industry, environmental and local community non-governmental organizations (NGOs), the latter often assuming important functions in the national implementation of the convention.

The in-depth reviews are conducted in a facilitative and non-confrontational manner. Further, the government of the country whose communication is being reviewed is invited to provide comments on a draft of the report, which are then taken into account by the IDR team. If, in the final draft, these comments are not treated to the satisfaction of the government in question, the latter has the opportunity of including remarks that would appear in a separate section of the report. While the comments typically provided by governments relate to both technical and factual information as well as policy-related statements, to date, no country has invoked its right to include its comments in a separate section of the report. The full text of the reports and their summaries are made available to all parties and accredited observers, and are also available to the public on the Climate Change secretariat's web site.

While IDRs allow a more detailed analysis of the individual country's report on implementation of commitments, there is limited time available to review the very extensive data that are generally made available by the government. The IDRs focus on verifying information in communications, reviewing compliance with guidelines for preparation of communications, filling information gaps, assessing progress in the implementation of policies, assessing the robustness of greenhouse gas emission projections, providing updates on information given in the communications and, to the extent possible, assessing consistency and comparability with the information in other communications. But there is neither the time available nor the mandate for IDRs to carry out an "audit" style of systematic and rigorous assessment of each individual country's implementation of the UNFCCC.

In the final phase of this review process, the COP, the Subsidiary Body for Implementation (SBI) and the Subsidiary Body for Scientific and Technological Advice (SBSTA) consider national communications, the synthesis reports and the IDRs, with a view to assessing the implementation of the convention, particularly in the light of the review of the adequacy of commitments toward achieving the convention's objective. So far, the process has focused on implementation of the convention by parties as a whole. Despite the fact that individual in-depth reviews of countries' communications have been carried out, there has not been a country-specific discussion of implementation in any of the organs of the convention, and consequently, no individual cases of non-compliance have been singled out.

The decisions of the COP on implementation of commitments by Annex I parties have been restricted to the conclusions that "for many Annex I Parties urgent further actions will be needed to return greenhouse gas emissions to their 1990 levels by 2000" and that "there is a need to address the concern expressed by some Parties that Annex II Parties are falling short of their commitments related to the transfer of technology and the provision of financial resources." The COP has also "urged" Annex I parties that have not complied with requirements to submit national communications and inventory data to do so as soon as possible. The COP has also adopted general conclusions on the extent to which the guidelines for preparing communications have been followed.

Article 7.2(f) of the convention also requires the COP to consider and adopt regular reports on implementation, which should be designed for the informed public and prepared in a style appropriate for public information and outreach.[34]

Non-Annex I parties

Communication of information

Non-Annex I parties have weaker commitments under the convention, both in terms of mitigation action required as well as communication of information on implementation. A different set of guidelines for the preparation of their communications reflects these weaker obligations. In addition to the requisite inventory of greenhouse gas emissions and general description of steps taken or envisaged to implement the convention, non-Annex I parties may also provide other information on, for example, financial and technological needs and constraints.

Non-Annex I parties are required to make their initial communication "within three years of the entry into force of the Convention, for that Party, or of the availability of financial resources in accordance with Article 4, paragraph 3" of the convention. Moreover, parties that are least developed countries "may make their initial communications at their discretion."[35] Most non-Annex I parties have chosen the "or" alternative, namely to submit their initial communication within three years of the availability of financial resources designed for this purpose,[36] provided by the GEF – the entity entrusted with operation of the financial mechanism of the convention. By the end of 1999, some 24 national communications from developing country parties had been received. Those parties that have submitted their initial communications may now begin preparations on their second one, including requests for the related funding by the GEF.

The consideration process

The COP, at its fourth and fifth sessions, defined a process for "consideration"[37] of the initial communications by non-Annex I parties. This process is similar to that in place for Annex I parties in that synthesis reports are to be prepared by the secretariat and reviewed by the COP. Further, the guidelines for non-Annex I party communications will also be subject to review and revision. There are no in-depth reviews of non-Annex I parties' communications, however. Instead, a consultative group has been set up of experts on non-Annex I party communications, mandated to improve the process of preparation of these communications. The consultative group will review the exchange of information and experiences, availability of financial resources and technical support, existing activities and support for the preparation of communications, difficulties in following the guidelines, and related data and methodological problems.

Implementation of commitments

Annex I parties

Returning greenhouse gas emissions to 1990 levels by the year 2000 (Article 4.2 (a) and (b))

One of the key commitments under the convention is "the aim of returning individually or jointly to their 1990 levels ... anthropogenic emissions of greenhouse gas emissions," and, elsewhere in the convention, "recognizing that the return by the end of the present decade to earlier levels of anthropogenic emissions of carbon dioxide and other greenhouse gases ... would contribute to modifying longer-term trends in anthropogenic emissions consistent with the objective of the Convention." In simpler terms, this language is generally taken to mean "aiming to return greenhouse gas emissions in 2000 to their 1990 levels," without affirming commitments beyond this date.

Apart from the fact that this limitation requirement is not a "hard" legally binding one, unlike those negotiated under the Kyoto Protocol, there is further flexibility in the way in which it is interpreted. Some countries view the limitation commitment to apply to each greenhouse gas separately, with others embracing the "basket approach," in which comparison is made of annual emissions of greenhouse gases aggregated by their global warming potential. Thus, a country may still achieve the "aim" if it emits in 2000 more than the 1990 amounts of one type of gas, but offsets this excess by emitting less of another. Further, some countries view the commitment to apply principally to carbon dioxide, which is the gas responsible for the lion's share of aggregate greenhouse gas emissions.[38] Countries often explicitly or implicitly state the way in which they interpret the "aim" in their national communication or in position papers, or through the voluntary self-imposed "hard" targets that many Annex I parties have passed at the national level.[39] Lastly, as countries must adopt polices and measures both to limit emissions and to protect and enhance greenhouse sinks and reservoirs, some parties adopt the "net" approach, which involves calculating total greenhouse emissions by subtracting removals by sinks[40] from gross emissions. Greater sequestration in the year 2000 than in 1990 could offset higher gross emissions, and therefore still allow a party to achieve the aim.[41]

The best indicators of compliance with the commitment to return greenhouse gas emissions in 2000 to their 1990 levels are the reported greenhouse gas emission inventories for 2000. Under current reporting requirements, which no doubt take into account the time required to collect and process the required information, these data will only be available by mid-2002. Apart from projections data for 2000, which are reviewed below, greenhouse gas inventory data for the years 1990–1997 are currently available,[42] and their levels and trends also serve as a useful proxy when assessing whether parties are likely to meet this aim.

On the basis of extrapolation of observed inventory data trends,[43] all Annex I parties with economies in transition will be below their 1990 (or other base year) levels of emissions of carbon dioxide (CO_2), methane (CH_4), and nitrous oxide (N_2O) in the year 2000.[44] All Annex II parties except five appear unlikely to achieve the aim of returning to 1990 levels in 2000 their levels of gross emissions of carbon dioxide, the most important contributor to global warming. The reverse trend is observed in extrapolations for Annex II parties' emissions of nitrous oxide and methane, with seven countries unlikely to achieve the aim. If one aggregates the emissions of these three greenhouse gases using global warming potentials, not surprisingly, the extrapolations mirror the results obtained for carbon dioxide.

As data collection improves and methodologies are refined, countries update their greenhouse gas inventory data for previous years, including for 1990. While this holds self-evident advantages, the constant changing of reference numbers also creates difficulties for assessing compliance.[45] As the limitation commitments in the convention are not hard and legally binding, the impact of this is not so serious. The protocol seeks to avoid these difficulties by establishing prior to the commitment period the values of certain key variables (e.g. carbon stocks, Article 3.4), agreeing on methodologies to be used in calculations (e.g. for greenhouse gas inventory, Article 5.2 and 5.3), and by establishing "a national system for the estimation of anthropogenic emissions by sources and removals by sinks of all greenhouse gases not controlled by the Montreal Protocol" (Article 5.1). An annex to the report of the COP at its third session fixes the total carbon dioxide emissions of Annex I parties in 1990 for the purposes of Article 25 (on entry into force). These values are based on the informtion submitted by Annex I parties in their first national communications, although these have since been revised to reflect improved methodologies and data collection.

The trend extrapolation exercise conducted above does not take into account the future expected values of a host of other variables that affect emissions, including, *inter alia*, the pace of implementation and effects of policies and measures. All Annex I parties are required to include projections of emissions in 2000, 2005, and 2010 in their national communications that take such factors into account. As the year 2000 approached, extrapolation of actual inventory data became a more powerful indicator of the countries' probable emissions in 2000. This is because it is difficult for countries to modify their trend (or business-as-usual) year 2000 emissions, as doing so requires implementing polices and adopting measures which generally involve time lags before the mitigation effects are felt.[46] Further, the process for implementing policies and measures frequently involves lengthy national processes, both in formulating the appropriate policy and the political process for approval and enactment of related legislation. Implementing policies and measures often also entails costs to the government, which generally need to be approved first.

Because of these time lags, the projection of baseline and "with measures" greenhouse emissions serves a critical purpose to national climate change policy-makers in determining whether the country is on the right path to meeting obligations.[47] Uncertainty, however, is inherent in these projections. Projected emissions may diverge from actual values if key variables in the models used to derive them turn out to be significantly different.[48] Alternatively, models may not be good approximations of reality. This may occur for example if the models do not represent properly the way in which the economic agents make choices or if the models contain implicit assumptions about political outcomes.[49] Any uncertainties in the calculation of inventories, for example in emission factors, will also be present in projections. Uncertainty arises also from the basic data in the model, as there is variability in the quality and reliability of these data, depending, for example, on data collection methods or survey techniques. Finally, a country's projections analysis itself may be suspect if there is likelihood that it has been prepared with political or negotiating considerations in mind.[50]

Based on countries' own projections provided in their second communications, only eight Annex II parties[51] will succeed in returning their gross carbon dioxide emissions to 1990 levels in 2000, while 10 Annex II parties expect growth of over 10 per cent, including the Annex II countries that emit the largest amounts. Only three Annex II countries predict longer-term stabilization or decline in carbon dioxide emissions up to the year 2010. On the other hand, only five Annex II parties expect to emit more methane in 2000 than in 1990, and most expect longer-term stabilization or decline. With regard to emissions of nitrous oxide, Annex II parties are evenly divided among those who expect to achieve the aim of returning emissions in 2000 to their 1990 levels and those who do not; these countries are also displaying differing longer-term growth prospects of these emissions. Universally, Annex I parties with economies in transition expect to emit less of all these three greenhouse gases in 2000 than in their base years, but expect their emissions to increase in the longer term as they emerge from recession, in some cases exceeding 1990 levels in 2010. Few countries have projected emissions of hydrofluorocarbons (HFCs), perfluorocarbons (PFCs), and sulphur hexafluoride (SF_6), but based on limited existing data mainly from Annex II parties, emissions of HFCs and SF_6 are projected to grow steeply, while a decline is expected in emissions of PFCs. Aggregating all these greenhouse gases suggests that, based on measures currently implemented, only seven Annex II parties will succeed in stabilizing their greenhouse gas emissions in the short and medium term.[52]

Communication of information (Articles 4.1, 4.2, and 12)

The requirement to communicate information related to implementation is often viewed as the strongest commitment in the convention, as the relevant articles of the convention and decisions of the COP are unambiguous, binding and contain little scope for individual countries' interpretation. Two sets of required information can be identified: the national communications and inventory data, the latter required on an annual basis. For both sets, countries have frequently failed to make their submissions by the agreed date. Delays generally arise from the often lengthy internal approval process by different ministries and from the extensive background studies necessary for the preparation of the material, rather than reluctance to disclose information.[53] Although these commitments are less pertinent to attaining the objective of the convention[54] than adopting mitigation and adaptation measures themselves, the failure to comply with these "harder" commitments does not augur well for performance on the "softer" commitments, nor encourage developing countries to submit their own communications on time.

Another aspect of compliance with commitments to communicate information is the extent to which the guidelines for communicating information have been followed. These guidelines are subject to continuous revision by the subsidiary bodies and the COP, with the aim of improving the quality of information communicated and to reflect changing requirements. The guidelines identify detailed sets of information that Annex I parties "should" include in the national communications, sets they are "encouraged" to include, and yet others that they "may" provide. This choice of weak language is partly grounded in the reluctance of delegations to include strong text such as "verification, monitoring and reporting." In practice, however, the "should" elements are viewed as compulsory, particularly as experience has shown that without adequate information from parties on steps undertaken by them to implement commitments, it is very difficult for the review mechanism developed under the convention for assessing implementation to function correctly.[55]

Provision of information required by the guidelines varies widely across parties. One might divide the types of information required into three categories. A first category includes numbers or data, for example, amounts of greenhouse gases emitted in the past and projected in the future, or financial contributions to the GEF. A second type of information includes "general descriptions" of actions undertaken to implement commitments (for instance, mitigation policies and measures, or public awareness programmes). Lastly, one can identify information on the methodologies used, particularly for inventory and projections calculations, the provision of which is principally designed to ensure transparency of methods and calculations.

Numerical data are generally well provided, with the following exceptions. A few EITs have only provided greenhouse gas inventory data for several years since 1990, rather than the full required 1990–1997 range. Some countries have not provided information on removals by sinks, for both inventories but especially for projections, generally owing to lack or unreliability of data. Inventory and projections data for emissions of HFCs, PFCs, and SF_6 are provided by little over one half of the countries.[56] Some countries have not provided projections of their emissions of gases other than carbon dioxide. Estimates of the mitigation effects of individual policies and measures are very often incomplete or missing.[57] Although required, only a few countries have provided an assessment of monitoring, for example through progress indicators. There are important information gaps on financial contributions to bilateral and multilateral institutions, particularly regarding "new and additional" resources.[58]

The guidelines require the inclusion of general descriptions of actions related to polices and measures education, training and public awareness, research and systematic observation, and vulnerability assessment and adaptation measures. These descriptions are generally provided, but naturally in varying degrees of detail. With regard to policies and measures, a minimum requirement is that the descriptions should provide a third party with a clear understanding of the action's "objective and degree of implementation." While the former criterion is generally met, frequently the latter is not. Information gaps also occur with regard to implementation of commitments related to the promotion and strengthening of education and training programmes in developing countries and on international cooperation to prepare for adaptation to the adverse effects of climate change.

Transparency requirements relate principally to greenhouse gas inventories and future projections of emissions. A variety of types of information add transparency, starting with a description of the methodology itself. Details of calculation methods for inventories, descriptions of models for projections, and for both inventories and projections, an explanation of the assumptions made are all necessary. A balance needs to be achieved between providing too sketchy a description and excessive detail. Taking the example of projections, the absence of a discussion of the key assumptions and sensitivity of model results to changes in the values in these assumptions makes it more difficult to interpret projections meaningfully. On the other hand, some projections, particularly for the energy sector, are comprised of hundreds of equations; it would not be useful to reproduce the full projections study containing all these numbers.

Transparency in inventories was generally satisfactory although in some cases adequate explanations were not provided when parties used emissions factors different from the IPCC default values. Projections methods, on the other hand, were frequently poorly described. Many of the elements that might assist the reader in understanding the models' strengths and weaknesses were missing, as was information on how parties expect the policies and measures they have implemented to result in the reported "with measures" projections.

Policies and measures at the national level (Article 4.1(b), 4.1(d), 4.1(f), and 4.2(a) and (b))[59]

Parties are required to formulate and implement national programmes containing measures to mitigate climate change, covering both emissions and removals by sinks. A starting point for almost all countries has been the establishment of a national climate change committee or unit, whose membership includes representatives of the principal ministries and agencies involved. In some cases, the committee oversees preparation of and amendments to a national climate change action plan, which is later approved by all ministries and parliament. These action plans usually contain national and/or sectoral targets of some variety, together with a prescribed set of measures. Although not always the case, ideally, parliamentary approval of plans is also accompanied by the approval of funds required for implementation of the prescribed measures. National communications contain descriptions of processes in place and policies and measures that are being implemented, agreed on or planned, with varying degrees of detail on status of implementation. In keeping with the guidelines for communicating information, national communications have included descriptions of all actions that have an impact on emissions reductions and sink enhancement. Most of these do not have as a primary objective the limitation of greenhouse gas emissions, but are part of other sectoral plans, for example on energy, forestry, or waste management. The sectoral discussion that follows does not attempt to provide an exhaustive discussion of implementation of policies and measures, as this would require a full volume in itself. Instead, each section provides a short description of the salient policies and measures being implemented, followed by a short qualitative assessment of the key features of policy implementation.

Energy sector plans[60] are of central importance to countries' climate change strategies, mainly because this sector is responsible for the largest share of greenhouse gas emissions, most of which are carbon dioxide. For example, in Annex I parties in 1995, fuel combustion contributed to 95 per cent of CO_2 emissions and 26 per cent of N_2O emissions. The energy and transformation industries alone contributed to 36 per cent of these CO_2 emissions. Countries have different profiles of measures implemented in the electricity generation sector, which depend, *inter alia*, on the countries' sources of energy supply, technological options used for electricity generation, market structure in electricity production and distribution and historical developments in each country's energy sector.[61] Countries with a significant percentage of primary energy supply from nuclear or hydroelectric power have lower greenhouse gas emissions than would otherwise be the case, but also have more limited options for reducing these emissions. In several countries, the political decisions on how to replace power from existing nuclear plants as these are decommissioned will be of central importance to those countries' future emission paths.

The energy efficiency of fossil-fuelled power plants may be improved by replacing old plants with newer, more efficient, technologies,[62] while existing plants may also be upgraded, and losses in transmission and distribution may be reduced.[63] Efficiency gains are also being achieved through the promotion of combined heat and power plants, including through the provision of guaranteed prices for small producers. Apart from improving energy efficiency, emissions may be reduced by measures that encourage shifts to less polluting sources of electricity generation. These types of measure include, for example, favouring the construction of new gas-fired power plants over more polluting coal-fired plants and the removal of subsidies to coal. Other methods of mitigation include policies such as the building of principles of demand-side management and integrated resource planning into legislation and electricity tariff structures. There are a few examples of pioneering initiatives on the sale of "green" electricity. Only a handful of countries have introduced energy or CO_2 taxes.[64] There has been little coordination among countries on the levels of these taxes, however, and exemptions are often granted to energy-intensive industries in order to preserve their international trade competitiveness.[65]

Against this background of policy implementation, there are two critically important patterns of reform in energy markets that may result in further energy efficiency and fuel switching. The first, observed in varying degrees in almost all Annex I parties, is a pattern of energy market reform. While some countries are mainly liberalizing energy prices, others plan to or have undertaken major changes to privatize and deregulate electricity and gas markets, including production, transmission, and distribution. These changes, which involve the removal of subsidies to fossil fuel production, will act to promote energy efficiency and a switch from coal to gas, provided prices of the latter remain low. Lower energy prices may, however, lead to increased demand, and thus theoretically the overall impact on greenhouse gas emissions is ambiguous. A second important structural change is the opening up of electricity markets to foreign suppliers. While this process of liberalization is still in its early stages, ultimately the impact on national patterns of electricity production, and therefore national greenhouse gas emissions, may be very significant.[66]

Measures to promote renewable energy include pilot or demonstration projects, tax exemptions, direct subsidies for investment in renewable sources, a minimum quota for the purchase of renewable energy by utilities, targets, improving access to grids, and research and development. The percentage of electricity generated with renewable sources remains low, except for some countries that have significant hydroelectric power, although in these countries the potential for expansion of hydroelectric power is limited. With a few exceptions, without policy intervention, most forms of renewable energy are not competitive at prevailing oil and gas prices.

Energy use in the industrial sectors of Annex I parties is an important source of CO_2 (20 per cent in 1995), as are the residential, commercial, and institutional sectors (15 per cent in 1995). These sectors together emitted 14 per cent of total 1995 N_2O emissions. Industrial sector measures aim both to lower the energy intensity of industry as well as improve the energy efficiency of industrial buildings. Voluntary agreements with industry are a popular policy choice, possibly because of fears of damaging international trade competitiveness. Several countries have reported positive mid-term results on the effectiveness of these programmes. A few countries have also carried out energy audits of firms. The improved energy efficiency of residential and commercial buildings is targeted by a range of measures, including building energy codes; insulation laws; renovation requirements linked to energy efficiency together with support to do so; new buildings energy rating schemes; and energy efficiency targets for buildings. Minimum energy performance standards for domestic appliances are widespread, as are labelling requirements for domestic and other appliances. Some countries have introduced mandatory standards for water boilers, and several have realized major gains through district heating.

In 1995, fuel combustion in the transport sector was responsible for some 24 per cent of CO_2 emissions and 12 per cent of N_2O emissions, emissions that have grown rapidly, by 7 per cent, between 1990 and 1995.[67] All countries expect this growth to continue, with expected rates especially high in EITs. Countries' transport strategies and plans generally do not aim directly to mitigate climate change, but rather to reduce local air pollutants, reduce traffic and congestion, improve safety, and improve public transport. Many of the measures in these plans have a direct impact on reduction of greenhouse gas emissions, although a few (such as improvement of road networks) may in fact encourage higher emissions. Targets and standards aim to increase vehicle fuel efficiency, as do taxes on fuel and on the purchase of vehicles. Other transport sector policies include parking management, introduction of speed limits, improvement of driving practices, promotion of cycling, carpooling and car-sharing, the strengthening and improvement in energy efficiency of public transport networks, and encouraging combined road and rail transport. While there are initiatives in both the public and private sectors to conduct research into or provide support for alternatives, such as biofuels, hydrogen, and electric cars, high expected growth in this sector's greenhouse gas emissions is likely to constitute a major challenge to Annex I parties in meeting their protocol commitments.

Industrial processes result in the emission of only a small percentage of CO_2 but of nearly 25 per cent of Annex I party N_2O (mainly from adipic acid and nylon production). Emissions also occur of HFCs (from refrigerators, aerosol propellants, and fire fighting agents), PFCs (during aluminum production), and SF_6 (from the manufacture of electrical equipment). Efforts to curb these emissions largely involve voluntary agreements with industry, although air quality laws in a few countries are also pertinent.

Agricultural activities lead to substantial emissions of methane in Annex I parties (28 per cent of total emissions of this gas in 1995) and of nitrous oxide (45 per cent). Methane emissions in this sector occur from enteric fermentation in animals, and are largely a function of the size of herds. Short of reducing numbers, only limited gains may be achieved, by varying diet, grazing habits, and storage of slurries. Reductions in farming subsidies and reforms under the EU's Common Agricultural Policy have resulted in declining size of herds, which has in turn led to lower emissions. Emissions of N_2O from agriculture occur from the use of nitrogen fertilizers, and have been declining in many Annex I parties, as practices in fertilizer use are improved.

Methane emissions from waste accounted for 28 per cent of total emissions of this gas in 1995 in Annex I parties. Waste management plans include traditional policies such as incineration, recycling schemes, waste separation, composting and measures to reduce waste volume (such as landfill taxes). Less frequent are efforts to generate electricity from flaring of methane collected from landfills or from the combustion of waste. Although these measures have succeeded in lowering emissions in some countries, between 1990 and 1995 they increased by 6 per cent.

Significant amounts of methane are also emitted from coal mining and the production and transportation of natural gas (35 per cent of total Annex I party emissions of this gas in 1995). A reduction in coal production in some countries has led to a decline in these emissions, as has replacement of old gas distribution systems with new low leakage systems. While there has been a decrease of 8 per cent of these emissions in Annex I parties overall between 1990 and 1995, the gas networks in EITs still have very high leakage rates.[68] Investment in improving these networks could lead to substantial reductions in emissions.

Most countries have forestry plans, of which some component measures result in the increase or preservation of carbon sequestration capacity. Forestry management plans typically promote sustainable timber management, pest control and the prevention of fires. Afforestation is also promoted through regulations, subsidies, and tax incentives. Countries with large forested areas, in particular those with a strong tradition in silviculture, tend to exhibit the greatest sequestration.[69] There are, however, significant uncertainties in the science of carbon sequestration, which varies over time with the age of trees and forest composition. These factors could mean that parties that rely heavily on sequestration in order to meet targets could run into difficulties if sequestration rates cannot be maintained, if it turns out that less sequestration is occurring than originally estimated or if fires or pests decimate forests.

Adaptation (Article 4.1(e) and 4.4)

All Annex I parties have undertaken assessments of the expected impacts of climate change on their countries, although almost none have identified adaptation measures. In some cases, this has been a conscious policy decision, as is it is felt, for example, that regular practices in coastal zone management are adequate for now. A few Annex II countries have engaged in bilateral activities to build capacity to carry out such assessments in developing countries.[70] Countries also make contributions to the GEF, which disburses funds to developing countries for activities related to adaptation.[71] As the COP has recently provided additional guidance to the GEF to finance the implementation of adaptation response measures themselves, rather than only the studies of possible impacts to climate change and related adaptation policy options, disbursement of GEF funds on these activities is likely to increase in the future.

Research and systematic observation (Articles 4.1(g) and 5)

All Annex I countries have undertaken activities at the national level related to research, systematic observation, and the development of data archives related to the climate system. Typically, the national meteorology department or agency is very active, including in countries with economies in transition. Most of these countries also participate in several important international efforts on global observing systems[72] and on data analysis,[73] while a few Annex II parties are also carrying out bilateral projects in developing countries to improve research capacities and capabilities on climate-relevant issues. This section does not attempt to estimate the impact of the private sector investment and research, although these contributions are important.

Education, training, and public awareness (Articles 4.1 and 6)

Public awareness campaigns are important elements in all Annex I parties' strategies to combat climate change. These measures are attractive for their relatively low cost, political acceptability (especially when compared with alternative measures such as carbon taxes) and the potential win-win gains that may be obtained, for example, through motivating households to greater energy conservation. The fact that the mitigation effects and effectiveness of such measures are difficult to measure has not prevented a wide range of initiatives, ranging from broad-based campaigns targeting the general public to specific training programmes to encourage fuel-efficient driving practices and the introduction of modules on climate change in curricula.

Activities implemented jointly under the pilot phase (Article 4.2(a) and (b))

Although investor parties do not acquire any credits for activities implemented jointly under the pilot phase (AIJ), possibly because of the relevance of AIJ to the protocol's joint implementation and clean development mechanism, there has been growing interest in AIJ, evidenced by the increasing number of projects implemented. The most recent synthesis report prepared on the subject[74] indicates that 8 Annex II parties are investing in projects in 24 host countries, two thirds of which are EITs. While most projects are on renewable sources of energy and on improving energy efficiency, the projects on carbon sequestration are responsible for the greatest reported reduction of emissions.

Provision of finance assistance and the transfer of technology (Article 4.1(c), 4.3, 4.4 and 4.5)

The GEF has been designated as the entity entrusted with the operation of the financial mechanism of the convention. Accordingly, financial assistance under the convention is provided by disbursements by the GEF. Annex II parties have contributed funds first to the pilot phase of the GEF and then to the restructured GEF. Of the funds disbursed so far, some 39 per cent, or US$775 million, have been allocated specifically to projects on climate change.[75] Of these funds, the bulk has been allocated to projects promoting the adoption of renewable energy (some 36 per cent of total funds for climate change) and to projects for the removal of barriers to energy efficiency and energy conservation (27 per cent). A third priority area – on reducing the long-term costs of low greenhouse gas emitting technologies – has received 13 per cent, while enabling activities projects (mainly for the preparation of initial communications) have been granted 9 per cent of total amounts for climate change, and "short term response measures" have received 15 per cent. Annex II parties also provide financial assistance through bilateral channels and through other multilateral institutions. The global amounts of these contributions are difficult to estimate, as a broad range of projects could be relevant, but data on these are not readily available. Except for cases where bilateral assistance projects target-specific climate-relevant activities, such as reforestation or energy efficiency programmes, donor countries themselves have difficulties in estimating the full amounts that can count towards implementation of these commitments.

While a specific sub-article of the convention is devoted to Annex II party commitments on the transfer of technology, it is not easy to isolate the elements of soft and hard technology transfer that have occurred as a result of the financial assistance provided through these various channels. These difficulties are reflected in gaps in reporting in Annex II party communications. A further difficulty is that much technology transfer occurs by private sector activities on which governments do not automatically have good information. Annex II parties are also required to indicate in their communications what "new and additional" financial resources they have provided, including how these resources have been determined as being "new and additional." Annex II parties have experienced difficulties in doing so, both because of problems in identifying what the amounts are new and additional to, and also because of difficulties in proving that the contributions in question are indeed "new and additional."[76]

The specific needs and concerns of developing country parties arising from the adverse effects of climate change and/or the impact of the implementation of response measures (Article 4.8, 4.9 and 4.10)

There are major uncertainties in the science of the impacts of climate change on vulnerable countries, although the recent IPCC Special Report on the Regional Impacts of Climate Change has advanced understanding of possible impacts. The few non-Annex I party communications received to date generally also include sections on the expected impacts on climate change in their countries. Limited action has been undertaken by Annex II parties related to funding and the transfer of technology to meet the specific needs and concerns of vulnerable developing countries, mainly through the GEF, but also in the form of bilateral assistance. This action has already been described in the section above on adaptation.

Still greater uncertainties exist in assessing the impacts of climate change mitigation policies on other countries. While the studies and model simulations that have been carried out so far have identified possible effects on various economic variables in other countries[77] resulting from mitigation policies and measures, the magnitude of impacts is not known, not least because the overall impacts are the net result of several changes that act in opposite directions. Work is already underway by Working Group III of the IPCC on a chapter focusing specifically on this subject in the upcoming Third Assessment Report (TAR). Parallel to this effort, however, negotiations will continue according to a two-year programme of work adopted by the COP at its fourth session in Buenos Aires. The programme aims first at filling gaps in information and knowledge on the impacts of climate change and of the implementation of response measures, and then on identifying appropriate actions.

Non-Annex I parties

Article 4.7 states that the "extent to which developing country Parties will effectively implement their commitments under the Convention will depend on the effective implementation by developed country Parties of their commitments under the Convention related to financial resources and transfer of technology." The most important commitment of non-Annex I parties is the periodic communication of information related to the implementation, for which guidelines have been developed. This requirement is linked to some of their other obligations, since preparation of the communications subsumes some of these other commitments, for example, the publication of inventories of national greenhouse gas emissions as well as some of the necessary related studies, such as on the expected impacts of climate change. Implementation of these commitments is contingent on receipt of the necessary funding through the convention's financial mechanism.

The submission of initial communications from non-Annex I parties has been slower than originally expected, in part as a result of the lengthy process of preparation of project documents for funding approval and delays in receipt of funding necessary for their preparation. By the end of 1999, only 23 had been received by the secretariat. The principal focus of these communications has been the section on inventories of national greenhouse gas emissions. Most communications also describe national efforts to promote education, training, and public awareness related to climate change, on research and systematic observation and on the expected impacts of climate change, a few also advancing possible adaptation measures. Descriptions vary of actions undertaken to develop and implement programmes to mitigate climate change. In a limited number of cases, communications provide information on technology needs, although a separate process for providing this information to the secretariat exists. At its fifth session, the COP reviewed a first compilation and synthesis report of available communications, and concluded that, in view of problems encountered in preparing communications (for example, quality and availability of data, emission factors, and methodologies), national capacities for reporting in non-Annex I parties should be enhanced, and that reporting parties are taking measures to address climate change and its adverse impacts.

NGO involvement and participation in the process

The complexity of the negotiating blocs that delegations have formed in the climate change process is reflected in the NGOs[78] that participate in the process. At least four distinct groups of NGO actors can be identified in the climate change negotiations,[79] each with differing positions and contributions. Local-level authorities promote networks to combat climate change at the local and municipal level; in some countries, these groups are also entrusted with implementation of national climate change goals. "Green" NGOs promote climate-friendly action in a range of different ways. There is a strong representation of other business interests to whom climate change mitigation may be detrimental, principally the fossil fuel industry and electricity utilities. Sustainable business industry is also represented, and regroups the interests of firms that seek to develop climate friendly technologies on a commercial basis. The NGO community has been actively involved in the climate change process since the earliest meetings on climate change. The discussion below does not seek to identify the impact of individual groups, but explores the ways in which NGOs have contributed to the process.

At the international level, NGOs play an important role during the negotiations themselves. The convention allows any NGO "qualified in matters covered by the Convention, and which has informed the secretariat of its wish to be represented at a session of the Conference of the Parties as an observer, may be so admitted unless at least one third of the Parties present object." The UNFCCC secretariat has the role of ascertaining whether an organization applying for observer status meets the criteria[80] of having activities of relevance to the convention and of being classified as "not-for-profit."

According to Draft Rule 7 of the draft rules of procedure that have been provisionally applied thus far, "[s]uch observers may, upon invitation of the President [of the COP], participate without the right to vote in the proceedings of any session in matters of direct concern to the body or agency they represent, unless at least one third of the Parties present at that session object."[81] While the draft rules of procedure state that meetings of the COP shall be held in public while those of the subsidiary bodies shall be held in private unless the COP decides otherwise, in practice, the meetings of the COP and of subsidiary bodies have been open to the participation of all duly accredited observers. Meetings are typically comprised of both public and closed meetings. Up until the fourth session of the COP, the practice has been followed of restricting this representation and participation to public (or open) plenary meetings, while informal consultations have been open only to delegations of parties.

A separate but related question is that of "access to the floor" during public meetings, which may be viewed as comprising two elements. Official participants to UN conferences are recognized as such by a "nameplate" or "flag," which is placed in front of their assigned seat and which, when raised, indicates the desire to make an intervention. A nameplate also entitles the participant to receive a copy of all official documentation introduced, which is distributed by the conference officer.[82] At the first COP, the practice was adopted of not allowing NGOs an individual seat on the floor (and nameplate), but periodically inviting NGOs to make general statements at plenary meetings, but without permitting interventions at will during discussion on specific agenda items. The Bureau of the COP[83] decided that these procedures may be altered at the discretion of the chairperson of the body in question. In practice, exceptions have been made at some sessions of the subsidiary bodies, through the provision of seats (with nameplates) to representatives from the NGO community, and permission to make interventions on points under specific agenda items. A decision of the COP at its fourth session has opened up informal meetings (or "contact group" meetings) to attendance by representatives of NGOs and intergovernmental organizations, providing there is no objection by the presiding officers of the convention bodies, by the presiding officers of the informal meetings, or by at least one third of the parties present. This constitutes a significant step forward to the opening up of the negotiation process, which does not exist in most other UN negotiations where major economic interests are at stake.

At official climate change negotiations, NGOs also carry out important lobbying functions "in the corridors," through the distribution of position papers, circulation of information, reporting on discussions in different meetings and the preparation of analysis and reports. Outside official negotiations, the larger "international" NGOs in particular carry out lobbying activities and campaigns.

At the national level, the convention specifically requires parties to promote and facilitate public participation in addressing climate change, which is done in a variety of ways directly involving NGOs, aside from public awareness campaigns. Several countries include NGOs in their national committees on climate change. Input has also been solicited from the general public and/or NGOs on the national climate change strategy or on the national communication itself. Most in-depth reviews of Annex I party communications include meetings of the in-depth review team with representatives of different NGO constituencies. A few countries have even made efforts to include, and to fund the participation of, representatives of NGOs on their national delegations to climate change negotiations.

But most action at the national level is taken by the NGOs themselves. Lobbying action (both advocating the mitigation of climate change and, in the case of those supporting fossil fuel interests, warning against the impacts of signing stringent climate change treaties!) comprises an important part of many NGOs' national level activities. In several Annex I countries, jurisdiction for implementing mitigation policies in several subsectors falls to local government. Perhaps most important at the national level is the role played by many NGOs in public education and information dissemination through public awareness campaigns.

Compliance: Resolution of questions regarding implementation and the settlement of disputes

Compliance is often described as a cooperative means of law enforcement. Non-compliance can be seen not as a "breach of a treaty" but in a less adjudicating way that acknowledges that a party to an agreement may not be in wilful non-compliance but may lack the ability to comply. In this regard, one needs to distinguish between implementation and compliance. As used by Edith Brown Weiss, "implementation" refers to the legislation, regulations, and other steps required to implement an agreement, whereas compliance is a matter of judgment that measures whether the obligations of the agreement have been met through a change in a state's behaviour in an effort to comply.[84] Thus, an implementation mechanism becomes an integral part of the whole compliance system: reporting and review is the first step in the process. Communications pursuant to Article 12, as well as the in-depth reviews, would provide crucial information to an Article 13 mechanism established under the convention. The in-depth reviews serve to build confidence in the implementation process, and, although they do not directly examine compliance issues, they have the potential to enhance a party's compliance by encouraging it to undertake the necessary measures on a domestic level to implement the agreement. Moreover, parties are keenly aware that their communications and the reports of the in-depth reviews are in the public domain. Thus, this information is available not only to the Conference of the Parties and observer states, but to, *inter alia*, NGOs and the media. In treaties and conventions in which many of the commitments are perceived to be of a relatively "soft" nature, such reports and reviews may have less import. However, in a convention such as the one on climate change, which now has a protocol containing legally binding commitments, such information becomes vital. It ensures that the COP and its subsidiary bodies, including any non-compliance regime, have the most up-to-date information in order to review overall individual implementation of the convention and its related legal instruments.

Parties to the UNFCCC have been discussing for more than five years the possibility of establishing a "dispute resolution/non-compliance" mechanism in light of the convention's Article 13. Article 13 is a one-sentence mandate that was written during the negotiations leading to the adoption in May 1992 of the text of the convention by delegates and secretariat officials, in an effort not to lose the opportunity to provide the convention with the possibility of establishing such a mechanism at a later stage. Prior to the drafting of this provision, Elizabeth Dowdeswell and Ambassador Robert F. Van Lierop, co-chairs of Working Group II,[85] proposed the creation of a dispute resolution process. Such a process was envisaged as without prejudice and complementary to Article 14, the traditional dispute settlement procedure laid down in the convention. Article 14 provides for a "hierarchy of procedures"[86] designed to respond to bilateral disputes or disputes between several parties. Under that article, should parties fail to settle their disputes through negotiation or other peaceful means, they may make avail of judicial settlement through the International Court of Justice (ICJ), or arbitration or conciliation under the auspices of the Climate Change Convention.

This proposal recognized that, with regard to international environmental treaties, traditional dispute-settlement procedures are rarely, if ever, invoked by parties. In the climate change context, given the global nature of greenhouse gas emissions and the difficulty of pointing the "finger of blame" at one particular party, the working group considered that a non-adversarial and non-confrontational approach was warranted. Many negotiators reasoned that dispute avoidance was preferable to dispute settlement in a climate change regime, particularly since incidents of non-compliance by one or more parties have an effect on all parties to the convention. This reality augured for a "forward-looking" approach to compliance, rather than looking at past behaviour of parties in order to assess blame and impose sanctions. In this regard, many countries viewed the Implementation Committee of the Montreal Protocol on Substances that Deplete the Ozone Layer and the dispute settlement panels of the General Agreement on Tariffs and Trade (GATT)[87] as models for climate change. However, many reluctant delegates were quick to point out that the GATT dispute-settlement mechanisms were too "hard" and quasi-judicial for the climate change regime and that the non-compliance mechanism in the Montreal Protocol was not "soft" enough. In fact, some delegates were averse to the use of language in the convention that even referred to the concept of non-compliance. Because of time constraints, negotiators were unable to agree on a mechanism; the result is a single sentence in Article 13: "The conference of the Parties shall, at its first session, consider the establishment of a multilateral consultative process, available to Parties on their request, for the resolution of questions regarding the implementation of the Convention." Those countries that were "soft" on compliance were appeased by the wording that the envisioned process was "multilateral" and "consultative," "available to Parties on their request [only]," and that it was possibly precluded from addressing questions of interpretation. Conversely, those countries wishing to establish a strong non-compliance mechanism were appeased by the fact that this one-sentence mandate was sufficiently vague to lend itself to broad interpretation in the future.

During the negotiations of the ad hoc working group on Article 13 (AG13), as the necessary elements of a compliance/dispute resolution mechanism in the climate change context were being debated, many contended, particularly NGOs, that the following elements seemed indispensable:

– As the COP is the supreme body of the convention and is mandated to keep under regular review the implementation of the convention and to make the decisions necessary to promote effective implementation, all final decisions regarding compliance would rest with it.

- The convention's secretariat would serve as the interface for coordinating all bodies involved in implementation. (It should be noted that in the Montreal Protocol, the secretariat is empowered to initiate a non-compliance procedure.)
- Provision should be made for the possible establishment of a standing committee to handle non-compliance issues (other than the SBI) with a limited membership that has an equitable geographical representation and the possible representation of members in their individual capacities.
- The process should be transparent and the standing committee should have access to information from many sources. It should have the power to request information from parties and to send visiting missions to member states to assess information. It should have the power to make specific recommendations to the COP on measures to assist parties in non-compliance.
- The compliance mechanism should provide that parties shall have standing to trigger the process *vis-à-vis* their own or another party's compliance.[88]

In 1996, AG13 asked parties to respond to a questionnaire relating to the establishment of a multilateral consultative process (MCP). A synthesis of their responses was drafted and circulated to parties by the UNFCCC secretariat, which articulated a number of difficult questions, including: could the process be invoked by entities other than parties, for example, the secretariat, subsidiary bodies of the convention, or NGOs? Should the process be allowed to interpret the provisions of the convention? How would such a process relate to a protocol to the convention? What would be the relationship of such a process to other provisions of the convention, particularly, settlement of disputes (Article 14)? Should the process be vested with formal decision-making powers or make non-binding recommendations? How would the phrase in Article 13, "available to Parties on their request," restrict standing?[89]

The AG13 allowed NGOs to contribute actively to its deliberations by responding to the questionnaire and by providing their views on issues raised in the discussions held during its sessions and even serving on panel discussions in this regard. This involvement reflects the great interest that NGOs have shown in the non-compliance aspects of the UNFCCC, as well as the willingness of parties to listen to their views (certainly with regard to this issue) in a manner other than behind the scenes. Consequently, during most of the AG13 deliberations, NGOs had the opportunity to contribute while at the same time safeguarding parties' sovereign role in the intergovernmental negotiations. During 1997, the

AG13 moved forward from the stage of organizing its work and review-ing the precedents, which occupied its first 12 months, to assessing what type of a MCP would be appropriate for the UNFCCC and how it might be designed.

In its progress report to the COP at its third session, held in Kyoto, Japan, the group agreed that the MCP should be advisory rather than supervisory in nature; and secondly, there was agreement that AG13 should not complete its work until after COP3. It was thought imperative by the AG13 that members need to know the approach to issues of com-pliance and any multilateral consultative process under the protocol before it could take final decisions about their own approach to an MCP for the convention. The group had moved from unfocused general debate to the consideration of a compilation text that set out in a precise way the functions and procedures of a possible MCP.

The design of AG13 was finally completed and adopted by the COP, with, however, several square brackets, at its fourth session held in Buenos Aires, Argentina, in November 1998. The final design is entirely advisory, rather than supervisory, and allows for its terms of reference to be amended by the COP "to take into account any amendment to the Convention, decisions by the COP or experience gained with the working of the process." [90] Two central issues remained outstanding, with options retained under square brackets. First, the size of the Standing Multi-lateral Consultative Committee established under the MCP could consist of 10, 15, or 25 members. Secondly, there was no agreement on the com-position of the MCC. On the one hand, members may be designated based on equitable geographical distribution and the principle of rotation or, on the other hand, with one half to be designated by Annex I parties and one half to be designated by non-Annex I parties. Outgoing members may be reappointed for one immediate consecutive term. The chair-persons of the subsidiary bodies of the convention may participate in the meetings of the committee as observers. [91]

The debate over this text is most certainly one between Annex I and non-Annex I parties, with the latter wishing to ensure equitable and geographical representation on the committee. In addition, increasing the number of members on the committee ensures them greater represen-tation, although its greater size may impede upon the progress of the work of the committee. Some parties objected to the phrase equitable geographical representation stating that it was not a well-established practice and was not applicable in this context, despite the fact that the concept of equitable geographical distribution was particularly important in the negotiations on the rules of procedure of the convention. In its final report, the AG13 noted that the representative of the G77 and China speaking on behalf of the group stated that the principle of equitable geographical representation is a "well-established practice of the United Nations." Until these issues are resolved, in spite of their advisory nature, the terms of reference have no legal import *vis-à-vis* the convention, and cannot become operational. These outstanding issues were not resolved at the fifth session of the COP, thus still depriving the UNFCCC of a non-compliance mechanism.

Article 18 of the protocol, however, anticipates the need to develop rules, procedures, and mechanisms capable of imposing binding consequences on a party in non-compliance. It is, therefore, assumed that these will be compulsory in their jurisdiction, binding in their outcome, and enforceable.[92] It is widely acknowledged that the overall credibility of the protocol, with its binding commitments for Annex I parties, depends critically on a more "robust" compliance mechanism. Many parties now perceive the need to back the protocol's binding targets with an enforcement mechanism that is mandatory and that would impose both automatic and discretionary penalties. This change from the AG13 approach may be due to a growing perception that a "soft" mechanism may not be sufficient for the protocol, and that states, "in their role as market actors, will weigh the costs and benefits of compliance, and tend to choose to comply only when the costs of non-compliance are made high through tough enforcement."[93]

Despite the inherent weaknesses of the MCP adopted by AG13, it is thought that it will still prove useful for, *inter alia*, the following reasons: any party may address the Standing Committee with a question regarding the implementation of the convention by another party. Once a question is raised, the committee may initiate consultations with the party concerned. This aspect seems to have the "flavour of compulsory jurisdiction" since the party could not reject this process. In addition, the committee has the authority to make specific recommendations to the COP on measures to assist or bring about compliance by a party. This allows the committee to form a preliminary conclusion as to whether or not a party is in compliance, and to make an initial assessment of why a party is failing to comply. The MCP may also clarify and resolve questions and reach conclusions that include measures it deems suitable to be taken by the party concerned to encourage effective implementation of the convention. There is no indication that the COP needs to review or approve these conclusions. The publication of a report in this regard could prove useful in bringing public and diplomatic pressure to bear on a party to comply.[94]

Before the Kyoto Protocol enters into force, the MCP may have a role to play in monitoring implementation of mechanisms that are piloted during this interim period. Once in force, the parties to the protocol may decide, given the close institutional relationship between the two treaties, that the MCP could perform the non-compliance functions developed under Article 18 of the protocol. Both mechanisms could run in parallel as long as the MCP is operated without prejudice to the mechanism established by Article 18. One could envisage a single committee operating both a facilitative MCP under the convention and a stronger non-compliance procedure under the protocol.

The question arises as to whether the protocol needs a weak MCP that will serve no greater role than as a "help line" when the protocol requires parties to establish "appropriate and effective procedures and mechanisms to address cases of non-compliance." The establishment of such "procedures and mechanisms" to address non-compliance could render the need for an MCP redundant. It may be more sensible and effective for the MOP to concentrate on establishing a strong and well-functioning non-compliance mechanism under Article 17 of the protocol, rather than establishing both, thereby possibly blurring the lines between an MCP and a non-compliance mechanism. This may be particularly true now that parties have agreed to establish an MCP under the convention. As the convention MCP is merely advisory, parties to the protocol may turn to it for problems of an advisory nature and could revert to the mechanism envisaged under Article 17 of the protocol for more serious transgressions and breaches of non-compliance. This approach would be feasible given that all parties to the protocol must be parties to the convention.

However, given that not all parties to the convention will necessarily be parties to the protocol, the convention MCP would ensure that at least all parties to the convention have recourse thereto. Parties to the convention may wish to consider the development of a mechanism for the COP and the MOP that would involve all parties and that would consist of an amalgamated body designed both to deal with the "resolution of questions" and with cases of non-compliance, both in the convention and in the protocol. Parties to the convention have always argued for creating the least amount of institutions as feasible under the convention and, in that spirit, such an amalgamation might prove more effective; more democratic and universal in participation and scope; and less costly.

Given that developed country parties have finally agreed to legally binding commitments, an effective monitoring and compliance mechanism would seem warranted. In fact, Article 16 of the Kyoto Protocol provides that the Conference of the Parties serving as the Meeting of the Parties (COP/MOP) shall, as soon as practicable, consider the application to this protocol of, and modify as appropriate, the multilateral consultative process referred to in Article 13 of the convention, in the light of any relevant decisions that may be taken by the Conference of the Parties.

Any multilateral consultative process that may be applied to this protocol shall operate without prejudice to the procedures and mechanisms established in accordance with Article 17.

Article 17 provides that the COP/MOP "at its first session, approve appropriate and effective procedures and mechanisms to determine and to address cases of non-compliance with the provisions of this Protocol, including through the development of an indicative list of consequences, taking into account the cause, type, degree and frequency of non-compliance. Any procedures and mechanisms under this Article entailing binding consequences shall be adopted by means of an amendment to this Protocol." The protocol does not address how this article will relate to a possible multilateral consultative process under Article 16 of the protocol. Moreover, it is not clear how the protocol MCP would operate in conjunction with the MCP that has been adopted for the convention. It seems that with the advent of the protocol, the AG13 decided for a weaker mechanism, one that might inevitably be subsumed or overtaken by the processes, procedures, and mechanisms established under the protocol. In any case, it was not likely that the mechanism would be operational before the year 2000 and it was now not anticipated that the protocol would enter into force then.

The COP decided in Kyoto that the discussions regarding the design of a non-compliance mechanism under the protocol would not be assigned to an ad hoc working group such as those created for AG13 and the Berlin Mandate (AGBM). Many parties have criticized AG13 for carrying out its work in what they perceive as isolation without taking into consideration the political input of the SBI. Many seemed threatened by too many lawyers possibly agreeing to the design of a strong process that would not be reflective of the political realities relating to stronger commitments. Consequently, the COP decided that the work in this regard would be undertaken under the aegis of the SBI. This will result in fuller participation by parties but it may weaken the eventual outcome of the design by possibly reducing the scope of the mechanism to that of a more political, rather than monitoring and non-compliance body. In addition, given the heavy workload of the SBI leading up to the entry into force of the protocol, non-compliance may lose its sense of importance and expediency as it may be treated as one of many programme activities to be tackled by the SBI. Further, the consultative group of experts on non-Annex I parties set up at the fifth session of the COP may provide a forum for raising many of the issues that might have been brought to the MCP, had the latter been operational.

But further discussions on the MCP have been relegated to the background by the growing prominence of negotiations on a compliance regime under the protocol. A Joint Working Group on Compliance was set up at the fourth session of the COP, with the aim of developing a compliance system by its sixth session. Delegates are strongly divided on many issues, some of which are only likely to be resolved in tandem with the fleshing out of the operational details of the flexibility mechanisms, the completion date for which has also been set at the sixth COP. The range of compliance issues on the negotiating table can be broadly grouped into "institutional" questions, related to the structure of any compliance and/or enforcement bodies to be set up under the protocol, and on the consequences of non-compliance.

Conclusions

The final text of the UNFCCC agreed upon in 1992 is typical of many of the Rio agreements, where a highly politicized discussion led to weakened texts. Unlike many of the other sustainable development issues, however, climate change negotiations have since advanced at an accelerated pace. Some ten years after the General Assembly launched negotiations on climate change, major steps have been taken to develop a global legally binding agreement to limit a broad range of greenhouse gases. This progress represents a singular achievement in light of the fact that the climate change question confronts some of the thorniest issues that were on the table at Rio, and which proved to be major stumbling blocks during that process, namely consumption patterns, the transfer of technology, investment required for sustainable development, and conflicts between international trade and environmental protection.

The indicators of implementation that are currently available – greenhouse gas emissions inventory data up to 1995 and countries' own estimates of their emissions in 2000 and beyond – suggest that only about five Annex II countries will succeed in meeting the convention's weak "aim" of returning greenhouse gas emissions in 2000 to their 1990 levels. As EITs emerge from recession, emissions in almost all Annex I countries will continue to grow to levels well above those of 1990. While there is growing national awareness of climate change issues, only a few policies and measures in a few countries are being introduced specifically with the objective of mitigating climate change.

The reporting and review mechanism developed to monitor implementation of Annex I party commitments has stopped short of discussing an individual country's implementation records. Although in-depth reviews have identified the cases where Annex I parties are not likely to meet the convention "aim," only very limited remedial action has been taken by the convention bodies. This may in part be a result of the fact that no specific procedures exist for cases of non-compliance and that negotiations have only just been completed on a multilateral consultative process for the resolution of questions regarding implementation.

The legally binding commitments under the protocol will shift the focus away from the question of whether or not Annex I parties are implementing mitigation measures and from the results of national greenhouse gas projections, towards the need for developing a structure for more detailed reporting, verification of compliance, and for designing non-compliance measures. While implementation of the protocol will require Annex I parties to adopt domestic mitigation measures, the agreement also allows these parties to achieve their targets through actions abroad, via the three "flexibility mechanisms" of joint implementation, the international trade of emission permits and the clean development mechanism. The operational details of these mechanisms have yet to be negotiated, agreement on which is likely to be a precondition for many countries to sign and ratify the protocol. In defining the mechanisms, the protocol explicitly acknowledges the need for proper arrangements for reporting, monitoring, and verification of these flexibility mechanisms.[95] The protocol also calls for the development of "appropriate and effective procedures and mechanisms to address cases of non-compliance," including "an indicative list of consequences," as well as the possible application of the multilateral consultative process referred to in Article 13 of the convention. While the process for review of information, defined in Article 8 of the protocol, is broadly modelled on the one developed under the convention, the protocol has the additional requirement that the COP/MOP consider any "questions of implementation" that may be identified through the review process. For these reasons, the review of implementation under the protocol is likely to differ significantly from the process that has been carried out so far.

As the AG13 mechanism is supervisory, some parties may find it to be more a "help-desk" than a mechanism with real teeth to combat non-compliance. A non-confrontational and non-adversarial approach may nevertheless build confidence among parties and facilitate their usage of the mechanism. This is particularly important given that the traditional dispute settlement mechanisms established in environmental conventions have rarely been invoked. Negotiators are increasingly aware, however, that the credibility and effectiveness of the protocol will require a more "robust" mechanism not only to encourage parties to comply but also to respond effectively to their potential non-compliance. The successful negotiation of a compliance system is linked to an agreement on the operational details of the protocol's flexibility mechanisms, particularly as the latter will help to define more fully the required "level of effort," and associated economic costs, for parties to comply with the protocol targets.

Notes

1. United Nations Framework Convention on Climate Change, 9 May 1992, 31 *International Legal Materials* (1992), p. 848.
2. This chapter does not review the negotiating history of the UNFCCC. A useful such discussion, although not of subsequent decisions of the subsidiary bodies and the COP, nor of the Kyoto Protocol, may be found in Daniel Bodansky, "The United Nations Framework Convention on Climate Change: A Commentary," 18 *The Yale Journal of International Law* (No. 2, Summer 1993).
3. The decision to convene UNCED and launch the related negotiating process was taken by the UNGA by its resolution 44/228.
4. See UNGA resolutions 43/53, 44/206, 44/207, and 45/212.
5. The UNGA decided to launch this process by its resolution 47/188 in December 1992.
6. The UNEP's Ad Hoc Working Group of Experts on Biological Diversity conducted preparatory work, and later its Ad Hoc Working Group of Technical and Legal Experts or Intergovernmental Negotiating Committee adopted the agreed text in Nairobi in May 1992.
7. For instance, Agenda 21 contains chapters on protection of the atmosphere, combating deforestation, protection of the oceans, as well as other sections that are relevant to climate change. Linkages exist between the Climate Change Convention and UNCCD, CBD, and the Montreal Protocol on Substances that Deplete the Ozone Layer. For a discussion of linkages between some of these agreements, see "Protecting our planet – securing our future," United Nations Environment Programme, United States Aeronautics and Space Administration (The World Bank, 1998).
8. States not party to the convention may only attend as observers during meetings of the Conference of the Parties and the Subsidiary Bodies (Articles 7.6 and 9). According to the draft rules of procedure (which are being provisionally applied, with the exception of Draft Rule 42 on "Voting"), "observers may, upon invitation of the President, participate without the right to vote in the proceedings of any session, unless at least one third of the Parties present at the session object."
9. This group of countries does not correspond to the definition of the UN or that of the UNDP of "developing countries."
10. The European Community is itself a party to the convention, and frequently presents an official position during negotiations.
11. JUSCANNZ is made up of Australia, Canada, Iceland, Japan, New Zealand, Norway, Switzerland, and the United States of America. Positions of these individual countries do not always coincide; nor do they present a single official position during negotiations. They do, however, meet as a group for closed informal consultations.
12. The UNFCCC has retained the UN practice of electing officers equally from the five regional groups, with the additional inclusion of one member from the small island developing states (see Rule 22, Draft Rules of Procedure of the Conference of the Parties and its Subsidiary Bodies, FCCC/CP/1996/2).
13. See "Climate Change 1995. The Science of Climate Change. Contribution of Working Group I to the Second Assessment Report of the Intergovernmental Panel on Climate Change," IPCC (1996).
14. See "Climate Change 1995. Impacts, Adaptation and Mitigation of Climate Change: Scientific-Technical Analyses. Contribution of Working Group II to the Second Assessment Report of the Intergovernmental Panel on Climate Change", IPCC (1996). See also "The Regional Impacts of Climate Change: An Assessment of Vulnerability. A Special Report of IPCC Working Group II," IPCC (1998).

15. The IPCC was established jointly by the World Meteorological Organization (WMO) and UNEP in 1988 to assess available scientific information on climate change, the environmental and socio-economic impacts of climate change, and to formulate response strategies.

16. Annex I parties may implement these polices and measures jointly.

17. Possible examples of such polices include subsidies to energy production and some agricultural practices.

18. While the convention explicitly states that Annex II parties shall provide financial resources to "developing countries," it does not define a list of countries, nor state whether they are those not included in Annex I, which has created some ambiguity as to which countries are eligible for funding.

19. Because of the transition process, all EITs exhibited drastic decreases in domestic consumption and output in 1990, which are reflected in correspondingly low greenhouse gas emissions in that year. The COP has granted the request made by five EITs to use a base year prior to 1990 to avoid having an "artificially" low reference.

20. The latter applies particularly to countries highly dependent on the production, consumption, and export of fossil fuels and energy-intensive products.

21. The analysis refers to decisions taken up until the fifth COP, November 1999.

22. This double 'trigger' is intended to ensure that contributions to the task of reducing emissions are significant without giving a veto to the United States (whose share of 1990 CO_2 emissions from Annex I parties is 36 per cent). The participation of the United States, however, is viewed as essential for the effective implementation of the protocol.

23. The guidelines for review (see Annex to decision 3/CP.4) define the objectives, methodology, and criteria for assessing conformity with relevant provisions and the effectiveness of provision of financial resources.

24. A Memorandum of Understanding between the GEF Council and the Conference of the Parties outlines the respective roles and responsibilities of the two institutions (see decision 12/CP.2 of the COP contained in FCCC/CP/1996/15/Add.1). An annex to this memorandum provides guidance on the determination of funding necessary and available for the implementation of the convention (see the annex to the report of the SBI at its fifth session, document FCCC/SBI/1997/6).

25. The COP has requested reports on implementation by Annex II parties of commitments regarding technology transfer based on information in national communications, on inventories of climate change environmentally sound technologies, on technology needs of developing countries, on technology information centres, on adaptation technologies, and on the terms of technology transfer.

26. See Article 4.2(a), 4.2(b), and 4.2(d).

27. See also Article 4.1(a) of the convention.

28. See Article 4.2(b) of the convention.

29. These guidelines also make recommendations on the additional elements on which only Annex II parties must report.

30. The reporting guidelines have been revised twice, at the second and fifth sessions of the COP. At the latter session, specific guidelines were also developed for reporting on global climate observing systems, for which developing countries may also be used on a voluntary basis by parties not included in Annex I.

31. The guidelines clearly play a critical role in any assessment of compliance and verification. Given the stronger commitments under the protocol, the verifiability of information communicated on implementation will be correspondingly more important.

32. The present section refers to the review process as implemented so far. At its fifth session, however, the COP defined a supplementary review process for a two-year trial

period starting in 2000 – "the technical review of greenhouse gas inventories." This is likely to provide valuable experience in developing the more rigorous reporting and assessment procedures that will be required by a credible Kyoto Protocol, refining rules and greenhouse gas emissions accounting criteria.

33. The Climate Action Network, a group of non-governmental organizations, periodically makes an alternative assessment of the Annex I parties' national plans for mitigating climate change.

34. See decision 7/CP.1 of the COP taken at its first session (FCCC/CP/1995/7/Add.1).

35. See Article 12 of the convention on "Communication of Information Related to Implementation."

36. There is some debate as to whether the "availability" of financial resources is the date of signature of GEF-funded projects for preparing initial communications, dates of disbursement of funds, or dates of receipt. This problem is further compounded by the fact that full amounts of financial resources are generally not released at the beginning of the project.

37. Non-Annex I parties preferred this term to "review" to reflect their weaker commitments and obligations.

38. In 1995, carbon dioxide accounted for 82 per cent of Annex I party aggregate greenhouse gas emissions.

39. A meeting of OECD countries in Toronto in 1988 resulted in several countries agreeing to adopt voluntary targets for the reduction of CO_2 emissions by 20 per cent in 2005 as compared to 1988 levels. This "Toronto" target or other reduction objective is often reflected in the country's national climate change strategy; in some cases, these targets are more stringent than the "aim" contained in Article 4.2 (a) and (b) of the convention.

40. Anthropogenic removals by sinks occur principally through carbon sequestration. While such removals of nitrous dioxide also occur in soil, there are large uncertainties on the extent of this phenomenon.

41. These ambiguities do not exist under the Kyoto Protocol, as it contains text explicitly defining how commitments are to be interpreted. It is interesting to note that the convention commitment to "communicate ... information related to implementation" has the counterpart language in the Kyoto Protocol to provide "information necessary to demonstrate compliance."

42. As at February 2000.

43. Authors' own extrapolations.

44. This phenomenon is largely the result of the recession in these countries affecting output and therefore also greenhouse gas emissions, a recession from which only a few of these countries are exhibiting signs of recovering.

45. For a technical discussion of some additional related data problems, see document FCCC/SBSTA/1998/7, "Methodological issues identified while processing second national communications: Greenhouse gas emissions," UNFCCC (1998).

46. The lags will vary considerably according to the type of measure. An energy tax can be expected to have a more immediate impact on emissions than a tax rebate for investment in more energy-efficient plant.

47. Baseline or "business as usual" projections estimate emission in the absence of additional action being taken. "With measures" projections or scenarios estimate emissions when a package of measures has been introduced. Projections also serve to communicate to the international community what the country expects its emissions path to be.

48. Examples of key variables in the macroeconomic models used to forecast carbon dioxide emissions in the energy sector include growth rates, world price of oil, and exchange

rates with the US dollar. Multiple "with measures" scenarios with a range of values of key variables or with different packages of measures help policy-makers assess outcomes in an uncertain world.

49. Examples of such political assumptions include decisions on future electricity supply through nuclear power generation or on the extent of future electricity trading between countries.

50. For example, during negotiations on future commitments, a "high" baseline projection may serve as a negotiating ploy to argue for a lower future commitment. A high "with measures" scenario suggests that a country is making considerable efforts to mitigate emissions.

51. These countries are Austria, Denmark, France, Germany, Luxembourg, the Netherlands, Switzerland, and the United Kingdom.

52. These countries are Denmark, France, Germany, Luxembourg, the Netherlands, Switzerland, and the United Kingdom.

53. For example, 23 of 36 Annex I parties submitted their first communications on time, and only eight their second communications. These documents have been up to one year late, and delays of six months are common (see documents FCCC/SB/1997/INF.1 and FCCC/SBI/1998/INF.1). The performance on submission of inventory data has been even less satisfactory.

54. See Article 2 of the convention.

55. A case in point might be commitments related to the transfer of technology by Annex II parties, although reporting problems are linked to difficulties in defining indicators of the implementation of commitments, as is discussed in the section on transfer technology below.

56. Parties were required to report on these gases for the first time in 1997. Gaps are largely the result of poor data availability.

57. Gaps in reporting arise from data gaps, lack of available methods, lack of capacity and expertise for using existing methods, and lack of funds for carrying out the required studies. See also "Greenhouse gas emission projections and estimates of the effects of measures: moving towards good practice," OECD Information Paper, ENV/EPOC(98)10, OECD (1998).

58. See also the section below on the provision of finance assistance and the transfer of technology.

59. This section is based principally on information from national communications, in-depth reviews and other UNFCCC secretariat documentation, relevant literature of the International Energy Agency and the Organization for Economic Co-operation and Development, and independent NGO evaluations of national plans for climate change mitigation.

60. Typically, these "energy sector plans" target energy use from electricity generation and fuel extraction and in the industrial, residential, commercial, and institutional sectors. Often, although not always, fuel combustion in the transport sector is targeted in a separate strategy.

61. Some countries have invested steadily in energy efficiency measures and energy conservation since the early 1980s as a result of energy security concerns arising from the oil price shocks. As a result, additional energy efficiency gains are generally more costly in these countries. While relatively cheap gains may be achieved in the countries that have not had this history of investment in energy efficiency, often significant initial capital outlays are nevertheless required, for example, for district heating systems.

62. For example combined cycle gas turbines and fluidized bed combustion technologies.

63. EITs expect to achieve significant gains in this manner.

64. These include Denmark, Finland, the Netherlands, Norway, and Sweden, while a law has been passed in Switzerland allowing the introduction of a CO_2 tax if other measures fail to achieve a specified 2010 reduction target.

65. Despite extensive negotiation, there has been no agreement in the EU on adopting a carbon tax. Nor has discussion on common actions between OECD countries resulted so far in agreement on any measures to be taken, although the dialogue and related studies have identified possible policy options for common action (see "Policies and Measures for Climate Change Mitigation: Compilation of executive summaries from studies on policies and measures for common action," OECD/IEA Annex I Expert Group on the UNFCCC (August 1997).

66. Significant trade flows in electricity occur between Nordic countries through NordPool, a Nordic electricity exchange, largely driven by the excess supply of cheaper electricity in Norway (mainly hydroelectric power) and Sweden (mainly hydroelectric and nuclear power). The EU is also developing an internal electricity market that will result in greater trade flows. In February 1999, the first phase came into effect involving the opening up of a minimum of 25 per cent of gas and electricity markets to competition from other EU producers. If countries increase their production of fossil fuel-based electricity for export purposes, this could significantly increase their greenhouse gas emissions, possibly threatening their ability to meet targets, while the converse is also true.

67. N_2O emissions have increased owing both to growth in the sector and to the introduction of catalytic converters.

68. Sixty-nine per cent of 1990 methane emission occurred from fugitive fuel in EITs, compared to 23 per cent in Annex II countries, mainly during the production and transportation of natural gas. This share was 56 per cent for the Czech Republic, 67 per cent for Estonia and Hungary, 40 per cent for Poland, 61 per cent for Romania, and 73 per cent for the Russian Federation.

69. Australia, Estonia, Finland, Ireland, Latvia, Lithuania, New Zealand, Norway, Russia, Slovenia, Spain, and Sweden exhibit the highest sequestration, in one case offsetting gross carbon dioxide emissions by 80 per cent. Figures for most other countries lie in the range of offsets of 2–10 per cent.

70. Notable examples are initiatives by the Netherlands, Japan, and the United States.

71. It is difficult to estimate the exact amounts of GEF funding that have been disbursed on adaptation-related activities. Only a few projects specifically target adaptation, while funding for these activities mostly occurs through projects for preparing initial communications, of which carrying out an assessment of the expected impacts of climate change is a small part.

72. These are the Global Climate Observing System, the Global Ocean Observing System, and the Global Terrestrial Observing System.

73. Noteworthy examples are the International Geosphere-Biosphere Programme and the World Climate Research Program.

74. See document FCCC/CP/1998/2.

75. All data related to funds disbursed by the GEF are derived from GEF reports as at September 1998.

76. ODA flows can serve as an indicator of additionality. However, ODA is not restricted to climate-change relevant projects and technology transfer. Further, ODA flows have declined in some countries in recent years simply because of national recession and budget constraints, without this being a direct reflection of spending on climate change projects.

77. For example, mitigation policies and measures may affect global and domestic prices of oil, coal, and natural gas, as well as the quantities produced and exported by different countries; domestic and global prices of energy-intensive goods, and related production

and trade patterns; domestic and foreign savings and investment patterns; national income in different countries; and exchange rates, and current account and trade balances.

78. The term NGOs is taken to refer to all organizations that are neither Party to the Convention, Observer States not Party to the Convention, or intergovernmental organizations. Some of these constituent organizations, such as local government authorities, would not normally refer to themselves as NGOs.

79. These four constituencies are those that are recognized by the UNFCCC secretariat in its management of NGO participation, and are subject to modification over time. Indeed, at the first meeting of the INC, only two constituencies were recognized – business and industry and environmental NGOs. Many other groups are, however, also active in the climate change process, for example, private sector financial institutions, academia and research institutes, parliamentary associations, labour unions, consumer unions, youth groups, religious associations etc.

80. The Intergovernmental Negotiating Committee (INC), the subsidiary body established by the UNGA to negotiate a convention on climate change, developed these criteria during its early meetings, but the possibility of extending participation to corporations has since been discussed.

81. See document FCCC/CP/1996/2.

82. Such documentation includes, for example, proposals made by the COP president or subsidiary body chairman of text for adoption. Generally, at climate change negotiations, extra copies of such documentation are placed at the back of the conference room, which also allows NGOs to obtain a copy.

83. The bureau of the COP is comprised of its president, seven vice-presidents, the chairmen of the subsidiary bodies and a rapporteur.

84. Edith Brown Weiss and Harold J. Jacobson, "Why Do States Comply with International Agreements," 1 *Human Dimensions* (1996).

85. The INC established two working groups: Working Group 1 on commitments and Working Group 2 on legal and institutional issues.

86. See J. Werksman, *Designing a Compliance System For the Climate Change Convention*, 27 October 1995 (Foundation for International Environmental Law and Development working paper, SOAS, University of London, UK).

87. During the negotiations of the text of the UNFCCC, from 1991 to 1992, the present "WTO Understanding on Rules and Procedures Governing the Settlement of Disputes" had not yet been established. The DSU strengthens the former GATT dispute settlement procedures and provides for establishing panels, at the request of members, to resolve disputes between members. These panels make recommendations in their panel reports to the Dispute Settlement Body (DSB) with regard to the course of action to be followed by a member in order to resolve a specific dispute. The DSB decides whether these recommendations should be implemented. A recommendation may be for the removal of the offending measure by a member. The DSB, in extreme cases, may administer sanctions (compensation, suspension of concessions, retaliation).

88. See J. Werksman, above n. 86, pp. 11–17.

89. See "Syntheses of responses to questionnaire on the establishment of a multilateral consultative process under Article 13," document FCCC/AG13/1996/1, UNFCCC, 1996.

90. See para. 14 of the terms of reference of the MCP, Annex to decision 10/CP.4 of the COP at its fourth session.

91. See para. 9 of the terms of reference of the MCP, Annex to decision 10/CP.4 of the COP at its fourth session.

92. See J. Werksman, *Responding to Non-compliance under the Climate Change Regime*, OECD Information Paper, ENV/EPOC(99)21/FINAL, (OECD, May 1999), p. 9.

93. *Ibid.*, p. 10.

94. *Ibid.*, p. 18.
95. By its Article 17, "[t]he COP shall define the relevant principles, modalities, rules and guidelines, in particular for verification, reporting and accountability for emissions trading." Article 6 of the protocol on joint implementation between Annex I parties states that the COP/MOP shall "further elaborate guidelines for the implementation of this Article, including for verification and reporting." Article 12 on the clean development mechanism stipulates that the COP/MOP shall "elaborate modalities and procedures with the objective of ensuring transparency, efficiency and accountability through independent auditing and verification of project activities."

Part Three

Non-state actors and conference follow-up and implementation

7

From consensus-building to implementation: The follow-up to the UN global conferences of the 1990s

Masumi Ono

Introduction

The major United Nations global conferences of the 1990s focused international attention on key aspects of global change and development, including the environment, human rights, population, social development, and women. These conferences generated bold pronouncements and, with much fanfare, set forth ambitious internationally agreed goals and commitments. But it is the implementation of those goals that will determine whether each conference is ultimately a success or failure. The United Nations, to play its part in the implementation, has had to adapt to a major change in development strategies. The approach to development has become more integrative and holistic, and as a result, the institutional structure of the UN in the economic and social areas also had to evolve to put in place appropriate mechanisms for tackling the full spectrum of development issues from multisectoral and cross-sectoral perspectives.

This chapter aims to: (1) discuss how the major UN conferences broadened the definition of development which gave rise to the need for coordination within the UN in implementing the commitments made at the conferences; (2) identify the new and established institutional mechanisms designed to achieve that coordination; and (3) outline what the UN can do to strengthen and better coordinate its conference follow-up.

The need for coordination as a result of broadened definition of development

Each conference has facilitated the creation of international norms and set action-oriented goals that have broadened the traditional definition of development. In the wake of the conferences, a consensus has emerged that economic development, social development, and environmental protection are interdependent and mutually reinforcing components of what is now commonly termed "sustainable development."[1] This new approach is based on the following core precepts:

1. economic growth is the fundamental factor in development, since it drives consumption and investment and generates the resources required for social progress and environmental protection;
2. the *quality* of that growth is just as important as its pace, and that good quality growth can only be achieved by investing in people and their social progress;
3. development is for people, and human welfare is at the core of development objectives;
4. the empowerment of women, the contribution of youth, and the participation of the weaker and vulnerable segments of society are critical to success, and a strong and vibrant civil society is essential for social justice and successful development;
5. development must be environmentally sustainable and social and economic needs can and should be met without undermining long-term resource availability or the viability of the ecosystems on which the world depends; and
6. development can be sustained only in conditions of peace and stability; democratic and accountable governance, the rule of law, and respect for human rights can ensure such conditions.

The global conferences held in the 1990s[2] should be seen as links in the same chain, each of which has helped forge and strengthen the concept "sustainable development," or as it is also sometimes termed, "people-centered development." Although each conference had a specific theme, all of them examined sustainable development in a comprehensive and holistic manner. Agenda 21 of the United Nations Conference on Environment and Development, for example, not only addresses sectoral environmental issues but also requests that specific actions be taken in the areas of poverty eradication, business and industry, consumption patterns, children and youth, education, and women. The World Conference on Human Rights was the first of its kind to address human rights in all their dimensions, including economic, social, and cultural rights, as well as the rights of women and children and the right to development. The International Conference on Population and Development was the third international meeting on population, but the first to address the relationships between population, economic growth, and sustainable development. The World Summit for Social Development addressed the problems of poverty, social integration, and employment within an integrated framework. The Fourth World Conference on Women identified 12 critical areas of concern that include wide-ranging issues such as poverty, health, armed conflict, economy, human rights, and the environment. The themes of each conference – children (1990), environment (1992), human rights (1993), population (1994), social development (1995), women (1995), food (1996), and human settlements (1996) – are all interrelated, integral pieces of the jigsaw that makes up sustainable development.

This new broadened definition of development, however, presents a challenge to those in the United Nations and elsewhere who are working for its implementation. It is no easy task to maintain a clear focus on the specific issues at the core of each conference, while at the same time, ensuring that all the conferences collectively advance a unified, comprehensive view of development. As a result of the broad, multidimensional approach taken at each conference, the issues addressed by one often overlap with the issues addressed by others, making it more likely that implementation will be characterized by redundant, rather than complementary efforts. While the conference agendas have tended to take a cross-sectoral approach, the UN system had tended to be organized along sectoral lines, as was the case with most governments. Most of the current institutional structure of the UN in the economic and social areas was not envisioned from the beginning. Rather it evolved incrementally, with an array of committees, commissions, working groups, and programmes being formed along the way in response to new sectoral and cross-sectoral issues or emerging dimensions of development. As the UN's organs, bodies, and programmes have proliferated, so has the need for greater coherence within the system. The sweeping, cross-sectoral approach adopted by the global conferences has made the need for coherence even greater.

Institutional mechanisms to ensure coordination in the implementation of conference goals

The momentum sparked by the conferences has galvanized efforts within the UN to adopt a coordinated institutional framework for setting common priorities and ensuring consistency in implementation across the UN at the intergovernmental, inter-agency, and country levels.

Intergovernmental level

Each major conference of the 1990s has either created, broadened the mandate of, or otherwise transformed related intergovernmental bodies. This has raised the need for improvements in the complementarity and coherence of the follow-up process to UN conferences. To ensure that value is being added at each stage of the review – from a functional commission to the Economic and Social Council to the General Assembly, ongoing efforts have been made to improve the functioning of the three-tiered review process.

Functional commissions

Responsibility for monitoring and assessing the implementation of the goals of each conference, as well as for the preparatory process of the five-year progress review by the General Assembly, has been invested in specific functional commissions. Those commissions include the Commission on the Status of Women (CSW), the Commission on Sustainable Development (CSD), the Commission on Human Rights (CHR), and the Commission on Population and Development. These commissions should be organized so that they facilitate the exchange of inputs on relevant issues. CSW, for example in 1997 discussed the issue of "women and the environment" (one of the critical areas of concern highlighted by the Beijing Conference), in order to contribute to the discussions at the Rio +5 special session of the General Assembly on the five-year review of the Rio Conference in June 1997. Contrary to expectation, however, CSW's views on the matter were largely overlooked by both CSD and in the GA special session. On the other hand in 1998, close cooperation and coordination between the Commission on the Status of Women and the Commission on Human Rights (CHR) has enabled the two commissions to successfully ensure an integrated approach to the issue of gender and human rights. How was this coordination achieved? First, reports submitted to the Commission on Human Rights, such as the reports of the special rapporteur on violence against women, were shared with the Commission on the Status of Women. Second, the Division for the Advancement of Women and the Office of the High Commissioner for Human Rights prepared a joint report for the 1998 CSW and CHR sessions on the full enjoyment of human rights by women.[3] As a result of this success, both commissions called for even stronger cooperation and coordination between the two commissions and between the Office of the High Commissioner for Human Rights and the Division for the Advancement of Women. This kind of exchange of input helps to improve coherence and avoid needless duplication of effort.

The functional commissions continue to provide an important forum for exchanging national best practice in order to refine the implementation of conference goals. In the Commission for Social Development in 1998, several government representatives gave an insightful presentation on national and regional efforts to implement the goals of the World Summit for Social Development. The Commission for Social Development encouraged governments to submit, on a voluntary basis, information on their own specific participatory initiatives so that the commission can periodically take stock of the lessons learned.[4] In its decision on the exchange of national experiences,[5] the Commission on Sustainable Development (CSD) encouraged governments to continue providing voluntary national communications or reports on the implementation of Agenda 21 at the national level, with the broad involvement of all sectors of society. Governments were also encouraged to continue making voluntary national presentations in the framework of the commission's sessions. The Commission on Population and Development, meanwhile, has requested that the UN Secretariat and UNFPA explore how to facilitate the exchange of information among all relevant actors concerning best practices and lessons learned in the implementation of the Program of Action of the International Conference on Population and Development. One well-received idea was to create an internationally accessible electronic database. Likewise, the Commission on the Status of Women at its session in 1998 reviewed the status of national action plans and strategies for the implementation of the Beijing Platform for Action that highlighted good practices,[6] and proposed that the UN establish a readily accessible database of good practices and lessons learned with regard to the issue of violence against women. It invited contributions of information from member states and NGOs.[7]

In an effort to encourage greater participation and the cooperation of civil society in the functional commissions, the Commission for Social Development, at its session in 1998, held panel discussions on "Participation and Social Justice" and "Enhancing Social Protection and Reducing Vulnerability." The Commission on the Status of Women held panels on "critical areas of concern," and the Commission on Sustainable Development held its first "industry segment," bringing together representatives of industry (both the business community and trade unions), NGOs, governments, and international organizations. These kinds of constructive interaction between the functional commissions and civil society should be further encouraged so that healthy diverse perspectives can be openly shared and reflected in intergovernmental deliberations.

Economic and Social Council

The Economic and Social Council (ECOSOC) as a charter body and a principal organ of the UN is mandated to promote international cooperation in the economic, social, and related fields under the authority of the General Assembly.[8] The council is responsible for coordination of the economic and social work of the UN and its specialized agencies.[9] Over the years, the council was perceived as not being fully equipped to coordinate the activities of the vast number of UN system organizations effectively or to guide the work of its subsidiary machinery sufficiently. Recently, however, a renewed effort has been made to revitalize ECOSOC's performance in both areas, especially as they relate to conference follow-up.

To develop a coherent and well-coordinated approach to the global commitments reached at the major conferences of the 1990s, ECOSOC's task is to ensure the harmonization and coordination of the agendas and work programmes of the functional commissions by promoting a more efficient division of labour and providing them with clearer policy guidance.[10] Since 1995, the council has been engaged in a systematic effort to ensure coordinated and integrated follow-up to, and implementation of, UN conference goals, focusing on cross-cutting themes such as poverty, the enabling environment, gender, and human rights. These themes common to many global conferences of the 1990s were drawn from the 12 themes[11] identified by the Secretary-General[12] to help ECOSOC formulate development policies in an integrated and coherent manner. Strong inter-agency cooperation and coordination are essential in order to ensure a fully integrated approach throughout the UN system.

The UN's institutional structure in the economic and social fields has also evolved as part of a larger UN reform process. For the last several years, there has been an ongoing effort to revitalize and strengthen ECOSOC and its role in providing guidance to the council's subsidiary bodies and the UN system organizations. ECOSOC has been reviewing its subsidiary bodies, including the functional commissions with responsibility for follow-up to major conferences, and working to enhance communication and coordination with the regional commissions.[13]

General Assembly

The General Assembly, as the final authority for the review and monitoring of progress, is in the process of holding special sessions for the five-year reviews of progress made for each of the major conferences – in 2000 for the World Summit for Social Development as well as for the Fourth World Conference on Women, and in 2001 for the United Nations Conference on Human Settlements (Habitat II). The special sessions for the five-year reviews of the Rio Conference on the Environment and of the International Conference on Population and Development were held in 1998 and 1999, respectively. ECOSOC will need to ensure, through consultations with the functional commissions, that the five-year reviews draw on the knowledge and expertise on these issues throughout the UN system.

Inter-agency level

The Administrative Committee on Coordination (ACC) has held policy discussions on integrated and coordinated follow-up to conferences, and on the cross-cutting themes of poverty eradication, gender mainstreaming, human rights, and the role of civil society.

In 1995, to provide coordination and integrated support at the inter-agency level, the ACC established three ad hoc Inter-Agency Task Forces (IATFs), each based on a broad theme arising from the conferences. The IATFs were on: (1) the enabling environment for social and economic development; (2) employment and sustainable livelihoods; and (3) basic social services for all. All three IATFs were time-bound and led by agencies with special competence to deal with the theme of their task force. The IATFs have achieved the following: (1) clarified the key elements of the policy framework for pursuing conference goals; (2) devised recommendations and guidelines for UN system programming; (3) produced country reviews and case studies; (4) made proposals on other areas requiring attention (the role of civil society, the elaboration of statistics and indicators); and (5) recommended institutional arrangements for follow-up to the work of the task forces.[14]

The task forces have been praised for helping to promote a clearer understanding within the UN system of the policy framework and development agenda at the country level. They have highlighted the need for continued dialogue, both among the agencies and between agencies and governments. The IATFs brought together some 20 organizations and have also improved the interaction between agencies at the headquarters and country levels. While their work is now over, the task forces revealed that the UN system shares a largely consistent view on the broad policy framework for implementing the goals of the conferences. Agencies still have differences; however, over what issues deserve the highest priority. But differences are not surprising, given the different mandates and competencies of each agency and the political motives of governments. Nonetheless, the recommendations made by the task forces for future action as well as the lessons learned from their experience could provide a solid basis for continued efforts to mobilize UN system support for the coordinated follow-up to conferences, particularly in putting conference goals into effect at the field level.

In addition to creating the task forces, the ACC established an Inter-Agency Committee on Women and Gender Equality (IACWGE) as a standing committee of the ACC to coordinate UN system-wide efforts to implement the Beijing Platform for Action, and to follow the progress made by the UN system in incorporating a gender perspective in institutional structures and in policies and programming.

Country level

It was agreed at the various global conferences that governments have the primary responsibility of formulating national plans of action and translating the conference goals into practical policies in line with their national priorities and circumstances. The UN's role, as often emphasized in the conferences, is to assist the governments in their efforts at country level. A key concern in implementing conference goals is to balance country-specific circumstances with the specific mandate and capabilities of each agency. Collaborative dialogue between governments and agencies is therefore vital to ensuring that balance. To this end, a dialogue has been actively pursued between governments and agencies to put conference goals into operation.

At the country level, there are various mechanisms for coordination, such as the resident coordinator system, Country Strategy Notes, field-level committees, thematic working groups, the programme approach, and the consultation process of the UNDP-led round tables and World Bank-led consultative group meetings. The resident coordinator system is meant to ensure that there is appropriate inter-agency dialogue with national authorities on the cross-sectoral implementation of conferences. Thematic groups have been established in many countries, to address such cross-cutting themes as poverty, women's empowerment, basic social services, employment and sustainable livelihoods, and HIV/AIDS. The effectiveness of these mechanisms and the extent to which they are used vary by country and by issue. Participants usually include government officials and UN agency representatives, and in some cases national experts and NGOs. Coordination mechanisms tend to work most effectively when they are formed around a specific concrete issue, as evidenced by the success of the HIV/AIDS programmes at the field level.

As part of the reform process initiated by Secretary-General Kofi Annan, a new common framework is being introduced for development cooperation by funds and programmes at the country level. The United Nations Development Assistance Framework (UNDAF) is designed to achieve goal-oriented collaboration, programmatic coherence, and mutual reinforcement among UN programmes, and so far has been experimented with in 18 countries with the cooperation of the Bretton Woods institutions and other UN specialized agencies. An assessment of UNDAF's effectiveness is expected to be completed by the year 2001, to evaluate UNDAF's effect on the performance of the United Nations system and its usefulness as a tool to harmonize and integrate efforts to promote poverty eradication and people-centered development.[15]

The regional, subregional and interregional dimensions of the follow-up to conferences also require further expansion and improvement, since much of the emphasis in follow-up is placed on national implementation. In some areas such as the environment, interregional exchange of lessons learned would obviously be beneficial. The regional commissions[16] are well situated to translate the recommendations and decisions adopted at regional and global levels that are suitable for each region. Their conference follow-up activities mainly consist of data collection and processing, analysis and research, advocacy and dissemination of information, monitoring and evaluation of the implementation of globally and regionally agreed plans and strategies, sponsoring regional ministerial conferences, organizing national workshops, NGO workshops, regional seminars, and expert group meetings. The scope of their involvement in the follow-up to conferences depends on regional specificity, the level of resources, and the mandate of each regional commission.

It has been noted in the Economic and Social Council that coordination does not come free. Indeed, the cost of coordination must be borne in mind in terms of time, effort, and financing. However, the benefits that arise through better coordination nearly always outweigh the costs in the long run: policies are made more coherent, work programmes are streamlined and the implementation of conference goals is made more effective. In any case, all current efforts to improve coordination within the UN are carried out using existing resources and incur no additional financial cost to the UN.

Maximizing the impact of the UN's activities in implementing conference goals

In recent years, global conferences have provided much of the impetus for conceptual advances in the field of development. Having entered the implementation phase with an improved institutional framework to promote coordination among intergovernmental bodies and the UN system organizations, what can the United Nations do in order to maximize the impact of its activities in implementing the goals and commitments of the global conferences?

The UN can contribute to the realization of conference goals in two major ways: first, it can translate global norms into useful policy advice to national governments; and secondly, it can support the efforts of governments to implement those norms through operational programmes.

Translating global norms into useful policy advice

The intergovernmental and inter-agency level institutional framework mentioned above corresponds to the first aspect of the UN's role – translating global norms into policy advice. Sustainable development should continue to provide a broad framework to guide the ongoing work of the system while pursuing the important related issues of mainstreaming human rights, environmental, gender, population, and children. The goal of poverty eradication, as reaffirmed by all recent global conferences, would also remain a fundamental commitment for the system. Nonetheless, given the complex interlinkage among the issues addressed at various UN conferences, the council, in its role of overseeing the co-ordinated follow-up to conferences and summits, must ensure that issues of a cross-cutting nature are addressed in a coherent and integrated way without duplicating the efforts of various intergovernmental bodies. Such coordination is an ongoing management task of ECOSOC. Indeed, some delegations strongly feel that the council should function as more or less a "board of directors," directing the work of its subsidiary bodies. That would be the council's added value in the three-tier review process.

In order to ensure the continued development of appropriate policy advice, progress made in the implementation of the conference goals also needs to be monitored and evaluated. The need for effective monitoring and the development of indicators was raised during ECOSOC's meetings in May 1998 and 1999. The demand for information and basic statistical data has increased as a result of the global conferences. A large number of indicators, ranging from 18 to 134 is required for the follow-up of conferences.[17] However, a serious gap exists between such demand and the supply of information by most developing countries, unable to cope with the overwhelming volume of data requests. In order to monitor progress at the country level effectively, the capacity of both the UN system and of countries to collect and analyse statistics needs to be strengthened. A coherent set of basic indicators would also need to be developed.

At present, the work on indicators is being carried out in various fora. For example, the Statistical Commission adopted a Minimum National Social Data Set (MNSDS) in 1997, taking a first step towards the creation of a coherent set of indicators for monitoring progress in conference implementation at the country level.[18] The commission stressed that the indicators in MNSDS should be considered as a minimum not a maximum list, and invited users to refine it to meet national needs and circumstances, and requirements in specific fields. The UN system will need to promote its use and adaptation to specific country situations.

In order eventually to rationalize a set of indicators, an inventory of indicators produced by the UN system is being developed. Inter-agency collaboration aimed to define a common set of indicators for goals from four or more conferences for common country assessment (CCA). Types of indicators include 40 socio-economic (including environment); seven governance and civil and political rights; and 10 key demographic and economic contextual. Supplementary thematic indicators are still being developed. The Inter-Agency Committee on Women and Gender Equality in 1997 had initiated efforts to develop gender-sensitive indicators. The Organization for Economic Cooperation and Development/ Development Assistance Committee (OECD/DAC), in collaboration with the United Nations and the World Bank, developed a core set of indicators for monitoring progress towards widely shared development goals and goals agreed upon at recent global conferences. Clearly, coordinating the work of these entities and other international organizations could enhance the effectiveness of the UN's monitoring capacities. Efforts have continued to be made to harmonize these core sets developed under various initiatives.[19]

The other issue related to monitoring implementation is the need to streamline national reporting processes. For if each of the conferences pursues its own separate reporting requirements, it would be likely to be duplicative, costly, and time-consuming. If data collection, monitoring, and reporting could be carried out around commonly agreed themes and goals, on the basis of shared definitions, concepts, and approaches, this would considerably reduce the reporting burden each government and other development actors may face. ECOSOC addressed this issue in 1995, and asked the Secretary-General to prepare a standardized and simplified format for national reporting. Subsequently, the General Assembly requested that the Secretariat prepare country profiles for the special session on the follow-up to the Rio Conference in June 1997. Similar efforts also need to be pursued in the follow-up to other conferences. Arrangements would need to be put in place to develop coordinated and consistent methodological approach to all the data requirements stemming from the global conferences.

Supporting the efforts of governments to implement norms agreed at conferences

The second aspect of the UN's role – implementing global norms through operational activities – points to the key challenge of conference implementation: linking the normative and operational parts of the work of the UN system. In this respect ECOSOC has an important role to play as the coordinating and oversight body of the UN system. The council could strengthen its links with the executive boards of funds and programmes

(UNDP, UNFPA, UNICEF, and WFP) and with the governing bodies of the specialized agencies to ensure that broad policies agreed at the level of ECOSOC are applied in the operations of these organizations.

In fulfilling the role of implementing global norms, the private sector and NGOs also have a vital part to play, both in the implementation of global norms and in the mobilization of resources. The potential roles of the private sector and civil society have received growing recognition and interest from the UN. Given the shrinking availability of public sector resources for sustainable development, the participation of the private sector, particularly through investment, has become ever more important, and has been recognized as such by various intergovernmental bodies. NGOs have been actively involved in increasing the public awareness about UN conferences and their implementation through an array of their own follow-up activities, including UN conference theme-related symposia, seminars, policy dialogues with governments at the national level, and follow-up within the UN. The UN, for its part, has recognized the need for greater NGO involvement in conference goal implementation, and has reviewed ways to improve arrangements for their participation.

The implementation of conference goals requires enormous financial resources. The UN Conference on Environment and Development estimated the average annual cost for implementation between 1993 and 2000 at over $600 billion, including $125 billion from the international community.[20] The International Conference on Population and Development estimated that, in developing countries and countries with economies in transition, the implementation of programmes in the area of reproductive health, including those related to family planning, maternal health, and the prevention of sexually transmitted diseases, as well as other basic actions for collecting and analysing population data, will cost $17 billion in 2000, $18.5 billion in 2005, $20.5 billion in 2010, and $21.7 billion in 2015 (these cost estimates were prepared by experts, based on experience to date in the four areas of reproductive health referred to above).[21] In reality, the evaluations made for the five-year review of the International Conference on Population and Development revealed that international assistance for population and reproductive health increased by 54 per cent from the pre-conference period, to slightly over $2 billion in 1996, which represents roughly 35 per cent of the target agreed at Cairo for international assistance. Domestic financial resources from governments and NGOs were estimated to have been about $7 billion annually during the period 1996–1997, and an additional $1 billion was estimated to have been provided by individuals and households.[22]

Despite the vast financial resources required to achieve the goals of global conferences, the discouraging downward trend in ODA levels has continued. According to OECD, total aid from member countries of DAC (OECD's Development Assistance Committee) has declined continuously for the last five years to reach a record low of 0.22 per cent of the combined GNP of DAC countries in 1997. These levels are far below the UN's aid target of 0.7 per cent of GNP. Furthermore, according to OECD/DAC, one quarter of ODA goes to countries which, as a group, are near to or have already achieved the OECD/DAC conference-inspired goals for 2015. Given the scarcity of resources, it would seem more appropriate that a greater share of ODA should go to the least developed and low-income countries that are furthest from achieving those goals. This is sure to be one of the major factors in the General Assembly as it prepares for a high-level consultation on financing for development to be held before the end of 2001.[23] The major issues on the agenda are likely to be: mobilization of domestic resources; mobilization of private financial flows; international financial cooperation; external debt; trade; innovative sources of finance; and governance of the international monetary, financial, and trade systems. However, progress in the area of financing is inevitably very slow, as the issue is politically charged for both donor and recipient countries. The search for new and innovative ways of generating funds continues, but the voluntary nature of development funds is still the agreed principle. Any attempt to raise funds on a global scale in order to tackle the global problems identified by the UN conferences will face vigorous resistance by governments who fear infringement of the traditional notion of sovereignty.

Conclusions

Ultimately, the responsibility for implementing conference goals rests with each national government. However, there is certainly a role to be played by intergovernmental and non-governmental organizations. The UN, through its series of global conferences, has contributed to building consensus and norms. The challenge it faces now is to operationalize those commitments and norms in a comprehensive and coherent way. The UN could contribute and support national efforts for the implementation of conference goals through operational activities and effective monitoring and evaluation. Coordination and collaboration within the UN system – as well as with other development partners – are essential, particularly in this age of shrinking financial resources for multilateral aid. The institutional structure of the United Nations system has evolved as it has been charged with new tasks by the global conferences. The value of these new institutional mechanisms will be judged by how effectively they help to implement the conference goals and commitments.

However, these mechanisms can only facilitate and support the implementation. The realization of the conference goals must be driven by the political will of each member country of the United Nations. The global conferences have initiated a continuous process for mobilizing such political will.

Notes

1. Agenda for Development, General Assembly resolution A/RES/51/240, June 1997.
2. The World Summit for Children (1990), The World Conference on Education for All (1990), The Second United Nations Conference on the Least Developed Countries (1990), The United Nations Conference on Environment and Development (1992), The International Conference on the Least Developed Countries (1992), The International Conference on Nutrition (1992), The World Conference on Human Rights (1993), The International Conference on Population and Development (1994), The Global Conference on the Sustainable Development of Small Island Developing States (1994), The World Conference on Natural Disaster Reduction (1994), The World Summit for Social Development (1995), The Fourth World Conference on Women (1995), The Second World Conference on Human Settlements (1996), The World Food Summit (1996).
3. *Report of the Secretary-General on women's real enjoyment of their human rights, in particular those relating to the elimination of poverty, economic development and economic resources, 1998* (E/CN.6/1998/11-E/CN.4/1998/22).
4. Agreed conclusions on promoting social integration, *Report of the Commission for Social Development, 1998* (E/1998/26).
5. Decision 6/5 of the Commission on Sustainable Development (E/CN.17/1998/L.8).
6. *Report of the Secretary-General* (E/CN.6/1998/6).
7. Resolution 42/3 of the Commission on the Status of Women on violence against women migrant workers, *Report of the Commission on the Status of Women, 1998* (E/1998/27).
8. Article 60 of the United Nations Charter.
9. Article 63 of the United Nations Charter.
10. Agreed Conclusions 1995/1, *Report of the Economic and Social Council, 1995* (A/50/3).
11. These are: (a) a stable macroeconomic policy framework conducive to development; (b) external debt and finance for development; (c) international trade and commodities; (d) science and technology; (e) eradication of poverty and hunger; (f) access to productive occupational opportunities, full employment, and family incomes; (g) gender equality, equity, and empowerment of women; (h) basic social services for all: primary health care, nutrition, education, safe water and sanitation, population and shelter; (i) promoting social integration; (j) environment and natural resources; (k) Africa and special categories; (l) participation, democracy, human rights, accountability, and partnership with major groups and non-governmental organizations.
12. *Report of the Secretary-General on coordinated follow-up to major international conferences in the economic, social and related fields* (E/1995/86), pp. 25–38, Table I.
13. Mandated by General Assembly resolutions A/RES/50/227 (ECOSOC res. 1997/322) and A/RES/52/12B.
14. *Report of the Secretary-General on integrated and coordinated implementation and follow-up of major United Nations conferences and summits* (E/1998/19).
15. United Nations, *Report of the Secretary-General on operational activities of the United Nations for international development* (E/1999/55).

16. These are: the Economic Commission for Africa, the Economic and Social Commission for Asia and the Pacific, the Economic Commission for Europe, the Economic Commission for Latin America and the Caribbean, and the Economic and Social Commission for Western Asia.

17. United Nations, *Report of the Secretary-General on Meeting on Basic Indicators: Integrated and coordinated implementation and follow-up of major UN conferences and summits* (E/1999/11).

18. The 15 indicators contained in the Minimum National Social Data Set are: (1) population estimates by sex, age and, where appropriate and feasible, ethnic group; (2) life expectancy at birth, by sex; (3) infant mortality, by sex; (4) child mortality, by sex; (5) maternal mortality; (6) contraceptive prevalence rate; (7) average number of years of schooling completed, by urban/rural, sex, and where possible, income class; (8) number of people per room, excluding kitchen and bathroom; (9) access to safe water; (10) access to sanitation; (11) monetary value of the basket of food needed for minimum nutritional requirement; (12) GDP per capita; (13) household income per capita (level and distribution); (14) unemployment rate, by sex; and (15) employment/population ratio, by sex and, where appropriate, formal or informal sector.

19. United Nations, *Report of the Secretary-General on Meeting on Basic Indicators: Integrated and coordinated implementation and follow-up of major UN conferences and summits* (E/1999/11).

20. United Nations, *Report of the United Nations Conference on Environment and Development* (New York: 1992) (UN document symbol A/CONF.151/26 (Vol. III)), para. 33.18.

21. United Nations, *Report of the International Conference on Population and Development* (New York) (UN document symbol A/CONF.171/13/Rev.1), 1994 para. 13.15.

22. United Nations, *Report of the Secretary-General on Meeting on Basic Indicators: Integrated and coordinated implementation and follow-up of major UN conferences and summits* (E/1999/11).

23. General Assembly resolution A/RES/52/179.

8

Making meaningful UN-sponsored world conferences of the 1990s: NGOs to the rescue?

*Michael G. Schechter**

The future of UN-sponsored world conferences hinges, in large part, on the conference follow-up activities including those by non-governmental organizations (NGOs).[1] The broadness of this organization category has led some to generate a "lexicon of descriptors," including Public Interest NGOs (PINGOs), Business and Industry NGOs (BINGOs), Environmental NGOs (ENGOs), Civil Society NGOs (CSOs), Private Voluntary Organizations (PVOs), Donor-organized NGOs (DONGOs), Government-run NGOs (GRINGOs), Government-organized NGOs (GONGOs), Grassroots organizations (GROs), Community-Based Organizations (CBOs) etc.[2]

The focus in this chapter is on international non-governmental organizations, sometimes referred to by the acronym INGOs, but more often NGOs. I am including organizations that lack consultative status with IGOs, but excluding those whose intent is to make profits (even though General Motors was an accredited NGO at the Earth Summit in Rio) or that operate in a single country, but whose impact transcends that base.[3] The definition used here is consistent with that adopted by the UN's Department of Public Information: "NGO refers to a non-profit citizens' voluntary entity organized nationally or internationally. Thus, professional associations, trade unions, religious organizations, women's and youth groups, cooperative associations, development and human rights

* I would like to thank Professor M. J. Peterson of the University of Massachusetts, Amherst, for her very helpful comments on an earlier version of this chapter.

organizations, environmental protection groups, research institutes dealing with international affairs and associations of parliamentarians are considered NGOs."[4]

The vision of NGOs in this chapter is not a romantic one. It is clearly understood that while *some* NGOs can rightfully be referred to as the "conscience of the world" and *some* can rightfully be credited with placing issues of social justice on the global agenda – including OXFAM's successful pushing of the critique of Structural Adjustment Loans and the elucidation of the environmental and cultural impacts of economic development – not all NGOs are moral or have emancipatory goals, much less are they often accountable or democratic in form.[5] Even NGOs that have redistributionist goals can be criticized for taking the pressure off wealthy states from providing foreign aid and blunting protests and calls for change of poor governments. Others, including the International Rescue Committee, are seen as not working with existing professional and civil societies and, as a consequence, lacking a focus on longer-term social programmes to supplement their important short-term help.

NGO activities *at* the various conferences have ensured that NGOs have a key role to play in the follow-up to the UN-sponsored world conferences of the 1990s. Whether this bodes well for the future of such conferences is less clear. To date, the record of policy and procedural implementation is spotty, varied, and obviously incomplete. Only part of that, of course, can be credited to the actions of NGOs. Much of it is due to the relatively short span of time since the conferences concluded. Moreover, the role of NGOs in policy implementation, as in the conference deliberations themselves, is as much a product of government actions, preferences, and funding as it is of the merit of their ideas and the cleverness of the NGOs' own tactics and strategies. Although NGOs can exert pressure on governments, IGO and conference secretariats, as lobbyists normally do, member *states* of the United Nations are ultimately responsible for setting the agendas, for policy development and setting priorities, and for passing the resolutions to convene UN-sponsored world conferences.[6] They are also obviously responsible for paying for them and issuing, or not issuing, invitations.[7] "National governments are [also] expected to assume primary responsibility for the implementation of the resulting plans of action."[8] Moreover, as the dearth of conferences in the 1980s underscores, structural constraints – in this instance economic, material, and ideational – clearly affect the rise and fall of conferences.

Still, it is the contention of this chapter that the success of the 1990s conferences and the future of UN-sponsored world conferences in the twenty-first century are to a considerable extent in the hands of NGOs. This key contention of this chapter logically follows from but is slightly bolder than Smith's conclusion that NGO "... participation in these events and their aftermath is vital to their realization of the tasks of drawing public attention to global problems and of sustaining institutions that effectively respond to such problems."[9] Attention here is focused on such evolving follow-up responsibilities of NGOs as sustaining pressure on governments to live up to the commitments they made at the conferences, monitoring of the global political process,[10] informing parties about how and when to apply effective pressure to maximize compliance,[11] the development of national and international follow-up "legislation," and the actual provision of services.[12] The focus on NGOs at world conferences should not be understood as an argument that that is the only site of their influence; indeed the trends in increased impact of NGOs on global policies at world conferences parallels that happening outside the conferences;[13] more so, as NGO influence on global public policy is expected to increase whether or not world conferences are pervasive in the twenty-first century.

In many of these activities, the success of NGOs' work depends on their cooperation with other non-state actors, including epistemic communities, resistance movements, transnational advocacy networks, grassroots organizations operating in single countries, social movements, and IGOs of various types. For example, the UNICEF staff's work in the 1980s on the provisions of the draft Convention on the Rights of the Child was "... directed through the ad hoc NGO group that had formed in Geneva to press its own agenda."[14] NGOs are often supported by IGOs because the latter "... see citizens' groups like Earth Action as a means of working beyond governments to generate support 'from below' for multilateral problem solving."[15] But only some NGOs perform such roles and are truly part of the "new multilateralism."[16] Others are quasi-state actors and, as a consequence, not considered part of civil society by some observers, and are thus unable to provide world conferences with the sort of legitimacy they seek as being more democratic and representative than most of the UN and its specialized agencies.[17]

What this chapter argues, then, is that while it is too early to say anything definitive about the success or failure of many of the items on the agendas passed at the various UN-sponsored world conferences or whether the conferences will prove to be worth their costs to members and the UN, preliminary indications are that, in some instances, NGOs are succeeding in helping effectuate the conferences' programmes of action or other conference agreements and in some they are not. Obviously the future of UN-sponsored world conferences in the twenty-first century depends on a high ratio of successes to setbacks as well as the quality of the conferees' decisions themselves (i.e. even if NGOs are successful in assisting in the implementation of the conference's decisions, the meaningfulness of past and the promise of future conferences depends on the degree to which those conferees appropriately address the global challenges within the relevant regime).

What this chapter also seeks to accomplish is to identify some of the reasons for those differential levels of NGO success and thus the conditions that must be met to ensure success of any future UN-sponsored world conferences. Key factors would seem to include: (1) cooperation amongst NGOs; (2) the ability of NGOs to form cross-sectoral coalitions; (3) the ability of NGOs to participate *on* government delegations; (4) the preciseness, responsibility, and relevance of the conference documents for follow-up action by NGOs; (5) the ability of NGOs to identify like-minded IGOs with which they can coordinate actions; (6) the intensity of networking amongst NGOs and their exploiting of communication technologies to facilitate exchange of information;[18] (7) the sympathies of the conference secretariat with NGO goals; (8) the development of innovative projects (like the alternative treaty project connected to UNCED); and (9) the willingness of NGOs to work with non-traditional potential allies, including the business community, social movements, epistemic communities, transnational advocacy networks, grassroots organizations focused on efforts in a single country, or IGOs often identified as pro-business.

This last observation points to something where the evidence in the chapter is only inferential. NGOs and IGOs are only some of the non-state actors involved in the global governance processes in the issues central to this chapter. Social movements, transnational advocacy groups, and so-called resistance movements (including the NGOs systematically excluded from UN-sponsored world conferences) are also key. They are key to providing alternative perspectives and new ideas. They are also often closely tied to grassroots movements where the knowledge of specific problems and solutions is greatest. As the recently concluded Landmines Treaty suggests, they can also be quite successful in processes of global governance (although the import of such a treaty without US participation is somewhat dubious).[19] In a slightly different direction, if resistance movements and grassroots movements are not brought into the process they have the capacity to thwart rather than support policy implementation. They are key to one of the reasons why NGOs have been turned to by the UN in the first place, offering a legitimate claim to inclusiveness. To use slightly different language, if the implementation process is only "top down" rather than involving "bottom up" elements, more akin to the established multilateralism rather than involving the new, then the prospects are somewhat bleak for successful implementation of the decisions taken in the 1990s and, thus for the convening of a large number of well-financed, attended, highly publicized and meaningful UN-sponsored world conferences in the twenty-first century.

The implications of this argument are complex, controversial, and potentially important. They are empirical, theoretical, normative, and policy relevant. For example, they suggest that yet another set of actors needs to be included in any assessment and prediction as to the success or failure of intergovernmental organizations in general and UN-sponsored world conferences in particular.[20] They also suggest that there may be a tension between those who support (or oppose) world conferences because of their democratic format – one country, one vote – and support for the enactment and implementation of global public policy in which non-democratic, often unrepresentative, non-transparent NGOs that lack significant governmental oversight play a major role.[21] For, as Deacon has suggested, only a bit hyperbolically: "International NGO intervention ... falls outside the frame of any democratically responsible policy framework."[22] Moreover, if the US Congress is to allow significant US financial support for world conferences in the twenty-first century, NGOs must succeed in very dramatic and public ways in effectuating the key goals of the world conferences of the 1990s.

NGOs and UN-sponsored world conferences

NGOs – however they are defined – have significantly increased numerically in the past decades, multiplied the roles they perform and the influence they wield in global governance in general, and specifically in relation to the United Nations.[23] This is especially true through the aegis of UN-sponsored ad hoc world conferences:[24]

Clearly, NGOs are more prominent on the international scene today than they were 20 years ago. Comparing Rio [the Earth Summit of 1992] to Rome [World Food Conference of 1974], the transformation of the NGO community from outsiders-looking-in to stakeholders has been dramatic. After UNCED [Rio, United Nations Conference on Environment and Development of 1992] – and Vienna [World Conference on Human Rights, June 1993], Cairo [International Conference on Population and Development, September 1994], Copenhagen [World Summit for Social Development, March 1995], Beijing [World Conference on Women: Action for Equality, Development and Peace, September 1995] and Istanbul [United Nations Conference on Human Settlements, Habitat II, June 1996] since – there is no longer any question that NGOs are to be involved in the policy circle at the international level. Agenda 21 promised to include NGOs at all stages of its implementation, the rules for NGO involvement have been loosened, and ECOSOC is revising its rules for NGO involvement such that UN debates can no longer be made without conscious reference to the NGO participation.[25]

The most visible and perhaps because of that, the most frequently noted and studied phenomenon relating to NGOs and world conferences is the evolution of so-called parallel conferences, fora or, in Richard Falk's terminology, counter-conferences.[26] Large attendance at such counter-conferences is uncontestable. Some 40,000 non-government personnel attended the Fourth Women's Conference, in Beijing. Fewer attended other conferences, but the numbers were still sizeable. Less obvious than the huge numbers of attendees – presumably implying something about NGO belief in their importance – is the degree to which they significantly influence the *official* conferences, that is, where the government delegates are often working on legally binding documents. Indeed, it has been argued that NGOs themselves "have found that the best time to wield influence over a world conference is [not during the counter-conferences but rather] during the preparatory process – at least 60 per cent of the final outcome of a UN global conference is determined during the preparatory process – often through expert-group meetings, which are almost always open to NGO participation."[27] But, as will be noted, the preparatory conference work is key, in part, because it is often there that decisions are made as to the roles that NGOs will play in the conferences and thus, in turn, in the implementation phase, including what sort of financial and other state support they will have in conference follow-up activities.

Also contestable is the desirability of labelling such gatherings global or international or transnational civil society,[28] especially given that states have some control over the invitation lists for NGOs and the fact that most social movements opt out of conference participation, often seeing participation as requiring a greater formality to their structure than they seek and preferring to avoid the close work with governments that are often part and parcel of such counter-conferences.[29] (It is also something of a convention to restrict the term social movements to those collectivities committed to significant change (such as resistance movements), whereas such a commitment is less characteristic of many of the NGOs involved in these conferences).[30]

However it is not contestable or indeed hard to demonstrate that NGOs have come to be accepted as integral actors at world conferences, at least in the post-Rio era. For instance during the Preparatory Committees for the Social Summit, whose wide-ranging and ambitious agenda focused on the eradication of poverty, full employment, and social integration, governments were actually complaining that there was not enough NGO participation.[31] As a consequence, the conference secretariat encouraged NGO attendance: of the 250 delegates who attended, an "unprecedented" 50 were from NGOs. Thereby NGOs were actively engaged throughout the negotiating process.[32] The consequences of their active participation throughout the process were significant. For example, Ruben notes that the original platform for action drafted for the Summit "... completely ignored the environment and sustainable development. But persistent efforts by a hastily formed NGO Environmental Caucus and the US EPA [Environmental Protection Agency] brought environmental issues into the discussions."[33]

More to the point here, however, are arguments that suggest that the greatest contribution of world conferences with respect to NGOs may be in terms of what happens post-conference. For example, Humphreys notes that the links and networks developed during the UNCED process "... will continue to play an important role in monitoring any UN activities ..."[34] and that all NGOs that attended UNCED were allowed to participate in subsequent UN environmental activities, most notably the work of the UN Commission on Sustainable Development (CSD).[35]

The CSD invitation is a revealing one. Hailed at the time by many as a great concession by the North and a major accomplishment of the Rio Conference,[36] Bennett is less sanguine about the establishment and future of the CSD. He notes that no *organization* can effectively deal with the environmental issues assigned to it. What is needed, rather, is an *institutional* solution, one that involves Southern-based NGOs with a firm grasp of micro issues and policies. But none, at least in Bennett's perspective, is up to that task and thus the hopes, up to the present, appear to have been exaggerated. Perhaps in the future, he opines, a network of NGOs might perform this role in civil society.[37] More to the point is the critique of the CSD from the perspective of a number of unorthodox economists and environmentalists. They argue that the CSD, perhaps because the so-called radical or resistance NGOs were *not* present at Rio, is ill-suited to cope with the environmental challenges of the day. The CSD's premises are seen to be pro-capitalist, implying faith in supply-demand processes to cope with any impending environmental disasters.[38] Extrapolating from examples of so-called overfishing (i.e. where the market is unable to prevent the exhaustion of a species of fish), such economists and environmentalists contend that ideas like slowing economic growth need to be considered, not simply defined away as they believe the establishment of a follow-up institution focused on "sustainable development" seems to do.[39]

Even making allowance for these noteworthy and policy relevant exceptions, it is clear that a huge number of NGOs are significantly involved in global policy-making as it relates to the UN. It is also clear that NGOs will be among the keys to the extent that follow-up institutions – like the CSD – achieve the goals set out for them. The reasons *why* the UN has increasingly turned to NGOs to assist it in meeting global challenges, however, are not all that obvious. As noted above they are often explained in the most general terms (e.g. the problems of the twenty-first century are global in nature and thus require involvement of civil society). Upon closer examination, however, NGO involvement seems to result from the increased demands placed on the UN in the post cold

war era, its financial crisis, its decreased authority relative to the international financial institutions (IFIs), former UN Secretary-General Boutros Boutros-Ghali's preferred approach to global governance[40] and, at
least in some quarters, the UN's decreased legitimacy. While it might be
overstating the case to suggest that the UN Secretariat thought this new
approach to working with NGOs would gain it "more moral authority
and political relevance";[41] it is obvious that the Secretariat as well as UN
member states have allowed, even encouraged, this trend to evolve.

One of the consequences of NGOs' increased roles and influence *at*
the conferences is that NGOs have been increasingly successful in having themselves empowered for effectuating the conferences' outcomes, be
they formal treaties or programmes of action.[42] This is evident in the
conference documents themselves. They frequently include statements
empowering NGOs to assist in the implementation of the conferences'
action items.[43] This phenomenon is usually traced to Agenda 21, coming
out of the 1992 United Nations Conference on Environment and Development (UNCED). Apropos, a recent UN report contends that although
"the need to improve UN system interaction with civil society has been
repeatedly emphasized in the recent past" and that "it formed a part of
the proposals for UN system reforms," it was "beginning with Agenda 21
[that] all programmes/platforms of action of global conferences have assigned important roles to civil society in conference follow-up." In this
context, the role of the resident coordinator system is singled out for
carefully assessing the "... country level situation on the role of civil
society organizations [which includes NGOs] in conference follow-up." It
is added that such "... assessment might include: identification of potential partners, on the basis of objectives, constituencies and thematic interests, for follow-up activities, and current levels of their participation
at national and local levels in conference-related activities, particularly
monitoring of progress on the implementation of global commitments."
Based on such an assessment, the resident coordinator system should
play a facilitation role in promotion of government–civil society interaction in conference follow-up activities, particularly through representation in councils established for the purpose, undertake information-
sharing on a selective basis, and, if necessary, assist in capacity-building.[44]
More specifically, paragraph 10(c) of Chapter 27 of Agenda 21, entitled
"Strengthening the Role of Non-governmental Organizations: Partners for Sustainable Development," speaks of the need to "involve non-
governmental organizations in national mechanisms or procedures established to carry out Agenda 21, making the best use of their particular
capacities, especially in the fields of education, poverty alleviation and
environmental protection and rehabilitation." Others trace the call for
NGO participation in the implementation phase to the Conference on the

Human Environment in Stockholm in 1972 or even back to the first World Food Congress of 1963.[45] Whenever the proper baseline, it appears that whether such conferences have meaningful results and thus future successors are to a much greater extent than ever before, the responsibility of NGOs.

While this *is* the overall trend – NGOs' implementation responsibilities are significantly greater coming out of the conferences of the 1990s than they were of the 1970s – important differences exist between conferences and thus issue-areas. In part this is a consequence of the fact that each conference is free to adopt and apply its own rules for NGO participation.[46] For example, the Second World Conference on Habitat (in Istanbul 3–16 June 1996) was the first where NGOs were given the right to participate in informal drafting sessions,[47] whereas the 14–24 June 1993 World Conference on Human Rights (in Vienna) largely excluded NGOs from the official process "... because of the efforts of many Arab and Asian states who argued for restricted NGO access at every opportunity."[48]

At times, there are even significant differences in terms of NGO opinion and influence *within* the same conference.[49] This too has consequences in terms of NGO implementation responsibilities and thus the likely and perceived meaningfulness of the conference. For example, toward the end of UNCED, the divisions had sharpened between the NGOs on whether a binding forestry treaty was warranted and, if so, what form it should take.[50] A group of 39 NGOs, half from the North and half from the South, under the leadership of Bill Mankin of the Sierra Club, advocated a statement of forest principles in accordance with four key concepts: (1) effective forest protection and expansion; (2) indigenous peoples to be accorded full control and legal authority over their traditional territories; (3) participation by all in decision-making, and (4) adherence to basic ecological and sustainable management. On the other hand, 25 NGOs, all except for three from the South, under the leadership of Anil Agarwal of the Center for Science and Environment (CSE), sought to prevent any post-Rio global forest convention.[51] The conference ended with a non-binding treaty, the so-called Non-Legally Binding Authoritative Statement of Principles for a Global Consensus on the Management, Conservation and Sustainable Development of all Types of Forests.[52] Subsequent follow-up efforts by sympathetic NGOs and states to get a binding treaty have thus far been abortive. "The success that NGOs did achieve in the UNCED forest debate was largely the result of the lobbying of the larger established groups on issues that the majority of NGOs could easily agree upon, such as the participation of local communities and the need for security of land tenure."[53] The forestry case also reveals that NGO influence on conference outcomes is the greater the earlier in the process they get involved. It seems especially critical that they get involved before states have publicly articulated their positions (e.g. there is no evidence of influence of the Agarwal initiative on Southern governments as they had already reached similar conclusions on their own) and even more so, if those public articulated positions are in clear opposition to those of other governments. In the forestry case, it appears as if NGOs had very little political space left for initiating new ideas or working out new compromises, owing to governmental disagreements at PrepCom3 between governments of the North and South.[54]

NGOs and specific UN-sponsored global conferences

The following section can do no more than refer to some past conferences to illustrate some of the chapter's major themes and to help us draw some tentative conclusions for the future of such conferences. More details about these and other conferences can be found in other chapters in this volume and in the references provided in Schaubman's chapter (Appendix B).

Women's conferences

In her review of NGOs and women's conferences, Carolyn Stephenson credits the women's caucuses, established prior to the various women's conferences, with empowering the counter-conferences/fora that were convened. An analogous set of activities, funded by the US Agency for International Development, via the Eurasia and ARD/Checchi foundations, occurred in Russia. Money was provided to US organizations, including the League of Women Voters Education Fund and the Network for East-West Women to organize research and training seminars in Russia prior to the conferences.[55] Stephenson credits the caucuses, but the same can be said for the research and seminars in countries like Russia, with the development in turn "... of both the international women's movement and the more formal governmental and intergovernmental infrastructures ... that would begin to serve as the basis for an international women's regime." Indeed, she sees the most important outcome of the first women's conference (in Mexico City, 19 June–2 July 1975), and particularly its counter-conference,[56] as being the construction of an organizational infrastructure and international communications network.[57] In this context, Stephenson singles out the International Women's Tribune Center Newsletter, which was produced quarterly and sent free to "third world" women and at a low cost to others. The official registration list from the Mexico forum was the starting point.[58] Lubin and Winslow, also surveying the range of women's conferences, reached a similar conclusion:

The opportunity to exchange opinions and experiences and to enjoy the mutual support of those with similar goals lighted brush fires that continued to grow long after the conferences had closed their doors. One direct outcome ... was the creation of new nongovernmental organizations – international, national, and local. Another was the establishment of new units for cooperation with nongovernmental organizations by intergovernmental bodies and by national governments. A third was a broad extension of networking among these organizations at every level, including grass roots groups.[59]

Konstantinova reports that in Russia, for example, the government worked with NGOs in setting up a new national structure to monitor the status of women and ensure the implementation of the conference's Platform for Action. She goes on to argue that NGO and media pressure will be "vital for the success of such projects; but their desire or ability to do this remains unsure." Her scepticism seems to arise from the fact that the Russian media largely ignored the Beijing Conference, "except for a few articles that (justifiably) attacked the position of the official Russian delegation."[60]

Central to the past and future success of the women's human rights regime and the related international advocacy network are the NGOs that work to keep up pressure for repeated women's conferences, something essential because unlike most world conferences, the women's conferences have not concluded with the establishment of a new UN body empowered for monitoring and implementing women's issues.[61] Stephenson boldly asserts that it would be hard to explain the progress to date on women's issues in and around the United Nations without regard to Women's International Non-governmental Organizations.[62] More specifically, she notes that NGOs became much more "visible" in the final reports of the women's conferences beginning with the Copenhagen Conference (14–30 July 1980). In its Programme for Action governments are called upon to "enable" NGOs to help in the realization of the conference's goals, taking into account NGOs' resources and roles. It also calls upon governments to provide financial support, especially for grassroots NGOs and those comprised of or working on behalf of the rural poor. Revealingly, the programme also calls on governments to develop strategies to implement NGOs' particular recommendations and to "promote solidarity among women's groups."[63] Stephenson credits this to the longstanding cooperation between NGOs, women in the UN secretariat, and women on various country delegations.[64] Those participating at the women's conferences have also continually pressured governments to produce documents that commit themselves to greater participation and equality of women. These documents, especially as international legal scholars joined the women's movement, were vital because they could be used for leverage.[65]

Focusing on the Beijing Conference, Morgan makes the point that "a sizable NGO presence *on* official country delegations themselves was in large part the reason for the emergence of as strong a document as the Platform for Action."[66] There the charge to "civil society including non-governmental organizations and the private sector" was more pointed than in the past. It called upon various actors in civil society, including NGOs

... to take strategic action in the following critical areas of concern: (1) The persistent and increasing burden of poverty on women; (2) Inequalities and inadequacies in and unequal access to education and training; (3) Inequalities and inadequacies in and unequal access to health care and related services; (4) Violence against women; (5) The effects of armed or other kinds of conflict on women, including those living under foreign occupation; (6) Inequality in economic structures and policies, in all forms of productive activities and in access to resources; (7) Inequality between men and women in the sharing of power and decision-making at all levels; (8) Insufficient mechanisms at all levels to promote the advancement of women; (9) Lack of respect for and inadequate promotion and protection of the human rights of women; (10) Stereotyping of women and inequality in women's access to and participation in all communication systems, especially in the media; (11) Gender inequalities in the management of natural resources and in the safeguarding of the environment; (12) Persistent discrimination against and violation of the rights of the girl child.[67]

In this context, a key actor was the Women's Environment and Development Organization (WEDO), a global activist, advocacy, and information organization founded in 1990 in response to the preparations for the women's conference. Claiming 20,000 women as part of its global network, it launched a post-Beijing programme to promote the Beijing Platform for Action "as a politically binding 'Contract with the World's Women'." Knowing that the platform was not *legally* binding, WEDO worked on the assumption that if it popularized the platform's key provisions it would help "ensure that promises and commitments made by governments in Beijing [would be] implemented in every nation and community." Through its "contract" campaign, WEDO and others with which it allied sought to ensure that NGOs provided accurate information about the content of the platform and its relationship to countries' public policies. It was WEDO's firm conviction that NGOs had to mobilize women for implementation of the platform and national implementing legislation and administrative actions. WEDO's post-Beijing plan also included strengthening the monitoring and accountability networks of NGOs and undertaking specific education and action campaigns to strengthen grassroots implementation capacities. Accordingly it prepared and disseminated monitoring tools and preliminary reports, conducted advocacy programmes directed at governments about their implementation progress to date and plans for the future, and issued anniversary reports on government implementation (the first was not very subtly named, "Holding Governments and International Agencies Accountable to Their Promises: Monitoring and Advocacy Strategies for Advancing Women's Agendas"). This was done because WEDO recognized that the "momentum generated during [even the most] promising conference process is difficult to sustain."[68]

Jocelyn Down, a Guyanese women's rights leader, explained another feature at Beijing that has proven vital to the influence of NGOs on women's issues. She notes that James D. Wolfensohn, President of the World Bank, was the only head of a major international financial institution (IFI) to meet in Beijing with the unofficial delegations. While he was roundly criticized at the meeting, it was clear several years later that he had been affected by his observations or conversations there, or at least that he had become an explicit and quite visible ally. For example, he subsequently established or strengthened several programmes for monitoring the impact of Bank policies on women and explored ways by which more funds could be channelled into projects that would assist women.[69] On the other hand, as Sum's discussion of Hillary Clinton's role at the Beijing Conference underscores, it would be naive to assume that decades of conferencing, networking, communicating, and IGO and NGO follow-up have eliminated differences in the foci, aspirations, and discourses of women and organizations from the North and South. Sum powerfully critiques Clinton's "... attempt to deploy the language of rights and give voice to a hegemonic discourse oriented to an 'imagined community of women'," as if a "gendered version of human rights ... represented the unity and empowerment of women located in diverse functional and geographical terrains."[70] Cook notes, however, that the Beijing platform seems to imply that "... affording support to a strong NGO community and civil society more generally is one of the best ways of ... encouraging the cross-cultural promotion of women's common interests in the understanding of human rights law."[71]

Environmental conferences

Like Stephenson about women's conferences, Jasanoff's conclusions about NGOs at environmental conferences are bold:

The 1992 United Nations Conference on Environment and Development (UNCED) held in Rio de Janeiro confirmed by numbers alone that NGOs had taken their place beside states and intergovernmental organizations (IGOs), in particular, those of the United Nations (UN) system, as rightful participants in environmental management. The Global Forum for NGOs held concurrently with the official Earth Summit drew representatives from some 7,000 organizations, outnumbering governments present by about one hundred to one. More important, the intense preparatory activity in the non-governmental sector leading up to and through the Rio conference showed that environmental NGOs had developed extensive skills in scientific and technical exchange, policy-making and policy-implementation, which supplemented their more traditional roles in campaigning, activism and ideological consciousness raising.[72]

NGO influence was also magnified at Rio because at least 14 countries had environmental NGO representatives *on* their national delegations.[73]

Kolk's detailed case study of NGOs and the Brazilian Amazon reveals some less obvious, but in the long run quite important effects of NGOs at world conferences. After observing that the UNCED process favoured the larger, Northern NGOs that were more experienced in international negotiations and lobbying, Kolk goes on to observe that "The North-South controversy which dominated UNCED also influenced NGO relations and brought issues of trade, debt and international inequality to the attention of Northern environmental NGOs." This, in turn, contributed to the "further internationalization of the NGO movement," which, in turn, contributed to large NGOs in Washington taking relatively radical positions on issues related to Brazil. These, in turn, significantly affected the direction of World Bank policy.[74]

Another innovation of note connected to the Rio Conference – this time at the counter conference – was agreement to a so-called alternative treaties project. In the project, various NGOs and social movements were encouraged – at Rio *and afterward* – to develop treaties in specific areas of interest to them. They were understood to be "open documents, ready to shift and grow" as the need arose. They were "managed" via NGO-Net, an electronic communications network, and ranged in topics from environmental concerns to how NGOs "can better cooperate with one another at how to shape relations with other social sectors such as the youth and women's movements." The decision to move into the treaty-writing arena has been described as evidence that "NGOs are increasingly gaining confidence in their legitimate claim to a voice in the global policy dialogue and implementation. They are asserting with growing conviction the need for an empowered civil society." Their motivations have been explained this way:

As UNCED approached without any evidence that governments were willing to take responsibility for the environmental and, underlying that, the developmental crisis facing the planet, NGOs grew increasingly angry that their counsel was not being heard. The treaties were a positive response to that anger, asserting that civil society is prepared to deal with the crisis.[75]

Not surprisingly, at the Rio +5 Conference in 1997, environmental NGOs were a critical audience as government conferees surveyed the lack of progress on the various items on Agenda 21.[76] It would be overstating the case, however, to suggest that there had been no progress in terms of Agenda 21.

As noted by Yongo, activities related to the Convention on Biological Diversity (CBD) exemplify:

The CBD is very liberal about those who can participate in and at its COP [Conference of Parties].[77] The CBD recognizes that in many ways environmental NGOs concerned with the conservation and sustainable use of biological diversity, such as the IUCN [World Conservation Union], Greenpeace and WWF [World Wide Fund for Nature], have made important contributions to increasing transparency in international processes. The Convention remains a fora [sic] in which NGOs remain deeply involved and committed. As such it represents an important fora [sic] for the principles and objectives of Chapter 27 of Agenda 21 ..."[78]

More specifically, EarthAction focused its post-Rio CBD activity on encouraging its national implementation and on the signing and implementation of ILO Convention 169, the Indigenous and Tribal People's Convention,[79] as there is a close connection between lands claimed by indigenous peoples and those subject to the various provisions of the CBD. The Amazon merely represents the most obvious example of this. Still, Yongo contends for NGOs (and industry) to be very effective in the follow-up to Rio, they "need to be provided with the direct and legitimate channel for providing reports to secretariats and having those reports considered in evaluating implementation and compliance." This would really allow them to "... assist in monitoring the implementation of the CBD locally, nationally and internationally."[80]

The same has been noted for the Convention on Climate Change, i.e. NGOs get credit for much of what has been accomplished, but complain that their efforts are constrained by the limitations on their participation that persist. Changes demanded by them are informal as much as they are formal.[81] Butler and Ghai's analysis of the dispute resolution/noncompliance mechanism of the Climate Change Convention supports the notion of accomplishments within clear constraints.[82]

Thus far, the AG13 [Ad Hoc Working Group on Article 13 of the Climate Change Convention] has allowed NGOs to contribute actively to its deliberations by responding to the questionnaire and by providing their views on issues raised in the discussions during its sessions. Moreover, several representatives from NGOs served as panelists at the "Panel Discussion" held on noncompliance and dispute resolution mechanisms convened during the second session of the Conference of the Parties in Geneva, Switzerland, in July 1996. This involvement reflects the great interest that NGOs have shown in this aspect of the Climate Change Convention, as well as the willingness of parties to listen to their views (certainly with regard to this issue) in a manner other than behind the scenes. The chair of AG13, Patrick Széll, has been particularly adept at providing NGOs with the opportunity to contribute while safeguarding parties' sovereign role in intergovernmental negotiations.[83]

EarthAction's experiences pursuant to the Climate Change Convention provides a similar picture. They followed up with messages to US President Clinton, worked toward national implementation by those developing countries that had agreed to the convention, called for a more demanding protocol on reducing greenhouse gas emissions, pressed for restructuring and full financing of the Global Environment Facility (GEF), and worked to influence the meetings of the Conference of the Parties and the convention's review conference. Smith expressed some satisfaction at EarthAction's success in increasing the transparency of the GEF decision-making processes, thereby increasing the chances of developing countries to get their views heard. He also expressed pride in EarthAction's ability to put pressure on the Canadian government, by arguing that it seemed hard to understand how Canada could be pressuring poor countries to save their rainforests and not take action to protect their own in British Columbia. On the other hand, Smith expressed frustration on behalf of EarthAction and its partners especially for the "timidity" of small island developing states in confronting more powerful countries like the US.[84] What EarthAction's activities evidence is the ability of transnational advocacy networks to affect the bargaining processes in the implementation phase of world conference actions. This is done by direct participation, where permitted, working closely with countries and groups of countries and through calls for greater civil societal participation (i.e. greater accountability and transparency). The results cannot be expected to be immediate or dramatic; significant power asymmetries remain and matter, especially when powerful governments consider the issues salient to their national constituencies.

More generally, EarthAction, a transnational advocacy network with more than 1,500 partner organizations in over 140 countries, has sought to put pressure on elected officials by informing their constituents about "the timing of negotiations, the terms of debate, and expert assessments of what is needed to resolve a crisis." It also provides "editorial advisories" in hopes that the media will understand the issues and report what they might not otherwise have focused upon. For example, it got CNN to rebroadcast its video news clip about threats to biological diversity. "Both directly and through its network of NGOs, EarthAction also monitors global political processes, informing partners about how and when effective pressure can be applied." In the post-Rio environment, NGOs' focus has been on getting countries to implement the biodiversity and climate change conventions, but they have also supported follow-up negotiations on the Convention to Combat Desertification, another goal of Agenda 21. Strategies have included letter-writing campaigns to national leaders. While the impacts of such letters, indeed of any of EarthAction's activities, are impossible to measure, Smith notes "it is clear that such pressures do make policymakers aware of citizens' concerns about their foreign policy activity." (Whether it is truly "citizen" concerns or those of the EarthAction's leadership, of course, is part of the recent debate over the lack of accountability, representativeness, and transparency of many NGOs). Smith continues: "Although the pressure brought to bear on decisions regulating CO_2 emissions, protecting biological diversity, and curbing desertification may not have influenced policymakers at that particular time, it could be a factor in subsequent decisions." In terms of the various review conferences, some of which are discussed in this volume, Smith contended that "without transnational efforts like those of EarthAction to draw public attention to them, such conferences are unlikely to effectively change government practices."

The Vienna Convention on Human Rights

As noted above, NGOs were largely excluded from the World Conference on Human Rights. As a result, the Vienna Declaration implicitly established restrictions on NGO activity. Gaer cites this as an example of the "... gap between, on the one hand, the dependency of UN expert human rights mechanisms on information supplied by human rights NGOs and, on the other hand, government resentment of NGO reports and activism."[85] As Dias sees it, human rights NGOs were among the "main losers" at the Vienna Conference, presumably meaning in terms of their long-term involvement with follow-up activities.[86] Indeed, in terms of implementation, Dias was not able to mask his disappointment: "While on the one hand the Vienna Declaration recognizes the important role of nongovernmental organizations in the human rights field, paragraph 25 [38] of the Declaration states that only 'nongovernmental organizations and their members *genuinely* involved in the field of human rights should enjoy the rights and freedoms recognized in the universal declaration of human rights, and the protection of national law.' "[87] This is seen to be coded language excluding NGOs from human rights monitoring.[88] Korey's summary judgement about the declaration is much more upbeat, crediting NGOs, notably including those based in the third world, with successfully fending off those (such as China and delegations from Southeast Asia) who wished to blunt the commitment to universal standards of human rights.[89]

The UN Secretariat has been portrayed at Vienna as "... attempting to exclude references to specific states in the parallel NGO Forum's program and in excluding the Dalai Lama from speaking at it. Despite this, large numbers of NGOs attended the parallel [non-official] conference activities which ... impacted on the official deliberations."[90] Most notable – in terms of the "sheer scale of their presence" and their impact – were women's groups. "[T]heir persistence and level of organization, ensured that the final conference document was less insubstantial than at least some of the diplomats might have wished." Most significant, at least at this point in time, appears to have been the acceptance of the notion that "women's rights are human rights," that is, agreement to integrate or mainstream in the UN system violations of women's rights. Thus no longer would women's groups have to rely on a committee located in Vienna, out of the human rights mainstream, to investigate violations of the Convention on the Elimination of Discrimination against Women. Rather, they could turn to a special rapporteur appointed by the Commission on Human Rights to pursue the problem of violence against women.[91] The NGOs' concern with women's rights as human rights was coordinated by the Rutgers-based Center for Women's Leadership. "The dialogue between NGOs and official delegates was crucial in ensuring that the recommendations made by women's groups were incorporated in the final document, since the drafting committee was closed to NGOs."[92]

In spite of considerable support for some of them, a number of key NGO demands, however, were not included in the Vienna Declaration and Program of Action. These included: (1) recognition of the right of self-determination of indigenous peoples; (2) detailed measures to protect the rights of groups such as minorities, the disabled, victims of AIDS, people of alternative sexual orientations; and (3) adoption of a holistic approach to the right to development that would include cutbacks in military expenditures, reform of structural adjustment programmes, and accountability of multinational corporations for human rights violations.[93]

Still or really because of this, five years after the Vienna Convention, NGOs (with the support of the Canadian government) convened the Ottawa International Forum. It brought together 250 representatives of 100 NGOs and indigenous peoples to assess the overall situation of human rights. The participants noted at least three positive developments since Vienna: (1) the post of High Commissioner for Human Rights had been created and strengthened; (2) the UN Secretary-General was making progress in reorganizing the entire UN system as it relates to human rights, and (3) the Special Procedures and Mechanisms of the Commission on Human Rights were in the process of review, with a view toward strengthening them. Much credit has been accorded to NGOs in these regards, especially to Amnesty International for the recommendation for the establishment of the High Commissioner post. Korey, for example, contends that "NGOs transformed the entire character of the conference, compelling it to demand the creation of an institution [the UN High Commission for Human Rights] that would seek to link and strengthen the various special UN mechanisms, while at the same time acting as a kind of moral conscience of the world."[94] The idea of a High Commissioner had been around since 1963, but had faced intense opposition from the Soviet Union and some third world countries, who feared criticism for their human rights practices. While the collapse of the Soviet Union was an important, perhaps necessary, facilitating condition, NGOs' participation in Vienna was also key. Their effectiveness there owed much to the "extraordinary effort" of newly evolving third world-based NGOs as well as INGOs. Moreover, their ability to work with the US delegates in Vienna appears to have been partly a consequence of Washington-based NGOs having won the Clinton administration's support for the High Commissioner idea.[95]

ECOSOC and the General Assembly also held follow-up reviews to Vienna. These were highly divisive and unproductive; and there was very limited NGO participation.[96] In many ways, then, the Vienna +5 process shows the limits to what NGOs can do in the way of policy implementation or even monitoring when many states are opposed. At the same time, the Vienna +5 process shows how vital is NGO involvement in this aspect of global governance, especially if the decisions taken by UN-sponsored global conferences are going to be meaningful.

Habitat II (Istanbul)

One of the more interesting occurrences at Habitat II was the seeming "rollback" of some of the commitments on women's rights made a year earlier in Beijing. This occurred in spite of an explicit pledge by the conference's Secretary-General Wally N'Dow that that would not occur. Instead, there were votes, with the Group of 77 (G77) in the lead, re-affirming the importance of parental rights; guaranteeing respect for member states' religious and ethical values; recognition of the family as the basic unit of society; and deletion of all references, save one, to "reproductive health." At least one observer explains this, in large part, by the active lobbying of pro-family NGOs who, "for the first time, had prolonged access to national delegates."[97] Their ability to have this major an influence is related to their unique role envisaged at Istanbul (and thereafter) by the conference organizers.

The discourse at Habitat II was one of partnerships, some of which were formed during the conference itself (i.e. between NGOs and caucuses – comprised of NGOs and some, especially municipal, government officials – on Appropriate Building Technology, Rural-Urban Linkages, Sustainable Science and Technology, Sustainable Communities and Societies, Human Settlements, Water, Energy, Elderly, Family, Youth for Habitat, Foundations, Resources, Children Rights, Professionals, Training and Research Partners, Trade Unions, Academies of Science and Engineering, Disabled, Human Solidarity etc.).[98] Indeed, the conference organizers describe Habitat II as having been "organized as a Conference of Partners" in order "... to provide the fullest opportunity to all actors in civil society to bring their experiences to the preparatory process and to the Conference itself."[99] Habitat II was the first major global UN conference to permit NGOs to make interventions from the floor during working group and committee negotiations; it was also the first conference to give official recognition to NGO amendments.[100] Further (or perhaps because of these precedents), the Habitat Agenda stated that

The effective implementation of the Habitat Agenda requires strengthening local authorities, community organizations and non-governmental organizations in the spheres of education, health, poverty eradication, human rights, social integration, infrastructure and improvement of the quality of life, and relief and rehabilitation, enabling them to participate constructively in policy-making and implementation.[101]

Networks of NGOs (and networks of NGOs and Community-Based Organizations) were looked at to publicize the plight of those lacking adequate shelter, but also to monitor government evictions and promote efficient and sustainable energy and water use.[102] The post-Istanbul work of Africaucus – the African NGO Habitat II caucus working on urban/ habitat issues – exemplifies this approach. Some of its accomplishments included convening workshops, networking, documenting African "urban realities," advocacy within international meetings, and working with the Economic Commission for Africa (ECA) and the Organization of African Unity (OAU). More participatory municipal planning is one of the programmes envisaged for the future.[103] Habitat II clearly exemplified the influence of NGOs both during and after global conferences, as well as the ideological spread amongst NGOs.

The Social Summit

The Social Summit provides us with an opportunity to learn more about NGOs and world conferences through critiques of their actions (and inaction) at such conferences and in the follow-up phase to such conferences. Some of Somavía's critiques of NGOs at the Social Summit are particularly interesting, not least of all because he is generally credited with the convening of the conference and "his generous spirit" has been praised for opening almost all of the conference's business to NGOs.[104] Among the most interesting comments he has made is the argument that the problem with NGOs

... overall is that they are organized around sectors: women's organizations mobilize around women's issues, ecologists around the environment, human rights bodies on human rights issues, and so on. While some of these have cross-sectoral links, my feeling is that there is often an enormous amount of energy dedicated to drawing on partial information, and this leads to very little joint action.[105] On the other hand there are some social actors who are playing what could be described as a structural role – such as consumers – who are largely not organized. We can talk about putting private business at the disposal of social development, the great merit of which is that both sides benefit. But in the final analysis, a company makes a profit because someone is consuming its product. It is misleading to imagine that, in the whole production process, one actor is more important than the other is. Investment is key, as is accumulation, and the capacity of private investment to generate wealth is essential since there can be no distribution without wealth. However, that wealth depends on consumers. Yet, with the exception of organizations such as Consumers International, consumers remain largely dispersed. I believe that consumers should begin to organize in a more political way, affirming our rights as consumers just as trade unions organized to affirm and defend the rights of workers. When I say that civil society is too diffuse, that consumers are insufficiently organized, that trade unions are not fully enough linked within the wider civil society, I am also, of course, affirming that a huge array of social actors could play a real role in resolving many of the issues under discussion – if they worked together.[106]

The critiques of the NGOs' actions subsequent to the summit are also revealing, although it should first be noted that the *immediate* NGO follow-up to the summit was typical[107] even though the summit has been portrayed as unique amongst the world conferences. This is because it took up issues that were not really "already on the table" (contra Rio, Vienna, Cairo, Istanbul, or Beijing) and it was as much about ideas (e.g. the need to focus on the impacts of globalization and trade liberalization) and values (especially "solidarity") as about programmes. Former UN Secretary-General Boutros Boutros-Ghali has put it this way:

The World Summit for Social Development at Copenhagen in March 1995 stressed the interconnectedness of the entire continuum of conferences. It is obvious that economic problems have social consequences and that social deterioration in turn undermines economies. The ills that societies feel most acutely all have social origins and social consequences, and the Copenhagen summit focused on these: the urgent and universal need to eradicate poverty, expand productive employment, reduce unemployment, and enhance social integration.

The decision to focus a summit entirely on the most deprived segment of global society was a dazzling statement. One hundred and eighty-seven countries were represented at Copenhagen, no fewer than 117 of them by their heads of state or government. The most innovative idea of the summer was endorsement of the principle of spending 20 percent of overseas development assistance on basic social services, in return for which poor countries would agree to devote 20 percent of their budgets to such programs.[108]

The International Council on Social Welfare (ICSW) exemplifies the "typical" immediate post-conference activity. It quickly involved itself in promoting and monitoring implementation of the summit's agenda. Specifically, it convened meetings of various civil society organizations at the regional and international levels and urged governments and IGOs to pursue implementation (e.g. by defining absolute poverty and setting target dates for its elimination and monitoring observance of the key elements of the International Covenant on Economic, Social and Political Rights). Subsequent to the summit, the World Bank reoriented some of its programmes toward poverty eradication and the OECD's Development Assistance Committee (DAC) endorsed that target. There is also an obvious and expected payoff – and follow-up – to one of the major foci of the NGO caucuses: solutions to problems were shared. For example, CAPE (Children's Alliance for Protection of the Environment) discussed problems and progress related to child labour in Kenya,[109] something that would be hard for the Kenyan delegation to have done at the IGO sessions, but something that is priceless for grassroots organizations trying to come to grips with the economic, social, legal, moral, and psychological issues surrounding child labour issues.

But NGOs have not done all that well to meet the Summit's challenge of "creating an enabling environment," deemed a requisite for addressing the underlying causes of poverty and exclusion. More specifically, NGOs have made little headway in addressing the summit documents' focus on "the adverse social impact of short-term speculative activity in international financial markets, which diverts resources from genuinely productive enterprises and deters governments from pursuing long-term policies that would enable sustainable economic development and foster social cohesion." To make headway in these and other macro-economic issues would require NGOs

... to familiarize themselves with areas which may seem complex and uncongenial, and to take a constructive approach towards the potential benefits of economic development and private enterprise. It will also mean developing the capacity and courage ... to research and propose economic policies that will prevent further pain and social damage – even where these policies are unappealing to their own donors.

Further, it has been suggested the NGOs should be more precise, relevant, or responsible in some of their recommendations. By doing so, presumably they would gain credibility. For example, many of the NGOs that campaigned on debt issues, initially at least, argued for unconditional write-offs for all highly indebted least developed countries. "But in the case of the former Zaire, for instance, this might simply have increased the personal wealth of the former president." Thus it was suggested that debt reduction might be best linked to some form of conditionality. Related, it has also been suggested that perhaps NGOs should refocus their efforts from follow-up lobbying of ECOSOC and the Commission for Social Development to non-UN bodies, including the G7/G8, the Bretton Woods institutions, the OECD, and various regional and subregional groups. "The question is whether to urge these institutions outside the United Nations system to expand further into the area of social policy, or to persist in trying to strengthen the ECOSOC structure."[110] Here, of course, the contention is that successful implementation may require NGOs to break with their traditional allies or at least to form new alliances if they seek to contribute meaningfully to the achievement of the goals of the conferences of the 1990s, goals they helped formulate.

Conclusions

The UN-sponsored world conferences of the 1990s differed from their predecessors in many ways. This chapter has focused on the success of NGOs in being more fully integrated into the conference policy-making process. In some instances, they have been involved in all phases of the process, notably including the official preparatory committees and conference follow-up. As has been shown, their role in conference implementation, in some instances, has been identified in various conference documents as key to the success of the conferees' agenda. They themselves, of course, were often instrumental in including such empowering provisos.

Our review of the follow-up to various UN-sponsored world conferences has evidenced the importance of NGOs, especially democratically run, non-government funded, and "grassroots" ones, to the successful implementation of some of the key decisions taken at the conferences. Not simply is the active participation of such NGOs important at conferences (and counter-conferences), but they are important in effectuating the goals of the conferees. Even the UN Secretariat has recognized this, knowing that its reform measures to better implement conference decisions can only supplement the work of other actors. More specifically, we have found NGOs particularly valuable as critical thinkers and as monitors, both of governments and IGOs in fulfilling the commitments that they made at the conference (and subsequently). Feedback from that monitoring, of course, is vital to implementing policies in a context sensitive way, for oftentimes only "grassroots" NGOs are on site. But the monitoring is also vital to legitimizing the process in the eyes of those concerned about civil societal involvement and to convincing the funders of UN-sponsored world conferences that their money was well spent. Thus the success of past and the value of future conferences seem to be closely connected to the activities of NGOs at and perhaps especially after they conclude.

Moreover, this chapter has focused attention on the quality of NGO skills in policy implementation (by themselves or in concert with other actors) as well as their success at information gathering, evaluation and dissemination, interest articulation, consciousness raising, campaigning, activism, policy advocacy, and lobbying – the traditional activities of NGOs on which scholars have for long focused their attention.[111] It has also reinforced our knowledge about the need to pay attention to the multiple and often contradictory relationships between NGOs and social movements (and transnational advocacy networks[112] and epistemic communities).[113] And perhaps more importantly, attention has been focused on the relations between NGOs and statist actors (states and IGOs), including a weighing of the costs and advantages of collusion and cooption. Somewhat related, it focuses one's attention on competition, conflict, and cooperation among NGOs and on the characteristics and consequences of NGOs that have historically remained, through choice or otherwise, outside the world conference circuit.

Thus the procedural challenge to those supporting world conferences is to seek inputs from these often highly disparate and less formally organized, sometimes counter-hegemonic groups. Not to do so decreases the likelihood that the agendas of the conferences of the 1990s will be successfully implemented. Not to do so risks – as the CSD example shows – developing programmes of action that are insufficient to meet the challenges of the day. Not to be grounded in the so-called "new" or "bottom up" multilateralism risks a widening of the circle of critics of the UN and some NGOs, as being less legitimate, transparent, and accountable than the governments whose actions they are seeking to ignite and, to some extent, supplement.[114] And that, in turn, is likely to ensure that few conferences will convened in the twenty-first century. Nor should they. Even if the problems are global, and the UN lacks adequate machinery to address the problems, without active, broad-based, NGO (including "grassroots" and Southern-based) involvement in all phases of the policy-making process, member state money can be better spent in other ways.

Notes

1. "As is frequently pointed out, NGOs can be used quite loosely to describe any association of people, from youth groups to the Mafia, from the Roman Catholic Church to Greenpeace, from the International Chamber of Commerce to an agricultural cooperative in rural India. It includes organizations that are operational, providing services such as Oxfam, and those that are advocacy-based, such as the Third World Network. The term makes no distinction between broad membership-based organizations and small ones lead [sic] by inspired individuals. It does not distinguish between associations of citizens and organizations of capital, or between NGOs that work in cooperation with the state or those that seek to overthrow it. It fails to distinguish between the 'big eight' that control the US$8 billion market for NGOs and the tens of thousands that struggle for funding." Riva Krut, with the assistance of Kristin Howard, Eric Howard, Harris Gleckman, and Danielle Pattison, *Globalization and Civil Society: NGO Influence in International Decision-Making*, UNRISD Discussion Paper No. 83 (Geneva: United Nations Research Institute for Social Development, April 1997).

2. This leads Rodolfo Stavenhagen to conclude that: "It is not very useful to group all of these organisations and movements under the single heading of 'non-governmental organisations.'" "In fact," he continues, "... the term NGO refers most aptly to independent, private institutions involved in so-called development aid. Very often, these are but surrogates of governmental aid agencies. They usually have their headquarters in some industrialised country and carry out their activities in the Third World. Truly non-governmental popular organisations, representing the interests and demands of certain social groups (ethnic minorities, indigenous and tribal peoples, peasants, migrant workers, urban squatters, relatives of the politically persecuted or 'disappeared ones' and so on) should not, to my mind, be lumped together with other non-governmental organisations." Rodolfo Stavenhagen, "Peoples' Movements: the antisystemic challenge," in *The New Realism: Perspectives on Multilateralism and World Order*, edited by Robert W. Cox (London: Macmillan, for the United Nations University Press, 1997), pp. 33–34.

3. Even though the UN Framework Convention on Climate Change (UNFCCC) chose to include "municipal leaders and local authorities" as one of its three main NGO constituencies, I will not be treating local governments as NGOs. UNFCCC, Subsidiary Body of Implementation, *Involvement of Non-Governmental Organizations* (Bonn, 8th Session, 2–12 June 1998, Item 11 of the Provisional Agenda), FCCC/SBI/1998/5, p. 4.

4. United Nations, Department of Public Information, UN Briefing Papers, *The World Conferences: Developing Priorities for the 21st Century*, DPI 1816 (New York: Department of Public Information, 1997), p. 14. For an elaboration of these definitional issues, see: Michael G. Schechter, *Historical Dictionary of International Organizations* (Lanham, MD: Scarecrow Press, 1998), pp. 1–4. See also: Leon Gordenker and Thomas G. Weiss, "Pluralizing Global Governance: Analytical Approaches and Dimensions," in *NGOs, The UN and Global Governance*, edited by Thomas G. Weiss and Leon Gordenker (Boulder, CO: Lynne Rienner, 1996), pp. 18–19.

5. ECOSOC's latest guidelines for granting consultative status to NGOs calls for them to have a "democratically adopted constitution" providing "for the determination of policy by a conference, congress, or other representative body, and for an executive organ responsible to the policy-making body." It also explicitly calls for accountable and transparent decision-making processes. Moreover, the "basic resources" of NGOs gaining consultative status "shall be derived in the main part from contributions of the national affiliates or other components or from individual members." If this last criterion is not met, an explanation needs to be provided and the ECOSOC Committee on

NGOs needs to accept such an explanation. Moreover "any financial contribution or other support, direct or indirect, from a Government to the organization shall be openly declared ..." ECOSOC, *Consultative Relationship between the United Nations and Non-governmental Organizations*, Resolution 1996/31 (49th Plenary Meeting, 25 July 1996), Part I, paras 10, 12, and 13.

6. Tatsuro Kunugi, "Introduction," in *World NGO Conference: Report of the First Preparatory Meeting, Held at UNU Headquarters, Tokyo, 23–24 September 1996*. ⟨http://www.unu.edu/hq/unupress/ngoconference.html#Introduction⟩

7. *Host* countries pay most of the costs. Countries attending pay the expenses of their delegates. Goshko reports that the UN spends between $5 million and $6 million per conference. John M. Goshko, "U.N. Conferences Come Under Fire: Critics Say World Body Can't Afford Meetings Amid Financial Crisis," *Washington Post* (25 November 1995), A16. The UN itself puts the figure at $1.7 million to $3.4 million per conference, excepting the very costly Earth Summit. *United Nations Conferences: What Have They Accomplished?*, DPI/1825/Rev.4 (New York: United Nations, Department of Public Information, August 1997).

8. United Nations, Department of Public Information, UN Briefing Papers, *The World Conferences: Developing Priorities for the 21st Century*, DPI 1816 (New York: Department of Public Information, 1997), p. 14.

9. J. Smith, "Building Political Will after UNCED: Earth Action," in *Transnational Social Movements and Global Politics*, edited by J. C. C. Smith and Ron Pagnucco (Syracuse: Syracuse University Press, 1997), pp. 190–191.

10. For example, the Women's Environment and Development Organization (WEDO) plays a key role in this regard taking the position that "it is not sufficient to influence the words agreed to in UN conference documents: women NGOs must monitor government compliance and mobilize for implementation." Susan Davis, "Making Waves: Advocacy by Women NGOs at UN Conferences," *Development: Journal of the Society for International Development* (No. 3, 1996), p. 45.

11. Smith, for example, credits Earth Action with doing this in regard to UNCED. "Building Political Will," p. 173, n. 9 above.

12. Hart and Thetaz-Bergman contend that "The very air, food, and water that children require to survive at the most basic physiological level to support healthy physical growth have been the primary subject of concern of nongovernmental forces." Stuart N. Hart and Laura Thetaz-Bergman, "The Role of Nongovernmental Organizations in Implementing the Convention on the Rights of the Child," 6 *Transnational Law and Contemporary Problems: A Journal of The University of Iowa College of Law* (Fall, 1996), p. 377. Perhaps an equally important example of NGOs as service agents is a negative one, the UN's reliance on NGOs in Rwanda to perform the tasks that it could not. The NGOs' lack of competence there may have contributed to even more deaths. Bob Deacon with Michelle Hulse and Paul Stubbs, *Global Social Policy: International Organizations and the Future of Welfare* (Thousand Oaks, CA: Sage, 1997), p. 158. More generally, see Thomas G. Weiss, *Beyond UN Subcontracting: Task-Sharing with Regional Security Arrangements and Security-Providing NGOs* (London: Macmillan, 1998).

13. For example, Humphreys credits the International Union for the Conservation of Nature and Natural Resources (ICUN) with getting government delegates to the International Tropical Organization to agree to give consideration to conservation issues and likewise to include a conservation clause in the 1983 International Tropical Timber Agreement, the first UNCTAD-sponsored commodity agreement to contain a conservation clause. David Humphreys, "Hegemonic Ideology and the International Tropical Timber Organisation," in *The Environment and International Relations*, edited by John Vogler and Mark F. Imber (New York: Routledge, 1966), p. 97.

14. The World Summit for Children's *Plan of Action for Implementing the World Declaration on the Survival, Protection and Development of Children in the 1990s* said this about the role of NGOs in the implementation of its programme: "All international development agencies – multilateral, bilateral and non-governmental – are urged to examine how they can contribute to the achievement of the goals and strategies enunciated in the Declaration and this Plan of Action as part of more general attention to human development in the 1990s. They are requested to report their plans and programmes to their respective governing bodies before the end of 1991 and periodically thereafter." The establishment of a firm reporting deadline is a bit unusual. ⟨http://www.unicef.org/wsc/plan.htm⟩, para. 35(1).

15. Smith, "Building Political Will," p. 182, n. 9 above.

16. These are concepts central to the Multilateralism and the UN System (MUNS) project. See, for example, Robert W. Cox, "Introduction," in *The New Realism: Perspectives on Multilateralism and World Order* (London: Macmillan, for the United Nations University Press, 1997).

17. This point is elaborated upon and documented by Michael G. Schechter, "Globalization and Civil Society," in *The Revival of Civil Society: Global and Comparative Perspectives*, edited by Michael G. Schechter (London: Macmillan, 1999).

18. Weyker offers a useful summary of the advantages of IT (information technology) for NGOs: "Computers have helped movements to create impressive new kinds of hard (cognitive) information. Camcorders put the creation of powerful affective symbolic imagery into the hands of anyone with something symbolic to record. Computer and fax communications networks allow for the creation of affective bonds and planning of strategy across long distances at low costs ... Electronic communication networks also allow direct application of pressure without regard for geography by those tied into the network." Weyker also notes a number of "pitfalls" of IT for these purposes: (1) "... engaging of more and more 'ground-level' members of the movement to communicate directly and instantly with the outside world without working through the movement's hierarchy," something that could "potentially damage the movement's precious credibility abroad"; (2) lack of readiness of audience to hear the message broadcast; (3) risk of government wiretapping, and (4) possibility of government countermeasures. Shayne Weyker, "Kayapó Spin Doctors and Truth Commission Computer Programmers: New Information Technology's Role in Progressive Social Movements," Occasional Paper No. 18, Harrison Program on the Future Global Agenda (October 1996), pp. 8–13. ⟨http://www.bsos.umd.edu/harrison/papers/paper18.htm⟩

19. See, for example, Richard Price, "Reversing the Gun Sights: Transnational Civil Society Targets Land Mines," 52 *International Organization* (Summer, 1998), pp. 613–664.

20. In this sense, the chapter augments Cox and Jacobson's powerful, but heavily statist, analytical framework for inquiry in which they instructed students of intergovernmental organizations of the necessity to recognize that decision-making at an organization's headquarters or any particular meeting of the organization is only one international subsystem of the decision-making system necessary to explain the direction, much less successive failure of any intergovernmental organization. Robert W. Cox and Harold K. Jacobson, "The Framework for Inquiry" and "The Anatomy of Influence" in *The Anatomy of Influence: Decision Making in International Organization* by Robert W. Cox and Harold K. Jacobson (New Haven, CT: Yale University Press, 1973).

21. Here unrepresentative is meant not simply in terms of the fact that some NGO leadership has been portrayed as unrepresentative of its membership, but also that small grassroots agencies often find it difficult to have ongoing and credible relationships with intergovernmental organizations that are used to dealing with NGOs with large

budget lines. Deacon, *Global Social Policy: International Organizations*, p. 186, n. 12 above.

22. *Ibid.*, p. 192. Interestingly, Van Rooy, relying heavily on Schweitz, contends it is a "... myth [to suggest] that NGOs must be *representative* organizations in order to be legitimate participants." Instead NGO "... legitimacy rests on at least three pillars: NGOs as sources of information and expertise, NGOs as deliverers of services, and NGOs as 'keepers of the moral flame'." Alison Van Rooy, "The Frontiers of Influence: NGO Lobbying at the 1974 World Food Conference, the 1992 Earth Summit and Beyond," 25 *World Development* (1997), p. 110.

23. Their increased influence in general has been explained by their increased financial resources and expertise, and technological breakthroughs have made it possible for them to communicate with each other without the interference of local governments. Richard Reitano, "Summits, Multilateral Diplomacy, and the United Nations," in *Multilateral Diplomacy and the United Nations Today*, edited by James P. Muldoon, Jr. et al. (Boulder, CO: Westview Press, 1999), p. 116.

24. Donini identifies an evolving source of NGO influence, wherein the UN and UN-related agencies often hire talented NGO employees. "No Amnesty International activist has yet been appointed to a senior position in the UN Centre for Human Rights, but this is the exception rather than the rule – and, to be fair, a former Amnesty International official was appointed to a very high position in the joint Organization of American States (OAS)-UN human rights monitoring mission in Haiti." The degree to which NGOs are able to use these personal links to effectuate their policy preferences is as yet largely unexamined, but it is intriguing to think of the influence channels, especially when it is remembered that an increasing number of countries are including NGO employees on government delegations. In the latter regard, Conca relying on Finger, reports that at least 14 countries at UNCED had environmental NGO representatives on their national delegations. Antonio Donini, "The Bureaucracy and the Free Spirits: Stagnation and Innovation in the Relations Between the UN and NGOs," in *NGOs, the UN, and Global Governance*, edited by Thomas G. Weiss and Leon Gordenker (Boulder, CO: Lynne Rienner Publishers, 1996), p. 86. Ken Conca, "Greening the UN: Environmental Organisations and the UN System," in *NGOs, the UN, and Global Governance*, edited by Thomas G. Weiss and Leon Gordenker (Boulder, CO: Lynne Rienner Publishers, 1996), p. 111.

25. Van Rooy, "Frontiers of Influence," p. 104, n. 22 above. Those revisions were adopted at ECOSOC's 49th plenary meeting on 25 July 1996 (resolution 1996/31).

26. "The Global Promise of Social Movements: Explorations at the Edge of Time", 12 *Alternatives* (1987), p. 173.

27. JoAnn Fagot Aviel, "NGOs and International Affairs: A New Dimension of Diplomacy," in *Multilateral Diplomacy and the United Nations Today*, edited by James P. Muldoon, Jr. et al. (Boulder, CO: Westview Press, 1999), pp. 159–160.

28. Thus while the use of the term international or civil society seems a bit premature and imprecise, it is probably fair to characterize such gatherings as "a new dynamic of embryonic participatory democracy to the global community and to the shaping of international law," while recognizing the NGOs are not necessarily highly accountable institutions. For a good discussion of NGO governance, including issues of accountability, see: Leon Gordenker and Thomas G. Weiss, "Devolving Responsibilities; A Framework for Analysing NGOs and Services," in *Beyond UN Subcontracting: Task-Sharing with Regional Security Arrangements and Service-Providing NGOs* (London: Macmillan, 1998), pp. 40–42.

29. Clark, Friedman, and Hochstetler "find evidence that the construction of a global society [centered around UN world conferences] is under way but is far from complete."

Ann Marie Clark, Elisabeth J. Friedman, and Kathryn Hochstetler, "The Sovereign Limits of Global Civil Society; A Comparison of NGO Participation in UN World Conferences on the Environment, Human Rights, and Women," 51 *World Politics* (October, 1998), p. 5.

30. It must be quickly added that it is hard to overstate the importance of evaluating the consequences of the non-invited to such conferences. For example, Van Rooy reports that only four organizations out of 1,418 were turned down in their request to attend the Rio Convention. Of course, the point is also that there are those that do not even apply. More interestingly perhaps, Van Rooy notes that some of the NGOs attending the 1974 World Food Conference had different views and policy recommendations from the government representatives because they had diagnosed the world food crisis as a "political" problem, "... based on the structure of North-South relations, while their governments interpreted the crisis largely as a problem of technical production, exacerbated by difficult weather." "Frontiers of Influence," pp. 95 and 101, n. 22 above.

31. Barbara Ruben, "Uniting for Action: Activists have a growing presence at UN conferences, but is the panoply of NGO voices being heard?" *Environmental Action* (Summer, 1995), p. 34.

32. Juan Somavía, "Post-Copenhagen: Personal Reflections," in *Advancing the Social Agenda: Two Years After Copenhagen: Report of the UNRISD International Conference and Public Meeting Geneva, 9–10 July 1997*, UNRISD/Conf/93/3 (Geneva: United Nations Research Institute for Social Development, December, 1997), p. 4.

33. "Uniting for Action," p. 34, n. 31 above.

34. Van Rooy makes a similar observation, noting that the World Food Conference was an important catalyst for NGO advocacy work and drew the attention of a whole new set of NGO actors to the international level. "Frontiers of Influence," p. 98, n. 22 above. The latter phenomenon is of particular importance given world conference fatigue and frustration amongst some long-involved NGOs.

35. Humphreys also writes of the precedents set at UNCED, most notably that the generous – but not unqualified – NGO accreditation processes used at UNCED were referred to the UN General Assembly for inclusion on a resolution suggesting that these procedures be used in subsequent UN-sponsored world conferences, something that has not really happened. "Hegemonic Ideology," p. 103, n. 13 above.

36. See, for example, Tariq Osman Hyder, "Environmental Rights: Multilateralism, Morality and the Ecology," in *Future Multilateralism: The Political and Social Framework*, edited by Michael G. Schechter (London: Macmillan, for United Nations Press, 1999).

37. J. Bennett, "Introduction: Recent Trends in Relief Aid: Structural Crisis and the Quest for a New Consensus," in *Meeting Needs: NGO Coordination in Practice*, edited by John Bennett (London: Earthscan Publications, 1995) pp. xv, xx–xxi. Morales' work, admittedly on a different subject, does not provide too much hope in this regard either. This theme is developed in Abelardo Morales-Gamboa, "Civil Society and the Regional Labyrinth in Central America," in *The Revival of Civil Society: Global and Comparative Perspectives*, edited by Michael G. Schechter (London: Macmillan, 1999).

38. See, for example, Peter Harries-Jones, Abraham Rotstein, and Peter Timmerman, "A Signal Failure: Ecology and Economy After the Earth Summit," in *Future Multilateralism: The Political and Social Framework*, edited by Michael G. Schechter (London: Macmillan, for United Nations Press, 1998), and Timothy Doyle, "Sustainable Development and Agenda 21: The Secular Bible of Global Free Markets and Pluralist Democracy," 19 *Third World Quarterly* (No. 4, 1998), pp. 771–786.

39. Peter Harries-Jones, Abraham Rotstein, and Peter Timmerman, "Nature's Veto: UNCED and the Debate Over the Earth," unpublished manuscript (February 1992, slightly revised January 1995).

40. As, for example, articulated in his *An Agenda for Peace: Preventive diplomacy, peace-making and peace-keeping*. Report of the Secretary-General pursuant to the statement adopted by the Summit Meeting of the Security Council on 31 January 1992. A/47/277-S/24111, 17 June 1992.

41. Krut, *Globalization and Civil Society*, n. 1 above.

42. Archer argues that the 1960 Congress and the one in The Hague seven years later "... were successful primarily as training grounds for NGOs. They provided one of the first opportunities for NGO representatives from East and West, North and South with a common interest in development issues to meet and exchange experiences. They provided an inspirational boost and a broader perspective for the individual NGO representatives working on particular projects in their own countries." Angus Archer, "Methods of Multilateral Management: The Interrelationship of International Organizations and NGOs," in *The US, the UN, and the Management of Global Change*, edited by Toby Trister Gati (New York: New York University Press, 1983), pp. 311–312.

43. See, for example, ⟨http://www.igc.apc.org/habitat/agenda21/ch-27.html⟩

44. The UN is quite candid as to its motivation: "The main objective of this effort is to build wider constituencies in support of UN system activities for conference follow-up as envisaged in the plans of action." United Nations Staff College Project, *Report of Inter-Agency Workshop on Field Level Follow-up to Global Conferences, Turin, 10–12 December 1997* (Turin, Italy: International Training Centre of the ILO, 1997), p. 9.

45. Although not the product of a world conference, *per se*, two authors argue that the provisions of the Convention on the Rights of the Child go "much further than previously existing international human rights treaties in recognizing the importance of nongovernmental entities." They specifically point to the "standards requiring that the Convention and mandatory reports of the States Parties be made public knowledge and encouraging use of competent bodies, beyond government agents, to submit reports and provide advice and technical assistance relevant to implementation." Hart and Thetaz-Bergman, "Role of Nongovernmental Organizations," p. 376, n. 12 above. They also provide a number of quite revealing, specific examples of the impacts of NGOs as by-products of such implementation activities (including national legislative enactments). *Ibid.*, pp. 377–379.

46. There are restrictions for meetings convened by ECOSOC (e.g. those of the UN Commission on Sustainable Development) and various specialized agencies of the UN, but not those called by the General Assembly. Thus there is a variety of accreditation programmes for global conferences.

47. Meaney notes that the US delegation and the women's caucus "... proposed that NGOs should also have the right to speak in the informal drafting sessions, a strategy widely perceived as designed to drown out the voices of small developing countries. As one Pakistani delegate warned, this increase of NGO influence at the expense of national delegations signals 'the privatization of diplomacy'." Mary Meaney, "Radical Rout," *National Review* (July 15, 1996), p. 25.

48. Felice D. Gaer, "Reality Check: Human Rights NGOs Confront Governments at the UN," in *NGOs, The UN and Global Governance*, edited by Thomas G. Weiss and Leon Gordenker (Boulder, CO: Lynne Rienner, 1996), p. 51.

49. There is some evidence of this at both Rio and Vienna. Smith, "Building Political Will," pp. 182 and 184, n. 9 above. Humphreys, "Hegemonic Ideology," pp. 97–98, n. 13 above. "Reality Check," p. 58, n. 48 above.

50. On the issue of a forest conservation treaty, Humphreys concludes that the North-South government tensions were paralleled by those amongst NGOs in spite of their best effort to present a united front. "Hegemonic Ideology," pp. 100–102, n. 13 above.

51. *Ibid.*, pp. 100–101.

52. ⟨http://www.igc.apc.org/habitat/agenda21/forest.html⟩

53. Humphreys, "Hegemonic Ideology," p. 101, n. 13 above.

54. *Ibid.*, pp. 102–103.

55. US foundations were also critical in paying for independent women's organizations to attend the Beijing Conference. Svetlana Konstantinova, "Russia's Portrait in the Women's World Gallery," 16 *SAIS Review* (Winter/Spring 1996), pp. 179–180.

56. Women's NGOs with ECOSOC consultative status had observer delegates at the official conferences, whereas others (prior to Beijing in 1995) were only able to attend the non-governmental forums. This included most of the feminist organizations established since the early 1970s. This bifurcation led to some competitive and conflictual dynamics amongst NGOs. Carolyn Stephenson, "Women's International Nongovernmental Organizations at the United Nations," in *Women, Politics, and the United Nations*, edited by Anne Wilson (Westport, CT: Greenwood Press, 1995), p. 138.

57. Although contending that "today's women's networks have their roots in the abolitionist moment of the 1800s and the subsequent international campaign for woman suffrage ...," Keck and Sikkink concur that the Mexico Conference was a key site in the "current wave of organizing internationally on women's issues ..." Margaret Keck and Kathryn Sekkink, *Activists Beyond Borders: Advocacy Networks in International Politics* (Ithaca, NY: Cornell University Press, 1998), pp. 168–169. Burch adds that the advent of computer technologies allowed the "networks to work far more effectively, particularly at the international scale, where information flow tended to be sporadic." During the Beijing Conference NGO delegations were able to keep in touch with their "grassroots" at home, "often generating feedback." She gives considerable credit to the APC (Association for Progressive Communications) Women's Networking Support Programme. Sally Burch, "ALAI: Networking with a Diversity Focus," 40 *Development* (No. 4, 1997), p. 48.

58. Stephenson, "Women's International", p. 144, n. 56 above. A useful example of the network in operation appears in International Women's Tribune Centre, "How it Happened – From Day to Day; Excerpts from Global FaxNet Bulletins, April 3–September 25, 1995," *Women's Studies Quarterly* (Nos. 1 & 2, 1996), pp. 18–39.

59. Carol Riegelman Lubin and Anne Winslow, *Social Justice for Women: The International Labor Organization and Women* (Durham: Duke University Press, 1990), p. 241.

60. Konstantinova, "Russia's Portrait," p. 185, n. 55 above.

61. On the traditional (limited) role and procedures of the UN Commission on the Status of Women, see Andrew Byrnes, "Toward More Effective Enforcement of Women's Human Rights Through the Use of International Human Rights Law and Procedures," in *Human Rights of Women: National and International Perspectives*, edited by Rebecca J. Cook (Philadelphia: University of Pennsylvania Press, 1994), pp. 209–210.

62. "Women's International," p. 150, n. 56 above.

63. *Programme of Action for the Second Half of the United Nations Decade for Women: Equality, Development and Peace*, A/CONF.94/35, paras 100–105.

64. Stephenson, "Women's International," p. 144, n. 56 above.

65. *Ibid.*, p. 150.

66. Robin Morgan, "The NGO Forum: Good News and Bad," *Women's Studies Quarterly* (Nos. 1 & 2, 1996), p. 52.

67. *Report of the Fourth World Conference on Women: Platform for Action*, A/CONF.177/20, para. 44.

68. Susan Davis, "Making Waves: Advocacy by Women NGOs at UN Conferences," *Development: Journal of the Society for International Development* (No. 3, 1996), pp. 45 and 47.

69. Barbara Crossette, "Women See Key Gains Since Talks in Beijing," *The New York Times* (8 March 1998).
70. Ngai-ling Sum, "The 'Hegemonic' Force of Hillary Clinton's 'United Sisterhood'," 1 *New Political Economy* (July, 1996), pp. 278–279.
71. Rebecca J. Cook, "Effectiveness of the Beijing Conference in Fostering Compliance with International Law Regarding Women," Chapter 4, this volume.
72. Sheila Jasanoff, "NGOs and the Environment: from Knowledge to Action," in *Beyond Subcontracting: Task-Sharing with Regional Security Arrangements and Service-Providing NGOs*, edited by Thomas G. Weiss (London: Macmillan, 1998), p. 203. See also: Fred Pearce, "No Southern Comfort at Rio?" *New Scientist* (16 May 1992), pp. 38–41.
73. Aviel, "NGOs," p. 160, n. 27 above. At the Cairo conference, NGO representatives "constituted a large part of many official delegations – half in the case of the U.S. delegation." *Ibid*.
74. Ans Kolk, *Forests in International Environmental Politics: International Organisations, NGOs and the Brazilian Amazon* (Utrecht, Netherlands: International Books, 1996), pp. 299–300.
75. Peter Padbury, *Non-Governmental Organization Alternative Treaties at the '92 Global Forum*, ⟨http://www.igc.org/habitat/treaties/ngoatgf.html⟩, June–July 1992.
76. Clark, Friedman, and Hochstetler see human rights NGOs as the role models for NGO monitoring of statist progress. "Sovereign Limits," p. 22, n. 29 above.
77. Article 23(4)(j) of the convention provides that: "The United Nations, its specialized agencies and the International Atomic Energy Agency, as well as any State not Party to this Convention, may be represented as observers at meetings of the Conference of the Parties. Any other body or agency, whether governmental or non-governmental, qualified in fields relating to conservation and sustainable use of biological diversity, which has informed the Secretariat of its wish to be represented as an observer at a meeting of the Conference of the Parties, may be admitted unless at least one third of the Parties present object. The admission and participation of observers shall be subject to the rules of procedure adopted by the Conference of the Parties."
78. Thomas Yongo, "Development, Implementation, and Effectiveness of the CBD Process," Chapter 5, this volume.
79. Smith, "Building Political Will," p. 183, n. 9 above.
80. Yongo, "Development, Implementation," n. 78 above.
81. United Nations, Framework Convention on Climate Change, *Involvement of Non-governmental Organizations*, pp. 6ff.
82. Jo Elizabeth Butler and Aniket Ghai, " The United Nations Framework Convention on Climate Change: Implementation and compliance," Chapter 6, this volume.
83. Jo Elizabeth Butler, "The Establishment of a Dispute Resolution/Noncompliance Mechanism in the Climate Change Convention," *Proceedings of the 91st Annual Meeting of The American Society of International Law* (Washington: The American Society of International Law, 1998), p. 254.
84. Smith, "Building Political Will," pp. 184–6, n. 9 above.
85. Gaer, "Reality Check," p. 51, n. 48 above.
86. I say this because Gaer goes on to note that NGOs' "presence and proposals heavily influenced the Conference's decision to recommend the appointment of a UN High Commissioner for Human Rights." Gaer, "Reality Check," pp. 59 and 60–61. It should be noted that the mandate of the Commissioner was less specific and activist than NGOs wanted, but, in any event, human rights NGOs seem to have made a positive impact *in* Vienna.
87. Clarence J. Dias, "The United Nations World Conference on Human Rights: Evalua-

tion, Monitoring and Review," Chapter 3, this volume. The article in its entirety reads: " While recognizing that the primary responsibility for standard-setting lies with States, the conference also appreciates the contribution of non-governmental organizations to this process. In this respect, the World Conference on Human Rights emphasizes the importance of continued dialogue and cooperation between governments and nongovernmental organizations. Nongovernmental organizations and their members genuinely involved in the field of human rights should enjoy the rights and freedoms recognized in the Universal Declaration of Human Rights, and the protection of the national law. These rights and freedoms may not be exercised contrary to the purposes and principles of the United Nations. Nongovernmental organizations should be free to carry out their human rights activities, without interference, within the framework of national law and the Universal Declaration of Human Rights."

88. Gaer, "Reality Check," p. 51, n. 48 above.
89. William Korey, "Human Rights NGOs: The Power of Persuasion," 13 *Ethics and International Affairs* (1999), p. 166.
90. Dianne Otto, "Nongovernmental Organizations in the United Nations System: The Emerging Role of Civil Society," 18 *Human Rights Quarterly* (No. 1, 1996), p. 119.
91. Kevin Boyle, "Stock-taking on Human Rights: The World Conference on Human Rights, Vienna 1993," 63 *Political Studies* (1995), p. 82.
92. Aviel, "NGOs," p. 161, n. 27 above.
93. Dias, "United Nations", this volume, n. 87 above.
94. Korey, "Human Rights NGOs," p. 164, n. 89 above.
95. *Ibid.*, p. 165.
96. Dias, this volume.
97. Meaney, "Radical Rout," pp. 25–26, n. 47 above.
98. *Guide for Civil Society on Implementing the Habitat Agenda,* Introduction, ⟨www.unhabitat.org/partners/civilsoc.html⟩
99. *Ibid.*, Part II, ⟨www.unhabitat.org/partners/civilsoc.html⟩
100. Aviel, "NGOs," p. 161, n. 27 above.
101. Habitat Agenda, para. 237.
102. *Guide for Civil Society on Implementing the Habitat Agenda*, Part IV, ⟨www.unhabitat.org/partners/civilsoc.html⟩
103. Africaucus: African NGO Habitat II Caucus, *Contribution to the preparation of the 17th session of CHS, Nairobi, 5–14, 1999* (Dakar, July 1998), ⟨http://habitat.unchs.org/chs17/contri.htm⟩
104. Claire Gaudiani, "A U.N. Focus on Poverty," 122 *Commonweal* (21 April 1995), pp. 4–5.
105. Clark, Friedman, and Hochstetler see some evidence of NGO-to-NGO exchange – for example environmentalists and women's activists – that has carried over into world conferences (e.g. at the women's tent in Rio). "Sovereign Limits," pp. 24 and 31, no. 29 above. Eccleston has developed a useful continuum on "global collaboration methods among environmental NGOs." He differentiates four styles of collaboration – networking, networks, coalitions, and alliances – varying by "degree" (of global contact and coordination) and costs of coordination, time, people, and resources. Alliances – presumably what Somavía would like to see – are portrayed as involving "*long-term* allegiance to common ideals among very trusted partners. Northern partners committed to *empowering* Southern NGOs. *Very regular* consultation by fax, IT [information technology] and personal meetings. Time investment *justified* by 'certainty' of shared values." Bernard Eccleston, "Does North-South Collaboration Enhance NGO Influence on Deforestation Policies in Malaysia and Indonesia?" in *NGOs and Environmental Policies: Asia and Africa*, edited by David Potter (London: Frank Cass, 1996),

p. 74. Emphasis in original. Smith argues that NGOs are often able to link issues together that IGOs and national governments never would. One of her examples is EarthAction's "campaign promoting the ILO convention on indigenous people's rights … [as] an alternative means of advancing the goals of the Convention on Biological Diversity and the negotiations on a forests treaty [at Rio]. Arguing that the recognition of indigenous peoples' land rights would curb environmentally unsustainable development in forest regions, EarthAction's campaign helped link these seemingly different multilateral efforts." "Building Political Will", p. 181, see n. 9 above.

106. Somavía, "Post-Copenhagen," p. 4, n. 32 above.
107. Jolly provides an overview of the initial UN follow-up. Richard Jolly, *Human Development: The World After Copenhagen*, 1996 John W. Holmes Memorial Lecture, ACUNS Reports and Papers, No. 2 (Providence, Rhode Island: Academic Council on the United Nations System, 1997). More generally, see Masumi Ono, "From Consensus-building to implementation: The follow-up to the UN global conferences of the 1990s", Chapter 7, this volume. Ono stresses the roles of specific functional commissions, including the Commission on the Status of Women (CSW), the Commission on Sustainable Development (CSW), the Commission on Social Development, the Commission on Human Rights and the Commission on Population and Development. She also notes that some of the Commissions collaborated with each other, some worked hard to prepare for the five-year review conferences that the General Assembly called for and some invited NGO input into some of their activities. *Ibid.*, pp. 4–6.
108. Boutros Boutros-Ghali, *Unvanquished: A U.S.-U.N. Saga* (New York: Random House, 1999), p. 171.
109. Gaudiani, "U.N. Focus," pp. 4–5, n. 104 above.
110. *Advancing the Social Agenda: Two Years After Copenhagen: Report of the UNRISD International Conference and Public Meeting Geneva, 9–10 July 1997* UNRISD/Conf/93/3 (Geneva: United Nations Research Institute for Social Development, December 1997), pp. 14–15, 19, and 59–60.
111. Peter Willetts, "Consultative Status for NGOs at the United Nations," in *"The Conscience of the World": The Influence of Non-Governmental Organisations in the U.N. System*, edited by Peter Willetts (Washington: Brookings Institution, 1996), pp. 48–52.
112. Keck and Sikkink, who have popularized the notion of transnational advocacy networks, have also spent some time discussing the relationships between such networks and NGOs (and social movements), *Activists Beyond Borders*, n. 57 above.
113. Humphreys notes, for example, that NGOs can contribute to the formation of epistemic communities by employing trained scientists to undertake research. They can, of course, also be part of NGOs themselves. Humphreys exemplifies his point by noting that individuals from, or employed as consultants by, NGOs helped to establish the links between deforestation and global warming, a sort of "textbook" example of the policy-making influence of epistemic communities (as well as underscoring the connections between them and NGOs). "Hegemonic Ideology", p. 108, n. 13 above. Deacon specifically sees NGOs, in alliance with IGO bureaucrats, as part of epistemic communities that have affected the "global social policy discourse" including at Rio and at Beijing. *Global Social Policy*, p. 200, n. 12 above.
114. While ECOSOC has tried to pre-empt some of these potential hazards by, as noted above, new guidelines calling for the credentialling only of transparent, accountable, and democratic NGOs, those guidelines are not binding on global conferences, much less NGOs more generally.

9

Conclusions

Michael G. Schechter

While global ad hoc conferences are not new, those of the 1990s were larger, more expensive, better publicized and more frequently attended by heads of state and government than ever before. Still, sceptics abound as to their substantive emphases, ideological orientation, and indeed their very worth. Accordingly, with the United States government in the lead, severe constraints have been placed on the future of such conferences until they prove their worth. It is the contention of this volume that the role of non-state actors, significantly including NGOs and the UN Secretariat itself, in the follow-up to the conferences, are among the keys to answering the sceptics' concerns. Of course, as the various studies herein document, the ability of non-state actors, including international lawyers, to effectuate global change in the direction sought by the various conference participants is related to the documents drafted at meetings preparatory to the conferences and agreed to at the conferences themselves. In those documents, often reflective of the work of NGOs themselves, states have, much more often than in the past, empowered non-state actors to assist in effectuating that change, including by monitoring the progress of states in fulfilling the commitments made at the conferences.

Jolly's chapter on the World Summit for Children offers a number of important answers to the critics of global ad hoc conferences. Jolly carefully documents the achievements of the WSC to date, as well as those goals not yet realized. Significantly, he also discusses the relationship between the World Summit and the widely-praised Convention on the

Rights of the Child, emphasizing that successful conferences are best understood as parts of processes rather than stand-alone, ad hoc events. Recognizing that preparatory and follow-up work and related activities are vital to the achievement of conference goals is essential in evaluating the worth of such conferences and in beginning to answer their critics. In addition to explicitly rejecting the notion that somehow the World Summit is the exception that proves the sceptics' generalizations, Jolly offers a number of factors "... that in principle ... can be applied to the follow-up of the goals endorsed at the other global conferences": (1) the necessity for widespread, governmental, and non-state commitment (intent in Rebecca Cook's language) to implementing the conferences' goals; (2) strong and determined national and international leadership; (3) broadly-based political and social mobilization; (4) a focused set of priority, reinforcing goals; (5) country-by-country implementation in pursuit of national plans of action; (6) ensuring that individual government plans of action cumulatively achieve universal goals; (7) doable low-cost strategies; (8) building on past successes; (9) support of a lead agency; and (10) teamwork with actors involved with related tasks. His analysis underscores that the WSC's widely hailed successes have been made possible by the presence of *many* of these factors. The authors of other chapters reinforce Jolly's conclusions, by noting the absence of many of these factors in less widely praised conferences. (Plus Cook underscores the importance of administrative, technical, and financial resources (capacity).) Thus the success or failure of conferences is related to process as well as subject matter. Of course, the process that governments and thus conferees follow – and the presence or absence of "Jolly's 10 factors" – is related to the salience and contentiousness of the subject matter of the conference as well. Few conferences demonstrate this point better than the Vienna Conference on Human Rights, the first such intergovernmental conference held on human rights for 25 years.

Actually, the UN World Conference on Human Rights is one of the most frequently criticized of the conferences of the 1990s. Critics note, for example, that, although it endorsed the universality of human rights, it failed to lay to rest once and for all the "ghost of cultural relativism." Similarly, while it recognized the important roles of NGOs in the human rights field, its key document – the Vienna Declaration – calls for national protection only of those NGOs whose members are "genuinely" involved in the human rights process. Presumably, it is left to state governments to determine which human rights organizations qualify. The ambiguity of the declaration reveals one of the truths of such conferences: they cannot paper over significant differences amongst governments and cultures on salient and contentious issues, especially when they are negotiated at a widely publicized global conference. While it is certainly possible to make an argument in favour of airing differences, many governments find it difficult to defend to their constituents the expenditure of scarce resources on conferences with such outcomes. Moreover, some governments are fearful that such conferences could result in the failure even to issue a final declaration or, worse yet, one which presented only one side of the debate, and not on their side. Indeed, Dias contends that such reasoning underlay the planning for the recently concluded Vienna +5 review. Fearing a possible renegotiation of the ambiguous, consensual document from Vienna, such governments saw Vienna +5 as a place for damage limitation and avoiding regression, rather than for making further progress in the human rights field. While that modest goal was achieved – "the Vienna consensus remains intact and undamaged" – the follow-up to this conference has done little to satisfy its critics.

The accomplishments, to date, of the Beijing and Rio Conferences – subjects of Part Two in this volume – seem to fall somewhere between the seeming extremes of the WSC and the Vienna Conference on Human Rights. Critics often still focus on these conferences, in part because of their size and expense. And, in the Republican-dominated US Congress case at least, because of the very visible presence of Hillary Rodman Clinton at the Beijing Conference. The three chapters in this part underscore the opportunities and limits to using international law as a means for effectuating change in state (and in the case of Beijing, personal) practice. All three chapters also evidence the importance of extensive preparation for the conferences, indeed why these cases are placed under the rubric of processes and not simply conferences.

Cook's analysis of the Beijing Conference also emphasizes the difficulties of meeting one of the sceptics' key concerns about UN-sponsored conferences, namely that they seek to focus on one major issue-area, whereas globalization makes that difficult, if not actually infeasible or dysfunctional. Simply recounting the areas of concern in the Beijing Platform underscores how organizers and participants at recent conferences have sought to respond to if not actually pre-empt this concern: poverty; education; health; violence; armed and other kinds of conflict; economic structures and policies; power and decision-making at all levels; institutional mechanisms; human rights; media and other communication systems; natural resources and the environment; and the girl child. All of the chapters in this part of the book further evidence how international lawyers go about trying to meet this concern, i.e. by developing increasingly "hard" law, bit by bit. The emphasis by Schechter, Jolly, and Dias on the necessity for coordination among conferences and amongst (especially non-state) policy implementers addresses this same point.

One of the most valuable lessons of Yongo's chapter is a reminder that the world is state-centric, even in areas outside of the military security regime. While Yongo's meticulous analysis documents the ways in which the legal instruments adopted in Rio "... confirmed and strengthened the bargains between countries at different levels of development," it also contends that "... if the UNCED process is to bear fruit, the North-South dialogue will have to concentrate more on activity and less on acrimony." For the South that means the provision of "new and additional funding" as promised in Article 20 of the Convention on Biological Diversity. Only governments can meet that demand. In a similar way it is only governments that can agree to the establishment of an effective monitoring mechanism for compliance with the CBD, or with the Convention on Climate Change, as argued by Butler and Ghai. Non-state actors can (and have) devised clever, flexible, potentially "robust" mechanisms. But the current international legal regime remains sufficiently statist that government acquiescence (and funding) is ultimately needed. (The same phenomenon, of course, explains the limits on global policy influence of attendees at counter-conferences).

The chapters in Part Three of the book note, however, the multiple, innovative, and creative ways by which non-state actors, to date chiefly NGOs and the UN secretariat, have gained access to the global conference policy-making process. Whereas Schechter argues that this process has not gone to its logical conclusion in that it remains less inclusive than it could or should be, both of these chapters (as well as those in earlier parts of the book) underline the necessity for going beyond the traditional focus on NGO activity *at* global conferences in order to assess their importance relative to other actors in the process. Indeed, as Schechter recounts, NGOs are aware of this. And it is because of that, that they have begun to seek to participate in the policy-making process throughout. While Dias's chapter in particular evidences the limits to their success in this regard, the critical point is that their past successes had resulted in states explicitly empowering them with conference follow-up activities. Thus the focus on follow-up requires a focus on non-state actors' activity as well as state compliance with the promises that they made in the heat of conference negotiations.

While it is too early in the conference processes to reach any *definitive* recommendations for the future of UN-sponsored global ad hoc conferences, it has been contended that these chapters provide a number of relevant insights. They have suggested that such conferences can have meaningful outcomes, especially on issues on which there are not significant cross-cultural divisions.

Throughout the volume, and summarized herein, we have also identified specific factors that can increase the likelihood that any such conferences in the twenty-first century would be more fruitful than those that have preceded them. We have argued that that success depends on the further empowerment of non-state actors, but also consistent positions by key governments. Moreover, several of the chapters have emphasized the role that international law (and lawyers) can play in effectuating peaceful change on globally salient issues. As much as anything else, however, the authors of this volume have tried to play a part in reframing the contemporary public policy debate and scholarly research about the pros and cons of UN-sponsored global conferences. Assessment of their worth and meaningfulness must include a focus on the follow-up to such conferences, for they are only a part – albeit the most highly publicized one – of processes aimed at addressing salient and enduring global problems.

Appendix A

Chronology of conference-related events[1]

Debbi Schaubman

1989

26 July	ICPD: adoption of ECOSOC resolution (1989/91) convening the conference
22 December	UNCED: adoption of GA resolution (A/RES/44/228) convening the conference

1990

5–16 March	UNCED: Preparatory Committee Organizational session (New York)
6–31 August	UNCED: Preparatory Committee session I (Nairobi)
29–30 September	**World Summit for Children** (New York)
14 December	FWCW: adoption of GA resolution (A/RES/45/129) convening the conference
18 December	WCHR: adoption of GA resolution (A/RES/45/155) convening the conference
21 December	FCCC: adoption of GA resolution (A/RES/45/212) establishing the intergovernmental negotiating process for the preparation by an Intergovernmental Negotiating Committee of a framework convention on climate change

[1] Some information has been drawn from Dag Hammarskjöld Library, UN-I-QUE ⟨http://www.un.org/Depts/dhl/unique⟩

1991

4–8 March	ICPD: Preparatory Committee session I (New York)
18 March–5 April	UNCED: Preparatory Committee session II (Geneva)
12 August–4 September	UNCED: Preparatory Committee session III (Geneva)
9–13 September	WCHR: Preparatory Committee session I (Geneva)

1992

20–24 January	ICPD: Expert Group Meeting on population, environment and development (New York)
2 March–3 April	UNCED: Preparatory Committee session IV (New York)
30 March–10 April	WCHR: Preparatory Committee session II (Geneva)
12–16 April	ICPD: Expert Group Meeting on population policies and programmes (Cairo)
3–14 June	**United Nations Conference on Environment and Development** (Rio de Janeiro)
4 June	**Framework Convention on Climate Change** opened for signature
5 June	**Convention on Biological Diversity** opened for signature
22–26 June	ICPD: Expert Group Meeting on population and women (Gaborone, Botswana)
19–27 August	ICPD: Fourth Asian And Pacific Population Conference (Denpasar, Indonesia)
14–18 September	WCHR: Preparatory Committee session III (Geneva)
October	UNCED: ACC establishes the Inter-Agency Committee on Sustainable Development to ensure system-wide coordination in implementing Agenda 21
26–30 October	ICPD: Expert Group Meeting on family planning, health and family well-being (Bangalore, India)
2–6 November	WCHR: Regional meeting in Tunis
16–20 November	ICPD: Expert Group Meeting on population growth and demographic structure (Paris)
11–12 December	ICPD: Third African Population Conference (Dakar, Senegal)
16 December	WSSD: adoption of GA resolution (A/RES/47/92) convening the conference
22 December	UNCHS: adoption of GA resolution (A/RES/47/180) convening the conference
	UNCED: series of General Assembly resolutions adopted, including A/RES/47/188, establishing an intergovernmental negotiating committee for the elaboration of an international convention to combat desertification and A/RES/47/189, convening

the Global Conference on the Sustainable Development of Small Island Developing States

1993

18–22 January	WCHR: Regional meeting in San José
	ICPD: Expert Group Meeting on population distribution and migration (Santa Cruz, Bolivia)
12 February	UNCED: Commission on Sustainable Development established
3–5 March	UNCHS: Preparatory Committee Organizational session (New York)
23–25 March	UNCED: Inter-agency Committee on Sustainable Development, first meeting (New York)
23–26 March	ICPD: European Population Conference (Geneva)
29 March–2 April	WCHR: Regional meeting in Bangkok
4–8 April	ICPD: Arab Population Conference (Amman, Jordan)
12–16 April	WSSD: Preparatory Committee Organizational session (New York)
15–16 April	SIDS: Organizational session of Preparatory Committee (New York)
19 April–7 May	WCHR: Preparatory Committee session IV (Geneva)
29 April–4 May	ICPD: Latin American and Caribbean Regional Conference on Population and Development (Mexico City)
10–21 May	ICPD: Preparatory Committee session II (New York)
14–25 June	**World Conference on Human Rights** (Vienna)
1 July	UNCED: High-Level Advisory Board on Sustainable Development created
30 August–10 September	SIDS: Preparatory Committee session I (New York)
8–10 September	UNCED: Inter-agency Committee on Sustainable Development, second meeting (New York)
20 December	WCHR: adoption of GA resolution (A/RES/48/141) creating office of High Commissioner for Human Rights

1994

31 January–11 February	WSSD: Preparatory Committee session I (New York)
2–4 March	UNCED: Inter-agency Committee on Sustainable Development, third meeting (New York)
7–11 March	SIDS: Preparatory Committee session I resumed (New York)
4–22 April	ICPD: Preparatory Committee session III (New York)

11–22 April	UNCHS: Preparatory Committee session I (Geneva)
25 April–6 May	**Global Conference on the Sustainable Development of Small Island Developing States** (Bridgetown, Barbados)
7–14 June	FWCW: Second Asian and Pacific Ministerial Conference on Women in Development (Jakarta)
14–16 June	UNCED: Inter-agency Committee on Sustainable Development, fourth meeting (Geneva)
22 August–2 September	WSSD: Preparatory Committee session II (New York)
5–13 September	**International Conference on Population and Development** (Cairo)
20–25 September	FWCW: Sixth Regional Conference on the Integration of Women into the Economic and Social Development of Latin Amerian and the Caribbean (Mar del Plata, Argentina)
10–14 October	FWCW: Expert Group Meeting on literacy, education, and training (Turin, Italy)
14–15 October	**International Convention to Combat Desertification in Those Countries Experiencing Serious Drought and/or Desertification, particularly in Africa** opened for signature
17–21 October	FWCW: High-Level Regional Preparatory Meeting of the Economic Commission for Europe (Vienna)
24–28 October	WSSD: Informal intersessional consultations (New York)
7–11 November	FWCW: Expert Group Meeting on women and economic decision-making (New York)
9–10 November	FWCW: Arab Regional Preparatory Meeting (Amman, Jordan)
16–20 November	FWCW: Asia/Pacific Regional NGO Symposium (Manila)
16–23 November	FWCW: Fifth African Regional Conference on Women (Dakar, Senegal)
21–23 November	FWCW: Expert Group Meeting on institutional and financial arrangements for the implementation of the Platform of Action (New York)
28 November–9 December	CBD: Conference of the Parties, first session (Nassau)
5–9 December	FWCW: Expert Group Meeting on peace (New York)
13 December	ICPD: Inter-Agency Task Force on the Implementation of the Programme of Action of the International Conference on Population and Development, first meeting (New York)

1995

16–27 January	WSSD: Preparatory Committee session III (New York)
1–3 February	UNCED: Inter-Agency Committee on Sustainable Development, fifth meeting (New York)
6–12 March	**World Summit for Social Development** (Copenhagen)
7 March	ICPD: meeting of the Working Group on Basic Education of the Inter-Agency Task Force on the Implementation of the Programme of Action (Paris)
28 March–7 April	FCCC: Conference of the Parties, first session (Berlin)
24 April–5 May	UNCHS: Preparatory Committee session II (Nairobi)
3 May	ICPD: meeting of the Working Group on Policy-related Issues of the Inter-Agency Task Force on the Implementation of the Programme of Action (New York)
4 May	ICPD: meeting of the Working Group on Common Approach to National Capacity-building in Tracking Child and Maternal Mortality of the Inter-Agency Task Force on the Implementation of the Programme of Action (New York)
16 May	ICPD: meeting of the Working Group on Women's Empowerment of the Inter-Agency Task Force on the Implementation of the Programme of Action (New York)
29 June	ICPD: meeting of the Working Group on Reproductive Health of the Inter-Agency Task Force on the Implementation of the Programme of Action (Geneva)
12–14 July	UNCED: Inter-agency Committee on Sustainable Development, sixth meeting (Geneva)
25 July	ICPD: Inter-Agency Task Force on the Implementation of the Programme of Action of the International Conference on Population and Development, second meeting (New York)
31 July–4 August	FWCW: Additional week of informal consultations (New York)
4–15 September	**Fourth World Conference on Women** (Beijing)
11–15 September	UNCED: Intergovernmental Panel on Forests, first session (New York)
19 October	ICPD: Working Group on International Migration of the Inter-Agency Task Force on the Implementation of the Programme of Action, first meeting (Geneva)

October	ICIF: mandate of the Inter-Agency Task Force on the Implementation of the Programme of Action of the International Conference on Population and Development expanded and Task Force re-named ACC Task Force on Basic Social Services for All; other task forces also created: ACC Inter-Agency Task Force on Full Employment and Sustainable Livelihoods and ACC Inter-Agency Task Force on an Enabling Environment for Economic and Social Development
4–17 November	CBD: Conference of the Parties, second session (Jakarta)
4 December	**Agreement for the Implementation of the Provisions of the United Nations Convention on the Law of the Sea of 10 December 1982 Relating to the Conservation and Management of Straddling Fish Stocks and Highly Migratory Fish Stocks** opened for signature

1996

25–26 January	ICIF: Task Force on Employment and Sustainable Livelihoods, first meeting
23 February	ICIF: Task Force on Basic Social Services for All, first meeting
5–8 February	UNCED: Inter-agency Committee on Sustainable Development, seventh meeting (New York)
5–16 February	UNCHS: Preparatory Committee session III (New York)
11–22 March	UNCED: Intergovernmental Panel on Forests, second session (Geneva)
22 March	ICIF: Task Force on the Enabling Environment for Economic and Social Development organizational meeting
April	FWCW: ACC establishes Inter-Agency Committee on Women and Gender Equality
17 April	ICIF: Task Force on Employment and Sustainable Livelihoods, second meeting
3–14 June	**United Nations Conference on Human Settlements** (Istanbul)
8–19 July	FCCC: Conference of the Parties, second session (Geneva)
9 July	ICIF: Task Force on Employment and Sustainable Livelihoods, third meeting
10–12 July	UNCED: Inter-agency Committee on Sustainable Development, eighth meeting (New York)

9–20 September	UNCED: Intergovernmental Panel on Forests, third session (Geneva)
22–23 October	ICIF: ACC Inter-Agency Committee on Women and Gender Equality, first session (New York)
4–15 November	CBD: Conference of the Parties, third session (Buenos Aires)

1997

10–21 February	UNCED: Intergovernmental Panel on Forests, fourth session (New York)
20–21 February	UNCED: Inter-agency Committee on Sustainable Development, ninth meeting (New York)
5–6 March	ICIF: ACC Inter-Agency Committee on Women and Gender Equality, second session (New York)
23–27 June	**UNCED: Special Session of the General Assembly to Review and Appraise the Implementation of Agenda 21 (Earth Summit+5)**
25 July	UNCED: ECOSOC Resolution 1997/65 establishes the Intergovernmental Forum on Forests
1 September	WCHR: Office of the High Commissioner for Human Rights and the Centre for Human Rights consolidated in thte Office of the United Nations High Commissioner for Human Rights
17–18 September	UNCED: Inter-agency Committee on Sustainable Development, tenth meeting (Geneva)
29 September– 15 October	CCD: Conference of the Parties, first session (Rome)
1–3 October	UNCED: Intergovernmental Forum on Forests, first session (New York)
1–11 December	FCCC: Conference of the Parties, third session (Kyoto)
11 December	FCCC: Kyoto Protocol adopted
19 December	UNCED: mandate of High-level Advisory Board on Sustainable Development terminated by General Assembly resolution A/RES/52/12B

1998

19–20 February	UNCED: Inter-agency Committee on Sustainable Development, eleventh meeting (New York)
25–27 February	ICIF: ACC Inter-Agency Committee on Women and Gender Equality, third session (New York)
4, 6, 11–13 March	FWCW: Commission on the Status of Women acting as the preparatory committee for the special session of the General Assembly entitled "Women 2000: gender equality, development and peace for the twenty-first century," first session (New York)

1–3 April	GEF: First Assembly (New Delhi)
4–15 May	CBD: Conference of the Parties, fourth session (Bratislava)
13–15 May	ICIF: Economic and Social Council Special Session on the Integrated and Coordinated Implementation and Follow-up of Major UN Conferences and Summits (New York)
19–22 May	WSSD: Preparatory Committee for the Special Session of the General Assembly on the Implementation of the Outcome of the World Summit for Social Development and Further Initiatives, organizational session (New York)
22–24 June	WCHR: Vienna +5 Global Forum (Ottawa)
28–29 September	UNCED: Inter-agency Committee on Sustainable Development, twelfth meeting (Geneva)
2–13 November	FCCC: Conference of the Parties, fourth session (Buenos Aires)
30 November–11 December	CCD: Conference of the Parties, second session (Dakar)

1999

6–7 February	ICPD: NGO Forum to parallel Hague International Forum
8–12 February	ICPD: Hague International Forum
23–26 February	ICIF: ACC Inter-Agency Committee on Women and Gender Equality, fourth session (New York)
8–9 March	UNCED: Inter-agency Committee on Sustainable Development, thirteenth meeting (New York)
15–19 March	FWCW: Commission on the Status of Women acting as the preparatory committee for the special session of the General Assembly entitled "Women 2000: gender equality, development and peace for the twenty-first century," second session (New York)
24 March–1 April	ICPD: Preparatory Committee for the Special Session of the General Assembly for the Review and Appraisal of the Implementation of the Programme of Action of the International Conference on Population and Development, first session (New York)
13–14 May	UNCHS: Preparatory Committee for the Special Session of the General Assembly for an Overall Review and Appraisal of the Implementation of the Habitat Agenda, organizational session (Nairobi)

17–28 May	WSSD: Preparatory Committee for the Special Session of the General Assembly on the Implementation of the Outcome of the World Summit for Social Development and Further Initiatives, first session (New York)
24–29 June	ICPD: Preparatory Committee for the Special Session of the General Assembly for the Review and Appraisal of the Implementation of the Programme of Action of the International Conference on Population and Development, resumed first session (New York)
30 June	FWCW: Commission on the Status of Women acting as the preparatory committee for the special session of the General Assembly entitled "Women 2000: gender equality, development and peace for the twenty-first century," resumed second session (New York)
30 June–2 July	**ICPD: Special Session of the General Assembly to Review and Appraise the Implementation of the ICPD Programme of Action (New York)**
13–20 September	UNCED: Inter-agency Committee on Sustainable Development, fourteenth meeting (Vienna)
25 October–5 November	FCCC: Conference of the Parties, fifth session (Bonn)
15–26 November	CCD: Conference of the Parties, third session (Recife)

2000

1–3 March	ICIF: ACC Inter-Agency Committee on Women and Gender Equality, fifth session (New York)
3–14 April	WSSD: Preparatory Committee for the Special Session of the General Assembly on the Implementation of the Outcome of the World Summit for Social Development and Further Initiatives, second session (New York)
15–26 May	CBD: Conference of the Parties, fifth session (Nairobi)
5–9 June	**FWCW: Special Session of the General Assembly to appraise and assess the progress achieved in the implementation of the Nairobi Forward-looking Strategies for the Advancement of Women and the Platform for Action (New York)**
26–30 June	**WSSD: Special Session of the General Assembly on the Implementation of the Outcome of the World Summit for Social Development and Further Initiatives**

2001
June   **UNCHS: Special Session of the General Assembly**
                              for an Overall Review and Appraisal of the Im-
                              plementation of the Habitat Agenda (exact dates
                              unknown)

Abbreviations

ACC	Administrative Committee on Coordination
CBD	Convention on Biological Diversity
CCD	Convention to Combat Desertification in Countries Experiencing Serious Drought and/or Desertification, Particularly in Africa
FCCC	Framework Convention on Climate Change
FWCW	Fourth World Conference on Women
GEF	Global Environment Facility
ICIF	Integrated and coordinated implementation and follow-up efforts
ICPD	International Conference on Population and Development
SIDS	Global Conference on the Sustainable Development of Small Island Developing States
UNCED	United Nations Conference on Environment and Development
UNCHS	United Nations Conference on Human Settlements II
WCHR	World Conference on Human Rights
WSC	World Summit for Children
WSSD	World Summit for Social Development

Appendix B

From PrepCom to follow-up: Researching the United Nations conferences of the 1990s

Debbi Schaubman

Even for the experienced researcher, studying the United Nations conferences of the 1990s can seem daunting. The volume of material, the initially arcane citations, the changes in organizational structure, all conspire to make this work appear more difficult than it is. This appendix furnishes the researcher with the necessary tools to begin such a research project. Section I contains a brief description of UN documentation and bibliographic resources in print and in electronic formats. Section II suggests some approaches to conducting UN research, with an emphasis on those strategies most relevant to studying the UN conferences and their follow-up. Section III focuses on finding information from and about non-governmental organizations (NGOs). Section IV introduces strategies for finding secondary source material. Finally, Section V provides a highly selective bibliography divided into several parts: material of general interest is followed by a section on each conference. The last part of the bibliography is devoted to materials on the efforts to coordinate and integrate conference follow-up.[1]

I. United Nations documentation

The United Nations is a very prolific publisher. Reports, press releases, background papers, resolutions, decisions, and notes appear in a seemingly never-ending stream. Researchers can be overwhelmed by the immense amount of available material. This issue is one that the UN itself has grappled with over the years. Attempts to reduce the bulk of documentation produced have met with mixed success and, indeed, have a mixed outcome for inquirers into UN activities.[2] Moreover, despite limited success by the organization to pare the number of pages produced each year, the numbers remain staggering.[3] In addition, the exponential growth in UN information available via the Internet has made information more readily available while simultaneously making it much more difficult to determine conclusively what *is* available.

To overcome the problems posed by this information deluge, it is important to develop an efficient technique for conducting UN-related research. An understanding of the UN's documentation system is the cornerstone to this process. As numerous reliable and detailed guides are available, only a general overview is provided here.[4] It is important to remember that the emphasis in this appendix is on information relevant to researching UN materials from the 1990s; for information relative to earlier decades, refer to the appropriate aforementioned guides. Furthermore, the documentation of the UN's specialized agencies is not treated in this appendix.[5]

The UN publishes two types of materials: documents and publications. "A document is a text submitted to a principal organ or a subsidiary organ of the United Nations for consideration by it, usually in connection with item(s) on its agenda" whereas "The term 'United Nations publication' refers to any written material which is issued by or for the United Nations to the general public, normally under the authorization of the Publications Board."[6] Although the lines between them are not always firm or sharp (it is, for example, not uncommon for a major *document* to receive subsequent distribution as a *sales publication*), the distinction is an important one. Methods of bibliographic access (i.e. ways to identify relevant materials), distribution patterns (i.e. where to find the materials), and citation rules (i.e. guidelines for referring to them), differ between the two.[7]

Sales numbers and series symbols

A UN publication may be available free of charge or as a sales publication. Those offered for sale are assigned a sales number consisting of letters and Roman and Arabic numerals separated by periods: e.g. E.97.I.5. The first of the four segments of the sales number is a language code, the second represents a year, and the third segment uses a Roman numeral to represent one of the more than 20 agency or topic-specific sales categories. The last segment is assigned sequentially as publications are issued in that sales category.

UN documents, on the other hand, are assigned "series symbols." This combination of letters and numbers separated by slashes provides a unique identifier for individual documents. Every element in the symbol has a particular meaning. Because of the delay before a document is indexed, an understanding of this system can be useful.[8]

The first element in the symbol identifies the main organ or body issuing the document. For example,

A	General Assembly	ST	Secretariat
E	Economic and Social Council	DP	UN Development Programme
S	Security Council	ACC	Administrative Committee on Coordination

The second element (and, in some cases, subsequent elements) frequently represents a commission, committee or conference. It may also designate the session or year the document was issued. For example, CN. denotes a commission:[9]

E/CN.4   Commission on Human Rights
E/CN.5   Commission for Social Development
E/CN.6   Commission on the Status of Women
E/CN.9   Commission on Population and Development (formerly, Population Commission)
E/CN.17   Commission on Sustainable Development

CONF. denotes a conference:

A/CONF.151   United Nations Conference on Environment and Development
A/CONF.157   World Conference on Human Rights
A/CONF.165   United Nations Conference on Human Settlements
A/CONF.166   World Summit for Social Development
A/CONF.167   Global Conference on the Sustainable Development of Small Island Developing States
A/CONF.171   International Conference on Population and Development
A/CONF.177   Fourth World Conference on Women

Subsequent elements in the symbol may identify the type of document:

/Add.	Addendum	/PV.	Verbatim record
/BP.	Background Paper	/R.	Restricted distribution
/Corr.	Corrigendum	/RES/	Resolution
/CRP.	Conference Room Paper	/Rev.	Revision
/INF.	Information series	/SR.	Summary record
/L.	Limited distribution	/WP.	Working paper

Table B.1 shows some typical document numbers.

Table B.1 Typical document numbers

Symbol	Explanation	Title
A/RES/52/100	100th resolution of the 52nd session of the General Assembly	"Follow-up to the Fourth World Conference on Women and Full Implementation of the Beijing Declaration and the Platform for Action"
E/1997/54	54th document of the 1997 session of the Economic and Social Council	*Annual Overview Report of the Administrative Coordination Committee for 1996*
E/CN.9/1998/4	4th document of the 1998 session of the Commission on Population and Development of the Economic and Social Council	*Health and Mortality: Report of the ACC Task Force on Basic Social Services for All*

Indexes (and other finding aids) for UN documentation

While an understanding of series symbols is helpful, it is more efficient to use finding aids to identify relevant material. There are a number of tools that enable researchers to identify UN publications and documents on particular subjects.

From 1979 until 1996, *UNDOC: Current Index* was the key index to UN information.[10] This print version of the catalogues of the Dag Hammerskjöld Library (DHL) and the UN Library in Geneva provided access to each document and publication by its subject, name, title, and series symbol. Although *UNDOC* was an improvement over its predecessors, the 1995 release of *UNBIS Plus on CD-ROM* was an even greater breakthrough in access.

Produced in arrangement with the DHL, *UNBIS Plus on CD-ROM* contains several interlinked databases. It includes the UN's bibliographic file (in essence, a continuing version of *UNDOC*), along with several other key databases (e.g. voting records, agenda items, indexes to the proceedings of the main organs, and the full texts of resolutions). To provide consistency, references in the *UNBIS Plus* bibliographic files are assigned subject headings according to the *UNBIS Thesaurus*, a specific set of subject terms devised by the DHL. The links between databases allow a researcher to search for resolutions by subject, read the text of the resolutions, and then view the corresponding voting information. The ease of this process is nothing short of miraculous to anybody who tried to do similar research as recently as 1994.

Although primarily a finding aid for a microprint/microfiche collection, the *Index to United Nations Documents and Publications on CD-ROM* published by Newsbank/Readex can also be used to identify relevant documents. The *Index* also includes the full text of resolutions and, since 1997, of selected proceedings. *AccessUN*, a web version of the *Index*, was launched in 1997. Taking advantage of the proliferation of UN information on the web, *AccessUN* includes hypertext links to the full text of selected documents.

In January 1997, an additional electronic resource became available to researchers: UN-I-QUE (UN Info Quest). It

... provide[s] quick access to document symbols/sales numbers for UN materials (1946 onwards). It does not give full bibliographic details nor does it replace existing bibliographic databases (UNBIS, UNBIS Plus on CD-ROM) produced by the Library. UN-I-QUE focuses upon documents and publications of a recurrent nature: annual/sessional reports of committees/commissions; monographic series; journals; annual publications; reports periodically/irregularly issued; reports of major conferences; statements in the General Debate, etc.[11]

Where to find UN documents and publications

Having determined what tools exist specifically to identify UN documents, the question of where to find these documents arises. To ensure that people have access to its materials, the UN created a depository library system in 1946. In most countries, the national library has been designated as a UN depository library. Other libraries may also apply for and be granted depository status.[12] All

United Nations Dag Hammarskjöld Library
UN-I-QUE (UN Info Quest): If cited, please provide attribution.

PREPARATORY COMMITTEE FOR THE INTERNATIONAL
CONFERENCE ON POPULATION AND DEVELOPMENT

NOTE: All meetings were held in New York.

3rd sess. (4–22 Apr. 1994): A/CONF.171/PC/9

2nd sess. (10–21 May 1993): E/1993/69

1st sess. (4–8 Mar. 1991): E/1991/47 + Add.1

Figure B.1 Sample output from UN-I-QUE

depository libraries receive sales publications, treaties, and the *Official Records*.[13]
Larger depositories also receive documents approved for general distribution.

One need not go to a UN depository, however, to find these materials. *United Nations Documents and Publications,* a microfiche set produced by Newsbank/Readex, is available for consultation at many libraries. Much of the material distributed to depository libraries is included, as are several categories of non-depository material. Most sales publications are not included in this set.

In recent years, an additional means of obtaining UN materials has become an essential part of the researcher's repertoire. Since the creation of the UNDP gopher in 1992, growth in the amount of UN documentation available via the Internet has been phenomenal. Materials from throughout the UN are available: resolutions of the main bodies, reports submitted to these bodies and their committees and commissions, press releases, background papers, fact sheets, and so on.[14] The availability of this information has not gone unnoticed by the public. According to a report of the Secretary-General issued a mere three months after the June 1995 opening of the UN web site ⟨http://www.un.org⟩, the site was accessed by an average of 5,000 users daily.[15]

Finally, although it has not yet been widely adopted for use outside the UN, the UN's Optical Disk System (ODS) will undoubtedly have a great effect on public access to UN documentation in the future. This fee-based service combines the indexing features provided by UNBIS with full-text delivery via the web. At present, ODS includes UN parliamentary documentation issued since 1993, as well as all resolutions and decisions from 1946 on. Changes in the pricing structure to permit discounted access to various user groups, including NGOs and depository libraries, are under discussion.[16]

II. Strategies for research

An important tip for the novice researcher (and a reminder to the more experienced): resist the temptation to dig right in and begin using the UN documentation! This can't be stressed too strongly. It is essential to gain a general sense of the issues addressed at a conference before beginning research with the official UN materials, thus familiarizing oneself with the important concepts and recurring themes.

Starting out: Learning the issues

There are numerous sources available to help one gain a general sense of the issues important at a specific conference. The titles mentioned below do not constitute a comprehensive list of sources; for additional suggestions, refer to Section V below.

A particularly useful starting place for a general audience is *World Conferences: Developing Priorities for the 21st Century*.[17] Each conference is described in 6–9 highly readable pages. An annex provides a brief overview of the Inter-Agency Task Forces established by the Administrative Committee on Coordination.

The *Yearbook of the United Nations*, published annually since 1947, is also a good starting point. Thematic chapters provide an overview of UN activities and a detailed index leads to references found in less obvious sections of the volume. Texts of key resolutions are also included. Quite valuable are the citations to key documents provided in the section endnotes. Unfortunately, despite efforts to reduce the delay to one year, publication of the *Yearbook* is still several years behind the calendar year.

Luckily, there are several other sources to which one can turn. The United Nations Association of the United States publishes the annual *A Global Agenda: Issues Before the General Assembly of the United Nations,* which provides a good summary of the current session's work. Citations to important documents are provided throughout the text.

The UN's quarterly magazine, *UN Chronicle*, is also useful for background material. In keeping with its more general purpose, however, it is not as detailed as the *Yearbook* nor does it provide the same profusion of document citations. Several conference-specific web sites also contain background information; these are included in Section V below.

Depending upon the subject matter of the conference under study, there may be many other UN-produced general sources available to the researcher. For example, the *United Nations Blue Books* series, begun in 1995, includes two volumes related to conference themes: *The United Nations and Human Rights, 1945–1995* and *The United Nations and the Advancement of Women, 1945–1996.* Written prior to the conferences, two volumes in DPI's *Notes for Speakers* series, *Social Development* and *The Advancement of Women,* provide useful background information. For additional suggestions, refer to the conference-specific parts of Section V.

Next steps ... Who's responsible for action?

Learning the details of the programme of action agreed to at the conference is the next step. A reading of the key outcome document(s) will enable the researcher

Item 3. General discussion on progress in the implementation of
Agenda 21, focusing on the cross-sectoral components of Agenda 21
and the critical elements of sustainability

In 1995, in accordance with the multi-year thematic programme of work
adopted by the Commission at its first session (E/1993/25/Add.1, chap. I,
sect. A, annex), this item is to focus on the following chapters of
Agenda 21:

chapter 3 (Combating poverty); chapter 5 (Demographic dynamics and
sustainability); chapter 8 (Integrating environment and development
indecision-making); chapters 23–32 on strengthening the role of major
groups; and chapter 40 (Information for decision-making).

. . . .

Documentation

Report of the Secretary-General on the role and contribution of major
groups (E/CN.17/1995/9)

Report of the Secretary-General on trade, environment and sustainable
development (E/CN.17/1995/12)

. . . .

Figure B.2 Excerpt from Commission on Sustainable Development, Provisional
Agenda (E/CN.17/1995/1), 22 March 1995

to determine which agencies and/or organs are responsible for implementing the
conference platform. Each agreement has a section focusing on institutional
arrangements or "follow-up to the conference" that details the specific implementation duties assigned to various UN bodies. For example, Agenda 21, the
programme of action agreed upon at the Rio Conference, includes a chapter
outlining the roles of the General Assembly, Economic and Social Council, Administrative Committee on Coordination, United Nations Environment Programme, and the United Nations Development Programme. It also requests the
establishment of two high-level bodies: a Commission on Sustainable Development and an advisory board of "eminent persons."

Having determined the responsible parties, one can begin to track their activities. This process is relatively straightforward if one uses the agendas issued by
the UN. An agenda is simply a list of topics to be discussed at a session of a UN
body. Prior to the convening of a session, a provisional agenda is released.[18] This
document contains the list of topics expected to be considered at the session and
assigns each an item number (Figure B.2). The provisional agendas issued by
the Economic and Social Council and its Commissions also include background
information for each item and a list of the documents to be submitted for

the discussion of that item. The *Provisional Agenda of the General Assembly* (A/session/150) does not include such annotations; these are found instead in the *Annotated Preliminary List of Items* (A/session/100). Once the agenda is finalized for a session, the title and number of the agenda item will not change. Keep in mind, though, that item numbers and titles do not necessarily stay consistent from session to session.[19] Furthermore, not every relevant document will be mentioned in the agenda; only the reports being brought directly before the body are mentioned in the list of documentation.

As can be seen from the example above, both the annotations and the list of documentation can be exceedingly useful for research. The item number and title also can be useful as both *UNBIS Plus on CD-ROM* and the *Index to UN Documents and Publications on CD-ROM* can be searched using this information.

If neither of these products is available, the item numbers and titles can still be important tools for researchers. Many documents are provided on the UN's web and gopher servers as full-text with complete identifying information. The web site provides a search engine ⟨http://www.un.org/search⟩, but without some planning, searches can result in too many false hits to be effective. This is due in part to the lack of subject indexing *per se*; researchers are entirely dependent on what words or phrases appear somewhere in the document. The inclusion of the agenda item information, however, provides researchers with a proxy subject heading. If searches are constructed based on these titles, the percentage of relevant results improves dramatically.

For example, as shown in Figure B.2, the Provisional Agenda for the 1995 session of the Commission on Sustainable Development, included Item 3: "General discussion on progress in the implementation of Agenda 21, focusing on the cross-sectoral components of Agenda 21 and the critical elements of sustainability." To use that information to locate materials on the UN's www and gopher sites, enter the following in the search box:

(agenda adj 21) implementation (cross-sectoral adj components)

Be sure to check the box marked "Match all of these words."

The UN web site search engine allows users to define a search using Boolean operators ("and," "or," "not") and proximity operators ("adj" means "adjacent," "w/#" means the second word follows the first word within the specified number of words, and "near"). If no operator is placed between two words in a "match all of these words" search, an "and" relationship is assumed. So, the example above translates to (agenda adjacent to 21) and implementation and (cross-sectoral adjacent to components).[20]

A list of documents matching these search criteria will be returned. (See Figure B.3 below for an example of a document retrieved by this search.) Undoubtedly, not all the documents will be what you want. Nonetheless, a well-crafted search is much more efficient than attempting to browse all parts of the UN's web and gopher sites.[21]

The UN has recently developed a new resource to improve tracking of the actions and responsibilities of its many bodies. The Integrated Meeting and Documentation Information System (IMDIS) is intended to be an "integrated,

```
                                              Distr.
                                              GENERAL

                                              E/CN.17/1995/15
                                              22 March 1995

                                              ORIGINAL: ENGLISH

COMMISSION ON SUSTAINABLE DEVELOPMENT
Third session
11–28 April 1995
Item 3 of the provisional agenda*

*   E/CN.17/1995/1.

       GENERAL DISCUSSION ON PROGRESS IN THE
IMPLEMENTATION OF AGENDA 21, FOCUSING ON CROSS-
  SECTORAL COMPONENTS OF AGENDA 21 AND THE
     CRITICAL ELEMENTS OF SUSTAINABILITY

       Demographic dynamics and sustainability

          Report of the Secretary-General
```

Figure B.3 Masthead of a CSD document on the UN's gopher ⟨gopher://gopher. un.org/00/esc/cn17/1995/off/95-15.en⟩ (emphasis added by the author)

process-oriented presentation of major Secretariat services, focusing in the first instance on those functions that fall within the economic and social areas."[22] When complete, users of the system will have access to a broad range of information by and about United Nations bodies including terms of reference, membership, journal of meetings, and agendas, resolutions, decisions, and agreed conclusions, and work programme reviews.

As previously noted, the Internet presence of the UN system is very decen-tralized. Not only do the specialized agencies maintain their own WWW and/or gopher sites, but numerous programmes and other bodies do, as well.[23] As a result, a search on the UN Headquarters site will not necessarily retrieve all the relevant documentation that has been made available. Complicating matters somewhat, not all the UN WWW sites have local search engines. All is not lost, however, as one can use an Internet-wide search engine (e.g. AltaVista, Hotbot etc.) to locate UN documentation. Several of these engines permit the user to specify that the search be limited to a particular host.[24] Researchers can also use UNIONS, the United Nations International Organizations Network Search, to search across the web pages mounted by several UN system web sites.[25]

United Nations documents themselves should not be overlooked as aids to finding other relevant information. Reports and resolutions usually include a prefatory or preambular section that provides the historical background of the

The General Assembly,

Recalling its resolutions 49/128 of 19 December 1994 and 50/124 of 20 December 1995,

Recalling also Economic and Social Council resolution 1996/2 of 17 July 1996 on the follow-up to the International Conference on Population and Development,

Acknowledging fully the integrated approach taken during the International Conference on Population and Development, which recognizes the interrelationship between population, sustained economic growth and sustainable development,

Having considered the report of the Secretary-General on the implementation of resolution 50/124, (1)
....

Figure B.4 Excerpt from General Assembly resolution 51/176: "Implementation of the Programme of Action of the International Conference on Population and Development" (A/RES/51/176)

document. These citations can be used to identify other documents useful for establishing the historical context of the current document (see Figure B.4).

Establishing the timeline

Having used the various finding aids and/or search engines to compile a list of relevant documentation, a plan for working through them must be developed. Strategies for researching the efforts to implement the recommendations of the UN conferences must take into account the time-specific nature of the work. That is, committees get formed, commissions get renamed, resolutions get passed, all of which have an effect on subsequent actions. Keeping track of the chronological sequence is essential to making sense of the information. Reading the documents in chronological order is highly recommended (or you may find yourself attempting to determine the actions of a committee that had ceased to exist).

Keep in mind, though, that the dates appearing on some documents can be misleading. For example, General Assembly resolution 50/161 was adopted at its 98th plenary meeting on 22 December 1995. This date may not be the most prominent one; a quick examination of the text posted on the UN gopher might lead one to believe that the resolution was adopted on 1 March 1996. However, this is simply the publication date. The date of passage is provided at the end of the resolution (see Figure B.5).

Similar confusions can occur as some items are available in multiple documents. For example, the annex to resolution 33/1 of the Commission for Social Development provides important information on the agenda-setting process for the Summit. This annex appears in several places including a Preparatory Commis-

Distr.
GENERAL
A/RES/50/161
1 March 1996

Fiftieth session
Agenda item 161

RESOLUTION ADOPTED BY THE GENERAL ASSEMBLY

[without reference to a Main Committee (A/50/L.66 and Add.1)]

50/161. Implementation of the outcome of the World Summit
for Social Development

The General Assembly,

Recalling its resolutions 46/139 of 17 December 1991, 47/92 of 16
December 1992 and 48/100 of 20 December 1993,

Recalling also Economic and Social Council decision 1991/230 of 30
May 1991, resolutions 1992/27 of 30 July 1992 and 1995/60 of 28 July
1995, and agreed conclusions 1995/1 of 28 July 1995, 1/

Having considered the report of the World Summit for Social
Development, held at Copenhagen from 6 to 12 March 1995, 2/
....

47. Decides to include in the provisional agenda of its fifty-first session
the item entitled "Implementation of the outcome of the World
Summit for Social Development", and to consider the implications for
a more coherent treatment of related items on its agenda in the
appropriate forums.

98th plenary meeting
22 December 1995

Figure B.5 Excerpt from A/RES/50/161 as presented on the UN gopher
⟨gopher://gopher.un.org/00/sec/dpcsd/ga/item161/ar50-161.en⟩ (emphasis added
by the author)

sion document (A/CONF.166/PC/2) and the Commission's report as presented in
the Economic and Social Council Official Records.[26] Each of these documents
bears a different date although each should also include the correct date for the
adoption of the resolution.

Press releases and news sources

Press releases can also be an invaluable source of information. By their very
nature, they are issued prior to or soon after an event, far in advance of any

meeting reports or summary or verbatim records. They are, therefore, an essential source of information on votes, draft resolutions, and programme recommendations. The UN web site provides a database of press releases issued since 13 October 1995. The database can be searched by keyword, document symbol, and category. Earlier press releases are available through the UNDP gopher ⟨gopher://gopher.undp.org:70/11/uncurr/press_releases⟩.

The numerous newsletters produced by the UN are also valuable sources of implementation-related information. *Development Update* provides bi-monthly updates on UN social and economic initiatives. Issues from January 1996 on are searchable on the UN website ⟨http://www.un.org/News/devupdate/⟩. Other newsletters are available through the web pages produced by various programmes and agencies; some of these resources are also available in print format. Specific titles are provided in the conference-specific parts of Section V.

III. Non-governmental organizations

Tracing the involvement of NGOs in the UN conferences of the 1990s and in the subsequent efforts to implement the programmes of action can pose problems of identification and acquisition for the researcher. The decentralized nature of NGOs results in the absence of any general NGO finding aids, thereby making it difficult to identify what publications have been produced. Acquiring the materials has historically been difficult and time-consuming. Although the growth of Internet access has made enormous amounts of NGO information available to a broader audience than ever before, only a relatively small subset of NGOs have a web presence. As a result, several strategies must be used to survey the field adequately.

First, it is important to use the resources already gathered. Numerous NGO documents were submitted to the Preparatory Committees and subsequently made available in the Newsbank/Readex microfiche collection and via the conference web sites. These documents and the list of NGOs accredited to the conference can be useful places to begin. This will, however, only be a subset of the organizations potentially involved in follow-up activities; many more NGOs were involved with the unofficial forums that paralleled the official proceedings. In addition, many NGOs have come into existence in response to the conferences themselves. Therefore, broader approaches should also be used.

There are many directories that identify NGOs working on a specific issue or focus on a specific geographic region; many of these listings combine the issue-oriented and regional approaches.[27] More general directory resources are also available. The *Yearbook of International Organizations*, published by the Union of International Associations (UIA), attempts to be a comprehensive directory of international organizations, including NGOs. The UIA has recently opened a WWW site ⟨http://www.uia.org⟩ providing directory information, links to organizational websites, and the texts of related research papers. In addition to providing address and telephone information, many directories will provide a list of recurrent publications.

NGOs themselves have been active in providing Internet services to other NGOs. The sites run by such organizations as the Association for Progressive Communications ⟨http://www2.apc.org⟩ and OneWorld ⟨http://www.oneworld.org⟩ host information from a number of organizations. Many of these "supersites" provide site-specific search engines to facilitate finding relevant information.

Of course, many NGOs have mounted their own web sites or are using servers hosted by other organizations or by commercial Internet service providers. As a result, it may be necessary to search across the web to locate specific NGO information. The lack of any predetermined subject terms on the web means that a thorough search will involve using synonyms for several aspects of the search. In addition, it may be advisable to further refine the search by excluding specific hosts. For example, a search for NGO materials relevant to UNCED follow-up activities must include numerous variations of the concept "follow-up" and the many synonyms for UNCED. This search may look like:

("follow up" or implement*) and (ngo or ngos or "nongovernmental organization"*) and ("Earth Summit" or (Rio near Conference) or "United Nations Conference on Environment and Development" or UNCED or "UN Conference on Environment and Development") and not (host:www.un.org or host:www.undp.org)[28]

The UN also provides access to NGO-related information. Resources such as *UN/ NGO Link* ⟨http://www.un.org:80/MoreInfo/ngolink/welcome.htm⟩ can provide useful leads on NGO actions. Additional information may be obtained from the United Nations Non-Governmental Liaison Service (NGLS). NGLS has recently launched a web site containing the full text of several of their major publications ⟨http://ngls.tad.ch⟩.

Finally, libraries should not be overlooked as potential sources of NGO material. Many libraries attempt to acquire a sample of the reports and issue papers published by NGOs; these may be identified by searching the library catalogue using the name of the NGO as an author. In addition, libraries may have collections of ephemeral material that do not appear in their catalogues. Be sure to check with the reference staff.

IV. Secondary Source Material[29]

Not surprisingly, the body of literature on the UN conferences of the 1990s is already quite substantial. Indeed, in many ways the problem is not one of locating books and articles on the conferences, but determining which ones to read.

Identifying monographic material is rather straightforward. Researchers with access to such bibliographic utilities as OCLC or RLIN can simultaneously search the catalogues of major research libraries in the United States. The catalogues of many individual libraries are also available via the Internet. Monographic material can be found by searching for the official conference name as a subject; materials emanating from the conference can by found by searching for the official conference name as an author. Unfortunately, there is no uniformity in using the conference name as a subject heading for works that are devoted to follow-up or implementation efforts.[30] As a result, researchers must use a more general keyword approach to locate these materials.

The periodical literature also abounds with material about the UN conferences. Articles and news items appear in such disparate sources as law reviews, magazines produced by NGOs, academic journals, and newspapers. Luckily for the serious researcher, there exist numerous indexes to this literature. Although it is beyond the scope of this appendix to enumerate all possible indexing sources, a few are particularly worth noting:

- the non-UN bibliographic file in *UNBIS-Plus on CD-ROM* contains "citations to monographs, serials, journal articles and publications of governments, international organizations, commercial publishers and other non-UN sources acquired by the Dag Hammarskjöld Library or the Library of the UN Office at Geneva."[31]
- *Alternative Press Index* provides bibliographic access to approximately 250 alternative, radical, and left-leaning publications. This resource can be especially useful for locating NGO-related materials.
- *Index to Legal Periodicals and Books* indexes articles from over 600 legal journals, yearbooks, government publications, and law reviews published in the United States, Canada, Great Britain, Ireland, Australia and New Zealand.
- *Public Affairs Information Service (PAIS) International* selectively indexes articles, books, conference proceedings, and government documents related to public affairs.

As previously noted, *UNBIS Plus* is on CD-ROM. The other titles are available in print, on CD-ROM and via the worldwide web (from fee-based services).

Using these indexes, although necessary, is not always straightforward. Each uses a different vocabulary to describe the material it covers. *PAIS*, for example, does not assign a conference-specific descriptor. Rather, the database uses "international conferences" and a word or phrase to describe the subject matter of the conference (e.g. "human rights"). Note, however, that the indexing is not always consistent. For example, "The Feminization of Human Rights: How the World Conference on Human Rights Brought Women onto the Agenda,"[32] although clearly about an effect of the WCHR, is not indexed as such.

As a result, just as in searching for monographic material, researchers hoping to be comprehensive should use both a structured approach and a more free-form keyword approach. However, just as with web searching, the lack of uniformity in referring to conferences in article titles and abstracts means one cannot depend on using only those keywords that appear in the conference name. For example, the United Nations Conference on Environment and Development has been referred to in the following ways:

- United Nations Conference on Environment and Development
- UN Conference on Environment and Development
- UNCED
- Rio Summit
- Earth Summit

Similarly, authors have referred to the Second United Nations Conference on Human Settlements as:

- Second United Nations Conference on Human Settlements
- 2nd United Nations Conference on Human Settlements
- UN Conference on Human Settlements (1996)
- City Summit
- Habitat II
- Habitat 2

The worldwide web, of course, provides access (both free and fee-based) to innumerable secondary sources. Newspapers as different as *The Earth Times* ⟨http://www.earthtimes.org⟩ and *The New York Times* ⟨http://www.nytimes.com⟩ provide varying numbers of issues free of charge. On the other end of the spectrum, the full texts of years of selected newspapers (US and foreign) are available in some of the full text services provided by the fee-based Lexis-Nexis. The resources available to researchers will vary from institution to institution; the local reference staff will provide advice based on the availability of specific resources.

It is not an understatement to say the amount of material available via the Internet is astounding. Researchers must, however, be cautious in their use of this material. Although it is true that critical thinking skills are important in all research endeavours, they are especially needed when using the web as a research tool. The issues of timeliness, authenticity, authority, and accuracy must be considered. When using materials acquired by a library, much of this evaluation work has already been done; in web-based research, it is up to the individual researcher to evaluate the materials.

V. Selective bibliography

A comprehensive bibliography of materials related to conference implementation is well beyond the scope of this appendix; instead, an attempt was made to include a broad range of resources. Key UN documents are listed (with URLs when WWW access is possible). Special emphasis has been placed on identifying NGO web sites devoted to follow-up efforts. Printed secondary source literature has, for the most part, been omitted. All entries are for materials available in English.

As worldwide web sites grow and develop, pages are added and others are dropped; indeed, the underlying structure may be totally reorganized. As such, it is considered correct bibliographic practice to include the date of access in a citation to a www page. I have chosen to omit that information from individual citations in favour of a general statement: all links were checked and found to be correct at the beginning of January 2000.

Following sections of general interest, the bibliography is organized by conference. The last section is devoted to the efforts to coordinate and integrate conference follow-up.

United Nations documentation and finding aids

Hajnal, Peter I., ed. *International information: Documents, Publications, and Electronic Information of International Governmental Organizations.* 2d ed. Englewood, CO: Libraries Unlimited, Inc., 1997.

Index to United Nations Documents and Publications. New Canaan, CT: News-bank/Readex (monthly).

Shaaban, Marian and Robert Goehlert. *UN Documentation: a Basic Guide*. Occasional Paper No. 16. Bloomington, IN: Indiana Center on Global Change and World Peace, 1993.

UNBIS Plus on CD-ROM. Alexandria, VA: Chadwyck-Healey, Inc. (quarterly).

UN. Dag Hammarskjöld Library. *UNDOC: Current Index* (ceased).

—— *United Nations Documentation: a Brief Guide*. NY: UN, 1994. (ST/LIB/34/Rev.2).

—— *United Nations Documentation: Research Guide*. ⟨http://www.un.org/Depts/dhl/resguide⟩

General resources on the United Nations

Earth Times. San Francisco: Earth Times, Inc. This newspaper on the environ-ment, sustainable development, and population is available in a bi-weekly print edition and a daily www edition ⟨http://www.earthtimes.org/⟩.

A Global Agenda: Issues Before the General Assembly of the United Nations. Lanham, MD: University Press of America (annual).

International Institute for Sustainable Development. *Linkages: a Multimedia Re-source for Environment and Development Policy Makers*. ⟨http://www.iisd.ca/linkages⟩. *Linkages* is an "electronic clearing-house for information on past and upcoming international meetings related to environment and development policy." The site provides access to the *Earth Negotiations Bulletin* (formerly *Earth Summit Bulletin*), "an independent reporting service that provides daily coverage of negotiations on environment and development at the United Nations," *Sustainable Developments*, reporting on conferences, workshops, and meetings not covered by the *ENB*, and */linkages/journal*, a source of "real-time information to decision makers on matters of environment and development policy."

UN Department of Public Information. *Basic facts about the UN*. New York: UN, 1995 (Sales no. E.95.I.31). Selected sections of this volume are available on the web ⟨http://www.un.org/aboutun⟩.

—— *UN Chronicle*. New York: DPI (quarterly).

—— *United Nations Publications Catalogue*. NY: UN. ⟨http://www.un.org/Pubs/sales.htm⟩

—— *Yearbook of the United Nations*. The Hague/Boston/London: Martinus Nijhoff (annual).

World Conferences: Developing Priorities for the 21st Century. UN Briefing Papers. NY: DPI, 1997 (DPI/1816; Sales no. E.97.I.5). The major accomplish-ments of the conferences of the 1990s are summarized. The chapters on the World Summit for Children, UNCED, and the Fourth World Conference on Women are also available on the UN web site ⟨http://www.un.org/geninfo/bp/worconf.html⟩.

Non-governmental organizations and the UN

Global Policy Forum. *Non-governmental Organizations (NGOs) and the United Nations.* ⟨http://www.globalpolicy.org/ngos⟩. This web site includes such articles as "NGO Review – 1996: an Analysis by NGLS – the UN's Non-Governmental Liaison Service" which provides a brief summary of the changes in NGO arrangements and "NGOs, Civil Society and Global Policy Making: an Analysis," an essay by James Paul.

"Non-governmental Organizations in Partnership with the United Nations." ⟨http://www.un.org/MoreInfo/ngolink/partners.htm⟩, January 1996.

Rice, Andrew E. and Cyril Ritchie. *Relationships Between International Non-governmental Organizations and the United Nations: a Research and Policy Paper.* ⟨http://www.uia.org/uiadocs/unngos.htm⟩. Paper first appeared in *Transnational Associations* 47, no. 5 (1995): 254–265.

UN Economic and Social Council. *List of Non-governmental Organizations in Consultative Status with the Economic and Social Council as at 10 February 1997: Note by the Secretary-General* (E/1997/INF/4), 26 March 1997. ⟨http://www.un.org/MoreInfo/ngolink/list.htm⟩

—— Resolution 1296 (XLIV): "Arrangements for Consultation with Non-governmental Organizations," 23 May 1968. ⟨http://www.igc.org/habitat/ngo-rev/1296.html⟩

—— Resolution 1996/31: "Consultative Relationship Between the United Nations and Non-governmental Organizations," 25 July 1996. ⟨gopher://gopher.un.org/00/esc/recs/1996/E-RES96.31⟩

Weiss, Thomas G. and Leon Gordenker, eds. *NGOs, the UN and Global Governance.* Boulder, CO: Lynne Rienner, 1996.

Willetts, Peter, ed. *"Conscience of the World": the Influence of Non-governmental Organisations in the UN System.* Washington, DC: Brookings Institution, 1996.

World NGO Conference: Report of the First Preparatory Meeting Held at UNU Headquarters, Tokyo, 23–24 September 1996. ⟨http://www.unu.edu/hq/unupress/ngo-conference.html⟩

Conference-specific materials

1. World Summit for Children (New York, 29–30 September 1990)

1.1 General resources

Black, Maggie. *Children First: The Story of UNICEF, Past and Present.* New York: Oxford University Press, 1996. Commissioned by UNICEF, this work focuses on the organizational history between 1979 and 1995. Particular attention is paid to the origin of the World Summit and its continuing importance. Black's earlier work, *The Children and the Nations: The Story of UNICEF* (New York: UNICEF, 1986), provides deeper coverage of UNICEF's first 40 years.

UNICEF. *Annual Report*. New York: UNICEF (annual) ⟨http://www.unicef.org/apublic⟩

—— *First Call for Children*. New York: UNICEF (ceased). This periodical publication provided general news on UNICEF activities. Each issue also included a section on NGO activities.

—— *State of the World's Children*. New York: Oxford University Press for UNICEF (annual). ⟨http://www.unicef.org/apublic⟩

1.2 Background and conference

Statements by Heads of State or Government at the World Summit for Children (New York, New York, September 29–30, 1990). New York: UNICEF, 1990 [ERIC document ED343707].

UNICEF. *Report of the Executive Board (16–27 April 1990)*. Economic and Social Council Official Records 1990, Supp. 8 (E/1990/28; E/ICEF/1990/13). The purpose of the Summit is outlined in this report. Prior events and obligations discussed as crucial to the context of the Summit include the Convention on the Rights of the Child, World Conference on Education for All, and *Development Goals and Strategies for Children: Priorities for UNICEF Action in the 1990s* (E/ICEF/1990/L.5).

—— *World Summit for Children Update* (ceased).

World Summit for Children. *World Declaration on the Survival, Protection, and Development of Children and Plan of Action for Implementing the World Declaration on the Survival, Protection and Development of Children in the 1990s*. New York: UNICEF, 1990. Both documents are also available on the UNICEF web site ⟨http://www.unicef.org/wsc/⟩.

1.3 Follow-up and implementation

Castillo, Carlos. *The Children Here: Current Trends in the Decentralization of National Programmes of Action*. Florence, Italy: UNICEF International Child Development Centre, 1995.

Chen, Lincoln C. and Sagari Singh. *Sustainability of the World Summit for Children Goals: Concepts and Strategies*. UNICEF Staff Working Papers: Evaluation, Policy and Planning Series, EVL-97-004.

Children's House. ⟨http://childhouse.uio.no/⟩. This cooperate initiative by AIFS, CIDEF, Children's Rights Centre, Childwatch, Consultative Group, CRIN, Family Life Development Centre, IIN, NOSEB, Radda Barnen, ISCA, UNICEF, UNESCO, World Bank, and WHO serves as a clearinghouse of children-related materials.

UN Committee on the Rights of the Child ... *Reports of States Parties* ... (CRC/C) [dates vary]. Available via Treaty bodies database at ⟨http://www.unhchr.ch/tbs/doc.nsf⟩. Under Article 44 of the Convention on the Rights of the Child, states parties must submit reports on measures adopted and progress made in giving effect to the rights promised by the convention. Although states are not obligated to state that a National Programme of Action (NPA) has been adopted, some have chosen to highlight the NPA in their reports.

UN General Assembly. *Progress at Mid-decade on Implementation of General*

Assembly Resolution 45/217 on the World Summit for Children: Report of the Secretary-General (A/51/256), 26 July 1996. ⟨http://www.unicef.org/reseval/pdfs/middecad.pdf⟩

—— *Implementation of General Assembly Resolution 45/217 on the World Summit for Children: Report of the Secretary-General* (A/47/264), 17 June 1992.

—— Resolution 45/217: "World Summit for Children" (A/RES/45/217), 21 December 1990. ⟨gopher://gopher.un.org/00/ga/recs/45/217⟩

—— Resolution 51/186: "Progress at Mid-decade on the Implementation of General Assembly Resolution 45/217 on the World Summit for Children" (A/RES/51/186), 16 December 1996. ⟨gopher://gopher.un.org/00/ga/recs/51/RES51-EN.186⟩

UNICEF. *Africa's Children, Africa's Future: Implementing the World Summit Declaration.* New York: UNICEF, 1990. Also of interest are two titles prepared for the OAU International Conference on Assistance to African Children (Dakar, Senegal, 25–27 November 1992): *Africa's Children, Africa's Future: Human Investment Priorities for the 1990s* and *Africa's Children, Africa's Future: Background Sectoral Papers.*

—— *Programme of Action for Achieving the Goals for Children and Development in the 1990s: a UNICEF Response to the Declaration and Plan of Action of the World Summit for Children* (E/ICEF/1991/12), 22 March 1991. UNICEF's organizational response to the Plan of Action is presented. Part I outlines "strategic programme actions" in such areas as reduction of maternal and child mortality rates, control of diarrhoeal diseases, AIDS, nutrition, water supply and sanitation, and basic education. Part II concerns "support measures" outlining the role of UNICEF in assisting countries in preparing NPAs, inter-agency mechanisms for support, and monitoring.

—— *Progress of Nations* (annual). ⟨http://www.unicef.org/apublic⟩. This annual publication provides national-level data on progress towards meeting the goals put forth at the Summit.

—— *Progress Report on Follow-up to the World Summit for Children* (E/ICEF/1996/15), 8 April 1996.

—— *Progress Report on Follow-up to the World Summit for Children* (E/ICEF/1997/14 and Corr. 1–2), 17 March 1997.

—— *Progress Report on Follow-up to the World Summit for Children* (E/ICEF/1998/8), 18 March 1998.

—— *Progress Report on Follow-up to the World Summit for Children* (E/ICEF/1999/9), 5 April 1999.

—— *Progress Report on the Follow-up to the World Summit for Children* (E/ICEF/1993/12), 9 February 1993.

—— *Progress Report on the Follow-up to the World Summit for Children* (E/ICEF/1994/12), 6 April 1994.

—— *Progress Report on the Follow-up to the World Summit for Children* (E/ICEF/1995/15), 7 April 1995.

—— *Suggested Guidelines for the Preparation of the Progress Report on the Implementation of the World Declaration on the Survival, Protection and Development of Children and the Plan of Action for Implementing the World Declaration on the Survival, Protection and Development of Children, Adopted*

by the *World Summit for Children* (E/ICEF/1991/17), 11 July 1991. The An-
nexes to this document include an outline for the preparation of NPAs and
UNICEF Executive Board Decision 1991/10: "The Role of UNICEF in World
Summit Follow-up."
—— Planning Office, Evaluation and Research Office. Programme Division.
*Monitoring Progress Toward the Goals of the World Summit for Children: a
Practical Handbook for Multiple-indicatory Surveys.* New York: UNICEF,
1995. ⟨http://www.unicef.org/reseval/pdfs/mics.pdf⟩

2. United Nations Conference on Environment and Development (Rio de Janeiro, 3–14 June 1992)

2.1 General resources

International Institute for Sustainable Development. *Earth Negotiations Bulletin.*
⟨http://www.iisd.ca/linkages/voltoc.html⟩. Each volume is devoted to a specific
conference, convention, or agency: Vol. 2, UNCED; Vol. 4, Convention to
Combat Desertification and Drought; Vol. 5, Commission on Sustainable
Development; Vol. 7, UN Conference on Straddling Fish Stocks and Highly
Migratory Fish Stocks; Vol. 8, Global Conference on the Sustainable Develop-
ment of Small Island Developing States; Vol. 9, Convention on Biological
Diversity; Vol. 12, UN Framework Convention on Climate Change; Vol. 13,
International Forest Policy.
Medina, Sarah. *Global Biodiversity.* UNEP/GEMS Environment Library, no. 11.
Nairobi: UNEP, 1993.
World Commission on Environment and Development. *Our Common Future.*
New York: Oxford University Press, 1987. A collection of the materials re-
viewed by the Commission is available on microfiche: *World Commission on
Environment and Development Archive Collection on Sustainable Development,*
Ottawa: International Development Research Centre, 1989.
World Resources Institute. *Global Biodiversity Strategy: Guidelines for Action to
Save, Study and Use of Earth's Biotic Wealth Sustainably and Equitably.* Washington, DC: World Resources Institute, 1992. This planning document was
produced by WRI, World Conservation Union, and UNEP in consultation with
FAO and UNESCO. Also of interest from WRI/IUCN/UNEP is *Global Biodiversity Strategy: a Policy-makers Guide* (Washington, DC: WRI), 1992. WRI
maintains an extensive collection of biodiversity-related materials on their web
site ⟨http://www.wri.org⟩.

2.2 From PrepCom to conference

Note: Preparatory Committee materials were issued as A/CONF.151/PC.
Convention on Biological Diversity. ⟨http://www.biodiv.org⟩. The text of the convention, ratification status, documents from the Conference of the Parties, and
information on the clearing-house mechanism are provided on this web site.
Earth Summit, the NGO Archives. Hamilton, Ontario: Canadian Centre for
Occupational Health and Safety, 1995. This CD-ROM contains the full text of
approximately 30,000 pages of text from NGO contributions to the UNCED
preparatory process, the conference, and the Global Forum.

Grub, Michael, Matthias Koch, Koy Thomson, Abby Munson, and Francis Sullivan. *The "Earth Summit" Agreements: a Guide and Assessment: an Analysis of the Rio '92 UN Conference on Environment and Development.* London: Earthscan, 1993.

Global Forum. *NGO Alternative Treaties.* ⟨http://www.igc.apc.org/habitat/treaties/index.html⟩

Global Partnership for Environment and Development: a Guide to Agenda 21, Post-Rio Edition. New York: United Nations, 1993 (Sales no. E.93.I.9).

Halpern, S. *United Nations Conference on Environment and Development: Process and Documentation.* Academic Council for the United Nations System (ACUNS) Reports and Papers, no. 2. Providence, RI: ACUNS, 1993. Also available on the www. ⟨http://infoserver.ciesin.org/docs/008-585/unced-home.html⟩. Halpern provides a detailed chronological digest of UNCED documents including material from the PrepComs, and the meetings of the Intergovernmental Panel on Climate Change, the Intergovernmental Negotiating Committee for a Framework Convention on Climate Change, and the Working Group of Experts in Biological Diversity (later renamed the Intergovernmental Negotiating Committee for a Framework Convention on Biological Diversity).

Mintzer, Irving M. and J. Amber Leonard. *Negotiating Climate Change: the Inside Story of the Rio Convention.* New York: Cambridge University Press, 1994.

United Nations Conference on Environment and Development. *Earth Summit.* Ottawa: International Development Research Centre, 1993. The full text of the official proceedings, including national reports, background papers, and preparatory committee materials are provided on this CD-ROM.

—— *Report of the United Nations Conference on Environment and Development, Rio de Janeiro, 3–14 June 1992* (A/CONF.151/26/Rev.1 and Corr. 1; Sales no. E.93.I.8). New York: United Nations, 1993. ⟨gopher://gopher.un.org/11/conf/unced/English⟩. Along with the final report of the conference, the texts of the Rio Declaration, Agenda 21, and the Statement of Forest Principles are included.

United Nations Framework Convention on Climate Change, UNFCCC. ⟨http://www.unfccc.de⟩. This web site includes the text of the convention and the Kyoto Protocol, documents from the Conference on the Parties and Subsidiary Bodies, executive summaries and in-depth reviews of national communications. (Documents of the INC/FCCC were issued under series symbol A/AC.237).

UN General Assembly. Resolution 44/228: "United Nations Conference on Environment and Development." (A/RES/44/228), 22 December 1989. ⟨gopher://gopher.un.org/00/ga/recs/44/228⟩

2.3 Follow-up and implementation

Earth Council. *The Earth Network for Sustainable Development.* ⟨http://www.ecouncil.ac.cr⟩. The Earth Council was founded in September 1992 to promote implementation of the Earth Summit agreements. The site includes "Rio +5: Moving Sustainable Development from Agenda to Action," co-sponsored by IISD. The Rio +5 pages include national and regional consultation reports, special focus reports, workshop summaries, and an overview report.

Earth Summit Watch. ⟨http://earthsummitwatch.org⟩

Global Environment Facility. ⟨http://www.gefweb.org⟩. GEF is the interim funding mechanism for the Convention on Biological Diversity and the Framework Convention on Climate Change.

International Council for Local Environmental Initiatives. *Local Government Implementation of Agenda 21.* ⟨http://www.iclei.org/la21/la21lgov.htm⟩

Non-Governmental Organization Steering Committee for the Commission on Sustainable Development. *Towards Earth Summit Two, Manhattan Island, New York, 23–27 June 1997.* ⟨http://www.igc.apc.org/habitat/csd-97/index.html⟩

UN Commission on Sustainable Development. *Assessment of Progress in the Implementation of Agenda 21 at the National Level: Report of the Secretary-General* (E/CN.17/1997/5), 18 March 1997. ⟨gopher://gopher.un.org/00/esc/cn17/1997/off/97--5.EN⟩.

—— *CSD Update.* ⟨http://www.un.org/esa/sustdev/csdup.htm⟩. Bimonthly newsletter of the Commission.

—— *Global Change and Sustainable Development: Critical Trends* (E/CN.17/1997/3), 20 January 1997. ⟨gopher://gopher.un.org/00/esc/cn17/1997/off/97--3.EN⟩

—— *Implementation of the Convention on Biological Diversity: Note by the Secretary-General* (E/CN.17/1997/11), 25 February 1997. ⟨gopher://gopher.un.org/00/esc/cn17/1997/off/97-11.EN⟩

—— *Intergovernmental Panel on Forests.* ⟨http://www.un.org/esa/sustdev/ipf.htm⟩

—— *Overall Progress Achieved since the United Nations Conference on Environment and Development: Report of the Secretary-General* (E/CN.17/1997/2 and Add.1–31), 31 January 1997. ⟨gopher://gopher.un.org/00/esc/cn17/1997/off/progress/97--2.en⟩

—— *Overview of Other Follow-up Processes to the United Nations Conference on Environment and Development Relevant to the Work of the Commission* (E/CN.17/1994/2/Add.1), 27 April 1994. ⟨gopher://gopher.un.org/00/esc/cn17/1994/off/1994--2.a1⟩. This report focuses on the Framework Convention on Climate Change, Convention on Biological Diversity, negotiations on the Convention to Combat Desertification, Global Conference on the Sustainable Development of Small Island States, and the Conference on Straddling Fish Stocks and Highly Migratory Fish Stocks.

—— *Progress in the Incorporation of Recommendations of the United Nations Conference on Environment and Development in the Activities of International Organizations, and Measures Undertaken by the Administrative Committee on Coordination to Ensure That Sustainable Development Principles Are Incorporated in Programmes and Processes Within the United Nations System: Report of the Secretary-General* (E/CN.17/1993/8), 7 June 1993. ⟨gopher://gopher.un.org/00/esc/cn17/1993/off/93--8.en⟩

UN Department of Economic and Social Affairs. *Commission on Sustainable Development.* ⟨http://www.un.org/esa/sustdev/csd.htm⟩

—— *Earth Summit +5: Special Session of the General Assembly to Review and Appraise the Implementation of Agenda 21, New York, 23–27 June 1997.* ⟨http://www.un.org/esa/earthsummit/⟩. This site serves as an official clearinghouse for Earth Summit +5 information. It provides access to the "Programme for the

Further Implementation of Agenda 21" (A/RES/S-19/2, Annex); delegate statements; reports of intergovernmental and related bodies; reports on Agenda 21 implementation, and background papers on sustainable development activities.

—— *Sustainable Development: United Nations System-wide Web Site on National Implementation of the Rio Commitments.* ⟨http://www.un.org/esa/agenda21/ natlinfo/index.html⟩. Country-level information is provided on this site. A description of the purposes and content of the site is provided in UN Commission on Sustainable Development, *National Reporting to the Commission on Sustainable Development: Report of the Secretary-General* (E/CN.17/1998/8), 24 March 1998. ⟨gopher://gopher.un.org/00/esc/cn17/1998/official/98--8.en⟩

UN Department of Public Information. *Earth Summit +5: Special Session of the General Assembly to Review and Appraise the Implementation of Agenda 21, New York, 23–27 June 1997.* ⟨http://www.un.org/ecosocdev/geninfo/sustdev/ indexsd.htm⟩

UN Development Programme. *Capacity 21 Programme.* ⟨http://sdnhq.undp.org/ c21⟩. Capacity 21 is an initiative to assist developing countries build their capacity to integrate Agenda 21 into their national development plans. Documents provided include Annual Reports, Monitoring and Reporting Strategy Summary, and Programme Summaries and Updates.

—— *Development Watch: Monitoring Progress on Sustainable Developments.* ⟨http://www.undp.org/devwatch/⟩. An outline of the Development Watch project is provided in Commission on Sustainable Development, *Recommendations and Proposals for Improving Coordination of Programmes Related to Development Data That Exist Within the United Nations System: report of the Secretary-General* (E/CN.17/1993/9) 4 June 1993. ⟨gopher://gopher.un.org/00/ esc/cn17/1993/off/93--9.en⟩

—— *Implementing the Rio Agreements: A Guide to UNDP's Sustainable Energy and Environment Division.* ⟨www.undp.org/seed/guide/intro.htm⟩. SEED was created in 1994 to strengthen UNDP's capacity to implement Agenda 21-related programmes. It is comprised of five units: Capacity 21, Energy and Atmosphere Programme, Global Environment Facility (in conjunction with the other GEF implementing agencies), Natural Resources, and the Office to Combat Desertification and Drought.

UN Division for Sustainable Development. *Assessment of the International Institutional Arrangements to Follow up the United Nations Conference on Environment and Development (Chapter 38).* Background Paper #4. New York: Department for Policy Coordination and Sustainable Development, 1997. ⟨gopher://gopher.un.org/00/esc/cn17/1997/background/BACK4.TXT⟩

—— *Terms of Reference: Inter-Agency Committee on Sustainable Development.* ⟨http://www.un.org/esa/sustdev/iacsdref.htm⟩

—— Human Development, Institutions and Technology Branch. *Compilation of Information on Initiatives of Countries and International Organizations to Implement the Objectives of Chapter 34 of Agenda 21.* Background Paper #6. New York: Department for Policy Coordination and Sustainable Development, 1997. ⟨gopher://gopher.un.org/00/esc/cn17/1997/background/BACK.6⟩

UN Economic and Social Council. Resolution 1993/207: "Establishment of

the Commission on Sustainable Development," 12 February 1993. ⟨gopher://
gopher.un.org/00/esc/cn17/enable/1993-207⟩.

—— Resolution 1997/65: "Establishment of an Ad Hoc Open-ended Intergovernmental Forum on Forests," 25 July 1997. ⟨gopher://gopher.un.org/00/esc/
recs/1997/E-RES97.65⟩. Documents of the IFF are available at ⟨http://
www.un.org/esa/sustdev/iff.htm⟩.

United Nations Environment Programme. *The UNEP Biodiversity Programme
and Implementation Strategy: a Framework for Supporting Global Conservation
and Sustainable Use of Biodiversity.* [Nairobi] UNEP, 1995.

—— *United Nations System-Wide Earthwatch.* ⟨http://www.unep.ch/earthw.html⟩.
The Earthwatch web site "provides a working tool for all the organizations co-
operating in Earthwatch, assisting in improving cooperation across the UN
system and beyond, and helping to identify opportunities for collaboration and
joint programming." Additional information on Earthwatch is available in
Commission for Sustainable Development, *Information for Decision-making
and Earthwatch: Report of the Secretary-General* (E.CN.17/1995/18), 24 March
1995. ⟨gopher://gopher.un.org/00/esc/cn17/1995/off/95-18.en⟩

—— Governing Council. Decision 19/1: "Role, Mandate and Governance of
the United Nations Environment Programme," 7 February 1997. ⟨gopher://
unephq.unep.org/00/un/unep/govcoun/decision/19-sess/19_1.txt⟩. The "Nairobi
Declaration on the Role and Mandate of the United Nations Environment
Programme" is included as an annex.

UN General Assembly. *Implementation of General Assembly Resolution 47/199
on the Institutional Arrangements to Follow up the United Nations Conference
on Environment and Development: Report of the Secretary-General* (A/48/442),
14 October 1993. ⟨gopher://gopher.un.org/00/esc/cn17/enable/a48-442⟩

—— *Outcome of the Nineteenth Special Session of the General Assembly: Report
of the Secretary-General* (A/52/280), 14 August 1997. ⟨gopher://gopher.un.org/
00/ga/docs/52/plenary/A52–280.EN⟩

—— Resolution 47/188: "Establishment of an Intergovernmental Negotiating
Committee for the Elaboration of an International Convention to Combat
Desertification in Those Countries Experiencing Serious Drought And/or
Desertification, Particularly in Africa" (A/RES/47/188), 22 December 1992.
⟨gopher://gopher.un.org/00/ga/recs/47/188⟩. A convention was subsequently
adopted. Information on the convention is available from the United Nations
Interim Secretariat of the Convention to Combat Desertification ⟨http://
www.unccd.ch⟩. (Documents of the INCD were issued under series symbol
A/AC.241.)

—— Resolution 47/189: "Convening of a Global Conference on the Sustainable
Development of Small Island Developing States" (A/RES/47/189), 22 December 1992. ⟨gopher://gopher.un.org/00/ga/recs/47/189⟩. The conference was
held 25 April–6 May 1994. The *Report of the Global Conference on the Sustainable Development of Small Island Developing States* (A/CONF.167/9; Sales
no. E.94.I.8 and Corr.) includes the Declaration of Barbados and the Programme of Action for the Sustainable Development of Small Island Developing
States. The report is also available on the www ⟨gopher://gopher.un.org/00/
conf/sids/conference/official/eng/poa.txt⟩.

—— Resolution 47/190: "Report of the United Nations Conference on Environment and Development" (A/RES/47/190), 22 December 1992. ⟨gopher://gopher.un.org/00/ga/recs/47/190⟩

—— Resolution 47/191: "Institutional Arrangements to Follow up the United Nations Conference on Environment and Development" (A/RES/47/191), 22 December 1992. ⟨gopher://gopher.un.org/00/ga/recs/47/191⟩

—— Resolution 47/192: "United Nations Conference on Straddling Fish Stocks and Highly Migratory Fish Stocks" (A/RES/47/192), 22 December 1992. ⟨gopher://gopher.un.org/00/ga/recs/47/192⟩

—— Resolution 47/195: "Protection of Global Climate for Present and Future Generations of Mankind" (A/RES/47/195), 22 December 1992. ⟨gopher://gopher.un.org/00/ga/recs/47/195⟩. This resolution sets forth the arrangements for the International Negotiating Committee for a Framework Convention on Climate Change to serve as the interim secretariat support of the convention.

—— Resolution S-19/2: "Programme for the Further Implementation of Agenda 21" (A/RES/S-19/2), 28 June 1997. ⟨gopher://gopher.un.org/00/ga/recs/spec/RES-S19.2⟩. Passed at the end of the General Assembly Special Session, this resolution endorses the "Programme for the further implementation of Agenda 21." The text of the programme is included as an Annex.

UN Non-Governmental Liaison Service. *Implementing Agenda 21.* ⟨http://ngls.tad.ch/english/pubs/21/21eng.html⟩

3. World Conference on Human Rights (Vienna, 14–25 June 1993)

3.1 General resources

Alston, Philip. "The UN's Human Rights Record: from San Francisco to Vienna and Beyond." *Human Rights Quarterly* 16 (1994): 375–390. "This is a revised version of the principal background paper commissioned for the NGO Conference ..."

UN. *The United Nations and Human Rights, 1945–1995.* New York: DPI, 1995.

—— Dag Hammarskjöld Library. "Special Topics: Human Rights" in *United Nations Documentation: Research Guide.* ⟨http://www.un.org/Depts/dhl/resguide/spechr.htm⟩

United Nations High Commissioner for Human Rights. *United Nations Human Rights Programme.* ⟨http://www.unhchr.ch/html/abo-intr.htm⟩

3.2 From Prepcom to conference

Note: Preparatory Committee materials were issued as A/CONF.157/PC/.

Reilly, Niamh, ed. *Testimonies of the Global Tribunal on Violations of Women's Human Rights at the United Nation's World Conference on Human Rights, Vienna, June 1993.* New Brunswick, NJ: Center for Women's Global Leadership, 1994. The texts of all testimonies presented at the tribunal, one of the NGO Forum activities, are included. *Demanding Accountability: the Global Campaign and Vienna Tribunal for Women's Human Rights* by Charlotte Bunch and Niamh Reilly (New Brunswick, NJ: Center for Women's Global

Leadership, 1994; New York: United Nations Development Fund, 1994) provides background information on the organizing efforts that led to the tribunal.

UN Centre for Human Rights. *Newsletter: World Conference on Human Rights, Vienna, Austria, June 1993.* Geneva: United Nations Centre for Human Rights.

UN General Assembly. Resolution 45/155: "World Conference on Human Rights" (A/RES/45/155), 18 December 1990. ⟨gopher://gopher.un.org/00/ga/recs/45/155⟩

UN High Commissioner for Human Rights. *World Conference on Human Rights.* ⟨http://www.unhchr.ch/html/menu5/wchr.htm⟩. This web site includes the text of the Final Report, regional reports, Vienna Declaration and Programme of Action.

World Conference on Human Rights. *Report of the World Conference on Human Rights: Report of the Secretary-General* (A/CONF.157/24 (Part I)), 13 October 1993. ⟨http://www.unhchr.ch/html/menu5/d/vienrep.htm⟩

—— *World Conference on Human Rights, Vienna, June 1993: the Contributions of NGOs: Reports and Documents.* Vienna: Manzsche Verlags und Universitäts-buchhandlung, 1994.

3.3 Follow-up and implementation

Dias, Clarence. "'The Spirit of Our Age and Realities of Our Time' – Vienna plus Five: Critical Ngo Review Needed." *Human Rights Tribune* 4, no. 4 (September 1997): 6–18. ⟨http://www.hri.ca/vienna+5/review/clarence-dias.shtml⟩

Human Rights Internet. ⟨http://www.hri.ca⟩. This multi-part site provides access to information from and about the UN (including reports on UN human rights bodies, resolutions and decisions, treaties), Vienna +5, and the full text of selected articles from the *Human Rights Tribune*, and *For the Record 1997: The UN Human Rights System*, produced in partnership with the Canadian Department of Foreign Affairs and International Trade.

UN Commission on Human Rights. *Interim Report of the United Nations High Commissioner for Human Rights* (E/CN.4/1998/104 and Corr. 1–2), 20 February 1998. Available via the Charter-based bodies database at ⟨http://www.unhchr.ch/huridocda/huridoca.nsf⟩.

—— *Report of the United Nations High Commissioner for Human Rights* (E/CN.4/1995/98), 15 February 1995. Available via the Charter-based bodies database at ⟨http://www.unhchr.ch/huridocda/huridoca.nsf⟩.

—— *Report of the United Nations High Commissioner for Human Rights* (E/CN.4/1998/122), 23 February 1998. Available via the Charter-based bodies database at ⟨http://www.unhchr.ch/huridocda/huridoca.nsf⟩.

—— *Report of the High Commissioner for Human Rights* (E/CN.4/1999/9), 2 March 1999. Available via the Charter-based bodies database at ⟨http://www.unhchr.ch/huridocda/huridoca.nsf⟩.

—— *Report of the United Nations High Commissioner for Human Rights: Building a Partnership for Human Rights* (E/CN.4/1997/98), 24 February 1997. Available via the Charter-based bodies database at ⟨http://www.unhchr.ch/huridocda/huridoca.nsf⟩.

—— *Report of the United Nations High Commissioner for Human Rights: "Making Human Rights a Reality"* (E/CN.4/1996/103), 18 March 1996.

Available via the Charter-based bodies database at ⟨http://www.unhchr.ch/huridocda/huridoca.nsf⟩.

United Nations Development Programme. *Integrating Human Rights with Sustainable Human Development: a UNDP Policy Document.* New York: UNDP, 1998. ⟨http://magnet.undp.org/Docs/policy5.html⟩

UN General Assembly. *Follow-up to the World Conference on Human Rights: Report of the Secretary-General* (A/49/668), 15 November 1994. An overview of the Programme of Action is provided in the context of reviewing the year's achievements in implementation.

—— Resolution 48/121: "World Conference on Human Rights" (A/RES/48/121), 20 December 1993. ⟨gopher://gopher.undp.org/00/undocs/gad/RES/48/121⟩

—— Resolution 48/141: "High Commissioner for the Promotion and Protection of All Human Rights" (A/RES/48/141), 20 December 1993. ⟨gopher://gopher.undp.org/00/undocs/gad/RES/48/141⟩. The post of High Commissioner for Human Rights was created by this resolution.

United Nations High Commissioner for Human Rights. *Five-year Review of the Implementation of the Vienna Declaration and Program of Action.* Geneva: Office of the High Commissioner, 1996–1999. ⟨http://www.unhchr.ch/html/50th/vdparev.htm⟩.

4. International Conference on Population and Development (Cairo, 5–13 September 1994)

4.1 General resources

International Institute for Sustainable Development. *Earth Negotiations Bulletin.* ⟨http://www.iisd.ca/linkages/vol06/0600000e.html⟩. Volume 6 of the *ENB* is devoted to the ICPD. Issue 40 is a summary, including coverage of the preparatory meetings, conference, and selected follow-up activities.

Johnson, Stanley. *The Politics of Population: the International Conference on Population and Development, Cairo 1994.* London: Earthscan, 1995.

Taub, Nadine. *International Conference on Population and Development.* Issue Papers on World Conferences, no. 1. Washington, DC: American Society of International Law, 1994.

UN *Population Bulletin of the United Nations.* (ST/ESA/SER.N). Issue No. 37/38 is devoted to the five regional conferences held prior to the ICPD.

United Nations Population Fund. *Populi* (quarterly).

—— *Dispatches: News from UNFPA, United Nations Population Fund* (10 issues/year). ⟨http://www.unfpa.org/publications/public.htm⟩. Early issues were distributed as a special insert in *Populi.*

—— *State of World Population* (annual). ⟨http://www.unfpa.org/SWP/SWPMAIN.HTM⟩. An overview of the Programme of Action is provided in the 1995 edition. The 1996 edition included an appendix, "Follow-up to the ICPD: Implementing the Reproductive Health Agenda." A special report, "Implementing the ICPD Programme of Action," was included in the 1997 volume. A statistical section, "Monitoring ICPD Goals – Selected Indicators," also appears in the 1997 volume.

United Nations Population Information Network. ⟨http://www.undp.org/popin/⟩. This web site includes links to documentation from the conference and from the Population Commission/Commission on Population and Development from the 27th session (1994) to the present. The recommendations of the Expert Group meetings held prior to the ICPD are also provided. (The proceedings of these meetings are available as UN sales publications.) The *Population Newsletter*, as well as numerous other publications and information services, is provided.

4.2 From Prepcom to conference

Note: The series symbol attached to materials emanating from the Preparatory Committee changed from E/CONF.84/PC to A/CONF.171/PC as a result in the change of status accorded the Committee under General Assembly resolution 48/186, 21 December 1993. ⟨gopher://gopher.un.org/00/ga/recs/48/186⟩

Dutt, Mallika, ed. *From Vienna to Beijing: the Cairo Hearing on Reproductive Health and Human Rights.* New Brunswick, NJ: Center for Women's Global Leadership, 1995.

ICPD 94. ⟨http://www.undp.org/popin/icpd/newslett⟩. Twenty-two issues of this newsletter (also known as *ICPD Newsletter*) focusing on the conference and its preparatory process were published between January 1992 and December 1994. The final issue provides an historical overview.

International Conference on Population and Development. *Report of the International Conference on Population and Development, Cairo, 5–13 September 1994* (A/Conf.171/13/Rev.1; UN Sales no. E.95.XIII.18). New York: United Nations, 1995. The report includes the text of the Programme of Action and of the reservations made by national governments and the Holy See. The Programme of Action has also been published in *Population and Development* (ST/ESA/SER.A/149; Sales no. E.95.XIII.7) and is available on the UNFPA web site ⟨http://www.undp.org/popin/icpd/conference/offeng/poa.html⟩. An overview, *International Conference on Population and Development: Summary of the Programme of Action,* is available from DPI. ⟨http://www.un.org/ecosocdev/geninfo/populatin/icpd.htm⟩

International Women's Health Coalition. *The Cairo Consensus: the Right Agenda for the Right Time.* ⟨http://www.iwhc.org/cairoindex.html⟩

UN Economic and Social Council. Resolution 1989/91: "Convening of an International Meeting on Population in 1994," 26 July 1989. ⟨gopher://gopher.un.org/00/esc/recs/1989/91⟩

—— Resolution 1991/93: "International Conference on Population and Development," 26 July 1991. ⟨gopher://gopher.un.org/00/esc/recs/1991/93⟩

4.3 Follow-up and implementation

Earth Summit Watch. ⟨http://earthsummitwatch.org/programs.html⟩. Includes "One Year After Cairo: Assessing National Action to Implement Their ICPD Commitments," a compendium of country reports.

International Planned Parenthood Federation. *IPPF and Cairo +5.* ⟨http://www.ippf.org/cairo/index.htm⟩

International Women's Health Coalition. *Beyond Cairo and Beijing.* ⟨http://www.iwhc.org/beyond.html⟩

Netherlands Interdisciplinary Demographic Institute (NIDI). *Financial Resource Flows for Population.* ⟨http://www.nidi.nl/resflows/⟩. As part of efforts to improve data collection and reporting on financial flows, UNFPA has contracted with NIDI to provide data collection and management services. NIDI and UNFPA have also made earlier years of the *Global Population Assistance Report* available on the web. ⟨http://www.nidi.nl/resflows/reports/gparsel.htm⟩

UN Commission on Population and Development. *Activities Conducted by Nongovernmental Organizations and Intergovernmental Organizations in Sexual and Reproductive Health and Rights: Three Years after the International Conference on Population and Development: Report of the Secretary-General* (E/CN.9/1998/5), 5 December 1997. ⟨http://www.undp.org/popin/unpopcom/31stsess/flowup5e.htm⟩. Prepared in response to Economic and Social Council resolution 1996/2, this is a revised version of the report the Secretary-General submitted to the Commission at its 29th session (E/CN.1996/5). The report submitted to the 30th session focused on international migration (E/CN.9/1997/5).

—— *Flows of Financial Resources in International Assistance for Population: Report of the Secretary-General* (E/CN.9/1997/6), 24 January 1997. ⟨http://www.undp.org/popin/unpopcom/30thsess/official/finaneg6.html⟩. Issued annually since the 29th session of the Commission, this report reviews the flow of resources and the funding mechanisms for implementing the Programme of Action. The two-year collaborative information systems project undertaken by UNFPA and the Netherlands Interdisciplinary Demographic Institute (NIDI) is described in Section IV. Related Commission reports include: *Flow of Financial Resources in International Assistance for Population: Report of the Secretary-General* (E/CN.9/1996/6), 2 January 1996, ⟨http://www.undp.org/popin/unpopcom/29thsess/official/resflows.html⟩; *Flows of Financial Resources for Population Activities* (E/CN.9/1998/6), 2 December 1997, ⟨http://www.undp.org/popin/unpopcom/31stsess/finance/finan6eg.htm⟩; *Flow of Financial Resources for Assisting in the Implementation of the Programme of Action of the International Conference on Population and Development: Report of the Secretary-General* (E/CN.9/1999/4), 2 February 1999.

—— *Health and Mortality: Report of the ACC Task Force on Basic Social Services for All* (E/CN.9/1998/4), 3 December 1997. ⟨http://www.undp.org/popin/unpopcom/31stsess/health/health4e.htm⟩

—— *Report of the ACC Task Force on Basic Social Services for All [with a special focus on international migration]* (E/CN.9/1997/4), 7 January 1997. ⟨http://www.undp.org/popin/unpopcom/30thsess/official/rptacc4e.html⟩

—— *Report on the Twenty-eighth Session (21 February–2 March 1995).* Economic and Social Council Official Records 1995, Supp. No. 7. (E/1995/27; E/CN.9/1995/8). New York: UN, 1995. ⟨http://www.undp.org/popin/unpopcom/28thsess/official/8cn91995.html⟩. The terms of reference of the "revitalized" commission are included as an Annex.

—— *Work of the Inter-Agency Task Force for the Implementation of the Programme of Action of the International Conference on Population and Development: Report of the Inter-Agency Task Force* (E/CN.9/1996/4), 10 January 1996. ⟨http://www.undp.org/popin/unpopcom/29thsess/official/task.html⟩

UN Economic and Social Council. Resolution 1995/55: "Implementation of the Programme of Action of the International Conference on Population and Development," 28 July 1995. ⟨gopher://gopher.un.org/00/esc/recs/1995/E-RES95.55⟩
—— Resolution 1996/2: "Follow-up to the International Conference on Population and Development," 17 July 1996. ⟨gopher://gopher.un.org/00/esc/recs/1996/E-RES96.2⟩

UN General Assembly. *Implementation of the Programme of Action of the International Conference on Population and Development: Report of the Secretary-General* (A/51/350), 25 September 1996. ⟨gopher://gopher.un.org/00/ga/docs/51/plenary/A51-350.EN⟩
—— *Implementation of the Programme of Action of the International Conference on Population and Development: Report of the Secretary-General* (A/52/208), 24 June 1997. ⟨gopher://gopher.un.org/00/ga/docs/52/plenary/A52-208.TXT⟩
—— *Report of the Ad Hoc Committee of the Whole of the Twenty-first Special Session of the General Assembly: Addendum* (A/S-21/5/Add.1), 1 July 1999. ⟨http://www.undp.org/popin/unpopcom/32ndsess/gass/215a1e.pdf⟩. Contains the "Key Actions for the Further Implementation of the Programme of Action of the International Conference on Population and Development."
—— Resolution 49/128: "Report of the International Conference on Population and Development" (A/RES/49/128), 19 December 1994. ⟨gopher://gopher.un.org/00/ga/recs/49/128⟩
—— Resolution 50/124: "Implementation of the Programme of Action of the International Conference on Population and Development" (A/RES/50/124), 23 February 1996. ⟨gopher://gopher.un.org/00/ga/recs/50/res50-en.124⟩
—— Resolution 51/176: "Implementation of the Programme of Action of the International Conference on Population and Development" (A/RES/51/176), 11 February 1997. ⟨gopher://gopher.un.org/00/ga/recs/51/RES51-EN.176⟩
—— Resolution 52/188: "Population and Development" (A/RES/52/188), 18 December 1997. ⟨gopher://gopher.un.org/00/ga/recs/52/RES52-EN.188⟩. The GA resolved to convene a three-day special session (30 June–2 July 1999) to review and appraise Programme of Action implementation.

UN Inter-Agency Task Force on the Implementation of the ICPD Programme of Action. *Guidelines for the Resident Coordinator System.* September 1995. ⟨http://www.undp.org/popin/unfpa/taskforce/guide⟩. The Inter-Agency Task Force on the Implementation of the ICPD Programme of Action (IATF) was created by the ACC to integrate follow-up activities. The *Report of the First Meeting of the Inter-agency Task Force on the Implementation of the ICPD Programme of Action* (13 December 1994) and the *Report of the Second Meeting of the ICPD Inter-Agency Task Force on the Implementation of the ICPD Programme of Action* (25 July 1995) are included as appendices to the *Guidelines.*

United Nations Population Fund. *ICPD* +5. ⟨http://www.unfpa.org/ICPD/ICPD.HTM⟩. This site is the official clearinghouse of ICPD +5 material. Information is provided on the ICPD, the Hague International Forum (a review of country-level progress), UNFPA preparations for the review, and NGO participation. The *ICPD +5 News Bulletin* is also provided.
—— Task Force on ICPD Implementation. *ICPD News: Newsletter of the*

UNFPA Task Force on ICPD Implementation. ⟨http://www.undp.org/popin/ unfpa/taskforce/icpdnews⟩. Only six issues of this quarterly were published from July 1995 to May 1997. The last issue refers readers to *Dispatches* for news on ICPD implementation.

United Nations Population Information Network. *Implementing the Decisions of the International Conference on Population and Development: 5-year Review and Appraisal of Implementation of the ICPD Programme of Action (ICPD +5).* ⟨http://www.undp.org/popin/icpd5.htm⟩

5. World Summit for Social Development (Copenhagen, 6–12 March 1995)

5.1 General resources

International Institute for Sustainable Development. *Earth Negotiations Bulletin.* ⟨http://www.iisd.ca/linkages/vol10/1000000e.html⟩. Volume 10 of the *ENB* is devoted to the WSSD. Issue 45 provides a year-end update.

UN Department of Public Information. *Notes for Speakers: Social Development.* New York: DPI, 1995 (DPI/1625/SOC/CON).

United Nations. *Social Policy and Social Progress* (semi-annual). The first issue focused on the Social Summit.

5.2 From Prepcom to conference

Note: Preparatory Committee materials were issued under series symbol A/CONF.166/PC.

Paul, James. *Incorporating Human Rights into the Work of the World Summit for Social Development.* Issue Papers on World Conferences, no. 3. Washington, DC: American Society of International Law, 1995.

UN General Assembly. Resolution 47/92: "Convening of a World Summit for Social Development" (A/RES/47/92), 16 December 1992. ⟨gopher://gopher.un. org/00/conf/wssd/ini/a-47--92⟩

UN Preparatory Committee for the World Summit for Social Development. *Consideration by the Commission for Social Development of the World Summit for Social Development and its Preparatory Process: Note by the Secretariat* (A/CONF.166/PC/2), 29 March 1993. ⟨gopher://gopher.un.org/00/conf/wssd/ini/ pc--2.enx⟩. The Annex to Commission for Social Development resolution 33/1 is included. It explains the Commission's thinking on the agenda-setting process and elaborates on the Summit's three core issues: eradication of poverty, productive employment, and social integration.

World Summit for Social Development. *Report of the World Summit for Social Development* (A/CONF.166/9). ⟨gopher://gopher.undp.org/00/unconfs/ wssd/summit/off/a--9.en⟩

5.3 Follow-up and implementation

Note: Documents from the Preparatory Committee for the Special Session of the General Assembly on the Implementation of the Outcome of the World Summit for Social Development and Further Initiatives are issued under series symbol A/AC.253/.

International Council on Social Welfare. *Social Development Review*. Each issue has a thematic supplement. Each of the first three issues focused on one of the Summit's three core issues.

—— *World Summit for Social Development: Report on Follow-up Activities.* ⟨http://www.icsw.org/social_summit/wssd.html⟩. Provides an overview of intergovernmental, governmental, and NGO activities.

—— and United Nations Development Programme. "Memorandum of Understanding Between the United Nations Development Programme and the International Council on Social Welfare," 4 July 1997. ⟨http://www.icsw.org/policies/policy_memorandum.htm⟩. According to this agreement "the principal areas for collaboration and interaction will concern reduction and eradication of poverty throughout the world, with special emphasis on pursuing and monitoring implementation of the relevant agreements made at the World Summit for Social Development (WSSD) and other global conferences."

Jolly, Richard. "Human Development: the World after Copenhagen," *Global Governance* 3 (1997): 233–248.

Social Watch. ⟨http://www.socwatch.org.uy/⟩. Social Watch is an NGO devoted to monitoring the commitments made by governments at the WSSD and the FWCW. To date, it has published four editions of an annual report on compliance.

UN Commission for Social Development. *Follow-up to the World Summit for Social Development: Note by the Secretariat* (E/CN.5/1995/8), 6 April 1995. ⟨gopher://gopher.un.org/00/esc/cn5/1995/1995--8.en⟩

—— *Future Role of the Commission for Social Development: Report of the Secretary-General* (E/CN.5/1996/2), 3 May 1996. ⟨gopher://gopher.un.org/00/esc/cn5/1996/off/96--2.en⟩. Suggestions for modifying the Commission's mandate, agenda, and methods of work are provided. The Annex includes a history of the Commission, its structure, membership, and mandate.

—— *Preliminary Assessment of the Implementation of the Outcome of the World Summit for Social Development. Report of the Secretary-General* (E/CN.5/1999/4), 16 December 1998. ⟨http://www.un.org/esa/socdev/social.htm⟩. Contains an annex titled "Progress Toward Targets."

—— *Report of the Secretary-General [on Follow-up to the World Summit for Social Development]* (E/CN.5/1997/2), 30 January 1997. ⟨gopher://gopher.un.org/00/esc/cn5/1997/off/ECN51997.2⟩

—— *Report of the Secretary-General on Productive Employment and Sustainable Livelihoods* (E/CN.5/1997/3), 23 January 1997.

UN Department of Economic and Social Affairs. *Commission for Social Development*, 1 November 1997. ⟨http://www.un.org/esa/socdev/social.htm⟩. This web site provides access to Commission materials including *Structure of the Agenda and Programme of Work*, terms of reference, and documents from the 34th session (1995) to the present.

—— *World Summit for Social Development*. ⟨http://www.un.org/esa/socdev/wssd.htm⟩. Materials about the Summit, as well as a substantial report on implementation, are provided via this web site. Materials on the Year 2000 review are also included.

—— and Department of Public Affairs. *World Social Summit and Beyond: Achieving Social Development for All in a Globalized World.* ⟨http://www.un.org/esa/socdev/geneva2000/index.html⟩. Includes a primer on the Special Session with details on the issues, process, and participation. Also contains the texts of key documents, including those from the Preparatory Committee for the Special Session of the General Assembly on the Implementation of the Outcome of the World Summit for Social Development (A/AC.253/).

UN Development Programme. *Progress Against Poverty: a Report on Activities since Copenhagen.* [n.p.]: UNDP, 1996.

—— *Poverty Eradication: a Policy Framework for Country Strategies.* NY: UNDP, 1995.

—— *Social Development and Poverty Elimination Division (SEPED).* [n.p.]: UNDP, 1998. ⟨http://www.undp.org/seped/homefile/brochur2.pdf⟩. A thematic guide to the workings of SEPED, the division within the Bureau for Development Policy responsible for providing policy guidance in three areas: poverty eradication, employment, and sustainable livelihoods, and gender and development.

—— Civil Society Organizations and Participation Programme. *CSOs/NGOs Contributions to the World Summit for Social Development: Poverty Eradication One Year after the World Summit for Social Development: A Guide to NGOs.* [n.p.]: UNDP/UN-NGLS, [n.d.]. ⟨http://www.undp.org/csopp/wssdpove.htm⟩

UN Economic and Social Council. Resolution 1995/60: "Social Development," 28 July 1995. ⟨gopher://gopher.un.org/00/esc/cn5/er95-60.en⟩

—— Resolution 1996/7: "Follow-up to the World Summit for Social Development and the Future Role of the Commission for Social Development," 22 July 1996. ⟨gopher://gopher.un.org/00/esc/recs/1996/E-RES96.7⟩

UN General Assembly. *Implementation of the Outcome of the World Summit for Social Development: Report of the Secretary-General* (A/50/670), 26 October 1995. ⟨gopher://gopher.un.org/00/ga/docs/50/plenary/670⟩

—— *Implementation of the Outcome of the World Summit for Social Development: Report of the Secretary-General* (A/51/348), 18 September 1996. ⟨gopher://gopher.un.org/00/ga/docs/51/plenary/A51-348.EN⟩

—— Resolution 50/161: "Implementation of the Outcome of the World Summit for Social Development" (A/RES/50/161), 22 December 1995. ⟨gopher://gopher.un.org/00/sec/dpcsd/ga/item161/ar50-161.en⟩

—— Resolution 51/202: "Implementation of the Outcome of the World Summit for Social Development" (A/RES/51/202), 17 December 1996. ⟨gopher://gopher.un.org/00/ga/recs/51/RES51-EN.202⟩

United Nations Research Institute for Social Development. *After the Social Summit: Implementing the Programme of Action. Report of the UNRISD Roundtable Seminar, Geneva, 4 July 1995.* ⟨http://www.unrisd.org/engindex/conf/ascconf.htm⟩

—— *Advancing the Social Agenda: Two Years after Copenhagen, 9–10 July 1997, Geneva.* ⟨http://www.unrisd.org/engindex/conf/asaconf.htm⟩

6. Fourth World Conference on Women (Beijing, 4–15 September 1995)

6.1 General resources

Cook, Rebecca J. *The Elimination of Sexual Apartheid: Prospects for the Fourth World Conference on Women*. Issue Papers on World Conferences, no. 5. Washington, DC: American Society of International Law, 1995. This exploration of the background of the conference focuses on issues related to the integration of women's rights into the machinery of international law.

—— and Valerie L. Oosterveld. *A Select Bibliography Of Women's Human Rights*. ⟨http://www.law.utoronto.ca/pubs/h_rghts.htm⟩

International Institute for Sustainable Development. *Earth Negotiations Bulletin*. ⟨http://www.iisd.ca/linkages/vol14/1400000e.html⟩. Volume 14 of the *ENB* is devoted to the FWCW. Issue 21 is a summary of conference activities, including coverage of the regional and expert group meetings that preceded it.

UN *The United Nations and the Advancement of Women, 1945–1996*. New York: DPI, 1996.

UN Commission on the Status of Women. *Second Review and Appraisal of the Implementation of the Nairobi Forward-looking Strategies for the Advancement of Women: Report of the Secretary-General* (E/CN.6/1995/3 and /Add.1–10), 10 January 1995. ⟨gopher://gopher.un.org/00/esc/cn6/1995/1995--3.en⟩. This report was also issued as a sales publication, *From Nairobi to Beijing: Second Review and Appraisal of the Implementation of the Nairobi Forward-looking Strategies for the Advancement of Women: Report of the Secretary-General* (Sales no. E.95.IV.5).

UN Department of Public Information. *The Advancement of Women: Notes for Speakers*. New York: DPI, 1995. (DPI/1674/WOM/CON/Reprint)

—— *Global Gender Agenda and the United Nations*. ⟨http://www.un.org/ecosocdev/geninfo/women/gender.htm⟩

6.2 From Prepcom to conference

Note: Preparatory Committee materials were issued as A/CONF.177/PC.

Forum '95: The Independent Daily of the NGO Forum on Women, Beijing '95. New York: International Women's Tribune Center, 1995. A compilation of the nine issues of the newspaper published over the course of the Forum.

NGO Forum on Women. *Look at the World Through Women's Eyes: NGO Forum on Women, Beijing '95 (30 August–8 September): Final Report*. [New York]: [NGO Forum on Women, Beijing '95, Inc.], [1996].

—— *Look at the World Through Women's Eyes: Plenary Speeches from the NGO Forum on Women, Beijing '95*. New York: NGO Forum on Women, Beijing '95, Inc., 1996.

Reilly, Niamh. *Without Reservation: The Beijing Tribunal on Accountability for Women's Human Rights*. New Brunswick, NJ: Center for Women's Global Leadership, 1996. This volume includes the texts of statements made at the tribunal, part of the NGO Forum proceedings.

UN Division for the Advancement of Women. *The United Nations Fourth World Conference on Women.* ⟨http://www.un.org/womenwatch/daw/beijing/index. html⟩. This web site includes links to official documentation (including such older material as the Nairobi Forward-looking Strategies for the Advancement of Women), background papers, information on NGOs, and public information materials.

UN Fourth World Conference on Women. *Report of the Fourth World Conference on Women, Beijing, 4–15 September 1995* (A/CONF.177/20/Rev.1; Sales no. E.96.IV.13). New York: UN, 1996. ⟨gopher://gopher.un.org/00/conf/fwcw/ off/a--20.en⟩

—— *Women on the Move.* ⟨gopher://gopher.un.org/11/conf/fwcw/pim/move⟩. Nine issues of this newsletter, issued by the Secretariat of the conference, were published between March 1994 and the beginning of the conference.

UN General Assembly. Resolution 45/129: "Implementation of the Nairobi Forward-looking Strategies for the Advancement of Women" (A/RES/45/129), 14 December 1990. ⟨gopher://gopher.un.org/00/ga/recs/45/129⟩

6.3 Follow-up and implementation

Social Watch. ⟨http://www.socwatch.org.uy/⟩. Social Watch is an NGO devoted to monitoring the commitments made by governments at the WSSD and the FWCW. To date, it has published four editions of an annual report on compliance.

UN Commission on the Status of Women. *Follow-up to and Implementation of the Beijing Declaration and Platform for Action* (E/CN.6/1998/2), 20 January 1998. ⟨gopher://gopher.un.org/00/esc/cn6/1998/official/98cn6-2.en⟩

—— *Mid-term Review of the Implementation of the System-wide Medium-term Plan for the Advancement of Women, 1996–2001: Report of the Secretary-General* (E/CN.6/1998/3), 6 January 1998. ⟨gopher://gopher.un.org/00/esc/cn6/1998/ official/98cn6-3.en⟩

—— *Progress Achieved in the Follow-up to the Fourth World Conference on Women and in Mainstreaming a Gender Perspective Within the United Nations System: Report of the Secretary-General* (E/CN.6/1997/2), 7 February 1997. ⟨gopher://gopher.un.org/00/esc/cn6/1997/official/97cn6-2⟩

—— *Synthesized Report on National Action Plans and Strategies for Implementation of the Beijing Platform for Action: Report of the Secretary-General* [E/CN.6/1998/6], 22 December 1997. ⟨gopher://gopher.un.org/00/esc/cn6/1998/ official/98cn6-6.en⟩

UN Committee on the Elimination of Discrimination Against Women. *Guidelines for Preparation of Reports by States Parties* (CEDAW/C/7/Rev.3), 26 July 1996. Available via the treaty bodies database at ⟨http://www.unhchr.ch/tbs/doc.nsf⟩. States parties to the Convention on the Elimination of Discrimination Against Women are encouraged "to include information on measures taken to implement the Platform for Action in order to facilitate the work of the Committee on the Elimination of Discrimination against Women in monitoring effectively women's ability to enjoy the rights guaranteed by the Convention." Selected states parties' reports are available through this web site.

UN Division for the Advancement of Women, United Nations Development Fund for Women, and United Nations International Research and Training Institute for the Advancement of Women. *WomenWatch: The UN Internet Gateway on the Advancement and Empowerment of Women.* ⟨http://www. un.org/womenwatch⟩. This web site serves as a gateway to UN information on women. Resources provided include: *Women 2000*, a newsletter "published to promote the goals of the Beijing Declaration and the Platform for Action" and *Follow-Up to Beijing,* providing links to materials on the national, regional, subregional, and international levels. The international material includes UN reports, statements, draft resolutions, press releases, and the National Plans of Action and Strategies to Implement the Beijing Platform for Action.

UN Economic and Social Council. *Report of the Economic and Social Council for 1997* (A/52/3), 18 September 1997. ⟨gopher://gopher.un.org/00/ga/docs/52/ plenary/A52---3.EN⟩. In its Agreed Conclusions 1997/2, the Council promoted "a coordinated and coherent policy of gender mainstreaming by further clarifying the concept of mainstreaming and the central principles associated with it ..." (This is a preliminary version of sections of the Official Records of the General Assembly, Fifty-second Session, Supp. 3 (A/52/3/Rev.1).)

—— Resolution 1996/6: "Follow-up to the Fourth World Conference on Women." 22 July 1996. ⟨gopher.un.org/00/esc/recs/1996/E-RES96.6⟩

—— *Proposed System-wide Medium-term Plan for the Advancement of Women, 1996–2001: Report of the Secretary-General* (E/1996/16), 16 April 1996. ⟨gopher://gopher.un.org/00/esc/docs/1996/96--16.EN⟩. The medium-term plan was originally endorsed by the Economic and Social Council in 1993. It recognized at that time that revisions taking into account the outcome of the FWCW would be necessary. This is the revised plan. It was subsequently adopted by Economic and Social Council resolution 1996/34: "System-wide medium-term plan for the advancement of women, 1996–2001." ⟨gopher://gopher.un.org/00/ esc/recs/1996/E-RES96.34⟩

—— *Ways and Means to Enhance the Capacity of the Organization and the United Nations System to Support the Ongoing Follow-up to the Fourth World Conference on Women: Report of the Secretary-General* (E/1997/64), 28 May 1997. ⟨gopher://gopher.un.org/00/esc/docs/1997/E97---64.EN⟩. The report of the previous year was subtitled *Information on Developments in United Nations Intergovernmental Forums and at the Inter-agency Level: Report of the Secretary-General* (E/1996/82), 10 July 1996. ⟨gopher://gopher.un.org/00/esc/docs/ 1996/E96--82.EN⟩

UN General Assembly. *Implementation of the Outcome of the Fourth World Conference on Women: Report of the Secretary-General* (A/51/322), 3 September 1996. ⟨gopher://gopher.un.org/00/sec/dpcsd/daw/ga/ga51st/A51-322.EN⟩

—— *Implementation of the Outcome of the Fourth World Conference on Women: Report of the Secretary-General* (A/52/281), 14 August 1997. ⟨gopher://gopher. un.org/00/sec/dpcsd/daw/ga/ga52nd/A-52-281.EN⟩

—— Resolution 52/100: "Follow-up to the Fourth World Conference on Women and Full Implementation of the Beijing Declaration and the Platform for Action" (A/RES/52/100), 26 January 1998. ⟨gopher://gopher.un.org/00/ga/recs/52/

RES52-EN.100⟩. The General Assembly decided to convene a high-level plenary review to assess the progress made in implementing the Nairobi Forward-Looking Strategies and the Platform for Action. The Commission on the Status of Women is designated the preparatory committee for this year 2000 review.

Women's Environment and Development Organization. *Beyond Promises: Governments in Motion One Year after the Beijing Women's Conference.* New York: WEDO, 1996.

—— *Keeping the Promises, Holding Governments and International Agencies Accountable: Monitoring and Advocacy Strategies for Advancing Women's Agenda.* New York: WEDO, [1996].

—— *Mapping Progress.* New York: WEDO, 1998.

—— *Promise Kept, Promise Broken.* New York: WEDO, 1997.

—— Women's Environment and Development Organization. ⟨http://www.wedo.org⟩. WEDO, a global NGO, is involved in peace, gender, human rights, environmental, and economic justice campaigns. Its web site includes a newsletter, *News and Views*; synopses of WEDO's publications; and information on its advocacy work at the UN.

WomensNet. *Beijing '95: Women, Power and Change: Follow up and Implementation.* ⟨http://www.igc.org/beijing/index.html⟩

7. United Nations Conference on Human Settlements (Istanbul, 3–14 June 1996)

7.1 General resources

International Institute for Sustainable Development. *Earth Negotiations Bulletin.* ⟨http://www.iisd.ca/linkages/vol11/1100000e.html⟩. Volume 11 of the *ENB* is devoted to Habitat II. Issue 37 is a summary of conference activities, including coverage of the regional and expert group meetings that preceded it.

Leckie, Scott. *Towards an International Convention on Housing Rights: Options at Habitat II.* Issue Papers on World Conferences, no. 4. Washington, DC: American Society of International Law, 1994. Leckie explores the background of Habitat II and the prospects of using that arena to create an international convention on housing rights.

United Nations Centre for Human Settlements. *Habitat Debate.* Nairobi: UNCHS. ⟨http://www.unchs.org/unchs/english/docs1.htm⟩

United Nations Conference on Human Settlements. *The City Summit: Habitat II, United Nations Conference on Human Settlements, Istanbul, Turkey, 3–14 June 1996.* New York: DPI, 1995.

UN General Assembly. Resolution 43/181: "Global Strategy for Shelter to the Year 2000" (A/RES/43/181), 20 December 1988. ⟨gopher://gopher.un.org/00/ga/recs/43/181⟩. Included as an Annex to this resolution are "Guidelines for steps to be taken at the national level" including considerations when formulating and implementing a national shelter strategy and "Guidelines for steps to be taken at the international level."

7.2 From Prepcom to conference

Note: Preparatory Committee materials were issued as A/CONF.165/PC.

Habitat II Secretariat. *Countdown to Istanbul.* Nairobi: UNCHS. Issues 2–5 (April 1995–November 1995) available at ⟨http://www.undp.org/un/habitat/ guide/index.html⟩.

United Nations Conference on Human Settlements. *Habitat Agenda and Istanbul Declaration: Second United Nations Conference on Human Settlements, Istanbul, Turkey, 3–14 June 1996.* New York: DPI, 1996. ⟨http://www.undp.org/un/ habitat/agenda/index.html⟩

UN General Assembly. Resolution 47/180: "United Nations Conference on Human Settlements (Habitat II)" (A/RES/47/180), 22 December 1992. ⟨gopher:// gopher.un.org/00/ga/recs/47/180⟩

United Nations Conference on Human Settlements. *Report of the United Nations Conference on Human Settlements (Habitat II): Istanbul, 3–14 June 1996* (A/ CONF.165/14), 7 August 1996. ⟨http://www.unhabitat.org/agenda/⟩. Additional conference documentation and other relevant materials including the *NGO Composite Suggestions to the Habitat Agenda, Implementation of the Habitat Agenda* (summarizing the implementation arrangements), and *Partners and the Implementation of the Habitat Agenda* (draft guides to implementation for governments, civil society, and the private sector) are available from the conference web site ⟨http://www.unhabitat.org/habitat2/⟩.

An Urbanizing World: Global Report on Human Settlements, 1996. Oxford; New York: Oxford University Press for the United Nations Centre for Human Settlements (HABITAT), 1996. Prepared in response to Decision I/2 of the Preparatory Committee, this report is a comprehensive review of conditions and trends in human settlements and urbanization.

7.3 Follow-up and implementation

Habitat II NGO Forum '96. ⟨http://www.ngoforum.org.tr⟩

Shelter for All: The Potential of Housing Policy in the Implementation of the Habitat Agenda (HS/488/97E). ⟨http://habitat.unchs.org/unchs/english/shelter/ contents.htm⟩

United Nations Centre for Human Settlements. *Implementation Of The Habitat Agenda: Guidelines for the United Nations Resident Coordinator System* (HS/ 509/98E), January 1998. ⟨http://www.unchs.org/unchs/english/hagenda/guide1/ contents.htm⟩

—— Istanbul +5. ⟨*http://www.istanbul5.org/*⟩. Clearinghouse of information regarding the June 2001 Special Session of the UN General Assembly for an Overall Review and Appraisal of the Implementation of the Habitat Agenda.

UN Commission on Human Settlements. *Review of the Working Methods of the Commission: Report of the Executive Director* (HS/C/16/4), 10 February 1997. ⟨http://www.undp.org/un/habitat/chs16/16__4.html⟩. This report includes a proposal to expand Commission membership by adding representatives of local authorities, NGOs, and the private sector. It also includes suggestions on strengthening the monitoring capabilities of the Commission.

—— *The Role of Local Authorities, the Private Sector, Non-governmental Organ-*

izations and Other Partners in the Implementation and Monitoring of the Habitat Agenda: Report of the Executive Director (HS/C/16/6), 21 January 1997. ⟨http://www.undp.org/un/habitat/chs16/16__6.html⟩

UN General Assembly. *Implementation of and Follow-up to the Outcome of the United Nations Conference on Human Settlements (Habitat II): Report of the Secretary-General* (A/51/384), 20 September 1996. ⟨gopher://gopher.un.org/00/ga/docs/51/plenary/A51-384.EN⟩

—— *Implementation of the Outcome of the United Nations Conference on Human Settlements (Habitat II): Report of the Secretary-General* (A/52/181), 1 July 1997. Issued jointly with the Economic and Social Council (E/1997/77). ⟨gopher://gopher.un.org/00/ga/docs/52/plenary/A52--181.EN⟩

—— Resolution 51/177: "Implementation of the Outcome of the United Nations Conference on Human Settlements (Habitat II)" (A/RES/51/177), 16 December 1996. ⟨gopher://gopher.un.org/00/ga/recs/51/RES51-EN.177⟩

—— Resolution 52/190: "Implementation of the Outcome of the United Nations Conference on Human Settlements (Habitat II)" (A/RES/52/190), 18 December 1997. ⟨gopher://gopher.un.org:70/00/ga/recs/52/RES52-EN.190⟩

—— Resolution 52/192: "Follow-up to the United Nations Conference on Human Settlements (Habitat II) and the Future Role of the Commission on Human Settlements" (A/RES/52/192), 18 December 1997. ⟨gopher://gopher.un.org/00/ga/recs/52/RES52-EN.192⟩. The terms of reference, work programme, and methods of work of the Commission are elaborated.

—— Resolution 53/180: "Special Session of the General Assembly for an Overall Review and Appraisal of the Implementation of the Habitat Agenda" (A/RES/53/180), 15 December 1998. ⟨gopher://gopher.un.org:70/00/ga/recs/53/res53-en.180⟩

Integrated and coordinated implementation

Selected references

International Labour Organization. Employment and Labour Market Policies Branch. *UN ACC Task Force on Full Employment and Sustainable Livelihoods Synthesis Report*, 27 March 1997. Geneva: ILO, 1998. ⟨http://www.ilo.org/public/english/employment/strat/polemp/prog4-5.htm⟩

Press Release ECOSOC/5753: "Economic and Social Council Begins Session on Integrated, Coordinated Follow-up of Major United Nations Conferences and Summits," 13 May 1998. ⟨http://www.un.org/News/Press/docs/1998/19980513.eco5753.html⟩

UN ACC Task Force on Basic Social Services for All. *Basic Social Services for All 1997: Achieving the Goals and Commitment of United Nations Conferences.* ⟨http://www.undp.org/popin/wdtrends/bss/bsstoc.htm⟩. This web site includes information on the goals of the conferences *vis-à-vis* basic social services and relevant data items (presented in tabular and map displays).

UN Administrative Committee on Coordination. *Report of the Inter-Agency*

Committee on Women and Gender Equality on its First Session (New York, 22 and 23 October 1996) (ACC/1996/22), 6 February 1997. Both the short-term and long-term work programme of the committee are outlined. The terms of reference of the committee are included as Annex III. The *Report of the Inter-Agency Committee on Women and Gender Equality on its Second Session (New York, 5 and 6 March 1997)* was issued on 2 June 1997 as ACC/1997/8. Subsequent reports include ACC/1998/3 (third session) and ACC/1999/3 (fourth session).

UN Development Programme. *Discussion Note on Relationship Between Employment and Sustainable Livelihoods: Prepared by UNDP for ACC Inter-Agency Task Force on Full Employment and Sustainable Livelihoods.* [New York]: UNDP, [1996]. ⟨http://www.undp.org/sl/publication/sliatf9.pdf⟩

UN Economic and Social Council. *Annual Overview Report of the Administrative Committee on Coordination for 1995* (E/1996/18 and Add.1), 22 May 1996. ⟨gopher://gopher.un.org/00/esc/docs/1996/E96--18.EN⟩ and ⟨gopher://gopher.un.org/00/esc/docs/1996/96--18A1⟩

—— *Annual Overview Report of the Administrative Committee on Coordination for 1996* (E/1997/54), 13 May 1997. ⟨gopher://gopher.un.org/00/esc/docs/1997/E97--54.EN⟩

—— *Annual Overview Report of the Administrative Committee on Coordination for 1997* (E/1998/21), 4 May 1998. ⟨gopher://gopher.un.org/00/esc/docs/1998/e98--21.en⟩. As part of the preparations for the General Assembly special session on Rio +5, the ACC reviewed the functioning of the Inter-Agency Committee on Sustainable Development and its Task Manager system. A summary of the review is included as Annex III.

—— *Annual Overview Report of the Administrative Committee on Coordination for 1998* (E/1999/48), 11 May 1999. ⟨http://www.un.org/esa/coordination/ecosoc/doc99-48.htm⟩

—— *Coordinated Follow-up to Major International Conferences in the Economic, Social and Related Fields: Report of the Secretary-General* (E/1995/86), 9 June 1995. ⟨gopher://gopher.un.org/00/sec/dpcsd/dspd/iyep/e95-86.en⟩. The report suggests that the conferences "should be viewed as a continuum that links the various dimensions of development within an integrated framework." It provides an overview of the outcomes of six conferences and outlines main issues for coordination and identifies the crosscutting themes from the conferences.

—— *Integrated and Coordinated Implementation and Follow-up of Major United Nations Conferences and Summits: A Critical Review of the Development of Indicators in the Context of Conference Follow-up: Report of the Secretary-General* (E/1999/11), 7 April 1999. ⟨http://www.un.org/esa/coordination/ecosoc/doc99-11.htm⟩

—— *Integrated and Coordinated Implementation of and Follow-up to Major United Nations Conferences and Summits: Report of the Secretary-General* (E/1999/65), 7 June 1999. ⟨http://www.un.org/esa/coordination/ecosoc/doc99-65.htm⟩

—— *Report of the Economic and Social Council.* Official Records of the General Assembly, Fiftieth Session, Supp. 3. (A/50/3/Rev.1) ⟨gopher://gopher.un.org/00/sec/dpcsd/ga/item12/a50---3.en⟩. Of particular relevance is Agreed Conclusions 1995/1: "Agreed Conclusions on Coordinated Follow-up by the United Nations System and Implementation of the Results of the Major International Conferences Organized by the United Nations in the Economic, Social and Related Fields."

—— Report of the Secretary-General [on integrated and coordinated implementation and follow-up of the major United Nations conferences and summits] (E/1997/73), 10 June 1997. ⟨gopher://gopher.un.org/00/esc/docs/1997/E97--73.EN⟩

—— Resolution 1997/61: "Integrated and Coordinated Implementation and Follow-up of the Major United Nations Conferences and Summits," 25 July 1997. ⟨gopher://gopher.un.org/00/esc/recs/1997/E-RES97.61⟩

—— Resolution 1998/44: "Integrated and Coordinated Implementation and Follow-up of Major United Nations Conferences and Summits," 31 July 1998. ⟨gopher://gopher.un.org/00/esc/recs/1998/e-res98.44⟩

Notes

1. Several people provided valuable feedback on earlier drafts of this work: Jane Arnold, Dale Grover, Mary Beth Lake, Terry Link, Steven Sowards, and Susanna Van Sant. I thank them for the many improvements they suggested.
2. These efforts have included recommendations to reduce the number of pages per document, to require that some reports be submitted biennially rather than annually, and to reduce the number and length of preambular paragraphs in resolutions. UNICEF has, for example, decided to stop producing summary records of its executive board meetings (Decision 1994/R.1/1: "Implementation of General Assembly Resolution 48/162 on Further Measures for Restructuring and Revitalization of the United Nations in the Economic, Social and Related Fields, Including Future Working Methods of the Executive Board," *Executive Board of the United Nations Children's Fund: Report on the First, Second and Third Regular Sessions and Annual Session of 1994*, Economic and Social Council Official Records 1994, Supp. 14 (E/1994/34/Rev.1, p. 106). Changes such as these may well adversely affect the ability of future researchers to do in-depth historical research.
3. It is estimated that the UN's documentary output in 1997 will approach 600,000 pages. This represents a 25 per cent reduction from the number of pages reproduced in 1995. (*Control and Limitation of Documentation: Implementation of General Assembly Resolution 50/206C: Report of the Secretary-General* (A/52/291), 22 August 1997, para 7.)
4. e.g., UN, Dag Hammarskjöld Library, *United Nations Documentation: A Brief Guide*, NY: UN, 1994 (ST/LIB/34/Rev.2); Marian Shaaban and Robert Goehlert, *UN Documentation: A Basic Guide*, Bloomington, IN: Indiana Center on Global Change and World Peace, 1993; UN, Dag Hammarskjöld Library, *United Nations Documentation: Research Guide* ⟨http://www.un.org/Depts/dhl/resguide⟩.
5. The documentation systems of the specialized agencies vary greatly. For a brief guide to the indexes and finding aids of these and other intergovernmental organizations, see Debbi Schaubman, *International Law and Organizations: Information by Organization.* ⟨http://www.lib.msu.edu/publ_ser/docs/igos/igoorg.htm⟩
6. *Administrative Instruction ... Regulations for the Control and Limitation of Documentation. Addendum. Distribution of Documents, Meeting Records, Official Records and Publications* (ST/AI/189/Add.3/Rev.2, para. 2 and para. 4, respectively), 17 December 1985, as quoted in *United Nations Documentation: Research Guide* ⟨http://www.un.org/Depts/dhl/resguide/symbol.htm⟩.

7. Two guides that are particularly strong on UN citation formats are Xia Li and Nancy B. Crane, *Electronic Styles: A Handbook for Citing Electronic Information*, 2d ed., Medford, NJ: Information Today, Inc., 1996; Diane Garner, *The Complete Guide to Citing Government Information Resources: A Manual for Writers and Librarians*, rev. ed., Bethesda, MD: CIS, Inc., 1993.

8. For example, the knowledge that the Commission on the Status of Women has a central role in monitoring the efforts to implement the Beijing Conference Platform for Action combined with the knowledge that the Commission's documents bear the symbol "E/CN.6," may give the researcher a means to identify relevant recent materials even before they appear in a bibliographic index or database.

9. There are exceptions to this rule, of course. For example, documents issued by the Commission on Human Settlements bear the symbol HS/C.

10. Full citations to *UNDOC* and other finding aids can be found in Section V.

11. UN, Dag Hammarskjöld Library, *UN-I-QUE* ⟨http://www.un.org/Depts/dhl/unique/⟩.

12. As of January 1998, there were over 350 depositories in 141 countries; a list is available on the UN web site: UN, Dag Hammarskjöld Library, *List of Depository Libraries Receiving United Nations Material* (ST/LIB/12/Rev.14), 15 April 1997, last updated 20 January 1998 ⟨http://www.un.org/MoreInfo/Deplib/index.html⟩

13. *Official Records* are issued for each session of the General Assembly, Security Council, and Economic and Social Council. They consist of plenary meeting records; supplements containing the session's resolutions and reports of committees, commissions and other bodies; and annexes that reprint key documents.

14. The decentralized nature of the UN's online presence makes it difficult to determine precisely how many unique documents are available via the Internet. What is clear is that all documents are *not* available.

15. UN General Assembly, *Questions Relating to Information: Report of the Secretary-General* (A/50/462), 21 September 1995, para. 19. ⟨gopher://gopher.un.org:70/00/ga/docs/50/plenary/462⟩

16. See, for example, UN General Assembly, *Access to the Optical Disk System: Report of the Secretary-General* (A/52/803), 25 February 1998. ⟨http://www.globalpolicy.org/ngos/ods2-98.htm⟩

17. NY: Department of Public Information, 1997. (DPI/1816; Sales No. E.97.I.5). The chapters on the World Summit for Children, UNCED, and the Fourth World Conference on Women are also available on the UN WWW site ⟨http://www.un.org/geninfo/bp/worconf.html⟩

18. The provisional agenda is not necessarily the only pre-sessional document relevant to tracking documentation. The General Assembly, for example, also issues a preliminary list of items and an annotated preliminary list. An explanation of the various agenda-related documents is provided in *United Nations Documentation: Research Guide*.

19. This is not to say that they are *never* consistent. General Assembly Resolution 49/128, for example, specified that the Assembly would include an item specifically entitled "Implementation of the Programme of Action of the International Conference on Population and Development" on subsequent agendas.

20. Web sites and search engines change constantly. At the time of writing, the suggested search strategy, while somewhat lengthy, did work. If difficulties are encountered, read the help pages provided.

21. This is especially true as the UN web and gopher sites are not always consistent in their arrangement. For example, the URL for the *Annual Overview Report of the Administrative Committee on Coordination for 1994* (E/1995/21) is ⟨gopher://gopher.un.org/00/inter/acc/e95-21.en⟩. The URL for the *Annual Overview Report of the Administrative Committee on Coordination for 1995* (E/1996/18), on the other hand, is ⟨gopher://

gopher.un.org/00/esc/docs/1996/E96--18.EN⟩. This lack of consistency makes it quite difficult to deduce a likely URL.

22. UN Department of Economic and Social Affairs, *Integrated Meeting and Documentation Information System,* Version 0.8 – May 1998 ⟨http://imdis.un.org⟩; site originally examined 8 June 1998. Revised version of the site is available at ⟨http://esa.un.org/imdis⟩. It is unclear to what extent this system will remain open to users outside the UN system.

23. The *Official WEB Site Locator for the United Nations System of Organizations* ⟨http://www.unsystem.org⟩ provides listings arranged both thematically and alphabetically.

24. For example, to search the UNCHS web site for information on sustainable energy, one can use the following search on AltaVista ⟨http://altavista.com⟩: ⟨+"sustainable energy" +host:www.unhabitat.org⟩.

25. Administrative Committee on Coordination, *UNIONS.* ⟨http://www3.itu.int/unions⟩. Not all sites are as yet included in UNIONS. Help screens should provide up-to-date information on its coverage.

26. *Commission for Social Development: Report on the Thirty-third Session (8–17 February 1993),* Economic and Social Council Official Records 1993, Supp. 4 (E/CN.5/1993/13; E/1993/24).

27. For example: *UNHCR and NGOs: Directory of Non-Governmental Organizations,* Geneva: UNHCR, 1996; *World Directory of Environmental Organizations: A Handbook of National and International Organizations and Programs – Governmental and Non-governmental – Concerned With Protecting the Earth's Resources,* Sacramento, CA: International Center for the Environment and Public Policy, 1996; *Directory of International Non-governmental Organizations in Cambodia, Laos, and Vietnam* [Khon Kaen, Thailand]: Mekong Community Coordination Program, Research and Development Institute, Khon Kaen University, 1994; *A Guide to NGO Directories: How to Find Over 20,000 Nongovernmental Organizations in Latin America and the Caribbean,* Arlington, VA: Inter-American Foundation, 1995; *International Co-operation for Habitat and Urban Development: Directory of Non-governmental Organisations in OECD Countries,* Paris: Development Centre of the Organization for Economic Cooperation and Development, 1997; *Directory of Environmental Information and Organisations in Southern Africa,* Harare: Southern African Research and Documentation Centre: IUCN Regional Office for Southern Africa, 1996.

28. This query worked using the advanced search form on the Altavista search engine ⟨http://altavista.com⟩ on 16 August 1999. Note that search engines can vary greatly in syntax and that, as search engines continue to be refined, the required syntax may change. Note also that search engines vary in more than just syntax; they vary, for example, in what parts of a web page are indexed and in how relevancy is determined. To cast the widest net, it is wise to conduct your search on several search engines.

29. Although the examples provided in this section are drawn entirely from English-language resources and US library practices, the theoretical points are more widely applicable.

30. e.g. many libraries have catalogued *Four in '94: Two Years After Rio: Assessing National Actions to Implement Agenda 21,* NY: Natural Resources Defense Council, 1994, with a single subject heading: "Sustainable Development – Developing Countries."

31. *UNBIS Plus on CD-ROM: User Manual,* Alexandria, VA: Chadwyck-Healey, Inc., 1995, p. A-6.

32. Arvonne S. Fraser, "The Feminization of Human Rights: How the World Conference on Human Rights Brought Women onto the Agenda," *Foreign Service Journal* 70 (1993), pp. 31–34.

Acronyms and abbreviations

ACC   Administrative Committee on Coordination
ACUNS   Academic Council for the United Nations System
AG13   Ad Hoc Working Group on Article 13
AGBM   Ad Hoc Working Group on the Berlin Mandate
AIJ   activities implemented jointly
AOSIS   Alliance of Small Island States
APC   Association for Progressive Communications
ASEAN   Association of Southeast Asian Nations
BINGO   Business and Industry Non-governmental Organization
CAPE   Children's Alliance for Protection of the Environment
CBD   Convention on Biological Diversity
CBO   Community-Based Organization
CCA   common country assessment
CEDAW   Committee on the Elimination of Discrimination Against Women
CHM   clearing-house mechanism
CHR   Commission on Human Rights
CITES   Convention on International Trade in Endangered Species
CMS   Convention on Migratory Species
CNN   Cable News Network
COP   Conference of the Parties
CSD   Commission on Sustainable Development
CSE   Centre for Science and Environment
CSO   Civil Society Non-governmental Organization
CSW   Commission on the Status of Women
CTE   Committee on Trade and Environment

DAC	Development Assistance Committee
DESA	Department for Economic and Social Affairs
DHR	Dag Hammarskjöld Library
DONGO	Donor-organized Non-governmental Organization
DSB	Dispute Settlement Body
ECOSOC	Economic and Social Council
EITs	economies in transition
ENB	*Earth Negotiations Bulletin*
ENGO	Environmental Non-governmental Organization
EU	European Union
FAO	Food and Agriculture Organization
FCCC	Framework Convention on Climate Change
FFF	Food supplementation, Family planning, Female education
FIELD	Foundation for International Environmental Law and Development
G7	Group of Seven
G77	Group of 77
G8	Group of Eight
GATT	General Agreement on Tariffs and Trade
GEF	Global Environment Facility
GNP	gross national product
GOBI	Growth monitoring, Oral rehydration, Breastfeeding, Immunization
GOBI-FFF	Growth monitoring, Oral rehydration, Breastfeeding, Immunization – Food supplementation, Family planning, Female education
GONGO	Government-organized Non-governmental Organization
GRINGO	Government-run Non-governmental Organization
GRO	Grassroots organization
HCHR	High Commission for Human Rights
HFA	Health for All
HFCs	hydrofluorocarbons
IACWGE	Inter-Agency Committee on Women and Gender Equality
IATF	Inter-Agency Task Force
ICIF	Integrated and coordinated implementation and follow-up efforts
ICJ	International Court of Justice
ICPD	International Conference on Population and Development
ICSU	International Council of Scientific Unions
ICSW	International Council on Social Welfare
IDRs	in-depth reviews
IEA	International Energy Agency
IFF	Intergovernmental Forum on Forests
IFI	International Financial Institution
IGO	Intergovernmental Organization
IISD	International Institute for Sustainable Development
ILO	International Labor Organization
INC	Intergovernmental Negotiating Committee
INCD	Interim Secretariat of the Convention to Combat Desertification
INGO	International Non-governmental Organization
IPCC	Intergovernmental Panel on Climate Change

IPF	Intergovernmental Panel on Forests
IPPF	International Planned Parenthood Federation
IT	information technology
IUCN	World Conservation Union
MCP	multilateral consultative process
MICS	multi-indicator cluster survey
MNSDS	Minimum National Social Data Set
MOP	Meeting of the Parties
MOU	Memorandum of Understanding
MSU	Michigan State University
MUNS	Multilateralism and the UN System
NGO	non-governmental organization
NIDI	Netherlands Interdisciplinary Demographic Institute
NPA	National Plan of Action
OCLC	Online Computer Library Center
ODA	official development assistance
ODS	Optical Disk System
OECD	Organization for Economic Cooperation and Development
OHCHR	Office of High Commissioner for Human Rights
OPEC	Organization of Petroleum Exporting Countries
OXFAM	Oxford Committee for Famine Relief
PFCs	perfluorocarbons
PHC	Primary Health Care
PINGO	Public Interest Non-governmental Organization
PrepCom	Preparatory Committee
PVO	Private Voluntary Organization
R&D	Research and Development
RLIN	Research Libraries Information Network
SAARC	South Asian Association for Regional Cooperation
SBI	Subsidiary Body for Implementation
SBSTA	Subsidiary Body for Scientific and Technological Advice
SBSTTA	Subsidiary Body for Scientific, Technical and Technological Advice
SEED	Sustainable Energy and Environment Division
SIDS	Global Conference on Sustainable Development for Small Island Developing States
STAP	Scientific and Technical Advisory Panel
TAR	Third Assessment Report
TRIPs	Trade-Related Aspects of Intellectual Property Rights
UDHR	Universal Declaration of Human Rights
UIA	Union of International Associations
UN	United Nations
UNCCD	United Nations Convention to Combat Desertification
UNCED	United Nations Conference on Environment and Development
UNCHS	United Nations Conference on Human Settlements
UNCTAD	United Nations Conference on Trade and Development
UNDAF	United Nations Development Assistance Framework
UNDP	United Nations Development Program

UNEP	United Nations Environment Program
UNESCAP	United Nations Economic and Social Commission for Asia and the Pacific
UNESCO	United Nations Educational, Scientific and Cultural Organization
UNFCCC	United Nations Framework Convention on Climate Change
UNFPA	United Nations Fund for Population Activities
UNGA	United Nations General Assembly
UNICEF	United Nations Children's Fund
UNIFEM	United Nations Development Fund for Women
UNRISD	United Nations Research Institute for Social Development
UNWCHR	United Nations World Conference on Human Rights
VDPA	Vienna Declaration and Program of Action
WCHR	World Conference on Human Rights
WEDO	Women's Environment and Development Organization
WFP	World Food Program
WHO	World Health Organization
WMO	World Meteorological Organization
WRI	World Resources Institute
WSC	World Summit for Children
WSSD	World Summit for Social Development
WTO	World Trade Organization
WWF	World Wide Fund for Nature
WWW	World Wide Web

Contributors

Jo Elizabeth Butler was employed by UNCTAD as Legal Officer to the Commodities Division before her secondment to the Climate Change Convention secretariat for six years as legal adviser. She has since rejoined the UNCTAD secretariat as Chief of Public Affairs, and has recently been appointed Secretary to the UN Economic Commission for Africa and Chief of the Cabinet Office.

Rebecca J. Cook is Professor and Director of the International Human Rights Programme of the Faculty of Law at the University of Toronto. She specializes in the international protection of human rights and in health law and ethics, and serves on the editorial advisory boards of several journals including *Family Planning Perspectives*, *Human Rights Quarterly*, and the *Third World Legal Studies Journal*, and is Ethical and Legal Issues editor of the *International Journal of Gynecology and Obstetrics*. Professor Cook is an occasional adviser to the Commonwealth Medical Association, the Ford Foundation, Profamilia Legal Services for Women, and the World Health Organization. Her publications include over a hundred books, articles and reports in the areas of international human rights, the law relating to women's health and feminist ethics. She is the author of *Women's Health and Human Rights* (World Health Organization, 1994) and is the editor of *Human Rights of Women: National and International Perspectives* (University of Pennsylvania Press, 1994).

Clarence J. Dias, formerly a faculty member of the Department of Law of the University of Bombay, is the

President of the International Center for Law in Development in New York City and the Chair of the Board of Human Rights Internet. He is also a member of the Board of Global Policy Forum. He was the co-author of the UN-commissioned paper for the World Conference on Human Rights, "Human Rights, Development and Democracy" (UN General Assembly, A/CONF. 157/PC/20), and author and resource person on the same topic at the Vienna NGO Forum.

Aniket Ghai is in charge of the Geneva Environment Network, a cooperative partnership of over 30 Geneva-based environment and sustainable development units and organizations, including the UN bodies, NGOs and the private sector. Before that, he was a consultant to intergovernmental organizations, NGOs and governments, on a range of environment and sustainable development issues. He previously worked for the Climate Change Convention secretariat, for a Swiss environmental NGO and for the secretariat of the UN Convention on Environment and Development (UNCED).

Masumi Ono is currently an Economic Affairs Officer with the International Trade and Economic Cooperation Division of UNESCAP (United Nations Economic and Social Commission for Asia and the Pacific). She is based in Bangkok. There she deals with trade facilitation issues, managing projects in the SAARC (South Asian Association for Regional Cooperation) region as well as in the Greater Mekong Sub-region. Prior to this assignment, she was an Associate Economic Affairs Officer in the Department for Economic and Social Affairs (DESA) of the United Nations Secretariat in New York; there she was closely involved with the coordinated follow-up to major UN conferences, particularly as it relates to the General Assembly and ECOSOC.

Debbi Schaubman is the International Documents Librarian at Michigan State University (MSU). She has also been the Head of the MSU Government Documents Library since 1994. Her current research interests focus on information policies of intergovernmental organizations and the visual representation of information on the Internet.

Michael G. Schechter is Professor of International Relations at James Madison College of Michigan State University. His most recent publications include authoring the *Historical Dictionary of International Organizations* (Scarecrow, 1998) and editing *Future Multilateralism: The Political and Social Framework* (Macmillan for the UNU Press, 1999), *Innovation in Multilateralism* (Macmillan for the UNU Press, 1999), *Revival of Civil Society: Global and Comparative Perspectives* (Macmillan, 1999), and with Preet S. Aulakh *Rethinking Globalization(s): From Corporate Transnationalism to Local Interventions* (Macmillan, 2000). He also served as the editor of the American Society of International Law's publication series, *Issue Papers on World Conferences.*

Thomas Yongo is Legal Officer to the Governing Council of the United Nations Environment Program (UNEP) in Nairobi. Prior to that he served as the Associate Legal Affairs Officer in the Biosafety Program of the Secretariat of the Convention on Biological Diversity. Earlier in his career, Mr. Yongo served as a legal fellow at the Foundation for International Environmental Law and Development (FIELD) at the School of Oriental and African Studies at the University of London. He has published a dozen articles and notes, mostly in the area of international environmental law and practice.

Index